Blender
FOR
DUMMIES®
2ND EDITION

by Jason van Gumster
Producer/animator for Hand Turkey Studios

WILEY

John Wiley & Sons, Inc.

Blender For Dummies,® **2nd Edition**

Published by
John Wiley & Sons, Inc.
111 River Street
Hoboken, NJ 07030-5774
www.wiley.com

Library of Congress Control Number: 2011924143

ISBN 978-0-470-58446-0 (pbk); ISBN 978-1-118-07581-4 (ebk); ISBN 978-1-118-07582-1 (ebk); ISBN 978-1-118-07583-8 (ebk)

WILEY

Manufactured in the United States of America

10 9 8 7 6 5 4 3 2

About the Author

Jason van Gumster got into animation when he realized that he wanted to create movies . . . but that actors are generally intolerant of having pianos dropped on them. Using open source tools at nearly every step in his production process, Jason has produced animations and visual effects for television, film, and video games in his official capacity as a Production Monkey for Hand Turkey Studios, the company he helped start in 2005. A Blender user since 1998, Jason is well recognized in the Blender community for his knowledge of the program and has given numerous live demonstrations and workshops on Blender internationally. In January 2008, Jason worked with the Blender Foundation to assemble the Blender Certification Review Board and led the launch of the Blender Foundation Certified Trainer (BFCT) program.

Based in Richmond, Virginia, Jason can often be found in cafés and diners drawing, espousing the virtues of open source software, or catching confused looks from strangers as he contorts his body to better visualize a pose in a scene he's animating.

Dedication

To Heather. I love you. No backsies!

Author's Acknowledgments

My first thanks go to Blender's team of developers, led by our "benevolent dictator," Ton Roosendaal. Without these developers, Blender would never exist in the state that it does today. Of course, equally deserving of gratitude is the overall Blender community, without which Blender would never have been made open source.

Thanks, also, to everyone at Wiley, particularly Kyle Looper, Kelly Ewing, and Colleen Totz Diamond. Without their patience and tolerance for the wacky scheduling involved with writing about open source software, this book would not see the light of day. I'm truly grateful for their ability to keep me on task and (mostly) on schedule. I'd also like to thank Bassam Kurdali for agreeing to work as the book's technical editor. He's one of the most knowledgeable and talented members of the Blender community, and I hate to think of how little sense this book would've made without his input.

In the first edition of this book, I gave thanks to the unsung genius who first filtered water through ground coffee. I still believe accolades are in order here, though I think I must also acknowledge pastries. They're horrible for you, but they're the most delicious kind of horrible.

And finally, I'd like to thank my dear friends and family. Be it your talents, your honest opinion, your patience, or a well-timed insult, you give me exactly what I need, whether I know it . . . or want it. I can't explain how much that means to me.

Publisher's Acknowledgments

We're proud of this book; please send us your comments at http://dummies.custhelp.com. For other comments, please contact our Customer Care Department within the U.S. at 877-762-2974, outside the U.S. at 317-572-3993, or fax 317-572-4002.

Some of the people who helped bring this book to market include the following:

Acquisitions, Editorial, and Vertical Websites

Project Editor: Kelly Ewing

Acquisitions Editor: Kyle Looper

Copy Editor: Kelly Ewing

Technical Editor: Bassam Kurdali

Editorial Manager: Jodi Jensen

Vertical Websites Project Manager: Laura Moss-Hollister

Vertical Websites Assistant Project Manager: Jenny Swisher

Vertical Websites Associate Producer:
Douglas Kuhn

Editorial Assistant: Amanda Graham

Sr. Editorial Assistant: Cherie Case

Cartoons: Rich Tennant (www.the5thwave.com)

Composition Services

Project Coordinator: Sheree Montgomery

Layout and Graphics: Claudia Bell, Andrea Hornberger, Corrie Socolovitch

Proofreader: Bonnie Mikkelson

Indexer: BIM Indexing & Proofreading Services

Publishing and Editorial for Technology Dummies

    Richard Swadley, Vice President and Executive Group Publisher

    Andy Cummings, Vice President and Publisher

    Mary Bednarek, Executive Acquisitions Director

    Mary C. Corder, Editorial Director

Publishing for Consumer Dummies

    Kathleen Nebenhaus, Vice President and Executive Publisher

Composition Services

    Debbie Stailey, Director of Composition Services

Contents at a Glance

Table of Contents

Introduction

*W*elcome to *Blender For Dummies,* 2nd Edition, your introduction to one of the most well-known free programs for creating 3D computer graphics. With Blender, you can create characters, props, environments, and nearly anything else your imagination can generate. You can then take those creations and use them in Blender to tell a story in an animation, entertain people in a video game, or add a special effect to some video footage. And with the most recent updates to Blender's user interface, many of these tasks are even easier for beginners to get started with. They still haven't quite designed a way for Blender to give you a foot massage if you've had a bad day, but in all seriousness, it's difficult to imagine a task in computer animation that you can't do with Blender. And just think: The developers of Blender have included all these features in a roughly 22MB package you can download for free. Crazy!

Blender sits at a very unique position in the world of 3D computer graphics. In the past, to get into 3D modeling and animation, you had only a few options, and most of them were too expensive, too limiting, or — *ahem* — too illegal for people just trying to see what this whole 3D thing was all about. Blender circumvents all those issues because it's free. A world full of developers and users constantly contribute to, adding enhancements and improvements at a mind-boggling pace. In the relatively short period of time since the first edition of this book hit shelves, Blender has had enough changes that, superficially, it barely resembles the program I wrote about just two years ago. Fortunately, under the hood, it still looks and behaves like the Blender we love — just better.

Of course, 3D computer graphics is a complex topic, and all software of this type is dense with buttons, options, settings, and unique ways of working. Perhaps more than any other program like it, Blender carries a pretty heavy reputation for being difficult to understand. Blender isn't typically viewed as software for beginners. But, if I've done my job right, this book will help simplify things. *Blender For Dummies,* 2nd Edition is not just a book on using Blender. Sure, I explain why things in Blender work in their peculiar Blenderish ways, but I also make a point to explain core principles of 3D computer graphics as they are relevant. There's no use in being able to find a button if you're not really sure what it does or how it works. My hope is that with this combined knowledge, you can actually take advantage of Blender's unique traits to create your own high-quality 3D art as quickly and efficiently as possible. Perhaps you can even become as addicted to it as I am!

About This Book

Blender is an extremely complex program used for the even more complex task of producing high-quality 3D models and animations. As such, I can't cover every single feature and button in Blender. For a more comprehensive manual, refer to the excellent online documentation available through Blender's Web site at `wiki.blender.org`.

Because I want to bring you up to speed on working in 3D space with Blender so that you can start bringing your ideas to life as soon as possible, I focus on introducing you to the fundamental "Blender way" of working. Not only do I show you *how* something is done in Blender, but I also often take the time to explain *why* things are done a certain way. This approach should hopefully put you on the fast track to making awesome work and also allow you to figure out new parts of Blender on your own when you come across them.

Throughout the book, I refer to the Blender community. Blender's user community is probably one of its most valuable assets, and I would be remiss to neglect bringing it up. Not only do many members of the community create great work, but they also write new code for Blender, write and edit documentation, and help each other improve. And understand that when I make reference to the Blender community, I include you in that community as well. As of right now, you are a *Blenderhead* — a fellow Blender user and therefore a member of the Blender community.

Blender is a truly *cross-platform* program, running on Linux, Windows, Macintosh, and even variants of the Unix operating system. Fortunately, not much in Blender differs from one platform to another. However, for the few things that are different, I'll be sure to point them out for you.

Conventions Used in This Book

As a long-time Blender user, I absolutely love hotkeys, and I use them generously in examples throughout the book. Blender makes use of nearly every key on your keyboard, so some keys are a bit difficult to put in writing, particularly punctuation keys like the period (.) or tilde (~). When I suggest that you press these keys, I do just as I did in the last sentence: I spell the symbol and then put the actual symbol in parentheses.

Blender does allow you to customize your hotkeys and mouse buttons. It also ships with some handy presets for people who may be migrating to Blender from another 3D tool. Just know, however, that if you do customize your hotkeys or use any preset other than Blender's default, the hotkeys in this book won't work for you.

I also make use of this cool little arrow (⇨) for indicating a sequence of steps. It could be a series of hotkeys to press or menu items to select or places to look in the Blender interface, but the consistent thing is that all these items are used for steps that you need to do sequentially.

Also note the somewhat peculiar way that Blender's menus work. The menus are ordered so that they flow outward from wherever you open them. For example, if a menu opens near the bottom of a window, its content will flow upward, with the first menu item at the bottom and the last menu item at the top. Throughout this book, I list menu items from the first option to the last. So if you look at Blender on your computer or at the screenshots throughout this book, it may look like I'm listing the menu items in reverse order when in actuality, the menu is just flowing upward from the bottom.

Foolish Assumptions

I wrote the first edition of this book for two sorts of beginners: people who are completely new to the world of 3D, and people who know a thing or two about 3D, but are completely new to Blender. With all the new interface changes in the latest version of Blender, this book is also targeted at another type of beginner: Blenderheads who have not yet made the plunge to using Blender since the heavy revisions were made in the 2.5 series.

Because of the various types of beginners this book addresses, I tend to err on the side of explaining too much rather than too little. If you're someone who is already familiar with another 3D computer graphics program, such as 3DS Max, Maya, Lightwave, or even an earlier version of Blender, you can probably skip a number of these explanations. Likewise, if you're a complete newbie, you may notice that I occasionally compare a feature in Blender to one in another package. However, that comparison is mostly for the benefit of these other users. I write so that you can understand a concept without having to know any of these other programs.

I do, however, make the assumption that you have at least a basic understanding of your computer. I assume that you know how to use a mouse, and I *highly* recommend that you use a mouse with at least two buttons and a scroll wheel. You *can* use Blender with a one- or two-button mouse, and I provide workarounds for the unfortunate souls in that grim state (*cough*Mac users*cough*), but it's certainly not ideal.

An exception is if you're using Blender with a drawing tablet like the ones produced by Wacom. Depending on the model, these devices have quite a variety on the number and type of buttons. For that reason, I focus primarily on using Blender with a mouse, although I will occasionally point out where having a tablet is helpful. Because Blender makes use of all your mouse buttons, I stipulate whether you need to left-click, right-click, or middle-click. And in case you didn't already know, pressing down on your mouse's scroll wheel typically accesses the middle mouse button.

I also assume that you're working with Blender's default settings and theme. You can customize the settings for yourself, but if you do, Blender may not behave exactly like I describe. Bearing in mind this point about Blender's themes, you may notice that the screenshots of Blender's interface are lighter in this book than you see on-screen because I created a custom Blender theme that would show up better in print. If I used Blender's default theme colors, all the figures in the book would appear overly dark. I include this custom theme in the companion DVD for this book for those of you who want your copy of Blender to match what's shown on these pages.

Remember that this book was written while parts of the latest version of Blender were still under development. As such, there may be a few inconsistencies between how things are shown in the book versus how they appear in the final release. That said, most of those inconsistencies should be pretty minor, and I document any differences on this book's companion Web site, www.dummies.com/go/blenderfd2e.

How This Book Is Organized

The book's chapters are grouped into relatively cohesive sections called parts. Like the chapters, each part is meant to be modular and stand on its own, but is also structured in such a way that each one adds to the next. The following sections describe the content of each part.

Part I: Wrapping Your Brain Around Blender

Not only is Blender complex, but it also has some pretty unique ways of approaching the problem of creating in three dimensions. This part is dedicated to melding your mind with the Blender way of thinking. If you've ever started up Blender and wondered, "Why in the world is it doing things *this* way?!," this part is well worth the read.

Part II: Creating Detailed 3D Scenes

Each chapter in this part is dedicated to getting your work to look good, focusing on the skills of modeling, adding materials, and lighting your scenes. The techniques here are geared primarily toward creating static images, but nearly all of it is also relevant to getting animations to communicate clearly and be believable (not to mention, totally sweet to look at).

Part III: Get Animated!

Motion! Motion! Motion! Very few things in the world compare to the excellent feeling of bringing an inanimate object to life. It's hard work and can be very time consuming, but the payoff of seeing a character move and watching people react to it is worth every little bit of toil you put into it. This part shows you the basics of rigging and animating and touches on getting Blender to do a little animating for you with simulated physics.

Part IV: Sharing Your Work with the World

You *could* sit in a room and create a mountain of awesome work just for yourself, but there's certainly something rewarding about putting your work out for the world to see. That's what this part is all about. I walk you through the adventures of rendering out still images and animations so that you ultimately have something worth sharing. This part also introduces the beautiful cheating that you can do with post production and video sequencing.

Part V: The Part of Tens

In a way, I really kind of wanted to write this entire book as a series of helpful lists that would help get you started in Blender, but that structure actually isn't the best for the entire thing. That said, I had a lot of fun writing this part. These three chapters are geared to making sure that your time with Blender is well spent, so I cover troubleshooting and tips on improving your experience.

Icons Used in This Book

As you flip through this book, icons periodically appear next to some paragraphs. These icons notify you of unique or valuable information on the topic at hand. Sometimes that information is a tip, sometimes it's more detail about how something works, and sometimes it's a warning to help you avoid losing data. The following are descriptions of each icon in this book.

This icon calls out suggestions that help you work more effectively and save time.

This icon marks something that I think you should try to keep in mind while working in Blender. Sometimes it's a random tidbit of information, but more often than not, it's something that you'll run into repeatedly and is therefore worth remembering.

Working in 3D can involve some pretty heavy technical information. You can usually work just fine without ever having to know these things, but if you do take the time to understand it, I bet you dollars to donuts that you'll be able to use Blender more effectively.

This icon doesn't show up often, but when it does, I definitely recommend that you pay attention. You won't blow up your computer if you overlook it, but you could lose work.

Quite a bit has changed with the refactoring work that was done in the 2.5 series. These icons point out things that are new or different in Blender so that you can get to be at least as effective (and hopefully *more* effective) with the current version as you were with past versions.

Where to Go from Here

Wondering where to start? The easy answer here would be to say "Just dive on in!" but that's probably a bit too vague. This book is primarily intended as a reference, so if you already know what you're looking for, flip over to the table of contents or index and start soaking in the Blendery goodness.

For those of you who are just starting out, I suggest that you merely turn a couple of pages, start at Chapter 1, and enjoy the ride. And even if you're the sort of person who knows exactly what you're looking for, take the time to read through other sections of the book. You can find a bunch of valuable little bits of information that may help you work more effectively.

Regardless of how you read this book, though, my one hope is that you find it to be a valuable resource that makes you as addicted to Blender as I am.

Part I
Wrapping Your Brain Around Blender

The 5th Wave   By Rich Tennant

DAD ADDS 3-D GRAPHICS TO THE TRADITIONAL CAMPFIRE STORY

In this part . . .

Typically, when people first come into contact with Blender, they feel an incredible shock of "Ahhh! What *is* this crazy thing?!" The purpose of this part is to ease you into the Blender swimming pool so that you can start to have fun with the rest of the Blenderheads in the world. You get an idea of how Blender thinks and how to start taking advantage of the tools it provides you. If you've got experience in another 3D program, these chapters explain some of the essential interface concepts that permeate nearly all tools and features in Blender.

Time to have some fun. Wheeeeeeee!

Chapter 1

Discovering Blender

In This Chapter

▶ Figuring out what Blender is and what it's used for

▶ Understanding how the current version of Blender is influenced by its past

▶ Getting familiar with the Blender interface

*I*n the world of 3D modeling and animation software, programs are usually expensive — like, thousands-of-dollars-and-maybe-an-arm expensive. And there are *some* valid reasons for that cost. Software companies spend millions of dollars and countless hours developing these programs. And the large production companies that buy these programs for their staff make enough money to afford the high cost, or they hire programmers and write their own in-house software.

But what about you and me, the little guys? We are the ambitious dreamers with big ideas, high motivation . . . and tight budgets. How can we bring our ideas to life and our stories to screen, even if only on our own computer monitors? Granted, we could shell out the cash (and hopefully keep our arms) for the expensive programs that the pros use. But even then, animation is a highly collaborative art, and it's difficult to produce anything in a reasonable amount of time without some help.

We need quality software and a strong community to work, grow, and evolve with. Fortunately, Blender can provide us with both of these things. This chapter is an introduction to Blender, its background, and its interface.

Getting to Know Blender

Blender is a free and open source 3D modeling and animation suite. Yikes! What a mouthful, huh? Put simply, Blender is a computer graphics program that allows you to produce high-quality still images and animations using three-dimensional geometry. If you've seen an animated feature film or watched a television show where they go behind the scenes and explain how they made an actor look like he's being chased by a giant monster although he's really just standing in a big green room, you've seen what can be done with 3D computer graphics. In the right hands, Blender is capable of producing this kind of work. With a little patience and dedication, *your* hands can be the right hands.

One thing that makes Blender different and special compared to other comparable 3D software is the fact that it is free and *open source*. Being free and open source means that not only can you go to the Blender Web site (www.blender.org) and download the entire program right now without paying anything, but you can also freely download the *source,* or the code that makes up the program. For most programs, the source code is a heavily guarded and highly protected secret that only certain people (mostly programmers hired by the company that distributes the program) can see and modify. Because it's open source, anybody can see Blender's source code and make changes to it. The benefit is that instead of having a small group of paid programmers work on the program, Blender can be improved by programmers all over the world!

Because of these strengths, Blender is an ideal program for small animation companies, freelance 3D artists, independent filmmakers, students beginning to learn about 3D computer graphics, and dedicated computer graphics hobbyists.

Blender, like many other 3D computer graphics applications, has had a reputation for being difficult for new users to understand. At the same time, however, Blender is also known for allowing experienced users to bring their ideas to life quickly. Fortunately, with the help of this book and the recent improvements introduced in the latest version of Blender, that gap is becoming much easier to bridge.

Discovering Blender's Beginnings

The Blender you know and love today wasn't always free and open source. Blender is pretty unique in that it's one of the few software applications that was "liberated" from proprietary control with the help of its user community.

Originally, Blender was an internal production tool for an award-winning Dutch animation company called NeoGeo, founded in the late 1990s by Blender's original (and still lead) developer, Ton Roosendaal. As interest in Blender grew, Ton spun off a new company, Not a Number (NaN), to market and sell Blender. Sadly, NaN was forced to shut its doors in 2002, despite Blender's growing popularity. Ironically, this is where the story starts to get exciting.

Even though NaN went under, Blender had developed quite a strong community, which was eager to find a way to keep its beloved little program from becoming lost and abandoned. In July 2002, Ton established a nonprofit organization called the Blender Foundation and arranged a deal with the original NaN investors to release Blender's source to the Blender Foundation. The price tag was set at €100,000 (which at the time was about $100,000),. Initial estimations were that it would take as long as six months to one year to raise the necessary funds. Amazingly, the community was able to raise that money in a mere *seven weeks*.

Because of the Blender community's passion and willingness to put its money where its metaphorical mouth was, Blender was released under the GNU General Public License on October 13, 2002. With the source in the community's hands, Blender had an avalanche of development and new features added to it in a very short time. Eight years later, the Blender community is larger and stronger than ever, and Blender is a powerful modern piece of software, competitive in terms of quality with similar software costing thousands of dollars. Not too shabby. Figure 1-1 shows screenshots of Blender from its early days to the Blender of today.

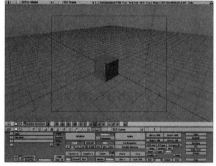
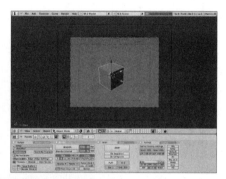
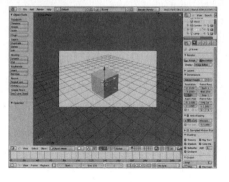

Figure 1-1: Blender through the years: Blender 1.8 (top left), Blender 2.46 (top right), and the major changes apparent in the Blender of today (bottom).

Making Open Movies and Games

One cool thing about the programmers who write Blender is that many of them also use the program regularly. They're writing code not just because they're told to do it, but also because they want to improve Blender for their own purposes. Part of this motivation has to do with Blender's open-source nature, but it also has to do with Blender's history as an in-house tool built on direct artist input and sometimes written by the artists themselves.

Seeking to get even more of this direct artist feedback to developers, the Blender Foundation launched Project Orange in 2005. The project's purpose was to create an animated short movie using open-source tools, primarily Blender. A small team of artists was assembled in Amsterdam, in the Netherlands, and roughly seven months later, *Elephants Dream* premiered and was released as the first *open movie*, meaning that not only was it created by using open-source tools, but all the production files — 3D models, scenes, character rigs, and so on — were also released under a permissive and open Creative Commons Attribution license. If you don't like *Elephants Dream,* you're free to change it to your liking or use the files for something else entirely! How many movies give you that luxury? You can see the film and all the production files at www.elephantsdream.org.

Due to the success of Orange, the Blender Institute was established in 2007 for the expressed purpose of having a permanent space to create open projects, as well as provide the service of training people in Blender. The first open project from the Blender Institute was Project Peach, which, following the model of Orange, assembled a team of artists who produced a short comedic animation called *Big Buck Bunny.* Like *Elephants Dream*, all production files for the Peach project were released under an open license. You can access them at www.bigbuckbunny.org.

Not being inclined to rest on its laurels, the Blender Institute launched Project Apricot as the team creating *Big Buck Bunny* was wrapping up its production. Apricot was a project similar to Orange and Peach, but rather than create an animated movie, the goal here was to create a video game. The result of this was *Yo Frankie!*, a game based on Frankie, the leader squirrel character from the *Big Buck Bunny* project. And, of course, all the content is freely available at the *Yo Frankie* Web site, www.yofrankie.org, under a permissive Creative Commons license.

With the completion of each project, the functionality and stability of Blender increased by a large degree. Orange brought improved animation tools, basic hair, and a node-based compositor. Peach provided enhanced particles for better hair and fur, optimizations for large scenes, improved rendering, and even better animation and rigging tools. Apricot revitalized Blender's internal game engine, which extended to better real-time visuals when modeling and animating in Blender.

And even as I wrote parts of this second edition of *Blender For Dummies*, artists at the Blender Institute were finishing up the latest open project, Project Durian. (A *durian* is a smelly Asian fruit with an exotic taste.) Durian is another short movie project, named *Sintel*, with the lofty goals of making Blender 2.5 production ready and adding features for epic scenes, including highly detailed sculpting, large environments, and highly detailed, high-resolution renders. You can see the film and access all the Durian project files at www.sintel.org. I've also included a copy of *Sintel* on the book's companion DVD, and the color insert of this book has still images from a few of the open movie projects.

All these projects continue to exhibit the strength of the Blender community. Each of them are financed in a large part by DVD presales from users who understand that regardless of the project's final product, great improvements to Blender are the result, and everyone benefits from that.

Getting to Know the Interface

Probably one of the most daunting aspects of Blender for newcomers and longtime 3D professionals alike has been its unique and somewhat peculiar interface. It's arguably the most controversial feature Blender has. In fact, at one time, merely calling the interface a feature would raise the blood pressure of some of you who tried using Blender in the past, but gave up in frustration when it did not behave as expected.

Although the interface wasn't the primary focus, the interface updates to Blender added in the 2.5 series of releases have made great strides toward alleviating that frustration. As a small example, when you first launch Blender, the splash image that appears is more functional now, providing you with quick links to online documentation as well as a list of recently opened files. Figure 1-2 shows the splash image you're presented with when you start Blender for the first time.

If you click anywhere other than the links provided by the splash image, the splash image goes away, and you're greeted with Blender's default scene, as shown in Figure 1-3. If you're looking at the interface for the first time, you may think it appears pretty daunting. However, the purpose of this book is to help you get the hang of Blender, explaining some of the design decisions in the interface and ultimately allowing you to be productive. Who knows, you might even start to like it and wonder why other programs don't work this way!

Figure 1-2:
The
new and
improved
Blender
splash
image.

Figure 1-2:
The
new and
improved
Blender
splash
image.

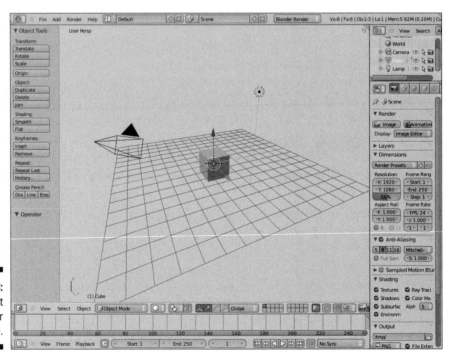

Figure 1-3:
The default
Blender
interface.

An interface that stays out of your way

The first thing to understand about Blender's interface is its basic organization. Figure 1-3 displays a single Blender window. Each Blender window can consist of one or more *areas* that you can split, resize, and join at will. In nearly all cases, an area defines the space of an *editor,* such as the 3D View, where you actually make changes and modifications to your 3D scene. Each editor can include one or more *regions* that contain additional features or tools for using that editor. An example of a region that all editors have is a header region at the top or bottom of the editor that typically includes menus and buttons to give you access to features in that editor.

Knowing this organizational structure, the next important thing to know is that Blender is designed to be as *nonblocking* and *nonmodal* as possible. Areas in Blender never overlap one another *(nonblocking)* and using one feature of Blender typically won't restrict you from using any of the others *(nonmodal).* As an example, in most software, if you want to open a new file or save your project, a file browser dialog pops up. This dialog is an overlapping window that not only blocks things behind it from view, but usually also prevents you from making any changes to your file. This setup isn't the case with Blender. In Blender, the file browser is an editor just like any other, and it makes perfect sense to be able to make a couple of tweaks to your scene before hitting the Save button. Figure 1-4 shows what it might look like to have a file browser open while you make tweaks.

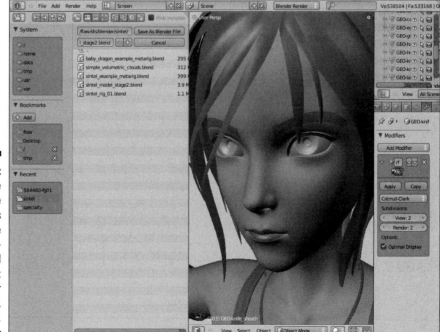

Figure 1-4: Doing those last couple of tweaks before finally saving (Model credit: Blender Foundation, *Sintel).*

At first, working in a nonblocking, nonmodal interface may seem to be really restrictive. How do you see different types of editors? Can you see them at the same time? Everything looks like it's nailed in place, so is it even possible to change anything? Fortunately, all these things are possible, and you get the benefit of never having your view of one area obstructed by another. Having an unobstructed workspace is a great way to be able to see at a glance what's going on in your file. Furthermore, as of the Blender 2.5 development series, if you absolutely *need* multiple windows that can overlap, you can have them. For example, you might have two computer monitors that are different sizes, and you'd like a full-sized Blender window in each. I show you how to do task later in this chapter in the "Duplicating an area to a new window" section.

Resizing an area

You can modify and change all the areas in a Blender window in the same way: Change the size of an area by left-clicking the border between two areas and dragging it to a new position. This method increases the size of one area while reducing the size of those that adjoin it. If you have only one area in your Blender window, it's exactly the same size as that window. To resize it, you need to either adjust the size of its parent Blender window or split a new area into that space.

Splitting and removing areas

While working in Blender, it's pretty common that the default layout isn't quite what you need to work efficiently. Sometimes you may need an additional 3D View, or you may want to see the UV/Image Editor in addition to the 3D View.

To create either of these layout changes, you need to *split* an existing area into two. Splitting a new area doesn't work like it used to in previous versions of Blender. In earlier versions, you'd split or join areas by right-clicking the border and choosing an option from a pop-up menu. As of Blender 2.5, a new system uses the corners at the bottom left and top right of any area. These *corner widgets* are marked as a triangular region indicated by diagonal lines.

To split any area into two, use the following steps:

1. **Left-click one of the corner widgets and drag your mouse cursor away from the area's border.**

2. **Drag your mouse cursor left or right to split the area vertically.**

   Dragging it up or down splits the area horizontally. As you drag your mouse, the areas update in real time so that you can see the result of the split while you're working. To cancel the operation, right-click or press Esc.

If you want to remove an area, the process is similar. Rather than splitting an area in two, you're joining two areas together. So instead of left-clicking the corner widget and dragging your mouse cursor away from the area border, drag it *toward* the border of the area you want to join with. This action darkens the area your mouse is in and draws an arrow to indicate which area you want to remove. Figure 1-5 shows the basic steps for splitting and joining areas.

Duplicating an area to a new window

In addition to the new way of splitting and joining areas, the Blender developers have also introduced a brand-new feature in the 2.5 series via corner widgets. You now have the ability to take any area and duplicate it to a new Blender window. You can move that window to a separate monitor (if you have one), or it can overlap your original Blender window. And within this new Blender window, you can split the duplicated area into additional ones as you like. This area duplication feature is a slight violation of Blender's non-overlapping principles, but the benefits it provides for users with multiple computer screens make it very worthwhile.

To take advantage of this feature, follow these steps:

1. **Shift+left-click one of the corner widgets in an area and drag your mouse cursor away from it.**

   This step duplicates the area you clicked in and creates a new Blender window to contain it. You can also achieve this effect from the menus in the header region of some editors by choosing View➪Duplicate Area into New Window.

2. **Close the additional Blender window by clicking the close button that your operating system adds to the border of the window.**

All editors in Blender areas have a horizontal region called the *header* running along either the top or bottom of the editor. The header usually features specialized menus or buttons that are specific to the editor you're using. Here are some ways you can customize the header:

✔ **Hide the header.** If you drag the seam all the way to the area border, then the header becomes hidden, leaving only a small plus icon (+) in the corner of the area. If the header is at the bottom of the editor, the plus icon appears at the bottom right. If the header appears at the top, it's at the top left. Left-click this icon, and the header reappears.

✔ **Change the location of the header.** You can also change the location of the header to either the top or bottom of the editor it belongs to. To do so, right-click the header and choose Flip to Top (or Bottom, depending on where your header currently is).

Create a new area

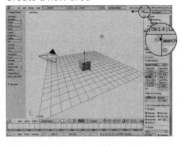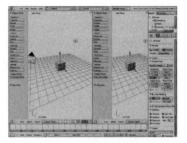

Remove an area

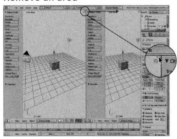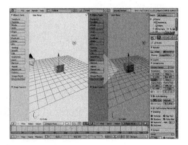

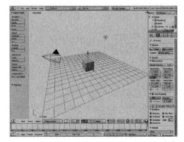

Figure 1-5:
Creating a
new area
and then
removing
that area.

Maximizing an area

When working in Blender, you also occasionally need to maximize an area. Maximizing an area is particularly useful when you're working on a model or scene and you just want to get all the other areas out of your way so that you can use as much screen real estate as possible.

To maximize any area, hover your mouse cursor over it and press Shift+spacebar. You can toggle back to the tiled screen layout by pressing Shift+spacebar again. These options are available in almost all editor types by choosing View⇨Toggle Full Screen from that editor's header or by right-clicking the header and choosing Maximize Area from the menu that appears. If the area is already maximized, then the menu item will say Tile Area.

Chapter 2

Understanding How Blender Thinks

*1*n this chapter, you get intimate with Blender. No, I don't mean you need to start placing scented candles around your computer. I mean that this chapter's focus is a detailed introduction to Blender's interface and how you can start finding your way around in it. First of all, it's pretty important to have an understanding of the various types of editors that Blender has and how to access them. These editors are the gateways and tools for creating whatever you want.

With the knowledge of what you can do with these editors, the next thing is actually building those creations. To do so, you need to understand how to work in a virtual three-dimensional space, and specifically, you need to understand how Blender handles that space. I also cover these topics in this chapter.

Looking at Editor Types

A Blender area can contain any editor type. You can see what editor types are available by left-clicking the button on the far left of that editor's header. Figure 2-1 shows the menu that appears when you press this button.

The editor types available through this menu are as follows. Next to each type is the hotkey sequence to bring up the editor type quickly:

- ✔ **3D View (Shift+F5):** Arguably the most-used editor in Blender, the 3D View shows you the three-dimensional view of your model or scene and allows you to modify it.

- ✔ **Timeline:** The Timeline editor offers you a convenient way to quickly jump from one part of your animation to another, as well as play back the animation.

- ✔ **Graph Editor (Shift+F6):** Blender's Graph Editor shows a graphical representation of animatable attributes in your scene as they change over time.

- ✔ **DopeSheet (Shift+F12):** The DopeSheet is where you create and adjust your overall animation by using actions or keying sets. You can use *actions* to animate all of a character's movement in a scene, or you can mix them together in the NLA Editor. *Keying sets* give you the ability to group together several different animatable attributes.

- ✔ **NLA Editor:** NLA stands for *nonlinear animation*. This editor allows you to mix pre-animated actions on a single character (such as mixing a waving hand animation with a walking animation to have your character walk and wave her hand at the same time).

- ✔ **UV/Image Editor (Shift+F10):** With the UV/Image Editor, you can do basic image editing as well as edit the texture coordinates for your models (see Chapter 7).

- ✔ **Video Sequence Editor (Shift+F8):** Blender's Video Sequence Editor (VSE) is a lightweight video editor. The VSE isn't as powerful as some other programs created specifically for editing video, but it's quite effective for stringing a sequence of scenes together and doing basic effects, overlays, and transitions.

Figure 2-1:
The Editor
Type menu.

✔ **Text Editor (Shift+F11):** Blender's integrated Text Editor is not only handy for keeping notes about your scenes and models, but it's also a convenient place to write and test your own Python scripts in Blender.

✔ **Node Editor (Shift+F3):** Blender has a Node Editor for materials and textures, as well as for compositing. This editor is where you modify these node structures. See Chapter 15 for more on using the Node Editor for compositing.

✔ **Logic Editor (Shift+F2):** Blender has an integrated game engine, allowing you to create your own custom video games directly within Blender. The Logic Editor is how you control the behavior in your game.

✔ **Properties (Shift+F7):** You can manipulate nearly all the different attributes for objects in your scene via this editor. You can find out more about this topic later in this chapter in the section "Working with the Properties Editor."

✔ **Outliner (Shift+F9):** The Outliner gives a hierarchical view of all the objects in your scene along with the ability to see how they're related to one another. It's also a quick way to select objects and do simple manipulations in a complex scene.

✔ **User Preferences:** Through the User Preferences editor, you can customize how you interact with Blender.

✔ **Info:** The Info editor contains Blender's main menu and displays basic information about your scene. It also serves as a report space where warnings and errors are logged. Advanced users and beginners alike can use the Info editor to figure out what happened if a feature doesn't work as expected.

✔ **File Browser:** This editor allows you to look through the files on your computer. It also allows you to look at the innards of your Blender projects to see how things are structured or for linking to other projects.

✔ **Python Console (Shift+F4):** The Console is a fairly handy editor that's often utilized by advanced users to help write custom Python scripts.

Working with the Properties Editor

After the 3D View, the Properties editor is probably the second most used editor type in Blender. You use buttons and values in this editor to modify the attributes of your scene and elements within it. Because this editor can manipulate so many parts of a scene, it's broken down and organized into a series of sections.

You can access each section by using the buttons in the header region of the Properties editor. These section buttons are ordered logically from large contexts (for example, Scene Properties) to progressively smaller contexts (for example, Object Data Properties) as you go from left to right. The available sections in the Properties editor can change, depending on your active selection in the 3D View. For example, if you have a camera object selected, the Modifiers section of the Properties editor isn't visible (because modifiers can't be applied to cameras). The following list describes each section of the Properties editor:

- **Render:** The Render Properties determine what the final output of your scene will look like when you decide to render it to an image or video. Chapters 14 and 15 cover these properties in more depth.

- **Scene:** These general properties dictate the nature of your scene, including things like the active camera, units of measurement, and the strength of gravity if you're using simulated physics.

- **World:** The buttons and values in the World Properties section control the environment that your scene is built in. They have a large influence on the final output of your scene.

- **Object:** Any object in your scene is going to have its own set of properties that you can modify. The Object Properties section allows you to make changes that affect an object as it relates to the scene.

- **Object Constraints:** When working in 3D — particularly with animation — it's often useful to constrain the properties of one object to that of another. Constraints automate parts of your scene and help make it much more manageable. Chapter 10 goes into constraints more deeply.

- **Modifiers:** A lot of work goes into building 3D models, so it's to your benefit to take advantage of your computer and let it take care of boring procedural steps while you focus on the more interesting parts of the process. Modifiers are great tools to facilitate these kinds of healthy shortcuts, and this subsection is where you manage those modifiers. You can find out more about modifiers in Chapter 5.

- **Object Data:** Like the previous four subsections, buttons and values in Object Data Properties change slightly depending on what sort of object you select, but their primary purpose is to give you the ability to work with the fundamental structural elements of your object.

- **Bone:** The Bone Properties section is available only if your active selection is an Armature object. *Armatures*, sometimes called skeletons in other programs, are used for animation in Blender, and they consist of a set of bone subobjects. Bone Properties are where you can adjust attributes of a specific bone that you've selected in the armature.

- **Bone Constraints:** Similar to the Object Constraints Properties, this section helps you manage constraints. The difference, however, is that this section is available only if your active selection is an Armature in

Pose Mode, and it manages constraints on bones, rather than objects. Chapters 10 and 11 cover constraints and the use of constraints on bones.

✔ **Material:** The controls in Material Properties allow you to dramatically change the appearance of objects in your scene. Chapter 7 goes into this subsection in much more detail.

✔ **Texture:** Textures can have a profound effect on how the surface of your 3D objects appears, making smooth, clean objects look rough, gritty, and believable. You can also use textures as custom brushes when painting and sculpting in Blender. This section is where you can edit those textures. You can find out more on texturing in Chapter 8.

✔ **Particles:** In computer graphics, particle systems are often used to create special effects or manage the behavior of groups of objects. This subsection of the Properties editor is where you manage particle systems in Blender. Working with particles is a pretty advanced topic. Chapter 13 gives you a brief introduction to the possibilities that they have.

✔ **Physics:** In the spirit of making your computer do as much work for you as possible, having the computer simulate physical behavior is sometimes helpful. It lends realism to animations and can often help you work faster. The Physics Properties section gives controls for simulating physics on your objects. See Chapter 13 for more on these topics.

Customizing Blender to Fit You

You can really tweak Blender's screen layout to virtually any configuration you can imagine. However, Blender's customization features go much deeper than just readjusting the areas in a Blender window. At this point in time, there are very few parts of Blender that, with a little time and effort, you can't completely overhaul to be as comfortable of a work environment as possible. This ability to customize is especially useful for people who are migrating to Blender from other 3D graphics programs. I won't say that you can make Blender behave exactly like any of these other programs, but sometimes little things like using the same keyboard shortcuts help make the transition smoother.

Although this section gives you the means to completely bend Blender's interface to your will, bear in mind that unless otherwise specified, this book relies on the default settings that ship with Blender. Unless you can remember your customized behaviors, it may be more helpful to use Blender's default settings (File⇨Load Factory Settings).

Using screen layout presets

You can make a variety of layouts depending on the sort of work you're doing. In Blender, these workspace layouts are called *screens,* and, by default, Blender comes with seven presets: Animation, Compositing, Default, Game Logic, Scripting, UV Editing, and Video Editing. When you first load Blender, you're in the Default screen layout. You can cycle through these screens by pressing Ctrl+← and Ctrl+→. If you prefer to use a menu, you can use the datablock (for more on datablocks, see the sidebar in this chapter) at the top of the window in the Info editor, shown in Figure 2-2, and left-click the screen icon next to the name of the current screen layout.

Figure 2-2:
The Screens
menu.

You can rename any screen to any name by switching to that screen and left-clicking its name in the screens datablock. Get used to the idea of naming everything in your projects. Trust me, being in the habit of using a reasonable name makes life infinitely easier when you come back to an old project, and you need to figure out what everything is.

The screens, and therefore the order that they're cycled through when you press Ctrl+← or →, are arranged in alphabetical and numerical order, for fast and logical organization. If you want to cheat a bit, you can give a specific order to the list by putting a number in front of each screen's name (such as 1-Default, 2-Animation, and so on).

To create a new screen, left-click the plus (+) icon next to the current screen name in the Info editor's header. Upon clicking this icon, Blender produces a duplicate of your existing screen layout. From here, you can make the changes create to your own custom layout, creating a horizontal Properties editor layout or a multimonitor layout with a separate window for each of your monitors. You can also delete screens (including the default ones that ship with Blender, so be careful) by clicking the button with the X icon to the right of the Scene datablock. When you're happy with changes you've made and you want to have these screens available each time you start Blender, save your settings by going to the User Preferences editor (Ctrl+Alt+U) and clicking the Save As Default button at the bottom of the editor or using the Ctrl+U hotkey.

Understanding datablocks: Fundamental elements in a Blender scene

In Figure 2-2, look at the widget that's used to manage screens. The interface gives you access to something called a datablock. A simple and obvious definition of a datablock is that it's literally a block of data. However, a datablock has more to it. Datablocks are used throughout both Blender's interface and its internal structure, so understanding how they work and how you can take advantage of them goes a long way to understanding Blender itself. Nearly every critical element in Blender is stored in a type of datablock, from screens and scenes to objects and textures.

Not only is a datablock a handy way to store information, but it also allows Blender to treat this information like a database. In particular, you can link datablocks and let them share

information. As an example, say that you create an excellent wood material, and you want to have two objects — a table and a chair — look like they're both made of the same wood. Well, rather than re-create that exact same material for each object, you can simply link both object datablocks to the same material datablock. Your computer uses less memory, and, more important, you have less work to do. And because datablocks are used throughout Blender, this same concept works in all kinds of situations: sharing textures between materials, sharing particle systems between objects, and even sharing worlds between scenes. It's an incredibly powerful feature of Blender and I refer back to datablocks a lot throughout this book.

Before creating a new screen that you want to keep around for future use, first return to your default setup by selecting File➪New or pressing Ctrl+N. When Blender saves your user settings, it saves them to a special .blend file called startup.blend that gets loaded each time it starts. So any models you have in the 3D View and any changes you make to other layouts are saved, too. Fortunately, if you made a mistake, you can always return to the default setup by choosing File➪Load Factory Settings and re-create your custom layouts from there.

When adjusting screen layouts, the menus and buttons in the header can be obscured or hidden if the area is too narrow. In this case, you can do two things:

✔ If the editor's header has menus, you can left-click the minus icon at the left of the header. The text menus collapse from view so that they're out of the way when you don't need them.

✔ If you still don't have enough space after collapsing the menus, Blender has another trick up its sleeve: Middle-click the header and drag your mouse left and right. The contents of the header move left and right so that you can bring those obscured buttons into view. You can also hover your mouse cursor over the header and user your scroll wheel. This feature is particularly handy for people who work on computers with small monitors.

Setting user preferences

This section on user preferences is by no means comprehensive. The number of options available in Blender's User Preferences editor is mind-bogglingly large. My intent here is to introduce you to the most helpful and relevant options to get you working effectively. For specific details on every single button, see the online documentation available at www.blender.org.

To change your user preferences, go to File⇨User Preferences (Ctrl+Alt+U), and Blender creates a new window just for the User Preferences editor. Although you can change any area to a User Preferences editor, it is sometimes nicer to use the File menu method because you don't have to replace or split any of your existing areas to get a User Preferences editor.

If you choose File⇨User Preferences, and you don't see a new window with the User Preferences editor, your window may be in a full-screen state and your operating system's window manager may not be allowing the window with User Preferences to sit atop that full-screen window. To get around this issue, toggle off the full-screen view by clicking the icon on the far right of the Info editor's header region or by pressing Alt+F11.

When you get the User Preferences to be the way you like, you can save them as your personal defaults by clicking the Save As Default button at the bottom of the User Preferences editor or by pressing Ctrl+U.

Interface

The first set of available options in Blender's User Preferences (shown in Figure 2-3) relate to how you interact with your scene within the 3D View. Moving from left to right, here are some of the more useful options:

- ✔ **Display:** The options in this column toggle the display of various informational elements in the 3D View, such as tooltips, object information, and the small mini axis in the bottom left corner.

- ✔ **View Manipulation:** The options in this column give you control over how you interact with the environment in the 3D View. For example, enabling Auto Depth and Zoom to Mouse Position in large scenes is often useful so that you can quickly navigate your way through your scene without becoming stuck.

- ✔ **Smooth View:** Smooth View is probably one of the coolest convenience options added to Blender in recent history and as such, it deserves explicit mention here. If you go to your 3D View and choose View⇨Camera (Numpad 0), the 3D View smoothly animates the change from the default perspective view to the Camera's perspective. Pretty slick, huh? The values in Smooth View are in milliseconds, with a maximum value of 1,000, or 1 second (although that's a bit slow for most tastes). The default value of 200 works nicely, but play with it on your own and see what works best for you.

✔ **Menus:** Some users prefer to have menus immediately pop open when they run their mouse cursor over them. The options under this heading facilitate that preference. It's disabled by default, but you can enable the Open on Mouse Over check box and then use the values below that to adjust the delay, or how long your mouse has to be over a menu's name before it pops up.

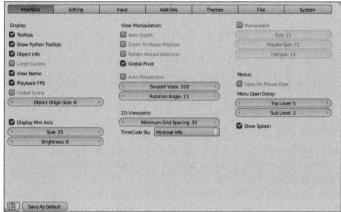

Figure 2-3:
The
Interface
options
in User
Preferences.

Editing

The next set of options is related to the act of editing objects. The most relevant options in this section relate to Blender's Undo feature. The options related to Undo are pretty important. From the Editing section, you can adjust how many steps of undo you have when working in Blender (default is 32), as well as toggle Global Undo on and off. Now, you may be wondering why in the world anyone would *ever* want to disable the ability to undo a mistake. The most common answer to this question is performance. Having undo enabled requires more memory from your computer, and each level of undo requires a little bit more. Sometimes, when working with very complex scenes or models, an artist might disable undo to dedicate all the computer's memory to the current scene rather than the steps used to create it. This decision occurs most when artists work with Blender's multiresolution sculpting tools (see Chapter 5).

Input

The settings and controls in the Input options of the User Preferences editor have the greatest influence over how you interact with Blender. As Figure 2-4 shows, this section is extensive.

Figure 2-4:
The Input
options
in User
Preferences.

The largest part of this section — the event editor on the right side — is actually covered later in this chapter in the section "Using custom event maps." However, the left-side column has quite a few useful settings as well:

- ✔ **Presets:** Blender ships with a small assortment of *application interaction presets* — a fancy way of saying hotkey and mouse configurations that match other 3D programs. You can use this datablocklike menu to choose an existing preset, create a new one, or delete a preset you never want to use.

- ✔ **Emulate 3 Button Mouse:** Blender was designed to be used with a three-button mouse. However, not all computers have three-button mice, particularly Macintosh machines and some tablet PCs. Enabling this option helps these users compensate by using Alt+left-click to do what is normally done with the middle-click.

- ✔ **Continuous Grab:** Continuous Grab is a cool feature added in Blender 2.5 that allows you to continue moving an object even after your mouse cursor has reached the edge of the editor. Continuous Grab is very useful and enabled by default, but it doesn't work as nicely for users working with a tablet interface, so you can disable it here if you need to.

- ✔ **Select With:** Blender's default behavior is to select objects with the right mouse button. However people migrating to Blender from other programs may be more comfortable selecting with the left mouse button. This control lets you switch between the two. A word of warning: Setting this value to Left disables the Emulate 3 Button Mouse feature.

- ✔ **Emulate Numpad:** This setting is a very handy option for laptop users. As you see in the next section, Blender makes use of the numeric keypad for quick access to top, front, side, and camera views in the 3D View. Unfortunately, most laptop users don't have an easily accessible numeric keypad on their keyboards. As a workaround, the Emulate Numpad option uses the number keys at the top of the keyboard to have the functionality that the corresponding Numpad numbers have. This control in User Preferences disables the normal layer-switching functionality that the number keys at the top of the keyboard normally perform, but the ability to quickly change views tends to be more valuable to users than the ability to quickly change layers.

✔ **Orbit Style:** By default, Blender uses the Trackball setting. However, users who are familiar with other 3D programs might prefer the Turntable setting. The difference may seem subtle to a new user, but it can be very disorienting for users of other software packages who may be used to turntable orbit style.

✔ **Invert Zoom Direction:** Similar to the Orbit Style option, some people are more comfortable scrolling forward to zoom out and back to zoom in. This setting gives users that option.

Add-Ons

Blender ships with an assortment of extensions, called *add-ons,* which provide users with additional capabilities within Blender. For example, if you're a veteran Blenderhead and you're used to the old Spacebar menu from earlier versions of Blender, there's an add-on that puts that feature back. Other add-ons modify Blender's interface, add new primitive objects, or provide additional tools that can help speed up your work. You can manage all add-ons from the Add-Ons section of User Preferences.

Add-ons come in primarily two types: Officially Supported and Community Supported. You can use the buttons on the left side of the Add-Ons section in User Preferences to filter which types you see. By default, all community supported add-ons that ship with Blender are disabled. Most officially supported add-ons are for importing and exporting file types to and from other programs. The bulk of these add-ons are enabled by default. To enable or disable a specific add-on, just left-click the check box on the right side of the add-on's box. Left-clicking the triangle on the left of the box expands it so that you can get more details about a specific add-on. All of Blender's add-ons are broken down into specific categories, and you can use the buttons on the left to see just the add-ons that are specific to a single category. Alternatively, you can use the search field above the category buttons.

Themes

Blender has quite a bit of flexibility in adjusting how it looks, thanks to the Themes options, as shown in Figure 2-5. I took almost all the screenshots for this book by using a variation of the Default theme, lightened for readability. However, when I work in Blender, I use my own theme that's a bit darker and easier on the eyes. Darker themes are particularly helpful if, like me, you're known for sitting behind the computer and working in Blender for 10- to 15-hour stretches (or more). In those situations, the less stress you can put on your eyes, the better.

Figure 2-5:
The Themes
options
in User
Preferences.

TIP

I include a copy of the theme I use as a Python script on the DVD that comes with this book. It's also available for download from this book's Web site, `www.dummies.com/go/blenderfd2e`. Feel free to use this theme for your Blender sessions or make your own! Everyone has their own tastes. In fact, one of the more popular Blender users, Pablo Vazquez (known as VenomGFX), has been known to use a theme that's completely purple and pink!

File

The File options relate to how Blender works with files. Figure 2-6 shows the settings in this section of the User Preferences editor.

The following list describes the important parts of this section:

✔ **File Paths:** Like most programs, Blender works with files. The values in this column show the default locations where Blender either places files or looks for them. Here you can indicate where your fonts are located, where you want to save your renders by default, and where to look for textures and sounds.

Probably the most important path in this section is the one for Temp. This location is where Blender stores Auto Save files, and it's also where it stores the notorious `quit.blend` file, which is great for recovering your last blender session. The default location for temporary files is `/tmp/`.

Unfortunately for users of Microsoft's Windows operating system, this location doesn't make any sense and actually doesn't even exist. If you're using Windows, I *strongly* advise that you change this location to `C:\Windows\Temp` or create a folder called `tmp` on your `C:\` drive. Linux users may also want to change this location because some Linux distributions like Ubuntu automatically clear the `/tmp` directory on each boot. I can't tell you the number of people who have closed Blender without saving their work and later realized that they couldn't recover any of their work because this path wasn't properly set.

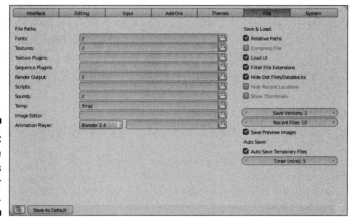

Figure 2-6:
The File
options
in User
Preferences.

✔ **Save and Load:** These options relate to how Blender opens and saves
project files. Of these options, the two most worth knowing about are
Compress File and Load UI, both of which you can modify from the File
Browser, but these check boxes define the default behavior.

The Compress File option is handy because it makes your `.blend` project files smaller when you save. The Load UI option is short for Load
User Interface, meaning that when you open a `.blend` file, Blender will
adjust your screen layout to match the one that was used to create that
file.

If you're opening a file that was created in earlier versions of Blender
that relied on the horizontal layout, you may want to disable the Load UI
option so that your file opens in the new Blender layout.

✔ **Auto Save:** Before Blender had undo functionality, users relied heavily
on its Auto Save features. Even in the age of undo, these options are a
lifesaver. For that reason, the following list goes into these settings in
more detail:

 • **Save Versions:** Each time you manually save a file in Blender, it
 takes your last save and stores it as an earlier version. You may
 have already created work in Blender and noticed some `.blend1`
 files in the same place you saved your `.blend` files. Those
 `.blend1` files are the earlier version. This option allows you to
 determine how many of these earlier versions you'd like Blender
 to retain for you. Each version has a number appended to the end
 of it, so if you have `MyFile.blend` and you have Save Versions
 set at 2, then after a few saves, you should see `MyFile.blend`,
 `MyFile.blend1`, and `MyFile.blend2` all in the same folder.

 • **Recent Files:** The number in this field tells Blender how many of
 your past files to remember when you go to File⇨Open Recent
 or press Shift+Ctrl+O. You can also use the File Browser (F1 or
 Ctrl+O) and look on the side region under the Recent heading.

• **Auto Save Temporary Files:** Enabled by default, this option is Blender's auto save functionality. It saves a copy of the current state of your file, or what I call a hot backup, in your Temp directory (adjustable in the File Paths options) every few minutes, as dictated by the Timer field below this button.

Some file paths begin with two forward slashes (//). These slashes are Blender's notation for a *relative path,* or file path as it relates to the location on your hard drive of your current file. In contrast is an *absolute path,* which is the full path to your file from the root of your file system. For example, if you have a file saved as `/home/user/Documents/project.blend`, then the absolute path to `project.blend` is `/home/user/Documents/`. Now say that you have a folder named `textures` in the same folder as your `project.blend` file, and in that folder is an image named `sandpaper.png`. The absolute path to that image is `/home/user/Documents/textures/`, while its relative path (relative to `project.blend`) is `//textures`.

System

Whereas the Interface options dictate how you interact with Blender, the options in the System section, shown in Figure 2-7, tend to dictate more how Blender interacts with you. Many options here are geared toward optimizing for performance, and generally the defaults work well.

Some of the more interesting options follow:

✔ **OpenGL:** If Blender is working sluggishly or if the interface looks really odd (noise, strange tears, repeating patterns), these settings are the first place to look to see whether you can get Blender working nicely. In particular, you may want to try enabling VBOs (Vertex Buffer Objects). With VBOs enabled, Blender's interface should be snappier on more modern video cards. However, on older hardware, VBOs may cause Blender's screen to behave strangely.

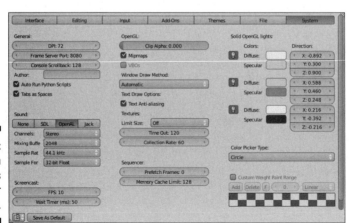

Figure 2-7: The System options in User Preferences.

✔ **Window Draw Method:** This drop-down menu is another fine place to look if Blender is displaying bizarrely on you. The default setting of Automatic should give you the best performance on your computer. However, if you're on an older machine, try seeing whether the Overlap or Full methods work better.

✔ **Color Picker Type:** Speaking of color pickers, the latest version of Blender added a new circular color picker widget, which is generally much faster to use for choosing colors when painting. However, everyone has different tastes in what color pickers they prefer to use, and some color pickers are better than others for specific purposes. For that reason, a drop-down menu contains a selection of different color pickers that you can use in Blender. Left-click the color swatches on the Solid OpenGL Lights and see which color picker suits you the best.

Using custom event maps

A primary inspiration for the deep structural changes introduced in Blender's code for the 2.5 series was to refactor Blender's *event system*. An event system is required for a complex program to interact with you and me, the users. Each time you press a button or move your mouse, it registers with the program as an *event*. The program then handles the event by performing an action of some sort. As an example, moving your mouse registers as an event, which then triggers your computer to perform the action of updating the location of the mouse cursor on your monitor. In earlier versions of Blender, the editors don't update until you release your mouse button.

With earlier versions of Blender, the event system was hard-coded and based on a design from the early 1990s. This setup not only made extending Blender difficult, but it also prevented Blender's interface from giving more instantaneous feedback. As an example, when you resize an area in Blender now, the editors in each area update while you're moving.

As an even more apparent benefit of the event system refactor, you've gained the ability to customize the event system to suit your needs, mapping events to a wide variety of possible Blender operations. Don't like using a particular hotkey in Blender's default configuration? You're free to change it!

If you refer to Figure 2-4, you should notice that the entire right side of the editor is devoted to modifying how events are handled within Blender. This list of events is particularly daunting to look at, and you can easily get lost among all those expanding and collapsing categories of events. Fortunately, you can modify how events are handled in a much easier way, and you don't even have to use the User Preferences editor if you don't want to. Instead, you can use the following steps:

1. **Find the operation you want to bind in Blender's menu system.**

   Say that you want to change the hotkey for opening a new project from Ctrl+N (the current hotkey) to Ctrl+X, the hotkey used in previous versions of Blender. You can find this operation by going to the Info editor's header and choosing File⇨New. Go to that menu item, but *don't click it* yet. Instead, proceed to the next step.

2. **Right-click the menu item for the operation and choose Change Shortcut from the menu that appears.**

   In this example, go to File⇨New, right-click it, and choose Change Shortcut. Blender prompts you for a new hotkey.

3. **When prompted, use the new hotkey that you want to assign.**

   In this case, you press Ctrl+X. Your new hotkey is assigned!

Figure 2-8 shows this process in action.

As of this writing, Blender doesn't currently warn you if you attempt to assign a hotkey that has already been bound to another operation. Blender simply double-binds the hotkey, favoring default behaviors over custom ones. Blender's interface will still say that your custom hotkey is assigned to the desired action, but it just won't work as expected. Currently, the only way to get around this problem is to make sure that your desired hotkey isn't already assigned.

Figure 2-8: Customizing a hotkey sequence directly from Blender's menus.

Of course, for ultimate control, the Input section of User Preferences is really the way to go. As daunting as this section may appear, it's actually pretty easy to use. The most effective way to make use of the event editor is to use the search feature, labeled Filter, in the upper right corner of the Input section:

1. **In the Filter field, type all or part of the operation you want to customize and press Enter.**

   The listing below updates with Blender's best guesses for the operation you're looking for. Alternatively, you can just drill down through the categories until you find the event you want.

2. **After you find the event you want, left-click the Edit button to the right of that event's category.**

   All available events for the category are now editable, and the Edit button changes to a Restore button. If at any time you decide that you want to revert to the system defaults, click the Restore button. Everything goes back to the way it initially was.

3. **Modify the event you want to change.**

   Changing an actual event is much like the process used to add hotkeys to menu items. It works like so:

   a. *Use the Type of Event Mapping drop-down menu displayed to the right or the operation name to stipulate whether the event is coming from a keyboard, mouse, text input, or some other source.* For example, if you're adjusting a hotkey, make sure that you've set it to Keyboard.

   b. *Left-click the Type of Event field that comes after the Type of Event Mapping menu.* It will either be blank or already have an event in it. Upon doing so, Blender prompts you for your new custom event (hotkey, mouse click, and so on.).

   c. *Set the event with the action you want assigned to it.* For example, if you're changing a hotkey, simply enter the key combination you want to use. If you decide that you don't want to change the event, just click anywhere outside of the Event Type field.

You can also use this interface to activate and deactivate events, delete events, and restore them to their initial values. Furthermore, if you expand the event's details by left-clicking the triangle to the left of the operation name, you have even more advanced controls. Figure 2-9 shows an expanded event.

Figure 2-9: Blender gives you a lot of custom control over its event system.

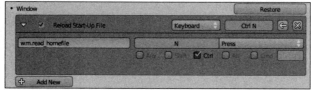

Customizing the event system can be a pretty involved topic, so if you're really interested in making extensive changes, it's to your benefit to play with the event system editor in the Input section of User Preferences a lot and make heavy use of the Restore buttons so that you can get Blender back to its defaults if something messes up.

After you have your events customized, you can save them to an external file that you can share with other users or simply carry with you on a USB drive so that your customized version of Blender is available wherever you go. To do so, click the Export Key Configuration button at the bottom of the User Preferences editor. A File Browser opens, and you can pick where you want to save your configuration file. The configuration is saved as a Python script. To load your custom configuration, it's possible to load your script in Blender and just run it. However, simply using the Import Key Configuration button at the bottom of the User Preferences editor is much easier.

Navigating in Three Dimensions

The 3D View is probably the most used window type in all of Blender. It also has some of the most unique interface decisions of any 3D software program. The purpose of this section is to guide you to understanding how to wield this part of Blender like a virtual 3D ninja!

All right, so perhaps I am a little over the top with the whole ninja thing, but hopefully this section takes you at least one or two steps closer to that goal.

Orbiting, panning, and zooming the 3D View

When trying to navigate a three-dimensional space through a two-dimensional screen like a computer monitor, you can't interact with that virtual 3D space exactly like you would in the real world, or as I like to call it, *meatspace*. The best way to visualize working in 3D through a program like Blender is to imagine the 3D View as your eyes to this 3D world. But rather than think of yourself as moving through this environment, imagine that you have the ability to move this entire world around in front of you.

The most basic way of navigating this space is called *orbiting*. Orbiting is the rough equivalent of rotating the 3D world around a fixed point in space. In order to orbit in Blender, middle-click anywhere in the 3D View and drag your mouse cursor around.

Occasionally, you have the need to keep your orientation to the world, but you'll want to move it around so that you can see a different part of the scene from the same angle. In Blender, this movement is called *panning*, and you do it by holding Shift while middle-clicking and dragging your mouse cursor in the 3D View. Now when you drag your mouse cursor around, the world shifts around without changing the angle that you're viewing from.

The third way of navigating 3D space is when you want to get closer to an object in your scene. Similar to working with a camera, this movement is called *zooming* the view. In Blender, you can zoom in two ways. The easiest method is by using your mouse's scroll wheel. By default, scrolling forward zooms in and scrolling back zooms out. However, this method doesn't always give you fine-grained control, and, even worse, some people don't have a mouse with a scroll wheel. In these cases, you can zoom by holding Ctrl while middle-clicking in the 3D View. Now, when you drag your mouse cursor up, you zoom in, and when you drag your mouse cursor down, you zoom out. If you prefer to move your mouse horizontally rather than vertically for zooming, you can adjust this behavior in the Input section of User Preferences.

Of course, if you happen to be working with a mouse that doesn't have a middle mouse button, you should go to User Preferences under Input and enable the Emulate 3 Button Mouse check box. With this check box enabled, you can emulate the middle mouse button by pressing Alt+left-click. So orbiting is Alt+left-click, panning is Shift+Alt+left-click, and zooming is done with Ctrl+Alt+left-click. Table 2-1 has a more organized way of showing these hotkeys.

Table 2-1   Keyboard/Mouse Keys for Navigating 3D Space

Navigation	Three-Button Mouse	Emulated 3-Button Mouse
Orbit	Middle-click	Alt+left-click
Pan	Shift+middle-click	Shift+Alt+left-click
Zoom	Ctrl+middle-click	Ctrl+Alt+left-click

Changing views

Although using the mouse to work your way around the 3D space is the most common way to adjust how you view things, Blender has some menu items and hotkey sequences that help give you specific views much faster and more accurately than you can do alone with your mouse.

The View menu

On occasion, you want to know what a model looks like when it's viewed directly from the front, side, or top. Blender has some convenient shortcuts for quickly switching to these views. The most obvious way is to use the View menu in the 3D View's header, as shown in Figure 2-10. This menu lets you choose a variety of angles, including the top, front, right, and the view from any of the cameras you may have in your scene.

Figure 2-10:
The View menu in the 3D View.

You can also use this menu to switch between orthographic and perspective views. The *orthographic* view of a 3D scene is similar to how technical drawings and blueprints are done. If two objects are the same size, they always appear to be the same size, regardless of how far away from you they are. This view is ideal for getting sizes and proportions correct in your models, especially if they're based on blueprints or technical drawings. The *perspective* view is more akin to how you actually see things. That is, objects in the distance look smaller than objects that are near you.

Behold the power of the numeric keypad!

The View menu is certainly helpful, but you can change your view in an even faster way: the numeric keypad. Each button on your keyboard's numeric keypad has an extremely fast way of changing your viewing angle in the 3D View. Figure 2-11 is an image of the numeric keypad with an indication of what each key does.

If the image in Figure 2-11 doesn't quite work for you as a reference, Table 2-2 shows what each key does in a table-based format.

In Figure 2-11, notice that the hotkeys are arranged in a way that corresponds with how you would expect them to be. Top view is at the top of the keypad at Numpad 7. The front view is accessed at Numpad 1, and if you move to the right on the keypad, you can see the right side view by pressing Numpad 3. Because it's the view you render from, the active camera is the most important and therefore gets the largest key at Numpad 0. Pressing Numpad 5 is a quick way to toggle between orthographic and perspective views. If you have View Name turned on in the Interface section of User Preferences, it actively informs you about which view you're using. And having the very cool Smooth View option enabled definitely helps you keep from getting disoriented while working.

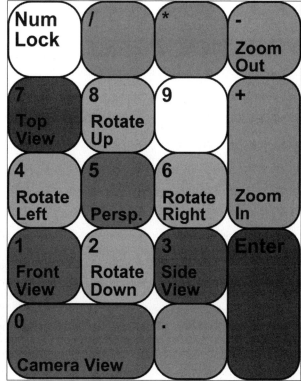

Figure 2-11: The numeric keypad is your ultimate tool for navigating 3D space.

The notions of what is left and right in the 3D View are relative to you, *not* the object or scene you're working in. That is, if you model a character who's facing you from the front view, pressing Numpad 3 (right side view) shows your character's *left* side. This setup can be a bit confusing in writing or conversation, but while you're working, it's really not much of an issue. I actually tend to think of the right and left side views as *side view* and *other side view* to avoid confusing myself.

Table 2-2		Hotkeys on the Numeric Keypad			
Hotkey	*Result*	*Hotkey*	*Result*	*Hotkey*	*Result*
1	Front	Ctrl+1	Back	+	Zoom in
2	Orbit back	Ctrl+2	Pan down	-	Zoom out
3	Right side	Ctrl+3	Left side	/	Toggle local view
4	Orbit left	Ctrl+4	Pan left	.	View selected
5	Ortho/Persp				
6	Orbit right	Ctrl+6	Pan right		
7	Top	Ctrl+7	Bottom		
8	Orbit forward	Ctrl+8	Pan up		
0	Camera view	Ctrl+0	Set active object as camera	Ctrl+Alt+0	Set user view as camera

Here is where the numeric keypad shows its real power. With the numeric keypad, you can just as easily view the opposite angle (bottom, back, or left side views) as you can the standard views. To see the opposite side of the standard views, press Ctrl while hitting the corresponding Numpad key. For example, if you want to see the bottom view, press Ctrl+Numpad 7.

Now, maybe you got a little bit excited and hit Ctrl+Numpad 0 to see what the opposite of the camera view is and had some unexpected results. Ctrl+Numpad 0 does something entirely different than pressing Ctrl in combination with the other Numpad numbers. The Ctrl+Numpad 0 hotkey actually allows you to treat any selectable object in Blender as a camera, with the view looking down the object's local Z-axis. You can also access this functionality from the View menu at View⇨Cameras⇨Set Active Object as Camera. If you're confused, take a quick look at the beginning of Chapter 3 for more explanation on local and global coordinate systems. The ability to treat any object as a camera may seem like a strange feature to have, but it can be really helpful for doing things like aiming lights and checking the line of sight of an object or a character.

TIP

Another cool thing you can do with Numpad 0 is to quickly snap the camera to your user view. For example, say that you've been working on a 3D model for a while from a certain angle, and you want to see what the model looks like in a render from that specific angle. Rather than try to grab and rotate your camera to get close to this same angle, you can simply press Ctrl+Alt+Numpad 0 or choose View➪Align View➪Align Active Camera to View, and the camera jumps directly to where you're viewing your model from. I find myself using this hotkey sequence quite a bit when I'm creating my models. Sometimes it's just easier to change your user view and snap your camera to it than it is to aim the camera how you want it.

The numeric keypad also gives you the ability to navigate your scene like you might normally do with your mouse. You use the 8, 4, 6, and 2 keys on the numeric keypad. Numpad 8 and Numpad 2 orbit the view forward and back, respectively, whereas Numpad 4 and Numpad 6 orbit it left and right. By default, Blender does these rotations in 15-degree increments, but you adjust this amount to be more fine or coarse in User Preferences under Interface with the value labeled Rotation Angle. Orbiting with the Numpad is a nice way to get a quick turntable view of a scene, particularly if you have your View rotation set to Trackball in User Preferences. You can also pan the view by pressing Ctrl in combination with any of these buttons. For example, Ctrl+Numpad 4 and Ctrl+Numpad 6 pan the view left and right. You can even zoom the view by using the Numpad Plus (+) and Numpad Minus (-) keys.

Two more useful hotkeys are on the numeric keypad: Numpad Slash (/) and Numpad Dot (.). These keys are somewhat more esoteric than the other keys, but they definitely come in handy.

Of the two, I tend to use Numpad Slash the most. Pressing Numpad Slash (/) toggles what Blender calls *Local View*. Basically, Local View hides everything in your scene except for the object or objects you've selected. Local View is really helpful for temporarily isolating a single object or set of objects in a complex scene so that you can work on it without anything else getting in your way.

Another key worth mentioning, although it's not exactly on the numeric keypad, is the Home key. Whereas using Numpad Dot (.) brings your selected objects into view, pressing Home zooms your view back until all objects in your scene are visible in the 3D View. Home is a very convenient key for getting an overall idea of what's going on in your scene.

Viewport shading types

Aside from changing the angle from which you view your 3D world, you may also want to change how the world is shown in the 3D View. In particular, I'm referring to what is called the *viewport shading*. By default, Blender starts in the Solid shading type, which shows your models as solid 3D objects, lit by the OpenGL lights you can set in Blender's User Preferences under System. You can change the viewport shading by going to the 3D View's header and left-clicking the button with a white circular icon, as shown in Figure 2-12.

Clicking this button reveals the following possible viewport shading types:

- ✔ **Textured:** The textured viewport shading type attempts to faithfully show you what your object will look like when textured and lit for the final render. The preview may differ a bit from what the final looks like, but short of rendering, it should give you the best idea to work from. Pressing Alt+Z quickly toggles between this viewport shading type and the solid one.

  If you have the a modern accelerated video card, you can enable GLSL (OpenGL Shading Language) shaders from the Properties region of the 3D View (View➪Properties or the N hotkey) under Display➪Shading. Change this drop-down menu from Multitexture to GLSL; when you use image-based textures, the textured viewport shading type will be more accurate. More on this topic is in Chapter 8.

- ✔ **Solid:** Solid is the default viewport shading type that Blender starts with. Press Z to toggle between solid and wireframe. Using solid is usually the standard work mode for working in Blender. If you have an older video card, the textured viewport shading types will perform much slower than this one.

- ✔ **Wireframe:** This viewport shading type shows the objects in your scene as transparent line drawings. The wireframe viewport shading type is a good quick way to get an idea of the structure of your models. And because wireframe is a bunch of lines, Blender doesn't have to worry about shading and therefore doesn't tax your computer's processor as much. On older computers, Blender is a lot more responsive using wireframe than it is when using solid or textured.

- ✔ **Bounding Box:** The bounding box viewport shading type replaces your 3D object with a wireframe cube that shows how much space your object takes up in the 3D world. This type isn't as commonly used as the others, but it does come in handy for quickly placing objects in a scene or detecting when two objects might collide. It can also be handy for scenes that feature a lot of complex geometry.

If you have more than one 3D View editor, they don't all have to have the same viewport shading. You can see the wireframe of your model in one editor while adjusting the lighting by using the textured viewport shading in another.

Selecting objects

How you select objects is one of the most controversial design decisions in Blender's interface: In nearly every other program, you select things — be they text, 3D objects, files, or whatever — by left-clicking them. This is not the case in Blender. When you left-click in the 3D View, all it seems to do is move around some strange crosshair thing. That thing is Blender's 3D cursor. I talk more about the 3D cursor later, but in the meantime, you're probably thinking, "How in the world do I select anything?"

The answer is simple: You select objects in Blender by right-clicking them. Multiple objects are selected and deselected by Shift+right-clicking them.

Although right-clicking to select certainly seems strange, there is actually a reason for doing it this way. This design decision wasn't made at random or just to be different for the sake of being different. There are actually two reasons for doing it this way. One is philosophical, and the other is practical.

- ✔ **Blender's approach to using the mouse:** In Blender, the left mouse button is intended to be used to perform or confirm an action. You left-click buttons or menus and left-click to confirm the completion of an operation like moving, rotating, or scaling an object, and you use it to place the 3D cursor. Selecting an object doesn't really act upon it or change it. So right-click is used to select objects as well as cancel an operation before it's completed. This setup is a bit abstract, but as you work this way, it does actually begin to make sense.

- ✔ **Prevention of Repetitive Stress Injury (RSI):** Computer graphics artists like 3D modelers and animators are known for working at a computer for insanely long stretches of time. Repetitive stress injury, or RSI, is a real concern. The more you can spread the work across the hand, the lower the chance of RSI. By making it so that you're not doing every single operation with the left mouse button, Blender helps in this regard.

Bottom line, the right-click-to-select paradigm really is a nice, efficient way of working in 3D space after you get used to it. However, if you try it and still don't like it, Blender offers you the ability to swap left and right mouse button usage in the Input section of User Preferences. Do note, however, that this book is written with the default right-click behavior in mind, so remember that as you read other chapters.

Taking advantage of the 3D cursor

"Okay," you say, "I can handle the right-click-to-select thing. But what's with these crosshairs that move to where ever I left-click? It seems pretty useless."

Those crosshairs are the 3D cursor. It's a unique concept that I've only seen in Blender, and this design is anything but useless. The best way to understand the 3D cursor is to think about a word processor or text editor. When you add text or want to change something, it's usually done with or relative to the blinking cursor on the screen. Blender's 3D cursor serves pretty much the same purpose, but in three dimensions. When you add a new object, it's placed wherever the 3D cursor is located. When you rotate or scale an object, you can do it relative to the 3D cursor's location. And when you want to snap an object to a specific location, you do it with the 3D cursor.

In terms of adjusting your 3D View, you can use the 3D cursor as a quick way to recenter your view. Simply place the 3D cursor anywhere in the 3D View by left-clicking. Now press Ctrl+Numpad Dot (.) and watch as the 3D View adjusts to put the cursor at the center of the window. This is similar to pressing Numpad Dot (.), except that you don't have to select any objects. Another convenient hotkey sequence is Shift+C. This combination relocates the 3D cursor to the origin coordinates of the 3D environment and then brings all objects into view. The Shift+C hotkey combination is like pressing Home with the added benefit of moving the cursor to the origin.

In Chapter 3, I cover the topic of grabbing, scaling, and rotating objects. Usually, you want to use Blender's default behavior of doing these operations relative to the median point of the selected objects. However, you can also perform any of these operations relative to the 3D cursor by pressing the Period (.) key on your keyboard or selecting 3D Cursor from the Pivot menu in the 3D View's header, as shown in Figure 2-13. You can use this menu to switch back to the default behavior or press Comma (,).

Figure 2-13:
The Pivot
menu in the
3D View.

The 3D cursor is also very useful for *snapping*, or moving a selection to a specific point in space. For a better idea of what snapping means, hover your mouse over the 3D View and press Shift+S. A menu like the one in Figure 2-14 appears.

Figure 2-14:
The Snap
menu.

Through this menu, you can snap your selected object to a fixed coordinate on the grid in the 3D View, the location of the cursor, or to the center of the grid, also known as the *origin* of the scene. You also have the ability to snap the 3D cursor to the middle of multiple selected objects, a fixed location on the grid, or to the active object in the scene. This method is a very effective way to move an object to a specific point in 3D space, and it's all thanks to the little 3D cursor.

New Features in Blender's 3D View Since 2.5

In addition to the massive changes Blender had under the hood for the 2.5 series with things like the event system refactor, veterans of earlier Blender releases should notice that Blender has had quite a face-lift performed on its interface. The organization of the Properties editor, covered earlier in this chapter in the "Working with the Properties Editor" section, is just one small example. Some of the most prominent updates to Blender's interface have been added to the 3D View. This section outlines a few of these changes.

Quad View

If you've used other 3D graphics programs, you may be used to something referred to as *Quad View*, where the 3D View is split into four regions: top, front, and right orthographic views and a user perspective view. In former versions of Blender, re-creating this layout was a somewhat arduous task of manually splitting areas and then setting up each area as a 3D View from each of those perspectives. And worse, with no way to lock those views in place, you could very easily change one of your orthographic views to user perspective on accident. Fortunately, this situation is no longer the case. Go to the 3D View's header and click View⇨Toggle Quad View or use the hotkey Ctrl+Alt+Q, and your 3D View will switch to look like the one in Figure 2-15.

When toggling back to Full View from Quad View, Blender chooses the view that your mouse cursor is hovering over when you do the switch. As a result, when you use the View menu (View⇨Toggle Quad View), you'll almost always pop back to the top view. However, if you use the Ctrl+Alt+Q hotkey with your mouse cursor over one of the other views, Blender will pick that one as Full View.

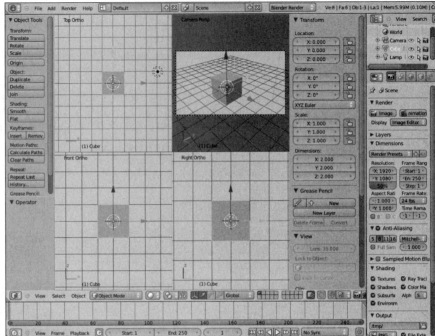

Figure 2-15:
Using the
Ctrl+Alt+Q
hotkey, you
can quickly
switch
between
Blender's
regular
viewport
and a
Quad View
viewport
like some
other 3D
programs
have.

Regions

Figure 2-15 also shows another addition to the 3D View: regions. Regions serve as a replacement for the floating panels of previous Blender versions. The major difference between regions and floating panels is that regions more closely adhere to Blender's non-overlapping philosophy.

You've actually had exposure to one type of region: the header. Like any region, you can collapse, expand, and flip the header region to the opposite side of the area.

Of course, the header isn't the only region available in the 3D View. In Figure 2-15, regions flank either side of the 3D View area. On the left is a Tool Shelf, and on the right is a region for modifying the properties of the 3D View, referred to as the Properties region or the Information region.

The Properties/Information region

You can toggle the visibility of the Properties region by going to View➪Properties in the header or by pressing N while your mouse cursor is in the 3D View. In fact, quite a few editors in Blender have a Properties region. And with the exception of the Text Editor, you can consistently open all of them by using the N hotkey.

In the 3D View, the Properties region serves two primary purposes. Most obviously, it allows you to directly modify your selected object by typing in explicit location, rotation, and scale values within the Transform panel. The rest of the region, however, is dedicated to customizing your 3D View. From here, you can control features like the location of the 3D cursor, which axis is displayed, the appearance of the grid floor, and the shading mode used for the textured viewport shading type (Multitexture or GLSL). This region is also where you go if you want to load a background image in the 3D View as a modeling reference. You can find out more about using background images for modeling in Chapter 5.

Because Blender has a Properties editor as well as a Properties region, you may find it useful to think of the Properties region as an Information region instead. It's a game of semantics, but by thinking of it as an Information region, the N hotkey is easier to remember.

The Tool Shelf

You can toggle the Tool Shelf's visibility by going to View⇨Tool Shelf in the header or by using the T hotkey. Think of the Tool Shelf as a place for frequently used tools or operators, referred to as *shortcuts*. Having shortcuts in the Tool Shelf is extremely helpful for helping you work faster, especially if you haven't memorized all of Blender's various hotkeys. This way, frequently used tools are only a single click away rather than the multiple clicks it might take you to hunt through the menu system.

The Tool Shelf holds an additional feature that's extremely useful. At the bottom of the Tool Shelf is the Last Operator panel. If you've just opened Blender, this panel should just have the heading of Operator. However, if you perform an action in Blender like moving your selected object or adding a new object, this panel updates to display values relevant to that operation. Using this panel, you can perform a quick, rough operation and then tweak it to be more precise. For example, if you add a UV sphere to your scene (Shift+A⇨Add Mesh⇨UV Sphere), Blender adds a UV sphere object to your scene at the location of the 3D cursor with 32 segments and 24 rings. Using the Last Operator panel of the Tool Shelf, you can not only adjust the location of your new sphere, but you can also modify the number of segments and rings it has. You can see more on how the Last Operator panel is used in Chapter 5.

You should note that the Last Operator panel is only relevant for the last operation you actually performed. It's not a construction history, and it doesn't persistently remain in memory after you perform subsequent operations. For example, if you add a UV sphere and then immediately rotate that sphere, there's no way for you to adjust the number of segments and rings in it from the Last Operator section. Even if you undo the rotate operation, those Last Operator values won't return. The Last Operation section relates to the last thing you did — no more, no less.

Don't know how to do something? Hooray for fully integrated search!

Blender's event system refactor provides one additional side effect that's incredibly useful, especially for new users: a search feature that's fully integrated into Blender's interface.

The benefit here is that if you know the operation you want to perform, but don't know where to go in Blender's interface to access it, you can simply search for that operation and perform it immediately. How's that for awesome?

The fastest way to access Blender's integrated search feature from any editor is to press spacebar. A menu with a search field at the top appears. Start typing the name of the operation you want to perform, and Blender updates the menu with search results that match what you typed. Furthermore, hotkeys show up to the right of the operator name in the menu so that you can remember the hotkey in the future. As an example, bring up the search menu (Spacebar) and type **save**. As you type, the menu updates with operations within Blender that relate to saving.

Using the integrated search feature is a great way to familiarize yourself with the way Blender works, especially if you're migrating from another program. In that case, you know the terminology for what you want to do; you just have to find out how Blender does it. Figure 2-16 shows Blender's integrated search menu.

Figure 2-16:
Blender's
integrated
search
menu is
a great
way to get
familiar with
Blender's
operators.

Chapter 3

Getting Your Hands Dirty Working in Blender

In This Chapter

▶ Understanding coordinate system orientations

▶ Making changes to 3D objects

▶ Speeding up the process with hotkeys

*B*lender is built for speed, and its design heavily emphasizes working as quickly and efficiently as possible for extended periods of time. On more than one occasion, I've found myself working in Blender for 10 to 15 hours straight (or longer). Although, admittedly, part of this ridiculous scheduling has to do with my own minor lunacy, the fact that I'm able to be that productive for that long is a testament to Blender's design. This chapter gets you started in taking full advantage of that power. I cover the meat and potatoes of interacting with three-dimensional (3D) space in Blender, such as moving objects and editing polygons.

If you've worked in other 3D programs, chances are good that a number of Blender concepts may seem particularly alien to you. Although this divide has been greatly reduced in Blender's recent update, to quote Yoda, "You must unlearn what you have learned" in your journey to become a Blender Jedi. If you've never worked in 3D, you may actually have a slight advantage over a trained professional who's used to a different workflow. Hooray for starting fresh!

Grabbing, Scaling, and Rotating

The three basic object operations in a 3D scene are the transformations known (by mathematicians) as translation, scale, and orientation. People who speak Blenderese use the terms *grab, scale,* and *rotate,* respectively. Other programs might also use the term *move* in place of *grab* or *size* in place of *scale.* You can use these three operations to place any object in 3D space at any arbitrary size and with any arbitrary orientation.

Also, because Blender tries to maintain consistency throughout its interface, you can use these transform operations in more than just the 3D View. For example, the same grab and scale operations work when you want to edit keyframes and motion curves in the Graph Editor! How's that for convenient?

In addition to having an emphasis on efficiency, Blender is designed to allow you to work for as long as possible while incurring the least amount of repetitive stress. For this reason, relatively few operations in Blender require you to hold down a key. Typically, you press and release a key to begin the operation. Then you confirm its completion by left-clicking with your mouse or pressing Enter. To cancel the operation, right-click or press Esc. In fact, this keyboard combination even works on some operations that require you to hold down a button. For example, if you try to split an area (left-click and drag a corner widget) and then decide you don't actually want to split it, you can right-click while adjusting the boundary between areas, and the operation stops.

Differentiating Between Coordinate Systems

Before you bound headlong into applying transformations to your objects, you need to understand how coordinate systems work in 3D space. All coordinate systems in Blender are based on a grid consisting of three axes: X, Y, and Z. The X-axis typically represents side-to-side movement, whereas the Y-axis represents front-to-back movement, and the Z-axis goes from top to bottom. This grid system with axes is referred to as the Cartesian grid. The origin, or center, of this grid is at the (0,0,0) coordinate. The difference in the coordinate systems within Blender lies in the way this grid is oriented relative to a selected 3D object. Figure 3-1 shows the Coordinate System Orientation menu in the 3D View header when you left-click it.

If you're coming from another 3D program, you may find the way Blender handles coordinates a bit disorienting. Programs like 3DS Max and Maya have the Y-axis representing vertical movement and the Z-axis going from front to back. Currently, you can't change the coordinate system in Blender to match these programs, so this system is one of those things that migrating users just need to get used to.

As Figure 3-1 shows, you can choose from five orientations: *View, Normal, Gimbal, Local,* and *Global.* Working in any of these coordinate systems gives you absolute control of how your object lives in 3D space. Depending on how you'd like to transform your object, one orientation may be more appropriate than the others. Blender also gives you the ability to create custom orientations. That topic is slightly more advanced than I have room to cover in this book, but after you create a custom orientation, it also becomes available on the Coordinate System Orientation menu.

Figure 3-1:
The
Coordinate
System
Orientation
menu.

This list describes details of the five possible orientations:

✔ **Global:** You see this orientation of Blender's base grid in the 3D View. In many ways, the Global orientation is the primary orientation to which everything else relates, and it's the base coordinate system described at the beginning of this section. The Z-axis, marked in blue, runs vertically in the space. The Y-axis is marked in green, moving along the front-to-back line, and the X-axis is in red, along the side-to-side line. The origin is located directly at the center of the grid.

✔ **Local:** In addition to the Global orientation, each 3D object in Blender has a local coordinate system. The base of this system isn't the same as the Global coordinate system's base. Instead, this coordinate system is relative to the center point, or origin, of your object. The *object origin* is represented by the orange dot that's usually located at the center of your 3D object. By default, when you first add a new object in Blender, its Local coordinate system of the object is aligned to the Global axis, but after you start moving your object around, its Local coordinate system can differ greatly from the Global orientation.

✔ **Gimbal:** When you rotate an object about its X, Y, and Z axes, the angles about those axes are known as Euler (pronounced like "oiler") angles. Unfortunately, a side effect of using Euler angles is that you have the possibility of running into *gimbal lock*. You run into this problem when one of your rotation axes matches another one. For example, if you rotate your object 90 degrees about its X-axis, then rotating around its Y-axis is the same as rotating about its Z-axis; they're *locked* together, which can prove to be a problem, especially when animating. This orientation mode in Blender is a way to help you visualize where the axes are so that you can avoid gimbal lock.

✔ **Normal:** The Normal orientation is a set of axes that's perpendicular to some arbitrary plane. When working with just objects, this description doesn't really apply, so the Normal orientation is exactly the same as the Local orientation. When you begin editing meshes, though, Normal orientation makes more sense because you have *normals* to work with. Blender also uses the Normal orientation for the local coordinate system of bones when working with Armatures for animation. A nice way to think about the Normal orientation is the "more local than local" orientation. Chapter 4 covers editing meshes in more detail, and Chapter 11 covers working with Armatures in depth.

✔ **View:** The View orientation appears relative to how you're looking at the 3D View. Regardless of how you move around in a scene, you're always looking down the Z-axis of the View coordinate system. The Y-axis is always vertical, and the X-axis is always horizontal in this orientation.

All these coordinate system explanations can be (please forgive the pun) disorienting. An easy way to visualize this concept is to imagine that your body represents the Global coordinate system, and this book is a 3D object oriented in space. If you hold the book out in front of you and straighten your arms, you move the book away from you. It's moving in the positive Y direction, both globally and locally. Now, if you twist the book to the right a few degrees and do the same thing, it still moves in the positive Y direction globally. However, in its local orientation, the book is moving in both a positive Y direction and a negative X direction. To move it in just the positive local Y direction, you move the book in the direction in which its spine is pointing.

To relate this concept to the View orientation, assume that your eyes are the View axis. If you look straight ahead and move the book up and down, you're translating it along the View orientation's Y-axis. Gimbal orientation would be if you rotate the book 90 degrees toward you, rotating about its X-axis. Then it's Y and Z axes are locked together. For a clear reference, the 3D manipulator in Figure 3-2 shows the difference between the coordinate systems.

Figure 3-2:
The Global, Local, View, Gimbal, and Normal coordinate orientations.

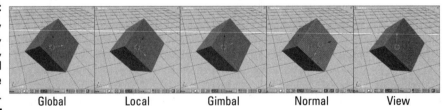

Global   Local   Gimbal   Normal   View

The last object you select is the *active* object. If you're using the Local, Gimbal, or Normal orientations and select multiple objects, the transform operations happen relative to the active object's orientation.

You can quickly change the coordinate system you're using by using the Alt+Spacebar hotkey.

Transforming an Object by Using the 3D Manipulator

In Blender's default configuration, the 3D *manipulator* is activated and viewable at the center of your selected object. You can use the manipulator to transform any object in a 3D scene. When Blender first starts, the manipulator is in Translate (Grab) mode, which you can determine in two ways:

- ✔ The manipulator itself looks like a set of colored axes located at the center of the selected object.

- ✔ In the 3D View's header, the button with the blue arrow icon on it is depressed to indicate that the manipulator is in Translate mode. By default, the manipulator is oriented to align with the Global axis.

In all coordinate system orientations under Blender, red represents the X-axis, green the Y, and blue the Z. If you think about the primary colors for light, a handy way to think of this is XYZ = RGB.

Switching manipulator modes

As you might expect, translation isn't the only transform operation available to you with the manipulator. If you refer to the 3D View's header to the left of where the Coordinate System Orientation menu is located, the button with the blue arc icon on it activates Rotation manipulator mode, and the button with the icon of a line connecting to the corner of a square activates Scale mode. Press the Rotation mode button to see the change in the look of the 3D manipulator. In this mode, the manipulator is a set of semicircles around the object's center, with the proper color representing each axis. Pressing the Scale mode button for the manipulator changes it to look much like it does in Translate mode, except that you see a small cube, rather than an arrow, at the end of each axis.

The 3D manipulator should be familiar to you if you've used other programs, where the corresponding tool might be called a *widget* or a *gizmo*. However, the Blender manipulator also does something else: It lets you activate multiple modes at the same time. Hold down Shift while pressing the appropriate button to activate a manipulator. You can then make any combination of transform modes active simultaneously. Many Blender users find this capability particularly helpful for animation, where some situations require quick access to translation and rotation but not necessarily to adjust the object's scale. Figure 3-3 shows the three separate modes of the manipulator, as well as the combo manipulator.

Figure 3-3:
The
Translate,
Rotate,
Scale, and
Combo
manipulator
modes.

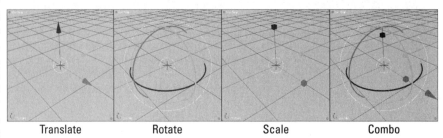

| Translate | Rotate | Scale | Combo |

Using the manipulator

To translate a selected object with the manipulator, follow these steps:

1. **Make sure that Translate mode is active by left-clicking the Translate manipulator mode button in the 3D View's header.**

2. **Left-click the manipulator arrow that points in the direction you want to move the object and drag to the location where you want to place your object.**

   For example, to move an object along the X-axis, left-click the red arrow on the manipulator. To cancel the operation, right-click or press Esc.

Notice also the white circle around the origin of the Translate manipulator in Figure 3-3. To translate a selected object in the X- and Y-axis of the View orientation, left-click and drag this circle. This convenient shortcut prevents you from having to continually switch orientation modes for the manipulator.

You can use the Ctrl and Shift while transforming to have more control. Move in fixed increments with default settings by holding down Ctrl. Hold down Shift while transforming an object to make adjustments on a finer scale. Hold down the Ctrl+Shift key combo while transforming to make adjustments in smaller fixed increments. Interestingly, these same modifier keys work when using any of Blender's value input fields.

This fixed-increment control is similar to the basic *snapping to the grid*, or *Increment* snapping, found in other 2D and 3D applications. Blender also offers the ability to snap your selected object to other objects (or parts of them), called *snap targets,* in your scene. Choices for snap targets are *Increment, Vertex, Edge, Face*, and *Volume*. You choose which snap target you want to use by left-clicking the Snap Element menu in the 3D View's header, as shown in Figure 3-4.

Figure 3-4:
The Snap
Target
Mode
button.

Holding Ctrl while transforming is actually a way to temporarily enable snapping behavior based on a chosen snap target. However, you may prefer snapping to be the default behavior (so you don't have to hold down Ctrl). You can enable snapping by left-clicking the magnet icon next to the Snap Element menu in the 3D View's header or by using the Shift+Tab hotkey. This option tells Blender to snap as default and that holding down Ctrl then temporarily disables snapping.

Here are the different available types of snap targets in Blender:

- **Increment:** In Blender's default behavior, your selection is snapped to fixed increments of Blender's base grid.

- **Vertex:** The vertex is the fundamental element of a mesh object in Blender. Using this target, the center of your selection snaps to vertices or points (for curves and armatures) in other objects.

- **Edge:** The line connecting vertices is referred to as an *edge.* Select this target to snap your selection to edges in objects of your scene.

- **Face:** Edges connect to one another to create polygons, referred to as *faces.* Choose this option to snap to them with your selection.

- **Volume:** When faces connect to create a surface, that closed surface is referred to as a *volume.* You can choose this option to snap your selection to an object's volume. This option is particularly useful when creating a rig for animating characters, as described in Chapter 11.

Snapping targets work in both Object mode as well as Edit mode. For more information on Edit mode, vertices, edges, and faces, see Chapter 4.

You can quickly change snap modes by using the Shift+Ctrl+Tab hotkey combination.

You can observe the changes made to your object in real time by looking in the 3D View's header as you transform it. Figure 3-5 shows how the header explicitly indicates how much you're changing the object in each axis.

Figure 3-5:
You can
view
changes
in the 3D
View's
header.

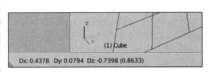

Dx: 0.4378 Dy: 0.0794 Dz: -0.7398 (0.8633)

Suppose that you don't want to move the object in the direction of just one axis. Instead, you prefer the freedom to move the object in the plane created by two axes, such as the XY, XZ, or YZ planes. Just Shift+left-click on the axis that's perpendicular to the plane in which you want to move. This axis is the one that's normal to the plane. For example, assuming that you want to scale the object in the XY plane, Shift+left-click the Z-axis cube of the Scale manipulator.

I use this technique a lot when modeling furniture and buildings. I can quickly scale a cube with the proper depth along a single plane to create a tabletop or a wall.

Transform operations are consistent across all manipulator modes in Blender, so you can apply any of these methods of interacting with the Translate manipulator in the Rotate and Scale manipulator modes. The only exception is that Shift+left-clicking an axis on the Rotate manipulator operates just like simply left-clicking the axis: It doesn't make sense to try to simultaneously rotate around two axes with any form of control. And don't forget that you aren't limited to working in just the Global coordinate system. You can choose any of the other four orientations from the Transform Orientation menu and the 3D manipulator adjusts to fit that orientation.

Saving Time by Using Hotkeys

Many professional Blender users find that the manipulator obstructs their view too much when working, so they disable it outright. To disable the manipulator, go to the 3D View's header near the manipulator mode buttons and click the button with the color axis icon. Alternatively, you can press Ctrl+Spacebar.

But wait, with the manipulator gone, how do I transform my objects? I'm glad you asked. Enter one of the most powerful features of Blender: hotkeys.

Part of the beauty of Blender's hotkeys are that they take a lot of pressure off of your mouse hand and shorten the distance of mouse-based operations. The accumulation of these little timesaving actions is what makes using hotkeys so powerful.

Transforming with hotkeys

You can access nearly every piece of major functionality in Blender with hotkeys. Transforms are no exception. *Translating* in Blenderese is called *grabbing*. That naming has specific significance as it pertains to hotkeys. To see what I mean, use the following steps to Grab/Translate your object:

1. **Select the object you want to move by right-clicking it.**

2. **Press G.**

   Congratulations! You're translating your object.

3. **Confirm the translation by left-clicking or pressing Enter.**

   Cancel by right-clicking or pressing Esc.

To rotate your object, press R. Scale it by pressing S. See a pattern here? The majority of Blender's default hotkeys are easy to remember. Most of them just use the first letter from the operation in question. And just like when using the manipulator, the familiar Ctrl, Shift, and Ctrl+Shift keypresses for snapping and fine adjustments still apply here.

Hotkeys and coordinate systems

By default, your transformations all happen in the View coordinate system when you use hotkeys. So no matter how you're viewing the scene, you're working in the XY-plane of the 3D View.

Suppose, however, that you want to grab your object and move it in the global Z-axis. You use a sequence of keypresses to do this action. Use the following steps to grab an object and move it to the global Z-axis:

1. **With your object selected, press G.**

   You're now in Grab/Translate mode.

2. **Without canceling this operation, press Z.**

   A blue line should appear that indicates the global Z-axis. Your object is locked to move only along that line. If you press Y, your object moves only along the global Y-axis and pressing X locks it to the global X-axis.

Pretty neat, huh? This method of using a sequence of hotkeys works with rotating and scaling as well (for example, R⇨Z rotates around the global Z-axis and S⇨X scales along the global X-axis).

What about the Local orientation? That's just one more keypress in the sequence. Follow these steps to grab an object and move it along its local Y-axis:

1. **Act like you are going to translate the object in the global Y-axis by pressing G⇨Y.**

2. **Press Y a second time.**

   You're translating in the local Y-axis. Pressing Y a third time brings you back into moving in the default View coordinate system.

If you want to use the Normal or Gimbal orientations, you can use the same preceding sequence. You just have to make sure that your Coordinate System Orientation is set to either Normal or Gimbal. Even though the 3D manipulator is disabled, Blender still pays attention to your choice here when you press the axis letter for the second time.

Again, this method of using a sequence of keypresses works with scaling and rotation as well. Keying the sequence R⇨X⇨X rotates around the local X-axis and S⇨Z⇨Z scales along the local Z-axis.

One of the more powerful features of the 3D manipulator is the ability to work in a plane rather than just one axis. You can work in a plane with hotkeys as well by using the same logic used in the manipulator. Use Shift plus the letter of the axis that's perpendicular to the plane you want to move in. For example, to scale your object in the global XY-plane, press S⇨Shift+Z. For the local XY plane, press S⇨Shift+Z⇨Shift+Z. This same methodology also works for the Grab operation (though, like with the manipulator, not for the Rotate operation).

Table 3-1 shows most of the useful hotkey sequences for transforming your objects.

Table 3-1   Useful Hotkey Sequences for Transformations

Grab	Scale	Rotate	Orientation
G	S	R	View
G⇨Z	S⇨Z	R⇨Z	Global Z-axis
G⇨Y	S⇨Y	R⇨Y	Global Y-axis
G⇨X	S⇨X	R⇨X	Global X-axis
G⇨Z⇨Z	S⇨Z⇨Z	R⇨Z⇨Z	Local Z-axis
G⇨Y⇨Y	S⇨Y⇨Y	R⇨Y⇨Y	Local Y-axis
G⇨X⇨X	S⇨X⇨X	R⇨X⇨X	Local X-axis
G⇨Shift+Z	S⇨Shift+Z	N/A	Global XY-plane
G⇨Shift+Y	S⇨Shift+Y	N/A	Global XZ-plane
G⇨Shift+X	S⇨Shift+X	N/A	Global YZ-plane
G⇨Shift+Z⇨Shift+Z	S⇨Shift+Z⇨Shift+Z	N/A	Local XY-plane
G⇨Shift+Y⇨Shift+Y	S⇨Shift+Y⇨Shift+Y	N/A	Local XZ-plane

An even faster way to constrain to axes involves using the middle mouse button. As an example, select an object and grab (G) it. Now move your mouse in roughly the direction of the X-axis and then middle-click. A red line should appear through your object's origin, and the object should be locked to moving along that line, constraining you to that axis. The same thing works in both the Y- and Z-axes. For an even more interactive way of constraining axes, hold down your middle mouse button while you're grabbing. All three axes appear, and your object locks to one of them as you bring your mouse closer to them. I absolutely *love* this feature.

While you're working with hotkeys to transform your objects in Blender, it's worth noting that Blender has a *tweak mode* that allows for making very fast grab adjustments with your mouse. To activate tweak mode, select (right-click) the object or subobject (vertex, control point, and so on) you want to move and drag your mouse in any direction. This shortcut takes you right into grabbing as if you'd selected the object and then pressed G, only faster! Many beginning users find themselves accidentally popping into tweak mode by moving their mouse while selecting. Now that you know how tweak mode works, you won't be caught by surprise, and you can take full advantage of this timesaving feature.

Numerical input

Not only can you use hotkeys to activate the various transform modes, but you can also use the keyboard to explicitly input exactly how much you would like your object to be transformed. Simply type the number of units you want to change after you activate the transform mode.

As an example, suppose that you want to rotate your object 32 degrees around the global X-axis. To do so, press R⇨X⇨32 and confirm by pressing Enter. Translate your object -26.4 units along its local Y-axis by pressing G⇨Y⇨Y⇨-26.4⇨Enter. These steps can be a very quick and effective means of flipping or mirroring an object because mirroring is just scaling by -1 along a particular axis. For example, to flip an object along the global Z-axis, press S⇨Z⇨-1⇨Enter. For consistency, these numerical input operations are also available when using the 3D manipulator.

The Properties region

One other way to explicitly translate, scale, and rotate your object is through the Properties/Information region (see Chapter 2) of the 3D View. To reveal this region, go to View⇨Properties in the 3D View's header or press N while your mouse cursor is in the 3D View. The Properties region sits along the right side of the 3D View and allows you to explicitly enter numerical values for Location, Scale, and Rotation. Close the Properties region the same way that you open it.

Blender's layer system

If, as a first-time Blender user, you rush to try to move your object around by attempting to use *M* as a hotkey, you may be surprised when Blender presents you with a funky pop-up panel of 20 unlabeled buttons. Interestingly, the *M* hotkey does activate a move function, but not like you'd expect. It allows you to move your object to one or more layers. Each button in the pop-up panel represents a single Blender layer. Left-click a button, and your selected object moves to that layer.

Blender's layer system is pretty unique among computer graphics software; the layers aren't layers in the traditional sense, where they're arranged in a stack and objects can live in only one layer at a time. Instead, Blender has exactly 20 layers and objects can simultaneously live on multiple layers. As a result, Blender layers tend to be treated as a quick way of grouping objects.

You can control which layers are visible by using the block of layer buttons in the 3D View's header. You can tell if a layer has objects in it at a glance by checking to see if the layer button has an orange circle within it. Shift+left-click a layer button to toggle its visibility. Left-clicking Shift+any layer button makes that layer visible and all others hidden. Press the Tilde (~) key makes all layers visible.

When in Object mode, the values in the Properties region don't change depending on which coordinate system you've selected. Location and Rotation are always in the Global orientation, whereas Scale is always in Local.

Chapter 4

Working in Edit Mode and Object Mode

*W*hen working on a scene in Blender, your life revolves around repeatedly selecting objects, transforming them, editing them, and relating them to one another. You shift from dealing with your model in Object mode to doing refinements in Edit mode.

And this process isn't only for modeling, but also for most of the other heavy tasks performed in Blender. Therefore, you can reuse the skills you pick up in this chapter in parts of Blender that have nothing to do with 3D modeling. Just as many of the transform operations work in editors other than the 3D View, many of the concepts here transfer nicely to other parts of Blender. Even if you don't know how to do something, chances are good that if you think like Blender thinks, you'll be able to make a successful guess.

Making Changes by Using Edit Mode

Moving primitive objects around is fun and all, but you're interested in getting in there and completely changing these objects to match your vision. You want to do 3D modeling. Well, you're in the right place. This section introduces you to Edit mode, a concept that's deeply embedded throughout Blender for editing objects. Even though this section is focused mostly on polygon modeling, also called *mesh editing,* most of the same principles apply for editing curves, surfaces, armatures, and even text.

When you understand how Blender thinks, figuring out unknown parts of the program is much easier.

Distinguishing between Object mode and Edit mode

In Chapter 3, you do everything in Object mode. As its name indicates, Object mode is where you work with whole objects. However, Object mode isn't very useful for actually changing the internal structure of your object. For example, select (right-click) the cube in the default scene. You know that you can turn it into a more rectangular shape by scaling it along one of the axes. But what if you want to turn the cube into a pyramid? You need to modify the actual components that make up the cube. These changes are made by entering Edit mode.

You can get to Edit mode in one of two ways: with the mouse or with a hotkey. To use the mouse method, left-click the Object Mode button in the 3D View's header. From the pop-up menu that appears, select Edit Mode (see Figure 4-1). Be aware that if you're working with an object other than a mesh, such as an armature, the contents of this menu may vary slightly to relate more to that object. However, with the exception of Empties (see Chapter 10), all objects have an Edit mode.

Figure 4-1:
The Mode button allows you to switch between Object mode and Edit mode for a selected object.

 Of course, Blender also has a hotkey to enter Edit mode. Actually, technically speaking, the hotkey toggles you between Object mode and Edit mode. Pressing Tab is the preferred way to switch between modes in Blender, and it's used so frequently that Blender users often use Tab as a verb and say they're *tabbing into* Edit mode or Object mode. This language is something you come across fairly often in Blender user forums and in some of Blender's online documentation.

Selecting vertices, edges, and faces

After you tab into Edit mode, the cube changes color and points form at each of the cube's corners. Each point is a *vertex*. The line that forms between two vertices is an *edge*. A *face* in Blender is a polygon that has been formed by three or four connecting edges.

Currently, faces in Blender are limited to only three-sided and four-sided polygons, often referred to as *tris* (pronounced like *tries*) and *quads*. In the not-to-distant feature, Blender — like many other programs — will support something called an *n-gon* that can have a virtually limitless number of sides. However, at this time, only some development versions of Blender have n-gon functionality. The current release is still limited to tris and quads. This situation isn't completely horrible, however, because you can still do a lot with just three- and four-sided faces. In fact, most detailed character models are made almost completely with quads and an occasional triangle, and all 3D geometry is reduced to triangles when it gets to your computer hardware. If you're interested, you can find more detailed information about Bmesh and n-gons in the "A word on Bmesh and n-gons" sidebar, later in this chapter

For polygon editing, you can use three different types of Edit modes, sometimes called *selection modes:* Vertex Select, Edge Select, and Face Select. By default, the first time you tab into Edit mode, you're in Vertex Select mode.

Two visual cues in the Blender interface clue you in to what selection mode you're using. First, for Vertex Select mode, you can see the individual vertices in the mesh. Second, as Figure 4-2 shows, three new buttons appear in the 3D View's header when you're in Edit mode. The button on the left (it has an icon of a cube with an orange dot over one corner) is enabled, indicating that you're in Vertex Select mode.

Figure 4-2:
The Edit
mode Select
buttons.

To the right of the Vertex Select button is a button displaying an icon of a cube with a highlighted edge. Click this button to activate Edge Select mode. When you do, the vertices are no longer visible on your mesh. Clicking the last button in this block, which has an icon of a cube with one side marked in orange, activates Face Select mode. When Face Select mode is active, vertices aren't visible, and each polygon in your mesh has a square dot in the center of it.

Now, you may notice that these buttons are blocked together, kind of like the 3D manipulator buttons. So, as with the manipulator, can you simultaneously activate multiple modes? Absolutely! Simply Shift+left-click the Select mode buttons to get this function. Some Blender modelers like to have Vertex Select and Edge Select modes active at the same time to speed up their workflow. This combination selection mode gives them immediate control at the vertex and edge level, and you can easily select the faces by using Blender's Lasso select (Ctrl+left-click+drag) across two edges. Figure 4-3 shows the default cube in each of the select modes, as well as a Combo Select mode.

Figure 4-3:
Vertex
Select, Edge
Select, Face
Select, and
Combo
Select
modes.

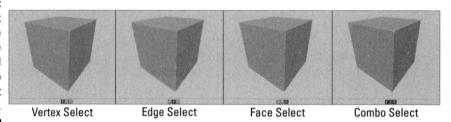

Vertex Select   Edge Select   Face Select   Combo Select

Of course, you can also use a hotkey sequence to access the various select modes. While you're in Edit mode, if you press Ctrl+Tab, you see a menu that lets you switch between modes. This menu doesn't let you set multiple modes; for combo selection, you still have to use the buttons in the 3D View's header.

Also, by default, the first time you tab into Edit mode, all vertices/edges/faces are selected. Selecting things in Edit mode works just like selecting anywhere else:

✔ Right-click any vertex to select it.

✔ Select and deselect multiple vertices by Shift+right-clicking them.

✔ Select large groups of vertices by using the Border Select tool (B), Circle Select (C), or Lasso Select (Ctrl+left-click+drag).

   • In Border and Circle Select, left-click and drag your mouse cursor to add to your selection. For Border Select, this action draws a box to define a selection area.

   • Circle Select is sometimes called Brush Select because selection is like painting. Any vertices that you run your mouse cursor over while holding down the left mouse button are selected.

   • Middle-click and drag to subtract from your selection and right-click or press Esc to exit Border or Circle Select.

   • To use Lasso Select functionality, Ctrl+left-click and drag your mouse cursor around the vertices you want to select. Anything within that selection region is added to your selection.

And, of course, all these selection tools work in Edge and Face Select modes, as well as in Object mode. Figure 4-4 shows what the various selection tools look like when in use.

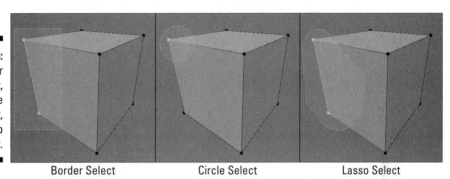

Figure 4-4: Border Select, Circle Select, and Lasso Select.

Border Select Circle Select Lasso Select

If you want to select everything (in Object mode, all objects; in Edit mode, all vertices in the active object), you can do so by pressing A. The A hotkey is a toggle, so anything previously selected when you press A is deselected. However, if nothing is previously selected, pressing A selects everything. Using this hotkey, you'll find yourself pressing A until you have either everything or nothing selected.

If you're using Blender's default settings, you can't see through your model. You can't select the vertices, edges, and faces on the back side of the model unless you orbit the 3D View to see those vertices or drop into the wireframe viewport shading setting. (Toggle between wireframe and solid by pressing Z.) On occasion, however, you may find it useful to see (and select) those hidden vertices while in solid viewport shading. To do so, click the Limit Selection to Visible button, sometimes referred to as the Occlude Background Geometry button. Located to the right of the Selection Modes block in the 3D View's header, this button has an icon of a cube with white highlighted vertices on it. (Refer to Figure 4-2.) By default, the Occlude Background Geometry button is enabled, but you can click this button to reveal the vertices, edges, and faces on the back of your model. The hiding of those rear vertices is often referred to as *backface culling*, and it's incredibly useful when you're working with complex models. I recommend that you keep it enabled and just temporarily switch to wireframe viewport shading (Z) if you need to quickly see or select those backface vertices.

Working with linked vertices

Another handy way to select things in Edit mode is by selecting linked vertices. *Linked vertices* are a set of vertices within a mesh that are connected by edges. In order to understand linked vertices better, go through the following steps:

1. **Select (right-click) your default cube in Blender and tab into Edit mode.**

   All the vertices are selected. If not, press A until they are.

2. **With all the vertices selected, press Shift+D or choose Add⇨Duplicate from the Tool Shelf or Mesh⇨Add Duplicate from the 3D View's header to duplicate your selection.**

   Blender creates a copy of your selection and automatically switches to grab mode, allowing you to move the duplicate set of vertices, edges, and faces immediately.

3. **Use your mouse to move your new cube off the original and confirm your placement by left-clicking a second time or pressing Enter.**

   None of the vertices in the original cube are selected. Each cube represents a set of linked vertices. So what if you want to select all the vertices in that cube, too? Sure, you can use the Border, Circle, or Lasso Select tools, but on complex meshes, these tools can get cumbersome. Instead, move to the next step.

4. **Place your mouse cursor near any vertex in the original cube and press L.**

   Blam! All the vertices in both of your cubes are selected.

Of course, the natural next question is, "How do I deselect linked vertices?" That's just as easy. Place your mouse cursor near any vertex on the duplicate cube you created and press Shift+L. All vertices connected to the one near your mouse cursor are deselected. I've found myself using L and Shift+L pretty heavily when trying to place teeth in a mouth I've modeled. These hotkeys are *very* handy.

Quite a few more selection options are available to you when working with meshes. I describe these selection methods in detail in Chapter 5.

While you're in Edit mode, you can work only with the current active object. You can't select and manipulate other objects while you're in Edit mode.

Still Blender's No. 1 modeling tool: Extrude

Besides transform operations (see Chapter 3), the most commonly used modeling tool in Blender is the Extrude function. In meatspace, *extrusion* is a process whereby some material is pushed through a shaped hole of some sort. When you were a kid, did you ever cut out a shape in cardboard and force clay or mud or Play-Doh through it? If so, you were extruding. If not, you certainly missed out on a good solid five to ten minutes of fun.

A word on Bmesh and n-gons

A longstanding criticism of Blender over the years is a relative lack of advanced mesh-editing features and tools. Some examples of such tools include per-edge beveling, clean boolean operations, and the notorious n-gon.

The reason Blender carried these limitations for so long has to do with its reliance on older code for Blender's mesh structures, called EditMesh among the Blender developers. In order to support these other powerful features, the EditMesh structure needed to be refac-

tored. For that reason, the Bmesh (short for Blender Mesh) project was launched. It's been slowly developing over the years, with only the attention of two developers working on it, and is slated to be included after the Blender 2.5 series finishes development and Version 2.6 is released. Not only does the Bmesh structure provide users with more powerful tools, but it's also more robust and may perform faster than the old EditMesh structure in some specific cases.

In 3D, extrusion follows a similar concept, except you don't have to create the hole to extrude through. Instead, that shape is determined by your selection and you can extend that selection in any direction. Use the following steps to extrude:

1. **Select the object you want to edit by right-clicking it.**

2. **Tab into Edit mode.**

3. **Select the vertices, edges, or faces you want to extrude.**

   Use any of the selection methods listed in the previous section.

4. **Extrude your selection in one of several ways:**

   • **Use the E hotkey.**

   • **Left-click Add⇨Extrude Region in the Tool Shelf.**

   • **Choose Mesh⇨Extrude Region from the menu in the 3D View's header.**

   After you extrude your selection, Blender automatically puts you into grab mode on the newly extruded parts.

Now, if you extrude a polygon, your new extrusion is constrained to move only along its normal. If you don't want this constrained behavior, middle-click your mouse (without moving it) and the constraint is removed, allowing you to freely move your extrusion around.

If you extrude an edge, your extrusion is constrained to a plane perpendicular to your newly extruded edge. If you extrude a single vertex, you're in a *free extrude* mode that's completely unconstrained. In order to use constraints in this case, you need to use the coordinate system constraint hotkeys described in Chapter 3.

Modeling organically with the Proportional Edit tool

Often, when you're modeling organic objects or objects with smoothly curved surfaces, such as characters, creatures, or sports cars, you may find yourself pushing and pulling a bunch of vertices to obtain that smooth surface. You can simplify this process by using Blender's *Proportional Edit Tool* (PET).

If you come from another 3D package, you might recognize PET as being similar to the *soft select* feature. You activate PET by left-clicking the PET button, which looks like two gray concentric circles in the 3D View's header. The hotkey for this operation is O. Now when you perform a transform operation, a circle appears around your selection. Your transformation influences any vertices that are within this circle with a gradual falloff.

You can adjust the influence of the PET by scrolling your mouse wheel or pressing Alt+Numpad Plus (+) and Alt+Numpad Minus (–). Additionally, you can control how gradual the falloff is by left-clicking the button with

the curve icon next to the PET button in the 3D View's header or by cycling through the options by pressing Shift+O.

PET has one more useful option. On complex meshes, you may want to use PET on one set of vertices that are connected to one another, but not to other nearby vertices in the same mesh. For example, say that you've modeled a character and her hand is at her side near her leg, and you'd like to smoothly edit her hand and pull it away from the leg without having to gradually adjust the vertices of the arm. PET is the perfect tool for this job. However, when you try to use PET, other leg vertices are within the PET's influence, and you end up moving those unintentionally. Wouldn't it be great if the PET could understand that you only want to move the hand? Well, I have good news: It can! Click the PET button in the 3D View header and select Connected or press Alt+O. The Connected option for PET only adjusts vertices that are connected to each other within its influence area. Neat, huh?

The selected orientation in the Coordinate Orientation menu is active even if you're transforming with hotkeys. So if you set that menu to the Normal orientation, you can press Z⇨Z, and your extruded region is constrained to its face. (Just pressing Z once constrains it to the global Z-axis rather than the face's normal.)

There are advantages and disadvantages to Blender's extrude function leaping directly into grab mode. The advantages are that you have all the transform functionality, such as axis-locking, snapping, and numerical input immediately available to you. The disadvantage is that, because of this autograb behavior, if you cancel the operation by right-clicking or pressing Esc, the newly extruded vertices, edges, or faces are still there, just located in exactly the same place as the vertices, edges, or faces that they originated from.

For this reason, if you cancel an extrude operation, make sure that your duplicate vertices, called *doubles*, are no longer there. A quick way to check is to press G after you cancel your extrusion. If it looks like you're extruding again, you have doubles.

You can get rid of doubles in a variety of ways:

✔ **If you still have the doubles selected, delete them.** You can activate the delete operation with hotkeys (X or Del), clicking Remove⇨Delete in the Tool Shelf, or by going to Mesh⇨Delete in the 3D View's header. You see a menu where you decide what elements of the mesh you want to delete. In this case, you choose Vertices. The disadvantage of this method is that it also removes the faces created by those vertices.

✔ **If the canceled extrusion operation was the last thing you did, undo it by pressing Ctrl+Z.** This solution is probably the quickest.

✔ **If you're unsure whether you have doubles from previous canceled extrusions, use Blender's special Remove Doubles function:**

1. **In Edit Mode, select all by choosing Select⇨Select/Deselect All from the 3D View's header or pressing A until all vertices are selected.**

2. **Press W⇨Remove Doubles, and Blender removes all doubles from your mesh.**

   You can find this option in Mesh⇨Vertices⇨Remove Doubles in the 3D View's header, as well as the Tool Shelf (Remove⇨Remove Doubles).

If you look in the Mesh menu of the 3D View, you have more than one Extrude option. A second Extrude operation, called Extrude Individual (Shift+E), works, depending on which selection mode you chose. If you're in Face Select mode, then the Extrude Individual operation extrudes each face you selected along its independent normal. Likewise, if you're in Edge Select mode, Extrude Individual extrudes each edge you selected independently of one another. And the same principle works on vertices if you're in Vertex Select mode and choose Extrude Individual.

When you're modeling, the most common type of extrusion you want is related to what you selected. For example, if you want to extrude an edge, you select that edge, or if you select a group of faces, chances are good that you want to extrude that as a region. As expected, Blender has shortcuts for these common modeling tasks.

To perform a quick extrusion:

1. **Select your object and tab into Edit mode.**

2. **Select the vertices, edges, or faces you want to extrude.**

3. **Ctrl+left-click where you'd like the extrusion to end.**

   Blender automatically decides what kind of extrusion you want and extrudes your selection right where you'd like. Working this way is particularly useful when you're doing a series of multiple extrusions, one right after the other, such as when you're roughing out a shape by "drawing" with vertices or edges.

Creating a simple model with Extrude

Although Ctrl+left-clicking for quick extrusion is convenient for creating rough models to start with, extruding with the E key certainly has workflow benefits. The biggest benefit is the quick access to your other transform tools. To illustrate this benefit, use the following steps to model a skyscraper from a single plane:

1. **Open Blender and tab into Edit mode on the default cube.**

2. **Change to right-side view.**

   You can do so by pressing Numpad 3 or going to View⇨Right from the 3D View's header.

3. **Translate everything by 1 unit in the positive Z direction (G⇨Z⇨1⇨Enter).**

4. **Orbit (middle-click+drag) the 3D View so that you can get a good view of the top face of the cube.**

5. **Switch to Face Select mode (Ctrl+Tab⇨Faces).**

6. **Select (right-click) the topmost face of the cube and delete it (X⇨Vertices).**

7. **Select all (A) and perform a multisubdivide with two cuts.**

   Use W⇨Subdivide, Add⇨Subdivide from the Tool Shelf, or Mesh⇨Edges⇨Subdivide from the 3D View's menu. This step creates a single subdivision cut. Increase the number of subdivisions by going to the Last Operator panel at the bottom of the Tool Shelf or pressing F6 and increasing the Number of Cuts value to 2.

8. **Switch to Edge Select mode (Ctrl+Tab⇨Edges).**

9. **Select the edges that form the corners of the plane.**

   Using regular right-clicking, Circle Select (C), or Lasso Select (Ctrl+left-click+drag) works best for this step.

10. **Extrude these edges and scale them by 1.1 in the XY-plane (E⇨S⇨Shift+Z⇨1.1⇨Enter).**

11. **Select all (A⇨A).**

12. **Extrude the region along the global Z-axis (E).**

    Your extrusion is constrained along the direction of the region's normal. Fortunately, because of the way you're working, that normal coincides with the global Z-axis. The height of this level can be whatever you like. I extruded mine by 3 units.

13. **With the region still selected, extrude again, but scale the region by 0.9 in the XY-plane (E⇨S⇨Shift+Z⇨0.9⇨Enter).**

14. **Translate this new region along the Z-axis by 0.1 units (G⇨Z⇨0.1⇨Enter).**

15. **Perform Steps 12 through 14 as many times as you'd like to get the skyscraper to your desired height.**

    I gave mine three layers.

16. **On your last extruded region, scale the selection in the XY-plane to a generally pyramid-shaped peak (S⇨Shift+Z).**

17. **Tab back into Object mode and behold the awesome beauty of your skyscraper!**

    Figure 4-5 shows an illustration of the major steps in this process.

Going through this process, notice how immediately after executing the extrude operation, you can scale the extrusion to create insets and outsets to grow your building from. Using extrusion with your transform tools in this manner gives you an immense amount of speed and flexibility when modeling.

Prior to Blender 2.5, PET worked only while you were in Edit mode. Now, PET works in Object mode as well. This capability can be really handy, but it can sometimes yield undesirable results if you want to use PET only while in Edit mode. For this reason, double-check your 3D View's header before performing a transformation to see whether PET is enabled.

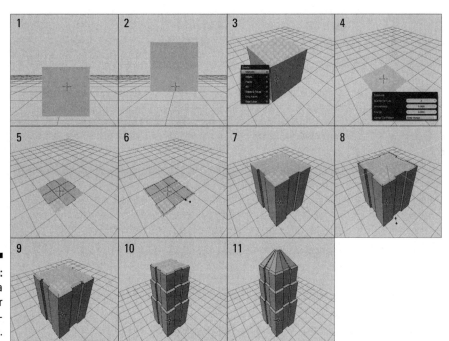

Figure 4-5:
Modeling a skyscraper from a single plane.

Adding to a Scene

There's got to be more to life than that plain default cube, right? Indeed, there is. Blender offers a whole slew of *primitives*, or basic objects, to build from.

Anytime you add a new object in Blender, the origin of that object is located wherever you placed the 3D cursor.

You may notice that for pop-up menus like the Dynamic Spacebar Menu (see sidebar), Blender places the last menu option you choose directly under your mouse cursor. This workflow feature helps increase your speed. The idea is that you often want to do the same task multiple times in a row. Blender makes repetitive tasks easier by shortening the distance you have to move your mouse with each function.

Adding objects

To add a new object to your scene, use the Shift+A hotkey and choose the type of primitive you want to put into the scene. You have the following choices:

- ✔ **Mesh:** Meshes are polygon-based objects made up of vertices, edges, and faces. They're the most common type of modeling object used in Blender.

- ✔ **Curve:** Curves are objects made up of curved or straight lines that you manipulate with a set of *control points*. Control points are similar to vertices, but you can edit them in a couple of ways that vertices can't. Blender has two basic forms of curves, Bèzier curves and NURBS (Non-Uniform Relational B-Spline) curves. You can also use curves as paths to control other objects.

- ✔ **Surface:** A surface is similar to a mesh, but instead of being made up of vertices, edges, and faces, surfaces in Blender are defined by a set of NURBS curves and their control points.

- ✔ **Meta ball:** Meta objects are unique primitives with the cool ability to melt into one another and create a larger structure. They're handy for a variety of effects that involve blobby masses, such as clouds or water, as well as quick, rough, claylike models.

- ✔ **Text:** The text object allows you to bring type into your 3D scene and manipulate it like other 3D objects.

- ✔ **Armature:** Armature objects are skeleton-like structures that consist of linked bones. You can use the bones in an armature to deform other objects. The bones are particularly useful for creating the puppetlike controls necessary for character animation.

Getting to know the toolbox menu

In previous versions of Blender, one of the quickest ways to access any feature in the 3D View is with a toolbox that was activated when pressing spacebar. To access the toolbox, you only had to hover your mouse in the 3D View and press spacebar. Sadly, this feature is no longer a default. Pressing spacebar now only pops up Blender's integrated search menu.

Fortunately, all is not lost! You can still have your good old toolbox back, thanks to Blender's Add-Ons system (see Chapter 2). Simply go to the Add-Ons section of User Preferences (Ctrl+Alt+U) and enable the Dynamic Spacebar Menu Add-On (it's in the 3D View category).

With this Add-On enabled, when you go back to the 3D View and press spacebar, a menu pops up with a variety of options beneath your mouse cursor.

The actual content of the menu changes, depending on context like what type of object you have selected or if you're in Edit mode or Object mode, but it's mostly a condensed form of what you find in Blender's Add and Object menus. If you want to use the integrated search feature that is normally bound to spacebar, that option is still there at the top of the Dynamic Spacebar Menu. Click that first option, and the familiar search menu appears.

✔ **Lattice:** Like armature objects, you can use lattices to deform other objects. They're often used in modeling and animation to squash, stretch, and twist models in a nonpermanent way. Lately, lattices are used less and less in Blender because users have gained the ability to deform objects with curves and meshes, but they're still very useful.

✔ **Empty:** The unsung hero of Blender objects, Empties don't show up in finished renders. Their primary purpose is merely to serve as a reference position, size, and orientation in 3D space. This basic purpose, however, allows them to work as very powerful controls.

✔ **Camera:** Like real-world cameras, camera objects define the location and perspective from which you're rendering your scene.

✔ **Lamp:** Lamp objects are necessary for lighting your scene. Just like in the physical world, if you don't have any light, you don't see anything.

✔ **Force Field:** In the simplest terms, a *force field* is an Empty that acts like the source of some physical force such as wind or magnetism. Force fields are used primarily with Blender's integrated physics simulation. I briefly touch upon force fields in Chapter 13.

✔ **Group Instance:** A group is a set of objects you define as being related to each other in some way. The objects in a group don't have to be the same type and are handy for organization as well as appending sets of objects from external files.

When adding new objects, be aware of whether you're in Object mode or Edit mode. If you add while in Edit mode, then your addition options are limited to the type of object you're editing. Also, your new object's data is joined with the object you're editing. If you don't want the object data to join, then make sure that you tab back to Object mode before adding anything new.

Meet Suzanne, the Blender monkey

Many 3D modeling and animation suites have a generic semicomplex primitive that is used for test renders, benchmarks, and examples that necessitate something a little more complex than a cube or sphere. Most of these other programs use the famous Utah teapot as their test model.

Blender has something a little more interesting and unique. Blender has a monkey head that's affectionately referred to as Suzanne, a reference to the ape in two of Kevin Smith's films: *Jay and Silent Bob Strike Back* and *Mallrats* (close to the end). You can add Suzanne to your scene by pressing Shift+A⇨Mesh⇨Monkey. If you look through the Blender community's forums and much of Blender's release documentation, you see Suzanne and references to her all over the place. In fact, the annual awards festival at the Blender Conference in Amsterdam is called the Suzanne Awards. Figure 4-6 shows a test render featuring Suzanne.

Figure 4-6: Suzanne!

Joining and separating objects

In the course of creating models for your scenes, you may need to join or separate objects — for example, if you accidentally add a new primitive while you're still in Edit mode. Of course, you can simply undo, tab into Object mode, and re-add your primitive, but why act like you made a mistake and go through all those extra steps?

There's another way. When you add a new primitive while in Edit mode, all the elements of your new primitive are selected, and nothing from your original object is selected. If only there were a command that would let you break this primitive away from this object and into an object of its own. Fortunately, there is. Press P⇨Selection, and your new primitive is separated into its own object. You can also access this function in the 3D View's header menu (Mesh⇨Vertices⇨Separate).

Tab back into Object mode and select (right-click) your new object. Its origin is located in the same place as its original object's origin. To put the origin of your new object at its actual center, press Shift+Ctrl+Alt+C⇨Origin to Geometry or click Object⇨Transform⇨Origin to Geometry in the 3D View's header. This Origin to Geometry operation checks the size of your object and calculates where its true center is. Then Blender places the object's origin at that location.

You can also specify that the object's origin be placed wherever your 3D cursor is located by pressing Shift+Ctrl+Alt+C⇨Origin to 3D Cursor or clicking Object⇨Transform⇨Origin to 3D Cursor.

A third option is similar to Origin to Geometry, but it moves the object's content rather than the origin itself. Do this operation by clicking Object⇨Transform⇨Geometry to Origin (Shift+Ctrl+Alt+C⇨Geometry to Origin).

As expected, you can also join two objects of the same type into a single object. To do so, select multiple objects. In Object mode, you can use the Border Select or Lasso Select tools, or you can simply Shift+right-click objects to add them to your selection. The last object you select is considered your *active object* and is the object that the others join into. With your objects selected, join them by pressing Ctrl+J or clicking Object⇨Join from the 3D View's header.

You can join objects of the same type only. That is, you can join two mesh objects, but you can't join a mesh object with a curve object. Using parenting or groups (discussed later in this chapter in the section "Discovering parents, children, and groups") may be more appropriate.

Creating duplicates and links

In the section "Working with linked vertices," earlier in this chapter, an example involved duplicating your selected vertices by using Shift+D (or Mesh⇨Add Duplicate). As you may expect, this operation also works in Object mode. This duplication method is great if you intend on taking an existing object and using it as a starting point to model another, more individualized object by tweaking it in Edit mode. However, suppose that you want your duplicated object to be identical to the original in Edit mode. And wouldn't it be nice if, when you do go into Edit mode, your changes happen to the original *as well as* to all the duplicates? For duplicated objects that you have to edit only once, you want to use the power of *linked duplicates*. Linked duplicates are objects that share the same internal datablocks.

Linking data between objects

Linked duplicates are similar to what other programs call instance copies. The process to create a linked duplicate is pretty straightforward:

1. **Select the object you want to duplicate by right-clicking it.**

2. **With the object selected, press Alt+D or Object⇨Duplicate Linked from the 3D View's header.**

    From here, the behavior is just like regular duplication.

    The object is automatically in grab mode.

3. **Place the object with your mouse and confirm its new location by left-clicking or by pressing Enter.**

You can use a few other methods to verify that this duplicated object is, in fact, a linked duplicate. The easiest way is to tab into Edit mode on the original object or on any of the duplicates. When you do, all the linked objects appear to go into Edit mode, and any changes you make here automatically update all the other objects immediately. Figure 4-7 shows three linked duplicates of Suzanne being simultaneously modified in Edit mode.

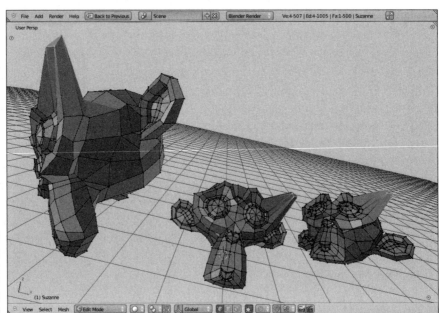

Figure 4-7:
Editing
duplicated
Suzannes!

A second way to verify the linked status of duplicates is to look in the Object Data section of the Properties editor. At the top of this panel, look at the top datablock field, which is the Datablock Name field. If a number appears to the right of the name, it is the number of objects linked to this datablock. In other words, this number is the count of your linked duplicates. Figure 4-8 shows how this panel looks when one of the Suzannes in the previous figure is selected.

Figure 4-8:
Three objects are sharing this datablock.

Another way to visualize linked data in Blender is to consider that Blender treats the internal structure of its .blend files like a database. As I cover in Chapter 2, all datablocks in your scene — including objects, materials, and mesh data — can be linked and shared between one another. The real power comes in allowing multiple objects to share with each other. For example, you can have objects share materials, mesh data, actions, and even particle systems. And different scenes can even share objects! Taking advantage of this feature not only reduces the size of your .blend files, but it can also seriously reduce the amount of redundant work you have to do. Figure 4-9 shows a data schematic for the previous scene involving the three linked duplicates of Suzanne. You can see how the datablocks in that scene relate to one another.

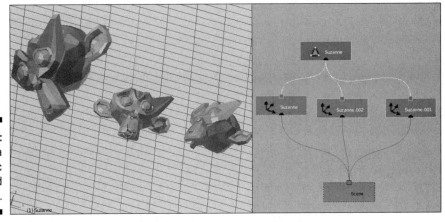

Figure 4-9:
A data schematic of linked Suzannes.

So say that you've been using Blender for a while without knowing about linked duplicates, and your .blend file is rife with redundant mesh data. Is there a way to get rid of those regular duplicates and make them linked duplicates? Of course! Follow these steps:

1. **Select all the objects that you want to share the same data.**

   Use any of the selection tools available to you (Border, Circle, Lasso, and Shift+right-click). All the objects must be of the same type, so you can't have a mesh object and a curve object share the same datablock.

2. **With each desired duplicate selected, select (Shift+right-click) the object with the datablock that you want to share with the others.**

   This step makes that last-selected object the active object.

3. **Press Ctrl+L or Object⇨Make Links from the 3D View's header menu to bring up the Make Links menu.**

4. **Choose the third option from the top, Object Data.**

   Kerplooie! All the selected objects now link to the same internal data.

Figure 4-10 shows the preceding process, using a bunch of cubes and a Suzanne object.

Figure 4-10:
Linking
cubes to
Suzanne.

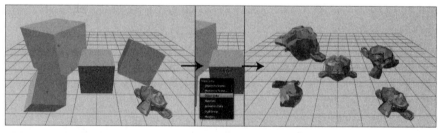

You probably noticed that the Make Links menu had some other interesting options. Following is a description of what each one does:

- ✔ **Objects to Scene:** If you have multiple scenes in your .blend file, you can make those scenes share the same objects. This option reveals another menu with all the scenes in the file. By choosing a scene, the object or objects that you selected have linked duplicates created in that scene.

- ✔ **Markers to Scene:** When animating in Blender, it's common to use *markers* in the Timeline, Dopesheet, and Graph Editor to indicate important moments in the animation. This feature allows you to share markers between Blender scenes.

✔ **Object Data:** This option is the one you used in the preceding example. Object Data links the internal data — be it a mesh, a curve, a lamp, or nearly any other object — of the selected objects to the internal data of the active object. For this option to work, all the selected objects must be of the same type. This is the only option where having objects of the same type is important.

✔ **Materials:** Choosing this option causes all the selected objects to share the same material settings. For more information on materials, see Chapter 7.

✔ **Animation Data:** This option relates directly to animation. It's the set of keyframes that describe the motion of an animated object, called *actions*. (Chapter 12 has more information on actions.) Choosing this option causes all your selected objects to share the same actions as the active object.

✔ **DupliGroup:** In the "Discovering parents, children, and groups" section of this chapter, you see how Blender allows you to organize your objects into groups. One cool thing about groups is that you can generate them as duplicated instances in a few ways. One of those ways is as a *dupligroup*. Choosing this option allows multiple objects to share the same dupligroup.

✔ **Modifiers:** A *modifier* is an operation that Blender performs on your object's data without permanently changing that data (see Chapter 5). Modifiers allow you to have very complex models that are still manageable, while retaining the simple editability of the original data. Unlike the other options in the Make Links menu, this option doesn't link the same modifier to multiple objects. What it really does is copy the modifier and its settings from one object to another. In the future, you may be able to treat modifiers as linkable datablocks, but that is not currently the case.

Unlinking datablocks

Of course, if Blender has a way to create links and duplicates, you'd logically (and correctly) think that you can convert a linked duplicate into an object with its own, nonshared datablocks. In Blender, this process is called giving that datablock a single user.

The reason for the *single user* terminology goes back to how these datablocks are tied together. From the perspective of the datablock, each object that's connected to it is considered a user. Refer to Figure 4-9: Each Cube object is a user of the Suzanne datablock. By choosing to Make Single User, you're effectively telling Blender to duplicate that datablock and make sure that it connects to only a single object. To make an object have single user data, select the object you want and then press U. You see a menu with the following options:

✔ **Object:** Use this option when you have an object that is linked to multiple scenes, and you want to make changes to it that appear only in the specific scene that you're currently working on.

✔ **Object & Data:** For cases like the preceding example with the linked Suzanne meshes where you have a linked duplicate that you'd like to edit independently of the other meshes, choose this option. Doing so effectively converts a linked duplicate into a regular duplicate.

✔ **Object & Data & Materials+Tex:** If you have an object that is not only sharing internal object data with others, but also sharing material settings, choose this option, and both of those datablocks are duplicated and singly linked to your selected object. Using this option is a pretty good way to make sure that your selected object isn't sharing with any other objects at all.

✔ **Materials+Tex:** In cases where you no longer want to share materials between objects, choosing this option makes sure that your selected object has its own material settings independent of all the other objects.

✔ **Object Animation:** This option is the inverse of the Make Links⇨Animation Data option. If your selected object is sharing actions with any other objects, choosing this option makes sure that it has actions of its own.

There is one other way to make object data a single user. In Figure 4-8, the number 3 is highlighted, showing that three objects share that particular datablock. If you left-click that number, you make that a single user datablock. This little button shows up in many places throughout the Blender interface. The datablocks that it operates on vary with context (for example, seeing this button in Material Properties means that it's working on a material datablock; seeing it in the Dopesheet means that it's working on actions, and so on), but it always means the same thing: Create a datablock like this one that has only the selected object as its user.

Discovering parents, children, and groups

Working in 3D, you may encounter many situations where you'll want a set of objects to behave like a single organizational group. Now, if the objects are all the same type, you can join them into a single object, but even with the L and Shift+L linked selection operations in Edit mode, this approach can get unwieldy. And joining them into a single object requires you to tab into Edit mode each time you want to work with an individual item. That's not very efficient, and it doesn't give you the flexibility of working with different kinds of objects as a single unit. The better way to organize your objects is with parent-child relationships or with groups.

Establishing parent-child relationships between objects

Creating parent-child relationships between objects, or *parenting* in Blenderese, organizes the objects hierarchically. An object can have any number of children, but no object can have more than a single parent:

1. **To make an object a parent, first select the objects you want to be children.**

   They don't have to be of the same type.

2. **Make your last selection (the active object) the object that you want to become the parent.**

3. **Press Ctrl+P⇨Object or click Object⇨Parent⇨Set in the 3D View's header menu.**

   After you confirm the operation by left-clicking or pressing Enter, Blender adds a dotted line from the origin of each child object to the origin of the parent. Now when you select just the parent object and perform a transform operation on it, it affects each of its children. However, if you select a child object and transform it, none of the other children or the parent object are influenced.

A good mnemonic device for remembering the correct order for selecting objects when you want to create a parent-child relationship is to think of the order people get off of a boat when they're abandoning ship: "Children first!"

Parenting is a great way to organize a set of objects that have a clear hierarchy. For example, say that you've modeled a dinner table and the chairs to go around it. Now you want to place that table and chairs in a room, but the room is scaled much smaller than the table and chairs. Rather than select, scale, grab, and move each object into place, you can parent each of the chairs to the table. Then you can just select and transform the table. When you do so, all the chairs transform right along with it, as if they were a single object! Woohoo! Figure 4-11 illustrates this example.

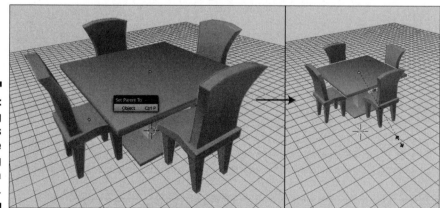

Figure 4-11: Parenting some chairs to a table and placing them in a room.

To clear a parent relationship, the process is only a click and a hotkey:

1. **Select the child object that you want to remove from the hierarchy.**

2. **Press Alt+P or click Object⇨Parent⇨Clear in the 3D View's header to clear the parent relationship.**

   You see a pop-up menu with three options:

   - **Clear Parent:** This option removes the parent-child relationship between your selected object and its parent. If the parent object was transformed after the parenting took place, the cleared child snaps back to the position, scale, and rotation that it was in before it was parented.

   - **Clear and Keep Transformation (Clear Track):** This option behaves the same as Clear Parent, except any transformations that were made while the selected object was a child are applied. This means that the cleared child does *not* snap back to its original pre-parented state.

   - **Clear Parent Inverse:** This option is a bit tricky to understand. It actually does not remove the link between the selected child object and its parent. Instead, it basically clears the parent's transformation from the child. Clear Parent Inverse is handy for situations where you've transformed an object before parenting it, and you want it to relate to the parent as if it had not been transformed prior to parenting. To be honest, I don't use this option very often, but it's certainly good to have around when you need it.

Creating groups

Of course, under some circumstances, parenting doesn't make sense for organizing a set of objects. A good example is a lighting setup that you want to adjust and reuse. Sure, you can rationalize that perhaps the key light is the most important light and therefore should be the parent, but that logic is a bit of a stretch and doesn't make much sense in more complex setups.

For these cases, Blender's *grouping* feature is ideal. To create a group, select all the objects you want to include in the group and press Ctrl+G or click Object⇨Group⇨Create New Group. All the objects in the group share a green selection outline rather than the default orange, to indicate that the object is a member of at least one group. The notion of an object being a member of at least one group highlights another example of how grouping and parenting differ. Whereas an object can have only one parent, it can be a member of any number of groups. If you go to the Object⇨Group menu, you have a number of options:

   ✔ **Create New Group (Ctrl+G):** This option is always available and creates a new group, adding your selected objects to it.

✔ **Remove from Groups (Ctrl+Alt+G):** This option is always available, and choosing it removes the selected objects from any groups they may be a member of. Removing all objects from all groups doesn't delete those groups while your Blender session is still active.

✔ **Add Selected to Active Group (Shift+Ctrl+G):** To use this feature, you need the active object to be the member of a group. Then any objects you have selected become members of all the groups your active object is a member of.

✔ **Remove Selected from Active Group (Shift+Alt+G):** Choose this option, and all your selected objects (including the active object) are removed from any groups in the active object.

Furthermore, it's worth knowing that groups have names. Check out the Object section of the Properties editor. This section contains a panel named Groups, listing the groups to which the selected object belongs. Left-click any group name to change it to something more relevant to that group's organization. Clicking the X next to the group name removes the selected object from that group. The set of layer buttons under the group name, labeled Dupli, have a special application for larger, more complex projects that involve linking groups between .blend files. Basically, if some objects in your group are on a layer that isn't enabled in these buttons, then those objects aren't visible when the group is linked to another file.

Selecting with parents and groups

When you're using parenting and groups, you gain the ability to rapidly select your objects according to their groupings. Press Shift+G, and you see a pop-up menu with a variety of options:

✔ **Children:** If you have a parent object selected, choosing this option adds all that object's children to the list of selected objects.

✔ **Immediate Children:** Similar to selecting all children, except this option traverses down the hierarchy by one step only. Children of children are not added to the selection.

✔ **Parent:** If the object you've selected has a parent object, that parent is added to the selection.

✔ **Siblings:** This option is useful for selecting all the children of a single parent. It does not select the parent object, nor does it select any children that these sibling objects may have.

✔ **Type:** This option is useful for making very broad selections. Use Type when you want to select all lamps or all meshes or armatures in a scene. This option bases its selection on the type of object you currently have selected.

> ✔ **Layer:** Use this option to select objects that live on the same layers. If an object is on multiple layers, any objects that share any layer with your selected object are added to the selection.

> ✔ **Group:** This option adds to the selection any object that is in the same group as your selected object. If the selected object belongs to more than one group, a secondary pop-up menu displays each of the group names for you to choose from.

> ✔ **Hook:** If you've added *hooks,* which are objects that control selected vertices or control points in an object, this option selects them. You can find more information on hooks in Chapter 11.

> ✔ **Pass:** Similar to layers, objects may have a PassIndex value that is useful for compositing and post-production work in Blender. Choosing this option selects any objects that share the active object's PassIndex value. You can find more information on passes and the PassIndex in Chapter 15.

> ✔ **Color:** This option allows you to select objects that have the same color, regardless of whether or not they link to the same material datablock

> ✔ **Properties:** If you use Blender's integrated game engine, it gives you the ability to add custom properties to objects that work in the game (like a Health property for characters). Choose this option, and all objects that have the same game properties are selected.

Saving, opening, and appending

Quite possibly the most important feature in any piece of software is the ability to save and open files. Having quick access to saving and opening files was especially useful for early versions of Blender, which lacked any sort of undo function. Blender users learned very quickly to save early, save often, and save multiple versions of their project files. One benefit is that Blender reads and writes its files *very* quickly, even for complex scenes, so you very rarely ever have to wait more than a second or two to get to work or save your project.

To save to a file, choose File⇨Save As from the main header or use the Shift+Ctrl+S hotkey. If you're used to older versions of Blender, you can still use the F2 hotkey to do the same thing. One strange thing that you may notice is that Blender doesn't bring up the familiar Save dialog box that Windows, Mac, or Linux uses. This is for three reasons. First and foremost, such a dialog box violates Blenders nonblocking interface concept (see Chapter 1). Not only that, but by Blender using its own File Browser interface, you can be guaranteed that no matter what kind of computer you use, Blender always looks and behaves the same on each platform. And as a third point, the Blender File Browser has some neat Blender-specific features that aren't available in the default OS save dialogs.

Take a look at the File Browser shown in Figure 4-12. The header for this editor features an assortment of buttons for navigating your hard drive's directory structure and filtering the files shown. If you've used the file browser that comes with your operating system, most of these buttons should be familiar to you. The majority of the options in the side region on the left of the File Browser are there to give you shortcuts to various locations on your computer's hard drive. However, at the bottom of the side region is a set of check boxes that change, depending on whether you're loading or saving your project.

The largest portion of the File Browser is devoted to actually showing files and folders. The topmost text field in this region is the current path on your hard drive to the folder/directory you're currently viewing. Below this text field is the text field for the actual name of your file. In this field, type your project's name. Pressing Enter or clicking the Save As Blender File button in the upper right corner saves the file for you. Below this button is a list of the files in the current folder. If you aren't familiar with Linux and Unix, the first item in this list might seem odd to you. This double-dot (..) is a shortcut for going up in the directory structure. Left-clicking it is just like clicking the Up button in the File Browser's header. It takes you to the parent directory of the one you're currently viewing. Figure 4-12 shows the Blender File Browser and labels the various buttons in it.

Saving after the first time

After you save your `.blend` file once, saving gets much quicker. To do a fast save while you're working, choose File⇨Save from the main header or, even faster, press Ctrl+S and confirm the overwrite by left-clicking or pressing Enter.

On larger projects, however, you may not want to continually overwrite the same file. In those cases, it's often more favorable to save progressive versions of your project as you work on it. You can open the File Browser and type a new name for each version — but it's slow. Often, when people save versions of a project file, they usually append a number to the end of the filename (for example, `file1.blend`, `file2.blend`, `file3.blend`, and so on). Blender knows this habit and aims to help you out.

The ultra-fast way is with the following hotkey sequence: F2⇨Plus (+)⇨Enter. Pressing Plus (+) while in the File Browser automatically appends that number to your filename for you. And if the file already has a number, it increments it by one. For logical consistency, pressing Minus (–) decrements that value. How's that for speedy? If you prefer to use your mouse, you can also perform the same function in the File Browser by left-clicking the Plus (+) and Minus (–) buttons after the filename text field.

New Folder

Display Options

Navigation/
Refresh

Sorting Options   Filter Options   Current File   Current Path   Files

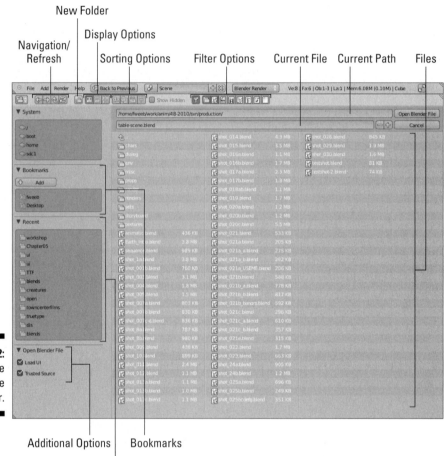

Figure 4-12:
The
Blender File
Browser.

Additional Options | Bookmarks

Recent Folders

Opening a file

Opening a `.blend` file is a straightforward task. Choose File↪Open from the
main header or press Ctrl+O. If you've used older versions of Blender, the
F1 hotkey still works, too. The File Browser loads again and allows you to
choose which file you want to load. To load the file, left-click the filename
and click the Open File button in the upper right corner. If you have a large
monitor and you don't want to move your mouse that far or you're just
interested in speedy shortcuts, you can quickly select and open a file by
double-clicking it.

Appending from an external file

Now, what if you have a model of a really excellent character saved in one .blend file, and you'd like to bring it into a scene that you've been working on in another .blend file? Wouldn't it be convenient if you could bring that character in and not have to remodel it from scratch? Of course, it would! This capability is precisely what Blender's Append feature is for.

To append an item from an external file, choose File➪Append from the main header or press Shift+F1. The File Browser opens, but now when you click on a .blend file, you can actually drill down into its structure. You can select any datablock in the file and bring it — as well as anything it's linked to — into your project. So if you select an object, you append that object, its object data (mesh, curve, and so on), any materials and textures it may have, and any animation linked to it. If you want to append just a material or texture, you can do that, too!

When appending, pay attention to the Link check box in the File Browser's side region. The default behavior is for the Link check box to be disabled. When disabled, any datablock that you append from another .blend file is completely copied into your current .blend file. From here, you can make custom changes to either file, and neither has any influence on the other. However, if you enable the Link check box, the datablock isn't actually copied into the current .blend. Instead, a reference is made that points to the datablock in the original file. I like to call this reference a *linked appendage*. The advantage of a linked appendage is that any changes you make to the original file are automatically updated in the file that links to it. These updates are really quite handy in large projects where you have a variety of models, materials, and other resources that you'd like to use over and over again. One complication of linked appendages, however, is that the linking file can't make any changes to the object that it links to. The only exception to this rule is groups.

When a group is made to a linked appendage, the linking file creates an Empty and binds the group reference to that as kind of a child, known as a dupligroup (I briefly touch on dupligroups earlier in this chapter in the "Creating duplicates and links" section). With this scheme, you can successfully transform and even animate your linked object. If you don't use groups and you want to modify an object appended with a link, your only option is to make that appended object local to the current file by selecting the appended object and pressing L➪Selected Objects. You can also choose Selected Objects and Data or choose All to completely confirm that you're no longer linked to that other file. Of course, making the object local increases the size of your .blend file and removes the collaborative benefit of working with linked appendages.

The moral of this story: If you're appending with links, it's probably in your best interest to create a group in the original file and create a linked appendage to that group from your new file. Using links to groups in external files is the primary way that artists use assets on medium-to-large animation projects.

Part II
Creating Detailed 3D Scenes

The 5th Wave   By Rich Tennant

In this part . . .

People don't start using a 3D computer graphics program to play with its interface. They use it because they want to create something awesome. That whole process starts with creating models. There are models for characters, settings, props, and even text and logos. The chapters in this part show you how to create meshes, curves, surfaces, and text objects in Blender. These are the building blocks used in CG to create incredible visuals.

In addition to modeling, lighting and materials can easily make or break a scene. To that effect, this part also shows how to set up lights effectively and how to use Blender's material system to get the models you create to look their best.

Chapter 5

Creating Anything You Can Imagine with Meshes

In This Chapter

▶ Working with vertices

▶ Using modifiers such as Mirror, Subdivision Surface, and Array

▶ Sculpting meshes to have extremely high detail

▶ Completing a practical example of modeling an eye for your characters

*P*olygon-based meshes are at the core of nearly every computer-generated 3D animation from video games and architectural visualization to television commercials and feature-length films. Computers typically handle meshes more quickly than other types of 3D objects like NURBS or meta balls, and meshes are generally a lot easier to control. In fact, when it comes down to it, even NURBS and meta balls are converted to a mesh of triangles — a process called *tesselation* — when the computer hardware processes them.

For these reasons, meshes are the primary foundation for most of Blender's functionality. Whether you're building a small scene, creating a character for animation, or simulating water pouring into a sink, you'll ultimately be working with meshes. Working with meshes can get a bit daunting if you're not careful, because you have to control each vertex that makes up your mesh. The more complex the mesh, the more vertices you have to keep track of. Chapter 4 gives you a lot of the basics for working with meshes in Edit mode, but this chapter exposes you to a bunch of handy Blender features that help you work with complex meshes without drowning in a crazy vertex soup.

Pushing Vertices

A *mesh* consists of a set of vertices that are connected by edges. Edges connect to each other to form either three- or four-sided faces. (Chapter 4 covers this in more detail, along with how to work with each of these mesh building blocks.) When you tab into Edit mode on a mesh, you can manipulate that mesh's vertices (or edges or faces) with the same basic grab (G), rotate (R), and scale (S) tools that work on all objects, as well as the very handy extrude (E) function. These actions form the basis for 3D modeling, so much so that some modelers like to refer to themselves as *vert pushers* because sometimes it seems that all they do is move little points around on a screen until things look right.

Of course, modeling has more to it. You actually have a choice between two primary methodologies when it comes to modeling:

- **Box modeling:** As its name indicates, *box modeling* starts with a rough shape — typically a box or cube. By adding edges and moving them around, the artist forms that rough shape into the desired model. Bit by bit, you refine the model, adding more and more detail with each pass. This technique tends to appeal to people with a background in sculpture because the processes are similar. They're both primarily subtractive in nature because you start with a rough shape and bring about more detail by cutting into it and reducing that shape's volume. If you need to add more volume to the mesh outside of the initial box shape, you select a set of edges or faces and extrude them out or pull them out. If you need to bring part of the mesh in from the initial box shape, you select those edges or faces and either extrude inward or just pull them in. Box modeling is a great way to get started in modeling, but you run a danger of ending up with really blocky models if you aren't careful about how you move your edges around.

- **Point-for-point modeling:** Point-for-point modeling consists of deliberately placing each and every vertex that comprises the model and creating the edges and faces that connect these vertices. The process is actually not as bad as it sounds. You can think about point-for-point modeling like drawing in three dimensions. And as you may expect, this technique appeals to people who come from a drawing background (or control freaks like me!). The advantage of this method is that you can control the final look of your model, and you're less inclined to end up with a boxy shape. However, some beginner modelers fall into the trap of getting too detailed too quickly with this technique, so you have to be careful.

Figure 5-1 shows the difference between a rough human head created by using box modeling techniques versus using a point-for-point method.

Although many modelers have a preference for one methodology over the other, most agree that each method has its advantages and often modelers take a hybrid approach. They may use a point-for-point technique to rough out the model and then make refinements by box modeling. With the advent of 3D sculpting, which I cover in the "Sculpting Multiresolution Meshes" section later in this chapter, this way of working has become even more popular.

Adding background images in the 3D View

When working with meshes or any other type of 3D object in Blender, reference images are often helpful for getting proper proportions and scale. If you have a separate monitor, you can choose to display your references there. However, you can use a reference more directly by loading an image into the background of the 3D View. To do so, go to the 3D View's Properties region (N) and look for the Background Images panel. Left-click the check box next to this heading and expand the panel by left-clicking the triangle to its left. You see an Add Image button. Left-click the Add Image button, and you get a panel for managing a background image. By default, your image (after you choose it) displays on all orthographic views in the 3D View. You can narrow this scope by using the Axis drop-down menu. For example, if you're modeling a person's face and have a profile photograph, then showing that background image in the front or top views

isn't useful, so you can use the Axis drop-down menu to just display the photo when you're looking from the right or left side view.

To pick an image for displaying in the 3D View, left-click the triangular icon to the left of the text that reads Not Set. Left-clicking that icon reveals an image datablock. Left-click the Open button, and Blender provides you with a File Browser for picking an image on your hard drive. When it's loaded, you can adjust the transparency, size, and positioning of your image. From here, you can continue to work, or you can add more images to display from other orthographic angles in the 3D View. People who model faces like to split the 3D View vertically, showing the front view in one 3D View and the right or left side view on the other. With reference photos of the same size set to display from the proper axis, it makes the process of modeling very speedy.

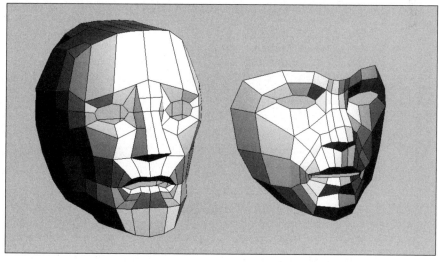

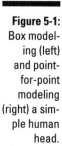

Figure 5-1: Box modeling (left) and point-for-point modeling (right) a simple human head.

Working with Loops and Rings

Regardless of whether you're box modeling or point-for-point modeling, understanding the concepts of *loops* and *rings* definitely makes your life as a modeler a lot less crazy.

Understanding edge loops and face loops

Generally speaking, an *edge loop* is a series of edges that connect to form a path where the first and last edges connect to each other — well, that's the ideal case anyway. I like to call this kind of *closed edge loop* a "good" edge loop.

Of course, then you probably want to know what a "bad" edge loop is. Well, you can have a path of edges that don't connect at the beginning and end of the loop, but calling these loops bad isn't really accurate. It's better to refer to edge loops that stop before reconnecting with their beginning as *terminating edge loops*. While you generally want to avoid creating terminating edge loops in your models, you can't always avoid having them, and sometimes you actually need them for controlling how edges flow along the surface of your mesh.

To get a better understanding of the difference between closed edge loops and terminating edge loops, open Blender and add a UV sphere (Shift+A⇨Mesh⇨UV Sphere) and leave the default settings for rings, segments, and radii. Tab into Edit mode on the sphere and Alt+right-click one of the horizontal edges on the sphere. This step selects an edge loop that goes all the way around the sphere like the latitude lines on a globe, as shown in the left image of Figure 5-2. This loop is a closed edge loop. Press A to deselect all and now Alt+right-click a vertical edge. When you do, you select a path of vertices that terminates at the top and bottom *poles*, or junctions of the sphere, as shown in the right image of Figure 5-2. That's a terminating edge loop.

The vertical loop doesn't go all the way around because, technically speaking, edge loops rely on *four-point poles*, or a vertex that's at the junction of four edges. Imagine that following an edge loop is like driving through a city. The four-point pole is like a four-way stop, where you have the option of going left, right, or straight. Well, to properly follow the loop, you keep traveling straight. However, if you come up to a fork in the road (a three-point pole) or a five-way (or more) intersection, you can't necessarily just go straight and be sure that you're following the loop. Therefore, the loop terminates at that intersection. That's why the horizontal edge loop in Figure 5-2, which is made up entirely of four-point poles, connects to itself, whereas the vertical loop stops at the top and bottom of the sphere, where all the edges converge to a single junction.

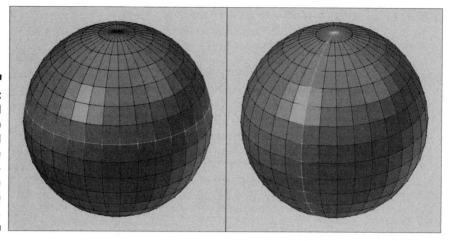

Figure 5-2:
A closed
edge loop
(left) around
a sphere
and a termi-
nating edge
loop (right)
on a sphere.

In addition to edge loops, you can also have face loops. A *face loop* consists of the faces between two parallel edge loops. Figure 5-3 shows horizontal and vertical face loops on a UV sphere. In Blender, you can select face loops when you're in Face Select mode (in Edit mode, press Ctrl+Tab⇨Faces) the same way you select edge loops in Vertex Select or Edge Select modes: Alt+right-click a face in the direction of the loop you'd like to select. For example, going back the UV sphere, to select a horizontal face loop, Alt+right-click the left or right side of one of the faces in that loop. To select a vertical face loop, Alt+right-click the top or bottom of the face.

In some Linux window managers, the Alt key manipulates windows, which supersedes Blender's control of it and prevents you from doing a loop select. Most window managers allow you to remap that ability to another key (like the Super or Windows key). However, if you use a window manager that doesn't offer that remapping ability, or you just don't feel like remapping that key, you can still select loops by using Shift+Alt+right-click. This key combination is actually for selecting multiple loops, but if you have no vertices, edges, or faces selected, it behaves just like Alt+right-click.

Selecting edge rings

Say that instead of wanting to select an edge loop or a face loop, you'd like to select just the edges that bridge between two parallel edge loops, as shown in Figure 5-4. These edges form an *edge ring*. You can only select edge rings from Edge Select mode (in Edit mode, press Ctrl+Tab⇨Edges). When you're in Edge Select mode, you can select an edge ring by using Ctrl+Alt+right-click. Trying to use this hotkey sequence in Vertex Select or Face Select mode just selects a face loop.

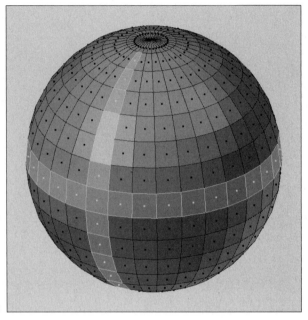

Figure 5-3:
Some
face loops
selected on
a sphere.

Being able to use rings and loops for selecting groups of vertices in an orderly fashion can be a huge benefit and timesaver for modeling. More importantly, when creating organic models like humans or faces, using edge loops effectively to control your *topology,* or the layout of the vertices, makes the life of a character rigger and animator a lot easier. (You can find out more on this topic in the sidebar "The importance of good topology," later in this chapter.)

Creating new loops

The ability to select loops and rings is nice, but the ability to create new loops is even more helpful when you want to add detail to a model. You can detail with what's called a *loop cut.* You can find this function in the Tool Shelf (Add➪Loop Cut and Slide). Alternatively, you can simply press Ctrl+R to access the loop cut operation directly. Regardless of how you choose to make a loop cut, when you run your mouse cursor over your model, a pink/purple line is drawn on the mesh, indicating where you might want to add your edge loop. After you decide where you want to cut, left-click to confirm (right-click cancels the whole operation). Doing so creates the edge loop and automatically enables the Edge Slide function on that loop. With Edge Slide, you can move your mouse around, and your loop travels along the surface of the mesh, allowing you to place it precisely where you want it to go when you left-click. If you ever want to use Edge Slide without creating a new loop, select the edge loop (or portion of an edge loop) that you want to slide and press Ctrl+E➪Edge Slide.

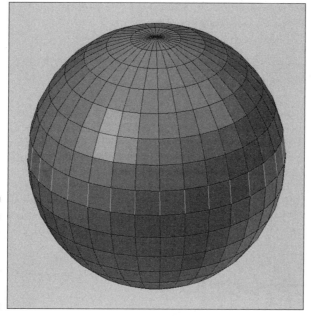

Figure 5-4:
An edge
ring
selected
on a UV
sphere.

When doing a loop cut, you can actually do multiple parallel loop cuts at the same time. When you activate the loop cut tool (Ctrl+R), scroll your mouse wheel, and you'll be able to add multiple loops all at the same time. If you don't have a scroll wheel on your mouse or you simply prefer to use your keyboard, you can adjust the number of loops in your cut by pressing Page Up and Page Down. Note that if you add multiple loops at the same time, Blender doesn't go into the Edge Slide functionality because it doesn't make sense to slide multiple parallel edges.

You can make cuts other than loop cuts. This feature is accessible with the Knife tool, by pressing K. Currently, the Knife tool is one of the few instances in Blender that requires you to hold down a key. To use the Knife tool, first select the edges or faces you want to cut. Then hold down K while left-clicking and dragging your mouse cursor across your model. A line appears across your mesh. Anywhere that line intersects with a selected edge in your mesh, Blender adds a vertex when you release K. After you have your initial cut in place, the Last Operator panel of the Tool Shelf has a drop-down menu, labeled Type, with a few additional options:

✔ **Exact:** Creates connected vertices exactly where the line from the Knife tool intersects selected edges.

✔ **Midpoints:** Creates connected vertices located at the midpoints of the edges that the Knife tool intersects. When I use the Knife, I tend to use this feature the most.

✔ **Multicut:** This option is the same as the midpoints option, but it creates edges based on the number of cuts you specify. All new vertices are spaced equally along the edges that the Knife tool's line intersects.

The settings in the Last Operator panel are also accessible from a pop-up panel in the 3D View that appears when you press F6. This panel is useful if, like me, you prefer to model with the Tool Shelf hidden.

Unlike the loop cut, the Knife tool works only on the edges that are currently selected. Of course, seeing the actual edges that you're cutting through is also helpful. I recommend switching to wireframe view or turning off the Limit Selection to Visible button.

With the Knife tool, you must select the edges you want to cut before using it.

Simplifying Your Life As a Modeler with Modifiers

Working with meshes can get complicated when you have complex models consisting of lots and lots of vertices. Keeping track of these vertices and making changes to your model can quickly become a daunting and tedious task, even with the ability to use loops and rings. You can quickly run into problems if you have a symmetrical model where the left side is supposed to be identical to the right, or if you need more vertices to make your model appear smoother. In these times, you really want the computer to take on some of this tedious additional work so that you can focus on the creative parts.

Fortunately, Blender actually has a feature, called *modifiers,* that helps tackle the monotony. Despite their rather generic-sounding name, modifiers are an extremely powerful way to save you time and frustration by letting the computer assume the responsibility for grunt work, such as adding smoothing vertices or making your model symmetric. Another benefit of modifiers is that they're *nondestructive,* meaning that you can freely add and remove modifiers to and from your object. As long as you don't apply the modifier, it won't actually make any permanent changes to the object itself. You can always return to the original, unmodified mesh.

You can access modifiers for your mesh in the Modifiers section of the Properties editor. Left-click the Add Modifier button to see a list of the modifiers that are available. Figure 5-5 shows the Modifiers section with the list of available modifiers for meshes.

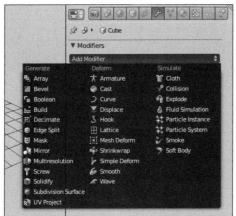

Figure 5-5:
All the modi-
fiers you
can use
on mesh
objects.

Because of space constraints, I can't give an extensive description on every modifier in the list, but I cover some of the most frequently used modifiers. That said, all Blender's modifiers share some of the same controls between them. Figure 5-6 shows the Modifiers section with two modifiers applied, Array and Bevel.

The first thing to notice is that the modifiers are stacked one below the other. This stacking is by design. What's more, the order in which the modifiers appear in the stack is important because one modifier feeds into the next one. So the second modifier — Bevel, in this case — doesn't operate on the original mesh data. Bevel actually operates on the new mesh data provided by the first modifier, Array, in this example.

The stacking order for modifiers is a little bit counter-intuitive if you think about it in terms of layers, where one builds on top of another. Blender's modifier stack doesn't work like that. Instead, you're better off thinking of Blender's modifier stack as a snowball rolling down a hill. Each modifier you hit on the way down the hill adds something or changes something about your snowball, modifying it more and more as it comes to the base of the hill. The topmost modifier is the first modifier and operates on the original mesh data. The modifier immediately below it works on the data that comes from the first modifier, and so on down the line.

In the preceding example, the object is first made into an array. Then the mesh that is created by the Array modifier has its edges beveled so that they're not as sharp cornered. You can change the stacking order by using the up/down arrow buttons on the right side of each modifier block. Left-clicking the up arrow raises a modifier in the stack (bringing it closer to being first), whereas the down arrow lowers it. You can left-click the X at the top right of any block to remove the modifier altogether. The downward triangle that's to the left of each modifier's name collapses and expands that modifier block when you left-click it. Collapsing the modifier block is useful for hiding a modifier's controls after you've decided upon the settings you want to use.

Figure 5-6:
The Array
and Bevel
modifiers in
Modifiers
Properties.

Between the modifier name field and the stacking order buttons are three or four additional buttons. From left to right, the first three buttons control whether the modifier is enabled for rendering (camera icon), viewing in Object mode (eye icon), and viewing in Edit mode (editing cube icon).

You may be wondering why you'd ever want to disable a modifier after you've added it to the stack, instead of just removing it and adding it back in later. The main reason is that many modifiers have an extensive set of options available to them. You may want to see how your object renders with and without the modifier to decide whether you want to use it. You may want to edit your original mesh without seeing any of the changes made by the modifier. If you have a slow computer (or if you want your fast computer to be as responsive as possible), you want to have the modifier enabled only when rendering so that you can still work effectively without your computer choking on all the data coming from Blender. Those buttons next to each name are for these situations.

Some modifiers, like Array, have an additional fourth button with an inverted triangle icon at the end of the button block. Its tooltip says that enabling this button will Apply Modifier to Editing Cage During Edit Mode. The editing *cage* is the input mesh, prior to any influence by the modifier. Enabling this button means that not only are the effects of the modifier visible in Edit mode, but you can also select and perform limited changes to the geometry created by the modifier.

Only two more buttons are common among all modifiers: the Apply and Copy buttons. Left-clicking the Apply button takes the changes made by the modifier and directly applies them to the original object. Applying actually creates the additional vertices and edges in the original mesh to make the mesh match the results produced by the modifier and then removes the modifier from the stack. While modifiers are nondestructive, meaning that they don't permanently change the original object, the Apply button is the one exception.

The Apply button works only if the object you're working on is in Object mode.

The Copy button creates a duplicate version of the modifier and adds it to the stack after the modifier you're duplicating. You probably won't be using this function very often, but it's useful when you need to double up a modifier, such as if you want to bevel twice to get a more rounded edge than a single bevel operation can get you.

Doing half the work (and still looking good!) with the Mirror modifier

When I was first learning how to draw the human face, I used to have all sorts of problems because I'd draw half the face and then realize that I still needed to do nearly the exact same thing all over again on the other side of the face. I found it tedious and difficult to try to match the first half of my drawing. Without fail, the first couple of hundred times I did it, something would always be off. An eye would be too large, an ear would be too high, and so on. I'm not embarrassed to say that it actually took me quite a long time to get drawings that didn't look like Sloth from *The Goonies*. (Some of my coworkers might argue that some of my drawings still look that way!)

Fortunately, as a 3D computer artist, you don't have to go through all that trial and error. You can have the computer do the work for you. In Blender, you use the Mirror modifier (Modifiers Properties⇨Add Modifier⇨Mirror). Figure 5-7 shows the buttons and options available for this modifier.

The Mirror modifier basically makes a copy of all the mesh data in your object and flips it along its local X-, Y-, or Z-axis, or any combination of those axes. The Mirror modifier also has the cool feature of merging vertices along the center seam of the object so that it looks like one unified piece. By changing the Merge Limit value, you can adjust how close vertices have to be to this seam in order to be merged.

Figure 5-7:
The Mirror
modifier.

The X, Y, and Z check boxes dictate which axis or axes your object is mirrored along. For most situations, the default setting of just the local X-axis
is all you really need. I nearly always enable the Clipping check box. This
option takes the vertices that have been merged — as dictated by the Merge
Limit value — and locks them to the plane that your mesh is being mirrored
across. That is, if you're mirroring along the X-axis, then any vertices on the
YZ plane are constrained to remain on that plane. This feature is great when
you're working on vehicles or characters where you don't want to accidentally tear a hole along the center of your model while you're tweaking its
shape with the Proportional Edit Tool (O). Of course, if you have to pull a
vertex away from the center line, you can temporarily disable this check box.

The next check box is labeled Vertex Groups. You can assign vertices in a
mesh to arbitrary groups, known as *vertex groups,* which you can designate in
the Object Data Properties, as shown in Figure 5-8.

Figure 5-8:
Vertex
groups are
created
with the
Object Data
Properties.

No Groups

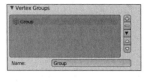

Object Mode

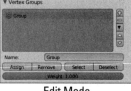

Edit Mode

Chapter 11 covers the actual process of creating vertex groups and assigning individual vertices to a group. However, the most basic way to create a
vertex group is to left-click the plus (+) icon to the right of the list of vertex
groups in the Object Data Properties while in Edit mode. A new vertex group
named Group appears. Now select some vertices in your mesh and press the
Assign button below the vertex group list. You've created a vertex group.

Here's how the Vertex Groups check box in the Mirror modifier works: Say that you've selected some vertices and assigned them to a group named Group.R, indicating that it's the group for some vertices on the right-hand side. And say that you've also created another group called Group.L for the corresponding vertices on the left-hand side, but because you have not yet applied the Mirror modifier, you have no way to assign vertices to this group. Well, if you have the Vertex Groups check box enabled, the generated vertices on the left side that correspond with the Group.R vertices are automatically assigned to Group.L. You don't even have to apply the modifier to get this result! This effect propagates to other modifiers that are based on vertex group names, such as Armatures.

Referring back to Figure 5-7, the U and V check boxes under the label of Textures in the Mirror modifier do the same kind of thing that the Vertex Groups check box does, but they refer to texture coordinates, or *UV coordinates*. You can find out about UV coordinates in Chapter 8. The simplest explanation, though, is that UV coordinates allow you to take a flat image and map it to a three-dimensional surface. Enabling these buttons on the modifier mirrors the texture coordinates in the UV/Image Editor and can possibly cut your texture unwrapping time in half. To see the results of what these buttons do, when you have a texture loaded and your model unwrapped, bring up the Properties region in the UV/Image Editor (View⇨Properties or N) and left-click the Modified check box. Hooray for nondestructive modifiers!

The last option in the Mirror modifier is the text field at the bottom labeled Mirror Object. By default, the Mirror modifier uses the object's origin as the basis for what to mirror. However, by clicking in this field and selecting or typing the name of any other object in your scene, you can use that object's origin as the point to mirror across. With the Mirror Object feature, you can use an Empty (or any other object) as a kind of dynamic origin. With a dynamic origin, you're able to do fun things like animate a cartoon character splitting in half to get around an obstacle (literally!) and joining back together on the other side.

Blender's text fields have integrated search, which means that you can type the first few letters of an object's name and if the name is unique, Blender displays a list of objects in your scene that match what you've typed.

Smoothing things out with the Subdivision Surface modifier

Another commonly used modifier, especially for organic models, is the *Subdivision Surface* modifier. Old-school Blender users may refer to the Subdivision Surface modifier as the *Subsurf* modifier. If you have a background in another 3D modeling program, you may know subdivision surfaces as *sub-ds* or *subdivs*.

If you're not familiar with subdivision surfaces, the concept goes something like this: Blender takes the faces on a given mesh and subdivides them with a number of cuts that you arbitrarily decide upon (usually one to three cuts, or *levels of subdivision*). Now, when the faces are subdivided, Blender moves the edges of these faces closer together, trying to get a smooth transition from one face to the next. The end effect is that a cube with a Subdivision Surface modifier begins looking more and more like a ball with each additional level of subdivision, as shown in Figure 5-9.

Now, the really cool thing about subdivision surfaces is that because they're implemented as a modifier, you get the smooth benefit of additional geometry without the headache of actually having to edit all those extra vertices. In the preceding cube example, even at a subdivision level of 6, if you tab into Edit mode, you control that form with just the eight vertices that make up the original cube. This ability to control a lot of vertices with a relative few is a very powerful way of working, and nearly all high-end 3D animations use subdivision surfaces for just this reason. You have the smooth organic curves of dense geometry with the much more manageable control of a less dense, or *low poly* mesh, referred to as a *cage*.

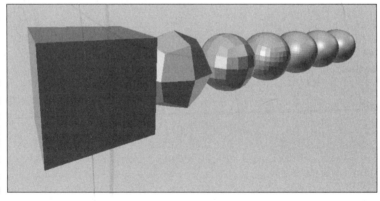

Figure 5-9:
A cube with increasing levels of subdivision from 1 to 6.

For a better idea of the kind of results you can get with the Subdivision Surface modifier, break out Suzanne and apply it to her with the following steps:

1. **Add a Monkey mesh (Shift+A⇨Mesh⇨Monkey).**

   Ooh! Ooh! Ooh!

2. **Set smooth rendering on the monkey (Tool Shelf⇨Shading⇨Smooth).**

At this point, Suzanne is pretty standard. She looks smoother than the faceted look she had when first added, but she's still blocky looking.

3. **Add a Subdivision Surface modifier to the monkey (Modifiers Properties⇨Add Modifier⇨Subdivision Surface or use the Ctrl+1 hotkey combo).**

Now *that's* Suzanne! Instantly, she looks a lot more natural and organic, even despite her inherently cartoony proportions. Feel free to increase the Levels number in the Subdivision Surface modifier to see how much smoother Suzanne can be. I caution you not to go too crazy, though. Setting Levels above 3 might choke your computer a bit if it's too slow.

4. **Tab into Edit mode and notice that the original mesh serves as the control cage for the subdivided mesh.**

Editing the cage with grab (G), rotate (R), scale (S), and extrude (E) directly influences the appearance of the modified mesh within the cage.

Figure 5-10 shows the results of each step.

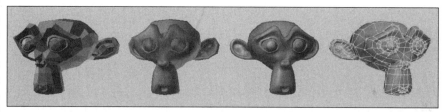

Figure 5-10: Adding the Subdivision Surface modifier to Suzanne.

As powerful as the Subdivision Surface modifier is, only a limited number of options come with it in the modifier stack. Figure 5-11 shows the Subdivision Surface modifier block as it appears in the Modifiers Properties. The first option is a choice between Catmull-Clark subdivision or Simple subdivision. The former is the default, subdividing and smoothing your mesh as expected. The latter works more like doing W⇨Subdivide multiple times while in Edit mode. It gives you more vertices in your meshes, but not the same kind of organic smoothness that the Catmull-Clark method provides. The simple subdivision method is good for some situations, though, so it's nice that the option is available to you.

The next set of values, labeled Subdivisions, allow you to set the level of subdivision that you see on your model. The first value, View, dictates the number of subdivisions your mesh uses in the 3D View. You can set View to a

whole number from 1 to 6. Because I like to keep my 3D View fast and responsive, I tend to keep this number down at 1. Occasionally, I push it up to 2 or 3
to get a quick idea of what it might look like in the final output, but I always
bring it back down to 1 or 0.

Figure 5-11:
The
Subdivision
Surface
modifier.

Beneath View is a similar value input labeled Render. When you create the
final output of your scene or animation, Blender uses this level of subdivision
for your model, regardless of which level you set for the 3D View. The Render
value has the same range that View does, but typically it's set to a higher
value because you usually want smoother, higher-quality models in your final
render. Don't go too crazy with setting this value. On most of my work, which
can get pretty detailed, I rarely ever use a setting higher than 3.

Use the Subdivide UVs check box for texturing. Like the U and V check boxes
in the Mirror modifier, enabling this option adds the additional geometry
to your UV map without requiring you to apply the modifier. Again, this
timesaver can be quite helpful when you're setting up your model for texturing. It's such a consistently useful feature that this check box is enabled by
default. Also, like the U and V options in the Mirror modifier, you can see the
results of the Subdivide UVs check box by enabling the Modified check box in
the UV/Image Editor.

The Optimal Display check box is something I typically like to leave turned
on all the time. Optimal Display hides the extra edges that are created by the
modifier when you view the model in wireframe view. On a complex scene,
hiding the edges can definitely help you make sense of things when working
in wireframe. Figure 5-12 shows the difference Optimal Display makes on a
Suzanne model with three levels of subdivision.

When working with the Subdivision Surface modifier, I typically like to have
the Optimal Display option enabled, along with the Apply Modifier to Cage
button at the top of the Subdivision Surface modifier panel. Everyone's different, though, so play with it on your own and see what works best for you.

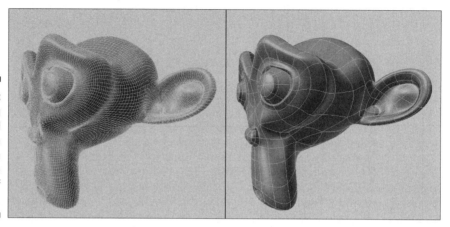

Figure 5-12:
Using
Optimal
Display on
a mesh
with three
levels of
subdivision.

Using the power of Arrays

One of the coolest and most-fun-to-play-with modifiers in Blender is the Array modifier. In its simplest application, this modifier duplicates the mesh a specified number of times and places those duplicates in line, evenly spaced apart. Have a model of a chair and need to put lines of chairs in a room to make it look like a meeting hall? Using a couple of Array modifiers together is a great way to do just that! Figure 5-13 is a screenshot of Blender being used to create that sort of scene.

You're not limited to using just one Array modifier on your object. I achieved the effect in Figure 5-13 by using two Array modifiers stacked together, one for the first row of chairs going across the room and the second to create multiple copies of that first row. Stacking multiple arrays is an excellent way to build a complex scene with just one object.

Blender's Array modifier is loaded with all kinds of cool functions that you can use in lots of interesting ways. Some ways facilitate a desire to be lazy by making the computer do as much of the repetitive, tedious tasks as possible. (For example, you can use the Array modifier to model a staircase or a chain-link fence or a wall of bricks.) However, you can also use the Array modifier to do some really incredible abstract animations or specialized tentacles or even rows of dancing robots!

The bulk of the power in the Array modifier lies in how it handles *offsets,* or the distances apart that the duplicates are set relative to one another. As shown in Figure 5-14, the Array modifier offers three different sorts of offsets, all of which you can use in combination with one another by enabling their check boxes:

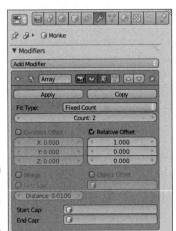

Figure 5-14:
The Array
modifier.

✔ **Constant Offset:** This offset adds a fixed distance to each duplicated object in the array. So setting the X value beneath this button to –5.0 shifts each of the duplicates five units in the negative X direction. The same behavior happens in the Y- and Z-axes when you set the values for those offsets as well.

✔ **Relative Offset:** Think of the Relative Offset as a multiplication factor, based on the width, height, and depth of the object. So no matter how large or small the object is, if you set the Z value to 1.0, for example, each duplicated object in the array is stacked directly on top of the one below it. This type of offset is the one that's used by default when you first add the Array modifier.

✔ **Object Offset:** The Object Offset is my personal favorite offset because of its incredible versatility. It takes the position of any object you pick in the Object field — I prefer to use Empties for this purpose — and uses its relative distance from the mesh you added to Array as the offset. But that's just the start of it! Using this offset also takes into account the rotation and scale of the object you choose. So if you have an Empty that's one unit away from your object, scaled to twice its original size and rotated 15 degrees on the Y-axis, each subsequent duplicate is scaled twice as large as the previous one and rotated an additional 15 degrees. Now you can make a spiral staircase like the one in Figure 5-15. And if you feel inclined to create an animation of a staircase where the stairs can be collapsed into each other and hidden, it's a simple as animating the offset object!

Figure 5-15:
(1) Model the step. (2) Add an Empty for Object Offset and rotate in Z. (3) Add the Array modifier. (4) Make it pretty.

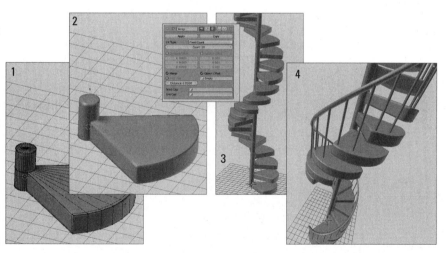

You also have a lot of control over how many duplicates the Array modifier creates, thanks to the Fit Type drop-down menu at the top of the Array modifier block. By default, the Fit Type is set to Fixed Count, and you explicitly enter the number of duplicates in the Count field below it. Fixed Count isn't your only Fit Type option, however. You actually have three:

✔ **Fixed Count:** This option lets you explicitly enter the exact number of duplicates you would like to create, up to 1,000.

Blender and real-world units

Previous versions of Blender didn't have any notion of real-world units. They had only a vague notion of *Blender units*, which you could mentally convert to any unit system available. The typical behavior was to assume that one Blender unit equaled one meter, but that wasn't a hard-and-fast rule. In the 2.5 series of releases, however, the Blender developers fixed this oversight and added support for real units. Blender defaults to the old behavior of using Blender units, but the Scene Properties has a panel labeled Units. If you need to explicitly use Metric (meters, centimeters, and so on) or Imperial (inches, feet, and so on) units, you can set those values here.

- ✔ **Fit Length:** This option creates the proper count of duplicate objects to fit in the distance that you define. Bear in mind that this length isn't exactly in whole units. It uses the local coordinate system of the object that you're making an array of, so the length you choose is multiplied by the scale of that original object, as shown in the 3D View's Properties region (N).

- ✔ **Fit Curve:** If you choose this option, you can choose the name of a curve object in the Object field below it. When you do, Blender calculates the length of that curve and uses that as the length to fill in with duplicated objects. Using this option together with a Curve modifier is a nice quick-'n-dirty way of creating a linked metal chain like the one on the cover of this book.

Another cool feature in the Array modifier is the ability to merge the vertices of one duplicate with the vertices that it's near in another duplicate. With the Merge check box enabled and some fine adjustment to the Distance value, you can make your model look like a single unified piece, instead of being composed of individual duplicates. I've used this feature to model rope, train tracks, and stair rails, for example. The First Last check box toggles to determine whether the vertices in the last duplicated instance are allowed to merge with the nearby vertices in the first object of the array. Use merging with Object Offset, and you can create a closed loop out of your duplicates, all merged together.

Say that you're using the Array modifier to create a handrail for your spiral staircase, and you don't want the handrail to simply stop at the beginning and end. Instead, you'd like the end of the handrail to have ornamental caps. You could model something and try to place it by hand, but that process can get problematic if you have to make changes or animate the handrail in the future. (Hey, this is computer graphics. Handrails that move and are animated make complete sense!) So another way to place ornamental caps on a handrail is to use the Start Cap and End Cap fields in the Array modifier. After you model what you want the cap to look like, you can pick or type the name of that object in these fields, and Blender places it at the beginning and the end of the array, respectively. Pretty slick, huh?

Sculpting Multiresolution Meshes

Over the years, as computers have gotten more powerful and more capable of handling dense high-poly models with millions of vertices, computer graphics artists have wanted more and more control over the vertices in their meshes. Using a Subdivison Surface modifier is great for adding geometry to make models look more organic, but what if you're modeling a monster and you want to model a scar in his face? You have to apply the modifier to have access and control over those additional vertices. And even though the computer may be able to handle having them there, a million vertices is a lot for you to try to control and keep track of, even with all the various selection methods and the Proportional Edit Tool. Fortunately, Blender supports *multiresolution meshes* and *Sculpt mode*.

Multiresolution (or *multires*) meshes address the problem of having to apply the Subdivision Surface modifier before you can directly control the vertices that it creates. With a multires mesh, you can freely move between a level 1 subdivision and a level 6 subdivision, just like with the Subdivision Surface modifier. However, the difference is that you can directly control the vertices of the level 6 subdivision just as easily as the level 1 subdivision by using Blender's Sculpt mode. And you can see changes made in either level — to varying levels of detail, depending on the level you're looking at. (If you make a very fine detail change in level 6, it may not be readily apparent at level 1.)

Something new: The Multiresolution modifier

Adding multires capabilities to a mesh used to be a process handled outside of the modifier stack. While this method worked fine, mixing the benefits of multires meshes with changes made by modifiers was difficult. You couldn't easily animate multires meshes with an armature or give them particle hair. As of Blender 2.5, those limitations no longer exist. Creating a multires mesh now is just like adding any other modifier to a mesh object. Figure 5-16 shows what the Multiresolution modifier block looks like.

Figure 5-16:
The Multi-
resolution
modifier
block with
a couple
levels of
subdivision
added.

The Multiresolution modifier is similar in appearance to the Subdivision Surface modifier. By default, the Multiresolution modifier starts with zero subdivisions on your mesh. Use the Subdivide button to increase the level of subdivision that you want to add to your mesh. Subdividing increments the values for Preview, Sculpt, and Render. Like the View and Render values in the Subdivision Surface modifier, these values control how many levels of subdivision you see in the 3D View, both while sculpting and when your model is rendered, respectively.

However, unlike with the Subdivision Surface modifier, you don't have exactly six levels of subdivision to switch between. In the Multiresolution modifier, the number can be as low as zero and as high as your computer's processor and memory can handle. And before adding a level, you have the option of choosing Catmull-Clark Subdivision or Simple Subdivision, like you can with the Subdivision Surface modifier.

The only caveat is that you can't freely change between subdivision types on a given level with the Multiresolution modifier. Changing from Catmull-Clark to Simple (or vice versa) has an effect on all multires levels.

If you have a Subdivision Surface modifier on your mesh, I recommend apply-ing it to your mesh or removing it from the modifier stack before adding the Multiresolution modifier. Because the Multiresolution modifier uses the same process to create subdivision levels, you really don't need to have both active at the same time.

After you have a level added, you have some additional options available. Clicking Delete Higher removes all subdivision levels greater than the level you're currently in. So if you have five levels of subdivision and you're at level 3, clicking Delete Higher effectively kills levels 4 and 5.

Enabling the Optimal Draw check box does the same thing that the corresponding check box does in the Subdivision Surface modifier: It prevents Blender from showing subdivided edges in the 3D View. Some 3D modelers who use sculpting tools like to overlay the model's wireframe on the mesh (Object Properties⇨Display⇨Wire check box) as they work so that they can have an idea of how their topology looks. (See the sidebar "The importance of good topology" in this chapter for more information.) Without Optimal Draw enabled, the 3D View of your model can quickly get cluttered, so enabling this check box simplifies the display for you.

Now, if you try to tab into Edit mode on a multires mesh, you still see only the vertices available to you in the cage provided by the base mesh. So how do you actually edit all those additional vertices created by the Multiresolution modifier? The answer: Sculpt mode. Sculpt mode treats your mesh very much like a solid piece of clay. You have a variety of sculpt brushes that help you shape and form your mesh to look exactly how you want. You can activate Sculpt mode from the Mode menu in the 3D View's header. When you're in Sculpt mode, the Tool Shelf (T) updates to show a whole set of options available to you for editing your mesh.

If you have a drawing tablet like the ones manufactured by Wacom, Sculpt mode takes advantage of the pressure sensitivity that a tablet offers.

When working in Sculpt mode and using the Multiresolution modifier, the general workflow is to start at low levels of subdivision to block out the rough shape of your model and then proceed to higher levels of subdivision for more detailed elements of your model. The process is very much like traditional sculpting in meatspace, as well as box modeling in the CG world. The only difference in this case is that the Multiresolution modifier allows you to freely move between high and low levels of subdivision, so you don't have to block out your whole model in a single go.

Nothing says that you're required to use the Multiresolution modifier when sculpting in Blender. In fact, Sculpt mode works just fine without any Multiresolution modifier at all. That said, you have far more flexibility and artistic control over your model if you do take advantage of the multiple levels of detail that the Multiresolution modifier provides.

Sculpting options

Figure 5-17 shows the contents of the Tool Shelf when you're in Sculpt mode. The buttons in these panels — Brush, Stroke, Curve, Texture, Symmetry, Options, Appearance, and Tool — are for customizing your sculpt brushes as you work.

Figure 5-17:
The Sculpt panel.

Brush types

As you work your way down the Tool Shelf, you get finer and finer control of your brush. In fact, the first panel, Brush, just contains a list of brush data-blocks, which serve as presets for all the subsequent settings in the Tool Shelf. Switch your brushes by clicking on the brush icon above the datablock and choose the preset brush you're interested in. By default, 19 presets appear in this list, each one modifying your mesh in a very specific way. All brushes work by left-clicking with the brush cursor over the mesh and dragging your mouse cursor around the 3D View. Due to this brush-style of editing, using a drawing tablet can be very beneficial.

Due to space constraints in this book, I can't cover each of the available sculpt brush presets. Here are brief descriptions of some of the most used sculpt brushes in the list:

✔ **Clay:** The Clay brush is pretty unique among Blender's sculpt brushes. Its primary purpose is to make large changes, adding or subtracting volume from your base mesh and dealing with details later. The Clay brush is also useful for merging unlinked meshes within the same object.

✔ **Flatten:** The Flatten brush lowers vertices to try and get them to be as flat, or *planar,* as possible. If you're sculpting a landscape and you decide to remove a hill, this brush is the one to use.

✔ **Grab:** When you left-click and drag your mouse cursor on a mesh with the Grab brush activated, the vertices that are within the brush cursor's circle are moved to wherever you drag your mouse to. Grab is like selecting a bunch of vertices in Edit mode and pressing G.

- **Inflate/Deflate:** When you run the Inflate brush over your mesh, vertices move outward along their own local normals. If the Subtract button in the Brush panel is enabled, the vertices move inward. This brush is good for fattening or shrinking parts of a model.

- **Layer:** The Layer brush is like the SculptDraw brush with a maximum height that it pulls the vertices, basically creating a raised mesa on the surface of your mesh.

- **Pinch/Magnify:** If you enable the Pinch brush, vertices are pulled toward the center of your brush cursor as you move it over the mesh. Pinch is a great way to add ridges and creases to a model.

- **SculptDraw:** The SculptDraw brush is the default brush and it basically pulls the surface of your mesh outward (or inward, if you enable the Subtract button in the Brush panel). By default, the brush works with an even falloff, so the raised areas you draw tend to flow smoothly back into the rest of the mesh.

- **Smooth:** If you have jagged parts of your mesh or undesirable surface irregularities created while sculpting, using the Smooth brush cleans up those bumpy parts and makes the surface of your mesh, well, smoother.

- **Snake Hook:** The Snake Hook brush is very similar to the Grab brush except it gives you more control over what you can do when you pull the vertices away from the main portion of your mesh. With enough geometry, you can actually sketch in 3D with the Snake Hook brush. It's useful for making things like spines, tentacles, and dreadlocks.

- **Twist:** Most of the other Sculpt mode brushes are primarily means of translating or scaling vertices. The Twist brush, in contrast, is a brush for rotating vertices in your mesh. When you left-click and drag your mouse on your mesh, the brush remains stationary and the position of your mouse cursor determines how much the vertices within the area of your brush rotate.

Brush controls

The Radius and Strength sliders below the list of brush datablocks control the size and strength of the brush you're currently using. You can use hotkeys for changing these values while in the 3D View so that you don't have to constantly return to the Tool Shelf:

- To change brush radius, press F, move your mouse until the brush cursor is the desired size, and left-click to confirm.

- To adjust the brush strength, press Shift+F and move your mouse cursor toward the center of the circle that appears to increase the strength or away from the center to decrease the strength. When you're at the strength you want, left-click to confirm.

The importance of good topology

If you listen to modelers talk or if you visit some of the Web forums where 3D modelers hang out, you'll hear the words *topology* and *edge flow* pretty often. These concepts are very important for a modeler, particularly if your model is destined to be animated. These terms refer to how the vertices and edges of your mesh lay out across its surface. Even when sculpting, 3D modelers will often use a base mesh that has good topology as their starting point. Or, when they're done sculpting, they'll take the model through a process known as *retopology* to give it a clean edge flow that's usable in animation. To that end, whether you're sculpting or just straight modeling, keep a few key guidelines in mind:

✔ **Use quads.** Try to avoid triangles whenever possible. Four-sided polygons look better when subdivided, and they also tend to deform more cleanly when an armature is used to animate them.

✔ **Minimize the use of poles that don't have four edges.** Remember that a pole is where multiple edges join at a single vertex. The UV Sphere mesh has two large poles at its top and bottom. Poles are harder to avoid than triangles, but you should do what you can to minimize their use because they can terminate edge loops, and they don't deform as nicely as four-edged poles. If you're forced to use a pole, try to put it in a place on the mesh that won't deform a lot when it's animated.

✔ **Holes such as mouths and eye sockets should be encircled by concentric edge loops.** This guideline is particularly important for character models that may be animated. Having concentric edge loops makes it easier to deform and animate these highly expressive parts of the face.

✔ **Edges should follow anatomy.** Following the flow of anatomy — particularly musculature — is important because doing so yields cleaner, more natural deformations. Arms don't pinch when you bend them; the crease from the side of the nose flows around the mouth. Following these little rules really makes the lives of riggers and animators much easier (and it helps make the final animation look better).

Additionally, if you happen to have a drawing tablet, you can bind the Radius and Strength values to the pressure sensitivity of your tablet. Each value slider has a button to its right with an icon of a hand pushing against a blue line with its index finger. Left-click this button on either slider, and Blender recognizes the pressure information from your tablet.

The next set of important controls available while in Sculpt mode are a pair of buttons in the Brush panel. Depending on which brush preset you're using, these labels may be named Add and Subtract, Flatten and Contrast, Inflate and Deflate, or they may not be there (for grabbing brushes like Grab, Snake Hook, and Twist). Regardless of what they're named, if they appear, the first button (Add, Flatten, Inflate) is the default behavior for sculpting brushes. If you enable the second button (Subtract, Contrast, Deflate), it does the inverse of the default behavior. For example, with Subtract enabled, the Clay brush pushes vertices into the volume of your mesh instead of pulling them out.

Also, note that regardless of whether you enabled the first or second button in this block, pressing Ctrl while using the brush does the opposite behavior. For example, if you're using the SculptDraw brush with Add enabled, the normal behavior creates a small hill wherever you move your mouse cursor. If you Ctrl+left-click and drag, you sculpt a small valley instead.

If you hold Shift while in Sculpt mode, Blender temporarily activates the Smooth brush, regardless of what the active brush is. The Smooth brush is handy if you find yourself bouncing between adding details and smoothing them out.

When working with brushes like SculptDraw, Inflate, or Layer, an additional check box, labeled Accumulate, appears under the Add/Subtract buttons. By default, when you use these brushes, they move the faces on your mesh relative to the normals that they have when you start making your stroke, regardless of how many times you paint over them in a single stroke. This default behavior is helpful because it prevents your mesh from quickly expanding uncontrollably. However, if you want to use a face's immediate normal when you run your brush over it, then you should enable this check box.

Other settings in the Sculpt mode Tool Shelf

The next few panels in the Tool Shelf while in Sculpt mode — Stroke, Curve, Texture, Symmetry, Options, Appearance, and Tool — are devoted to creating custom brushes. The next section gets into custom brushes in more detail. The following describes each panel in a little more detail:

- ✔ **Stroke:** The Stroke panel holds settings that dictate what happens when you're dragging the brush over your mesh. The most valuable setting in this panel is Stroke Method. The options in this menu dictate how your brush movement influences your mesh. For fun, choose the Layer brush and set the Stroke Method to Anchor. When you left-click and drag your brush over your model, you get a neat mesh tsunami that originates from the location you clicked.

- ✔ **Curve:** Within this panel are settings for adjusting how the influence of your brush changes from its center to its extremities.

- ✔ **Texture:** Any texture you can create in Blender can be used in a brush. The Texture panel is where you assign a texture to your current brush. See Chapter 8 for more information on creating textures.

- ✔ **Symmetry:** This panel controls how the sculpt brushes modify your mesh relative to the object's local axes. For example, if you left-click the X check box, anything you do on the left side of the mesh automatically also happens on the right side of the mesh. Symmetry is an excellent timesaver for doing involved tasks like sculpting faces.

✔ **Options:** The settings in this panel are commonly used to speed up your performance while sculpting. In particular, the Show Brush and Fast Navigate check boxes are very helpful. Show Brush (enabled by default) toggles the visibility of the brush's circle of influence around the mouse cursor and Fast Navigate (disabled by default) drops the subdivision level of your mesh while orbiting in the 3D View.

✔ **Appearance:** From the Appearance panel, you can stipulate what color to use for your brush's outline. Also, if you have an image that you'd like to use as a custom icon for your custom brush, you can enable the Custom Icon check box and point Blender to the location of that image on your hard drive. Then that image will appear as the representation of your custom brush in the brushes menu at the top of the Tool Shelf.

✔ **Tool:** You can base any brush in Blender on 16 different base tools. The Tool panel is where you define which tool your custom brush uses. You can also indicate whether the brush is used only for sculpting or if it can be used in Blender's other paint modes.

Creating custom brushes

Using the controls in the Tool Shelf while in Sculpt Mode, you can customize existing brush datablocks or create your own. Assuming that you want to do the latter, you need to first create a new brush datablock by clicking the Plus (+) button in the datablock beneath the list of brushes in the Brush panel at the top of the Tool Shelf. For efficiency, use an existing brush as a starting point by selecting that brush before adding your custom one. After clicking the Plus (+) icon, name your new brush by typing in the datablock field. Now you can go about customizing your brush.

Using Blender's texture system to tweak brushes

In the Texture panel, you can pick a texture to influence the behavior of your brush. You can use any texture you made in Texture Properties as a brush when you sculpt. Textured brushes are an excellent way to get more details added to your mesh while sculpting. Choose an existing texture by left-clicking the texture square in this panel and picking from the thumbnail images that appear. (See Chapter 8 for more information on creating and loading textures in Blender.) Refer to Figure 5-17 to see the Texture panel in Sculpt mode's Tool Shelf.

You may want to choose the Rake option from the Angle drop-down menu when you've loaded a texture. With this option chosen, the texture is rotated as you sculpt to match the motion of the brush. Using Rake helps you avoid creating unnatural patterns from your textures when you sculpt.

Sculpting with a high level of subdivisions can be taxing on your computer, using a *lot* of memory to store all those additional vertices. If you use too many levels of subdivision, your computer may run out of memory, and Blender may lock up or crash. In an effort to prevent a crash and give themselves more vertices to play with, many 3D modelers who use Blender's

Multiresolution modifier often go to the User Preferences under Editing to disable Global Undo and change the number of undo steps from the default value of 32 down to 0. This modification removes the safety net of undo, but it can often improve Blender's performance while sculpting.

Practical Example: Modeling an Eye

If you're modeling characters, chances are good that those characters are going to need eyes. Granted, there's a chance that all your characters may be robots, moles, and worms, but I'll assume that's not the case. Eyes carry the life of a character, so you want to get them right. This example walks you through producing a nice eye model that you can make quickly and even reuse in future projects. It also gives you a good opportunity to practice mesh modeling techniques covered in this chapter. As a bonus, this book's companion DVD and Web site feature a video version of this example.

Starting with a primitive

You're starting your eye model. First things first: Delete the default cube in the 3D View (X); it's not the ideal primitive to start this model. Of course, you have to start with something. Exactly what that something is depends on what you're modeling. People who do box modeling typically start with a cube. Point-for-point modelers often start with a plane and extrude faces and vertices from that mesh.

In the case of this specific eye model that you're creating, it's most prudent to take a box modeler's approach, though, with a primitive that more closely matches the base shape you need. That means you're going to use a sphere. If you go to add a new mesh object in the 3D View (Shift+A⇨Mesh), you might notice that Blender ships with two different sphere primitives: UV sphere and icosphere. Figure 5-18 shows these two types of spheres in Edit mode so that you can see the differences between them.

The primary difference between the UV sphere and the icosphere is topology. The UV sphere is made up predominantly of quads, whereas the icosphere is composed entirely of equilateral triangles. In the case of this model, you can take advantage of the radial topology at the top and bottom of the UV sphere primitive to more easily form some of the eye's features. For that reason, the UV sphere is what you want to add (Shift+A⇨Mesh⇨UV Sphere).

 After adding the sphere, notice that the Last Operation panel at the bottom of the Tool Shelf updates to show Add UV Sphere and provides some settings for you to adjust. You can use these values to tweak your initial base mesh. In this case, the default values work just fine, but you're welcome to play with these settings. If you hid the Tool Shelf (T), you can quickly pull up these settings after adding your sphere by pressing F6 in the 3D View.

Figure 5-18:
The UV
sphere (left)
features
topology
like a globe,
while the
icosphere
(right) is
built from
a set of
equilateral
triangles.

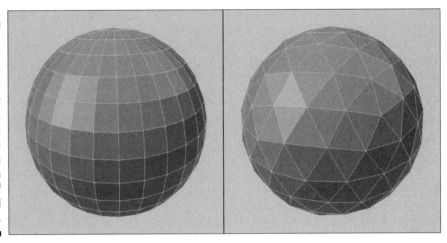

After you add your UV sphere, tab into Edit mode and rotate the vertices of your sphere by 90 degrees about the X-axis. If you like using the 3D manipulator, switch it to rotate by clicking its icon in the 3D View's header. Then you can click the red X-axis control and rotate by 90 degrees. Remember that you can see how much you're rotating by in the bottom-left corner of the 3D View's header. Also, hold Ctrl as you're rotating so that you can rotate in exact fixed increments. Of course, the fastest way to do this rotation operation is with the following hotkey sequence: R⇨X⇨90⇨Enter.

Creating the pupil and iris

After you rotate your UV sphere, you can form the basic structure of the eye. This process starts with forming the pupil and iris area. Use the following steps:

1. **Select the pole vertex at the front of your UV sphere.**

   It may be helpful to do this step from the front (Numpad 1) or right side view (Numpad 3) to make selection easier.

2. **Enable the Proportional Edit Tool (O).**

   This step allows adjustments to your selected vertex to influence some of the vertices near it.

3. **Grab your pole vertex and move it along the Y-axis toward the center of your sphere (G⇨Y).**

   While moving this vertex, use the scroll wheel on your mouse or the Page Up and Page Down buttons on your keyboard to adjust the influence of the Proportional Edit Tool. The area of influence should include the first two concentric edge loops around your pole vertex.

With those steps completed, you have the basic structure for your eye
model. The reason for building the iris and pupil this way is a bit of a lighting
trick. Because of the lens in the eye, the iris appears to reflect light in a pretty
unique way. By pulling that pole vertex and the edge loops surrounding it
slightly inward, you provide a surface for the light to reflect off of. Figure 5-19
shows what your eye model should look like at this point.

Technically, if you're working on a low polygon model, you could probably
just stop here. However, assume that you want to add a bit more detail to
your eye. You may be tempted to just add a Subdivision Surface modifier and
be done with it, but try a slightly more sophisticated approach. In order to
take that approach, you need a little more geometry on your mesh. In particular, you need to add detail in the pupil and iris areas. To do so, you need to
add some more edge loops. Start with the easy loops in the iris.

A good general rule when you model is that you should try to keep the faces in
your mesh roughly square and roughly all the same size.

If you look at the iris of your model, those faces are stretched and rectangular. You can make the faces more proportional by adding an edge loop
along the middle of them. You start this process by clicking the Loop Cut
and Slide button on the Tool Shelf or pressing Ctrl+R. Then run your mouse
cursor over your mesh until the pink preview loop shows the loop you want
to create at the midpoint of the edge loops that define the iris. Left-click to
confirm the loop cut and either slide the loop into place manually or simply
right-click, and Blender automatically places the edge loop at that midpoint.

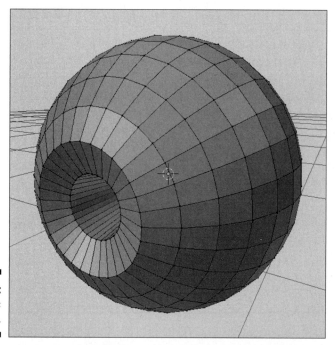

Figure 5-19:
Your basic
eye model.

Taking a knife to your pupil

Now you need to create some edge loops to more clearly define the pupil. However, one loop you should add is in the cone that forms the pupil. Edge loops terminate at poles that don't connect exactly four edges. For this reason, the Loop Cut and Slide feature (Ctrl+R) can't create a new edge loop in the cone. Instead, you need to use the Knife tool. Something to remember about the Knife tool is that it operates only on selected edges and faces, so you first need to select the faces you're interested in. A quick way to do make that selection is using this handy two-step process:

1. **Select the pole vertex at the center of your pupil.**

   In solid viewport shading, that vertex is sometimes hard to select. You may have to quickly switch to wireframe viewport shading (Z).

2. **Increase your selection by pressing Ctrl+Numpad Plus (+).**

Neat, huh? Now you can go ahead and use the Knife tool. You may find it easiest to do these next steps after toggling wireframe viewport shading (Z) and switching to the right side view (Numpad 3).

1. **With your desired faces selected, use the Knife tool to cut a new loop.**

   Hold down K and then left-click and drag your mouse to draw a line where you want to cut. When you release your mouse button and K, anywhere your line crossed an edge, a new vertex is created. This *Exact* type of cut is the Knife tool's default behavior. Of course, exact cuts are ugly looking, so use the next step to fix that problem.

2. **Using the Last Operation panel in the Tool Shelf or the F6 pop-up panel, change the cut Type from Exact to Midpoints.**

   Your newly created edge loop cleans up immediately. What you're going to do now is use your new edge loop to form the base of the pupil.

3. **Grab the edge loop and move it along the Y-axis toward the pole vertex at the center of the pupil (G⇨Y).**

   After the pupil is more clearly defined, you again have rectangular faces in your mesh, this time leading from the interior iris edge loop back to your new edge loop. It's not super critical that you deal with these faces, but taking care of them isn't a bad idea.

4. **Add a new edge loop along the faces that define the pupil.**

   From this point, you can tweak to taste. The next steps are optional, but they're something I like to do.

5. **(Optional) Select the innermost edge loop of the iris (Alt+right-click).**

6. **(Optional) Enable Proportional Editing (O).**

7. **(Optional) Scale (S) the edge loop down to make the pupil area a bit more cylindrical.**

   Use your mouse's scroll wheel to adjust the influence of the Proportional Edit Tool to taste.

8. **Disable Proportional Editing (O).**

At this point, the detailed eye is nearly done. It should look something like the image in Figure 5-20.

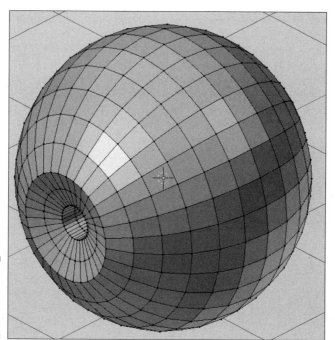

Figure 5-20:
A more detailed eye model.

Smoothing out the eye interior

Now it's time for some polish. Up to this point, you've been working with a faceted, flat-shaded model. The next step is to smooth things out a bit:

1. **Select all vertices in your mesh (A⇨A).**

2. **Set the shading type on the selected faces to Smooth.**

   Simply click Shading⇨Smooth in the Tool Shelf or press W⇨Shade Smooth. You're off to a good start, but assume that you're working with a model that allows for a high polygon count. The facets on your eye model are still somewhat noticeable. The next step can help.

3. **Add the Subdivision Surface modifier.**

   You can add this modifier in Modifiers Properties or quickly tab out to Object mode, use the Ctrl+1 hotkey, and tab back into Edit mode.

This smoother eye looks pretty nice, but the iris has lost a bit of its definition. Fortunately, you can easily add definition with just a little bit more geometry, two edge loops to be exact. You add one near the outer edge of the iris and another near the inner edge. Uses the same process as when adding an edge loop along the center of the iris: Loop Cut and Slide (Ctrl+R) where you want the new loop, left-click to confirm and create the loop, move your mouse cursor to slide the edge into place, and left-click again to confirm its location. When you're done, you should have an eye model like the one in Figure 5-21.

Building the eye's exterior

At this point, the hard part is done. All that remains is creating the exterior shell of the eye. Medically speaking, the shell would be the cornea and the sclera. For this model, form them as a single mesh. Now, the temptation here is simply to create a new UV sphere and make it slightly bigger than your eye model — and this approach actually would work fine. However, the downside of this technique is that it puts a pole right at the center of the eye, and the triangles caused by that pole can sometimes cause some ugly artifacts when you try to render your model. Fortunately, you can create this shell using a subdivided cube and Blender's handy To Sphere operator:

1. **Tab into Object mode, if you haven't already.**

2. **Add a new Cube mesh (Shift+A⇨Mesh⇨Cube).**

3. **Tab into Edit mode on your new cube mesh.**

4. **Smoothly subdivide the cube (W⇨Subdivide Smooth).**

5. **In the Last Operator panel, change the Number of Cuts value to 6.**

6. **Use the To Sphere operator and make the cube fully sphere-shaped (Shift+Alt+S⇨1⇨Enter).**

7. **Set shading to smooth (W⇨Shade Smooth).**

8. **Add a Subdivision Surface modifier (Tab⇨Ctrl+1⇨Tab).**

   You've just turned a cube into a sphere! It should look something like the image in Figure 5-22.

Now you just have to get that sphere to fit the eye you've already modeled and make a bulge for the cornea. You can easily do so with the following steps.

1. **Scale (S) your spherized cube down to fit the size of your eye model.**

   I find that the best method is with the viewport in wireframe (Z) and from the front view (Numpad 1). You may also want to hold down Shift while scaling so that you have more refined control.

2. **Switch to Face Select mode (Ctrl+Tab⇨Face) and select the polygon at the center front of your mesh, right in front of the pupil.**

   This face is what you're going to use to create the bulge for the cornea.

3. **Enable Proportional Editing (O), grab the selected face (G), and move it along the Y-axis, away from the center of the eye.**

   Use your mouse's scroll wheel to adjust the influence of the Proportional Edit Tool. It may be useful to work from the right side view (Numpad 3) as a wireframe (Z). You may also want to look on the Web for an illustrated reference of how far this bulge sticks out. I've exaggerated the cornea a little for this example so that it's visible in figures.

4. **Disable Proportional Editing (O).**

At this point, the model for your eye is essentially done. Clean things up a bit by selecting both of the meshes you created and joining them (Ctrl+J) as a single object. Also, go to the Object Properties and name your model something logical, like eye. Figure 5-23 shows what your final model should look like.

You have an eyeball!! Save this model because you can use it again for the materials and texturing example in Chapter 7.

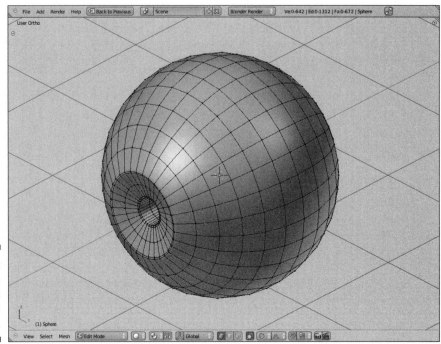

Figure 5-21:
Your eye
model, all
smooth and
nice looking.

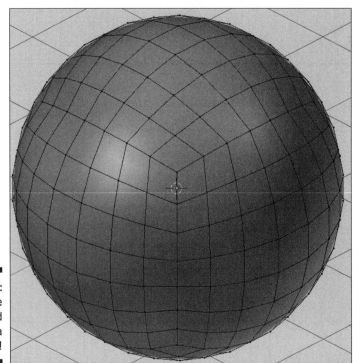

Figure 5-22:
It used to be
a cube, and
now it's a
sphere!

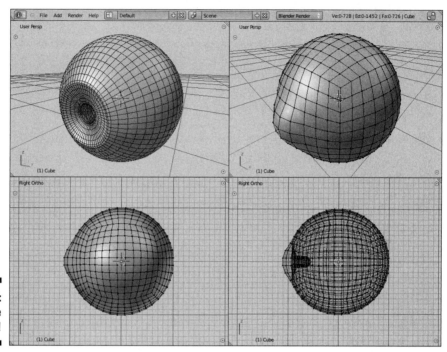

Figure 5-23:
Eye see
you!

Chapter 6

Using Blender's Nonmesh Primitives

Although polygon-based meshes tend to be the bread and butter of modelers in Blender, they aren't the only types of objects that are available to you for creating things in 3D space. Blender also has curves, surfaces, meta objects, and text objects. These objects tend to have somewhat more specialized purposes than meshes, but when you need what they provide, they're extremely useful.

Curves and surfaces are nearly as general purpose as meshes; they're particularly handy for anything that needs to have a smooth, nonfaceted look. They're also important for models that require mathematical precision and accuracy in their appearance. Meta objects are great at creating organic shapes that merge into one another, such as simple fluids. You can also use them to make a roughly sculpted model from basic elements that you can detail further in Sculpt mode. Text objects are exactly what they sound like: You use them to add text to a scene and manipulate that text in all three dimensions. This chapter tells you more about working with all these types of objects.

Using Curves and Surfaces

So, what's the biggest difference between curves and surfaces when compared to meshes? *Math!* Okay, I'm sorry. That was mean of me; I know that math can be a four-letter word for many artists, but don't worry; you won't have to do any math here. What I mean to say is that you can describe curves and surfaces to the computer as a mathematical function. You describe meshes, on the other hand, using the positions of all the individual vertices that they're composed of. In terms of the computer, curves and surfaces have two advantages:

- **Curves and surfaces are very precise.** When you get down to it, the best that a mesh can be is an approximation of a real object. A mesh can look really, really good, but it's not exact. Because curves are defined by math, they're exactly the correct shape, which is why designers and engineers like them.

- **Curves and surfaces take up less memory.** Because the shape is mathematically defined, the computer can save that shape by saving the math, rather than saving all the individual points. Complicated curves and surfaces usually take up quite a bit less hard drive space than the same shape made with meshes.

Of course, these advantages come with some caveats, too. For one, curves and surfaces can sometimes be more difficult to control. Because curves and surfaces don't really have vertices for you to directly manipulate, you have to use *control points*. Depending on the type of curve, control points can sit directly on the shape or float somewhere off of the surface as part of a control *cage*.

Even though curves and surfaces are perfect mathematical descriptions of a shape, the computer is actually an imperfect way of displaying those perfect shapes. All 3D geometry is eventually tessellated when the computer processes it (see Chapter 5). So even though curves and surfaces can take less memory on a computer, displaying them smoothly may actually take more time for the computer to process. To speed up things, you can tell the computer to use a rougher tessellation with fewer triangles. As a result, what you see in Blender is an approximation of that perfect curve or surface shape. Do you find yourself thinking, "But hey, I thought curves were supposed to be perfect mathematical descriptions of a shape. What gives with these facets?" Well, the curve *is* perfect. It's just hard for the computer to show it to you directly.

But despite these minor disadvantages, using curves and surfaces is a really smart move in quite a few cases. For example, most designers like to use curves for company logos because curves can scale in print to any size without looking jagged or *aliased* around its edges. As a 3D artist, you can import the curves of a logo design and give the logo some depth, dimension, and perhaps even some animation.

And speaking of animation, curves have quite a few handy uses there as well. For example, you can use a curve to define a path for an object to move along. You can also use curves in Blender's Graph Editor to display and control the changes to an object's properties over time. For modeling purposes, curves are great for pipes, wires, and ornate organic shapes. Figure 6-1 shows a park bench. Only curves were used to model its sides.

Figure 6-1:
With the exception of the slats for the seat and back, this entire park bench was modeled with curves. (Model credit: Bob Holcomb.)

A set of curves used to define a shape in three dimensions is a *surface*. In some ways, curve surfaces are very similar to meshes that have the Subdivision Surface modifier applied because they both have a control cage defining the final shape that's created. The difference is that the curve surface has space and precision benefits that meshes don't have. Also, surfaces are a little bit easier to add textures to because you don't have to go through the additional step of *unwrapping*, or flattening the surface, so you can apply a two-dimensional texture to it. When you use a surface, you get that unwrapping for free because it's already done for you.

For these reasons — especially the precision — architects, industrial designers, and engineers prefer to work with surfaces. Someone designed just about everything in your house, including your water faucet, your coffee maker, your television, your car, and even the house itself. If an item was manufactured within the last 20 years, chances are good that it was designed on a computer and visualized with surfaces. Also, before the advent of subdivision surfaces, early characters for computer animations were modeled using curve surfaces because they were better at achieving organic shapes. Of course, if you're seen using curves to build a character these days, you may be viewed as a bit of masochist . . . especially if you try to do it in Blender.

Understanding the different types of curves

In Blender, you can add curves by using Shift+A⇨Curve and choosing the type of curve you'd like to use from the menu that appears. As shown in Figure 6-2, you can use two main kinds of curves: *Bézier curves* and *NURBS curves.* (The Path curve is a specific type of Bézier curve.) You generally use Bézier curves more for text and logos. Bézier curves work in three dimensions by default, but you can get them to lock to a single 2D plane if you need to. You can tell that you're using a Bézier curve because if you tab into Edit mode to look at it, each control point has a pair of handles that you can use to give additional control over the curve's shape.

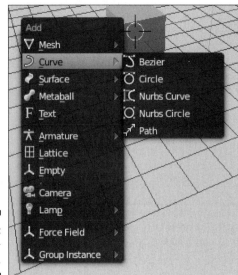

Figure 6-2:
The Add⇨
Curve menu.

NURBS stands for *Non-Uniform Relational B-Spline.* The control points in NURBS curves don't have handles like Bézier curves do. By default, NURBS control points don't normally even touch the curve shape itself. Instead, the control points are *weighted* to influence the shape of the curve. Control points with higher weights attract the curve closer to them. Figure 6-3 shows the same curve shape made with Bézier curves and with NURBS curves.

Although curves can work in three dimensions and can even create three-dimensional shapes like the park bench in Figure 6-1, you can't arbitrarily join them to create a surface. If you want to create a surface, you need to actually navigate to the Surfaces menu (Shift+A⇨Surface), as shown in Figure 6-4. Notice that NURBS Curve and NURBS Circle are also options on this menu. Be aware, however, that Blender treats these types of NURBS differently than the NURBS curves available in the Curve menu. In fact, Blender doesn't even allow you to perform a Join (Ctrl+J) between NURBS curves and NURBS surface curves. This limitation is a bit inconvenient, I know, but the situations where you'd actually want to do something like that are rare enough that you don't need to worry about it that much.

Figure 6-3: An arbitrary shape created with Bézier curves (left) and NURBS curves (right).

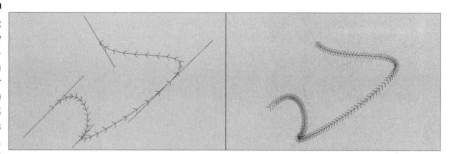

Figure 6-4: The Add⇨ Surface menu.

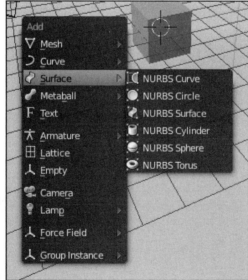

Working with curves

Surprisingly few specialized controls are specific to curves. Grab (G), rotate (R), and scale (S) work as expected, and, like with meshes, you can extrude a selected control point in Edit mode by either pressing E or Ctrl+left-clicking where you would like to extrude to. You can join separate curves in Edit mode by selecting the end control points on each curve and pressing F, like making a face with meshes.

If the two control points you select are at the start and end of the same curve, pressing F closes the curve, or, in Blenderese, you're making the curve *cyclic*. You can also make a curve cyclic with any control point selected (not just the start or end) by pressing Alt+C while in Edit mode or going to Curve⇨Toggle Cyclic in the 3D View's header. Figure 6-5 shows a cyclic (closed) and noncyclic (open) Bézier curve.

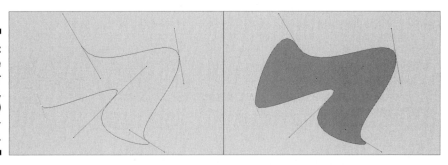

Figure 6-5:
The same Bézier curve, cyclic (left) and noncyclic (right).

If you make a 2D curve cyclic, it creates a flat plane in the shape of your curve. And putting one cyclic curve within the borders of another curve actually creates a hole in that plane. However, this trick doesn't work with 3D curves because they aren't planar. In those situations, you want to use a surface.

Changing 3D curves into 2D curves

Curves are initially set to work in three dimensions by default. Working in three dimensions gives you the ability to move curve control points freely in the X-, Y-, or Z-axes. You can optionally lock curve objects to work in any arbitrary two-dimensional plane you want. In this case, the control points on the 2D curve are constrained to its local XY plane.

To lock the curve to working only in two dimensions, go to Object Data Properties (see Figure 6-6) and left-click the 2D button.

When you tab to Edit mode on a 3D curve, you may notice that the curve has little arrows spaced along it. These arrows are *curve normals* and indicate the direction of the curve. To adjust the size of these curve normals, change the Normal Size value in the Properties region of the 3D View in the Curve Display panel. You can hide curve normals altogether by deactivating the Normals check box that is also in the Curve Display panel. In 2D curves, curve normals aren't displayed.

That said, all curves have direction, even cyclic ones. The direction of a curve isn't normally all that important unless you're using the curve as a path. In that situation, the direction of the curve is the direction that the animated object is traveling along the curve. You can switch the direction of the curve by choosing Curve➪Segments➪Switch Direction from the 3D View's header, clicking the Curve➪Switch Direction button in the Tool Shelf, or pressing W➪Switch Direction.

Figure 6-6 shows Object Data Properties when a curve is selected.

Figure 6-6:
The controls for editing curves.

The controls in Object Data Properties are relevant to all curves, regardless of type. Some of the most important ones are in the Shape panel. You've already seen what the 2D and 3D buttons do. Below them are the Preview U and Render U values. These values define the resolution of the curve. Remember that Blender shows you only an approximation of the real curve. Increasing the resolution here makes the curve look more like the curve defined by the math, at the cost of more processor time. That's why you see two resolution values:

✔ **Preview U:** The default resolution and it's also what you see in the 3D View.

✔ **Render U:** The resolution that Blender uses when you render. By default, this resolution is set to 0, which means Blender uses whatever value that is in Preview U.

Extruding, beveling, and tapering curves

The controls in the Geometry panel pertain primarily to extruding and beveling your curve objects. The Offset value is the exception to this rule. It's pretty interesting because it allows you to offset the curve from the control points. The effect of the Offset value is most apparent (and helpful) on cyclic curves. Values less than 1 are inset from the control points, whereas values greater than 1 are outset.

The ability to inset or outset your curve with the Offset value is a quick way to put an outline on a logo or text because Blender doesn't have a stroke function for curves like Inkscape or Adobe Illustrator does.

The Extrude value is probably the quickest way to give some depth to a curve, especially a 2D curve. However, you don't want to confuse the curve Extrude value with the extrude capability you get by pressing E. The Extrude value affects the entire curve in Object mode, rather than just the selected control points in Edit mode. On a cyclic 2D curve, the flat planar shape that gets created extends out in both directions of the local Z direction of the curve object, with the caps drawn on it. And you can even control whether Blender draws the front or back cap by enabling or disabling the Front and Back check boxes in the Shape panel. If you extrude a noncyclic curve, you end up with something that looks more like a ribbon going along the shape of the curve. The ribbon look is also what happens when you increase the extrude value on a 3D curve. Figure 6-7 shows some of the different effects that you can get with an extruded curve.

Figure 6-7:
Some of the different things you can do with an extruded curve.

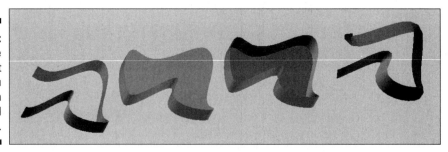

Of course, one drawback to extruding a curve is that you get a really sharp edge at the corners of the extrusion. Depending on what you're creating, harsh edges tend to look "too perfect" and unnatural. Fortunately, Bevel can take care of that for you. To give an extruded curve more natural corners, simply increase the Depth value under the Bevel label. When you do, the bevel is really kind of simple: just a cut across the corner. You can make the bevel smoother by increasing the Resolution value. Like the Preview U and Render U values, this value increases the resolution of part of the curve. In this case, it's the resolution of the bevel. Increasing the Resolution value makes a smoother, more curved bevel. Beveling works on both cyclic and noncyclic curves.

But say that you want something more ornate, kind of like the molding or trim you'd find around the doorway on a house. In that case, you want to use a *bevel object*. Using a bevel object on your curve basically means that you're going to use the shape of one curve to define the bevel on another.

To get a better idea of how you can use bevel objects, use the following steps:

1. **Create a Bézier circle (Shift+A⇨Curve⇨Circle).**

   In Object Data Properties, make sure that the circle is a 2D shape. Scale up the circle nice and large with S so that you can see what's going on.

2. **Extrude the circle by increasing the Extrude value in the Geometry panel of the curve's Object Data Properties.**

   The circle doesn't have to be excessively thick, just thick enough to give it some form of depth.

3. **Create a Bézier curve (Shift+A⇨Curve⇨Bézier Curve).**

4. **Tab into Edit mode and edit this curve a bit to get the bevel shape that you want.**

   Keep the curve noncyclic for now.

5. **When you're done editing, tab back out to Object mode.**

6. **Select your Bézier circle and, in the Bevel Object field of the Geometry panel in the curve's Object Data Properties, type or click the name of your Bézier curve.**

   If you didn't rename it (although you should have!), it's probably called something like `Curve` or `Curve.001`. After you select your bevel object, the corners of your Bézier circle are beveled with the shape defined by your Bézier curve. Now for fun, follow the next step.

7. **Go back and make the bevel object curve cyclic (Alt+C).**

   Doing so actually removes the front and back planes from the extrusion. You're left with a curve shape that follows the main Bézier circle's path

8. **For extra kicks, select the Bézier circle and tab into Edit mode; select any control point and press Alt+S to shrink or fatten the beveled shape around that control point.**

   Slick, huh?

When you use a bevel object, you're essentially handing control of the curve's shape over to the bevel object. That being the case, after you use it, changing the values for Extrude, Bevel Depth, and Bevel Resolution has no effect on the curve for as long as you have the bevel object there.

Figure 6-8 shows the results of these steps.

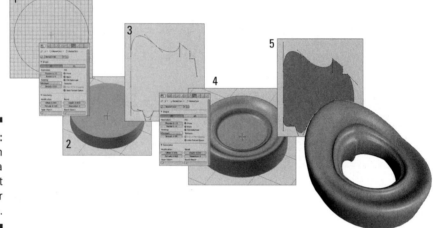

Figure 6-8:
Having fun by adding a bevel object to a Bézier circle.

If you're using a curve to model anything roughly cylindrical in shape such as a pipe or a tube, you actually don't need to use a bevel object curve at all. It's a bit of a hidden function, but you can get the same effect by just beveling the curve. I know that sounds odd (how do you bevel something that doesn't have any corners?), but trust me, it works. You bevel the curve by disabling both the Front and Back check boxes in the Shape panel and then increasing the Bevel Depth. Increasing the Bevel Resolution value makes the cross-section more circular. Hooray! One less bevel object to hide!

In the preceding example, I show that you can use Alt+S on individual control points to shrink or fatten the thickness of the extrusion. However, perhaps you'd like to have more control along the length of the curve. This situation is where you'd use the *Taper Object* field. Like bevel objects, the taper objects use one curve to define the shape of another. In this case, you're controlling the thickness along the length of the curve, and it works in very much the same way: Create a separate curve that dictates the taper shape and then type the name of that curve in the Taper Object field of the curve you'd like to control. Figure 6-9 shows how a taper object can give you complete control of a curve's shape along its length.

TIP

I prefer to create my bevel object and taper object curves in the top view (Numpad 7) along the X-axis. This way, I have a good frame of reference for the curve's center line. That's important because bevel objects use the center line to define the front and back of a curve's extrusion. You can think of taper objects as a kind of profile that revolves around its local X-axis. Bringing your control points to the center line makes the tapered curve come to a point, whereas moving them away from the center line increases the thickness.

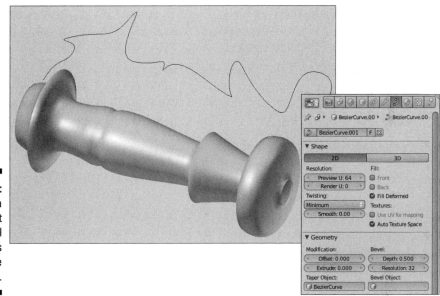

Figure 6-9:
Using a
taper object
to control
a curve's
lengthwise
shape.

Adjusting curve tilt

One other thing that you can control on curves is the *tilt* of the control points. In other programs, the tilt may be called the *twist* property. To get a good idea of what you can do with tilt, try the following steps:

1. **Create a Bézier Curve (Shift+A⇨Curve⇨Bézier) and tab into Edit mode.**

2. **Make the curve cyclic (Alt+C).**

   You may also want to select (right-click) the handles and rotate (R) them so there's a cleaner arc.

3. **Select one of the handles and press Ctrl+T or click the Tilt button in the Tool Shelf.**

   Move your mouse cursor around the selection in a clockwise fashion and watch how the Tilt value in the 3D View's header changes.

4. **Confirm completion (left-click or Enter).**

If you increase the Extrude and Bevel Depth values, you should now have something that looks a bit like Figure 6-10.

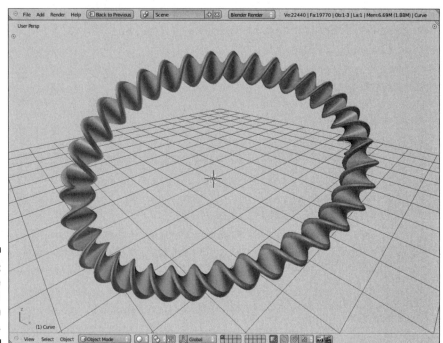

Figure 6-10:
Fun with the
tilt function!
Mmmmmm
. . . twisty.

Editing Bézier curves

The most defining aspect of Bézier curves are the handles on their control points. You can switch between the different types of handles by pressing V in the 3D View or choosing Curve⇨Control Points⇨Set Handle Type. Handles on Bézier curves are always tangential to the curve and come in one of four varieties in Blender:

- ✔ **Automatic:** These handles are set by Blender to give you the smoothest possible result in the shape of your curve. They appear in yellow and generally form a straight line with equal lengths on either side. If you try to edit an Auto handle, it immediately reverts to an aligned handle.

- ✔ **Vector:** Vector handles are broken like free handles, but they point directly to the next control point. The shape of the curve is an exactly straight line from one control point to the next. Editing a handles on a vector control point turns it into a free handle.

✔ **Aligned:** Aligned handles are always in a straight line, and they display in a pinkish color. If you grab (G) and move one handle on a control point, the other moves in the opposite direction to balance it out. You can, however, have aligned handles of differing lengths.

✔ **Free:** Free handles are sometimes referred to as *broken* handles. They display in black and don't necessarily have to be in a straight line. Free handles are best suited for giving you sharp points that smoothly flow to the next control point.

Figure 6-11 shows four curves with the same exact control points, but each with different types of handles. And, yes, you can mix handle types in a single curve. It's actually quite handy when you need a figure to be smooth in some parts and pointy in others.

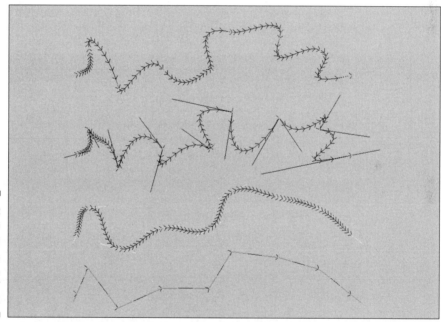

Figure 6-11:
The same curve with aligned, free, auto, and vector handles.

Editing NURBS curves and surfaces

NURBS are a different kind of beast in terms of controls. They also have control points, but NURBS curves are conspicuously without handles.

Blender treats a NURBS curve differently than a NURBS surface curve. With that caution in mind, though, whether you're dealing with a curve or a surface curve, the following things generally apply to all NURBS:

✔ **Each control point has a weight.** The weight, which is a value between 0 and 1, influences how much that control point influences the curve. In Blender, you set the weight in the Transform panel of the 3D View's Properties region (N). There, for any selected control point, you have the ability to directly modify the X, Y, or Z location of the control point as well as its weight, indicated by the W value. The value in the W field is averaged across all selected control points.

✔ **NURBS have knots.** In math terms, *knots* are vectors that describe how the resulting curve is influenced by the control points. In Blender, you have three settings that you can assign to knots from the Active Spline panel in the curve's Object Data Properties: Uniform, Endpoint, and Bézier. By default, with the Bézier and Endpoint check boxes disabled, NURBS are assigned uniform knots. You can tell they're uniform because the curve doesn't go all the way to the end control points. Those control points' weights are factored in with all the other control points. Endpoint knots, in contrast, bring the curve all the way to the last control points, regardless of weight. Bézier knots treat the control points like they're free handles on a Bézier curve. Every three control points act like the center and two handles on a Bézier curve's control points.

✔ **NURBS have an order.** An *order* is another math thing. What it really means, though, is that the lower the order, the more the curve directly follows the lines between control points. And the higher the order, the smoother and more fluid the curve is as it passes the control points. You can also change the values for order in the Active Spline panel below the Bézier and Endpoint check boxes.

Figure 6-12 shows the influences that curve weights, knot types, and order can have on a NURBS curve.

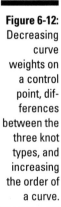

Figure 6-12: Decreasing curve weights on a control point, differences between the three knot types, and increasing the order of a curve.

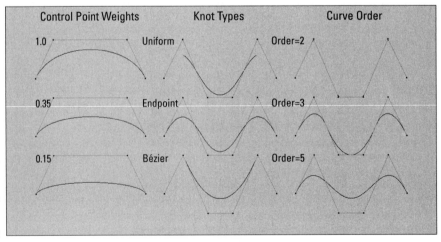

You might notice in the Active Spline panel that you can independently set the knot, order, and resolution controls for a U or a V value. If you're dealing with just a curve, the U direction is all you need to worry about and, therefore, all that Blender shows you. However, a NURBS surface works in two directions: U and V. If you add a NURBS Surface (Shift+A⇨Surface⇨NURBS Surface), you can visually tell the difference between the U segments, which are reddish, and the V segments, which are yellow.

One really cool thing you can do easily with NURBS surfaces that's difficult to do with other types of surfaces is a process called *lofting*. (Other programs may call it *skinning*, but because that term actually means something else for rigging, I use lofting here.) Basically, lofting is the process of using a series of NURBS surface curves with the *same number of control points* as a series of profiles to define a shape. The cool thing about lofting in Blender is that after you have the profiles in place, the process is as simple as selecting all control points (A) and pressing (F). The classic use for lofting is modeling the hull of a boat, as you see in the following steps and in Figure 6-13:

1. **Add a NURBS surface curve (Shift+A⇨Surface⇨NURBS Curve) and tab into Edit mode.**

2. **Select All and Rotate –90 degrees around the X-axis (A⇨R⇨X⇨–90).**

   The bottom of your boat forms.

3. **Model a cross-section of the boat's hull.**

   You can add more control points using extrude (E or Ctrl+left-click) and move them around with grab (G). When modeling your cross-section, it would be a good idea to press Alt+C and make the curve cyclic.

   Try to keep the cross-section as planar as possible. I like to work from the front view (Numpad 1).

4. **Select all control points in your cross-section and duplicate it along the Y-axis (A⇨Shift+D⇨Y).**

5. **Make adjustments to the new cross-section to suit your tastes, but *do not add any control points*.**

   Lofting requires that each cross-section has the exact same number of control points. If you add or remove control points from a cross-section, it doesn't work.

6. **Repeat Steps 4 and 5 until you're satisfied.**

7. **Select All and press F.**

   You've made a canoe!

A quick note on paths

You might be begrudging the fact that I glazed over adding a Path curve (Shift+A⇨ Curve⇨Path). The reason is that you can turn just about any curve into a path. By default, when you add a path, it's really a shortcut for adding a NURBS curve with one check box enabled in the curves Object Data Properties: Path Animation. By enabling this check box, Blender understands that this curve is a path that you can use to control the movement of an animated object. To make any NURBS or Bézier curve into a path, all you have to do is left-click this check box. I get more into the use of paths as animation controls in Chapter 10.

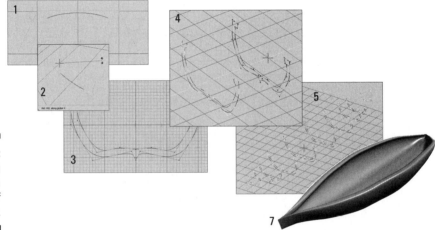

Figure 6-13: Using lofting to create a the hull of a boat.

Understanding the strengths and limitations of Blender's surfaces

When compared to other tools that work with NURBS surface, Blender admittedly falls short in some functions. You can extrude surface endpoints, do lofting, and even *spin* surface curves (sometimes called *lathing* in other programs) to create bowl or cup shapes. However, that's about it. Blender currently doesn't have the functionality to do a ton of other cool things with NURBS surfaces, such as using one curve to trim the length of another or project the shape of one curve onto the surface of another.

However, there's hope. It's been slow coming, but Blender has recently made more progress on the integration of better NURBS tools. If all goes well, the next version of Blender should show marked improvement. Ultimately,

NURBS may even be able to use a large quantity of the modifiers that you enjoy using on meshes.

Using Meta Objects

Meta objects are cool little 3D surfaces that have been part of computer graphics for a long time. Sometimes meta objects are referred to as *blobbies*. The principle behind meta objects is pretty simple: Imagine that you have two droplets of water, and you begin moving these two droplets closer and closer to each other. Eventually, the two droplets are going to merge and become a single, larger droplet. That process is basically how meta objects work, except you have complete control over when the droplets merge, how much they merge, and you can reseparate them again if you'd like.

You can also do something that's more difficult in the real world: You can subtract one droplet from the other, rather than add them together into a merged object. They're a ton of fun to play with, and there are some pretty neat applications for them. Figure 6-14 shows two metaballs being merged.

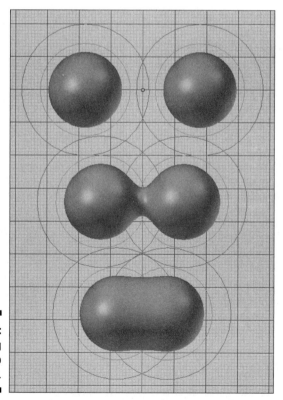

Figure 6-14: Merging two metaballs.

Meta-wha?

Meta objects are a bit like curves and NURBS in that their entire existence is defined by math. However, unlike NURBS or even meshes, you can't control the surface of a meta object directly with control points or vertices. Instead, the shape of their surface is defined by a combination of the object's underlying structure — a point, a line, a plane, a sphere, or a cube — and its proximity to other meta objects.

There are five meta object primitives:

- ✔ **Ball:** The surface in this primitive is based on the points that are all the same distance from a single origin. You can move and scale a metaball uniformly, but you can't scale it in just one direction.

- ✔ **Capsule:** Whereas the basis for a metaball is a single point, the basis for a meta capsule is the line between two points. You can scale the surface uniformly, like a metaball, but you can also scale it in its local X-axis.

- ✔ **Plane:** The meta plane's underlying structure is, as you may have guessed, a plane. You have both the local X- and the local Y-axis for scaling, as well as scaling uniformly.

- ✔ **Cube:** The meta cube is based on a three-dimensional structure — specifically, a cube. You have the ability to scale this primitive independently in the X, Y, or Z directions.

- ✔ **Ellipsoid:** At first glance, you might mistake this meta object for a metaball. However, instead of being based on a single point, this object is based on a sphere. So if you keep the local X, Y, and Z dimensions equal, a meta ellipsoid behaves just like a metaball. However, like the meta cube, you can also scale in any of the three individual axes.

A cool thing about meta objects is that while you're in Edit mode, you can change from one primitive to another on the fly. To do so, use the Active Element panel in the meta object's Object Data Properties. Figure 6-15 shows each of the primitives along with the default settings for them in the Active Element panel.

The Active Element panel always displays the Stiffness value for the selected meta object. This value controls the influence that the selected meta object has on other meta objects. The Stiffness value is indicated visually in the 3D View with a green ring around the meta object's origin. You can adjust the Stiffness value here in the panel, or if you select the green ring (right-click), you can Scale (S) to adjust the Stiffness visually. By right-clicking the reddish, pinkish ring outside of that green ring, you can select the actual individual meta object.

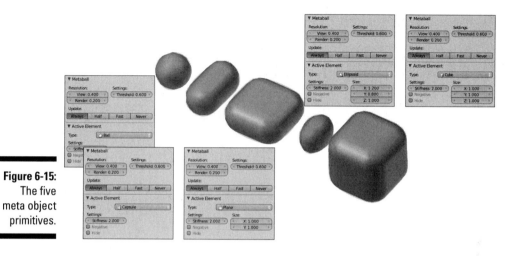

Figure 6-15:
The five
meta object
primitives.

And depending on the type of meta object primitive you're using, other values of X, Y, and Z may appear in the Active Element panel while you're in Edit mode. You can adjust these values here or in 3D View by using the S⇨X, S⇨Y, and S⇨Z hotkey sequences. At the bottom of the panel are buttons to either hide the selected meta object or give it a negative influence, subtracting it from the positive, and therefore visible, meta objects.

When you tab back out to Object mode, you can move your combined meta object (a meta-meta object?) as a single unit. Note, however, that even though you've grouped these meta objects into a single Blender object, they don't live in a vacuum. If you have two complex Blender objects made up of metas, bringing the two of them together actually causes them to merge. Just keep that as something you may want to bear in mind and take advantage of in the future.

As a single Blender object, though, you can control a few more things using the Metaball panel, as shown in Figure 6-16. This panel is always available to meta objects, whether in Object mode or Edit mode, and it sits at the top of the Object Data Properties.

Figure 6-16:
The
Metaball
panel.

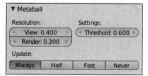

The first two values in the Metaball panel are resolution values:

✔ **View:** Controls how dense the generated mesh is for the meta object in the 3D View. Lower values are a finer mesh, whereas higher values result in much more of an approximation.

✔ **Render:** Does the same thing as the View value, except it has an effect only at render time. The reason is that meta objects can get really complex quickly, and because they're generated entirely by math, these complex combinations of meta objects tend to use a lot of computer-processing power.

Working at a larger View size in the 3D View helps keep your computer responsive while you work, whereas a finer Render value keeps things pretty on output.

The Threshold value is an overall control for how much influence the metas in a single Blender object have over each other. This value has a range from 0 to 5, but in order for a meta object to be visible, its individual Stiffness value must be greater than the Threshold value.

Below Threshold are four buttons that control how the meta objects get updated and displayed in the 3D View:

✔ **Always:** The slowest and most accurate, this setting is the default. Every change you make in the 3D View happens instantly (or as fast as your computer can handle it).

✔ **Half:** This option reduces the resolution of the meta object as you move or edit it, increasing the responsiveness of the 3D View. When you finish transforming the meta object, it displays in full resolution again.

✔ **Fast:** As the name implies, this setting is nearly the fastest. When you enable this button, Blender hides the meta objects when you perform a transform and then re-evaluates the surface when you finish. Fast works very nicely, but the downside is that you don't get the nice visual feedback that Always and Half give you.

✔ **Never:** This method is certainly the fastest update. Basically, if you try to edit a meta object, it hides everything and never updates in the 3D View. Although Never may not seem useful at first, if you decide to bind your meta object to a particle system as a way of faking fluids, turning this setting on definitely increases performance in the 3D View.

What meta objects are useful for

So what in the world can you actually use meta objects to make? I actually have two answers to this question: all sorts of things, and not much. The reason for this seemingly paradoxical answer is that you *can* use meta objects to do quick, rough prototype models, and you *can* also use them with a particle system to generate simple fluid simulations. However, with the advent of advanced modeling tools like multires sculpting and subdivision surfaces, meta objects don't get used as often for prototyping. And with more advanced fluid simulation and rendering technology, meta objects are also used less for those applications as well. They have a tendency to use a lot of computer-processing power and don't often give good topology by themselves.

That said, even though meta objects are used *less* for these purposes, that doesn't mean that they're never used. In fact, not too long ago, I used a set of metaballs with a glowing halo material to animate the life force being forcefully pulled out of a guy. I could probably have used a particle system or fluid simulator to do this effect, but using metaballs was actually faster to set up, and I had more direct control over where everything was placed on the screen. So don't count meta objects out just yet. These little suckers still have some life left. Besides, they're still fun to play with!

Adding Text

Over the years, working with text in Blender has come a long, long way. The way you work with text in Blender has quite a few differences from what you might expect of word-processing software like OpenOffice.org or Microsoft Word. What you may not expect is that Blender's text objects share a few features in common with desktop publishing programs like Adobe InDesign or QuarkXPress.

Blender's text objects are really a specialized type of curve object. Nearly all the options I describe for curves also apply to text. (See the section "Using Curves and Surfaces," earlier in this chapter.) For example, you can quickly bring text objects into the third dimension using the Extrude, Bevel, and even the Bevel Object and Taper Object fields. Figure 6-17 shows an example of the interesting things you can do with a single text object in Blender.

Figure 6-17:
Taking advantage of the curve-based nature of Blender text objects.

Adding and editing text

You add a text object in Blender the same way you add any other object. Press Shift+A⇨Text, and a text object appears at the location of your 3D cursor with the default content of the word *Text*.

To edit the text, you tab into Edit mode. After you're in Edit mode, the controls begin to feel a bit more like a word processor, although not exactly. For example, you can't use your mouse cursor to highlight text, but if you press Shift+← and Shift+→, depending on where the text cursor is located, you can highlight text this way.

Shift+Ctrl+←/→ highlights whole words at a time. Backspace deletes text and pressing Enter gives you a new line.

In addition, formatting controls appear in the Font panel of Object Data Properties for text objects, as shown in Figure 6-18.

Figure 6-18:
The Font panel.

In the Paragraph panel is a block of alignment buttons to help you align your text relative to the origin of the text object. You have the following options:

- ✔ **Left:** Aligns text to the left. The text object's origin serves as the left-hand guide for the text.
- ✔ **Center:** All text is centered around the text object's origin.

- ✔ **Right:** Aligns text to the right. The text object's origin serves as the right-hand guide for the text.

- ✔ **Justify:** Aligns text both on the left and on the right. If the line is not long enough, Blender adds spacing, or *kerning,* between individual characters to fill the space. This option requires the use of text boxes. (See the next section, "Working with text boxes," for more details.)

- ✔ **Flush:** This option works similar to the way Justify does, but with one exception: If the line is the end of a paragraph, it forces the text to align both sides. Like Justify, this option requires the use of text frames.

Working with text boxes

Both the Flush and the Justify options require the use of something called *text boxes.* The Left, Center, and Right align options all work relative to the location of the text object's origin. However, if you want to align your text on both the left and the right side, you need more than one reference point. Text boxes are a way of providing those reference points, but with a couple of additional benefits as well. Basically, text boxes are a rectangular shape that defines where the text in your text object lives. Text boxes are similar to the *frames* you might use in desktop publishing programs. They're also one of those things that you normally don't see in 3D software.

To work with text boxes, you use the block of values in the panel labeled Text Boxes. The X and Y fields under the Offset label determine where the top-left corner of the text box is located, whereas the Width and Height fields define its size. As you adjust these values while in Edit mode, you should see a dashed rectangle in the 3D View.

Now, the cool thing about text boxes is that you can actually define more than one and place them arbitrarily in your scene. Add a text box by left-clicking the Add Textbox button in the Text Boxes panel. If you have more than one text box defined, the text can overflow from one box into another. Using multiple text boxes is an excellent way to get very fine control over the placement of your text. You can even do newspaper-style multicolumn text this way, as shown in Figure 6-19.

A particularly cool feature for text objects is Paste File (from Edit mode, Text⇨Paste File). If you already have a bunch of text created and don't feel like retyping it in Blender, choose Paste File and use the File Browser to find the text file you want to load. After you do, the content of whatever is in that text file is added from the location of the text cursor.

If you're working with a lot of text, you may find that Blender doesn't perform as speedily as you'd like while editing. If you left-click the Fast Editing check box in the Shape panel, Blender uses just the outline to the text in the 3D View while in Edit mode. This adjustment gives Blender a bit of a performance boost so that you're not waiting for characters to show up seconds after you finish typing them.

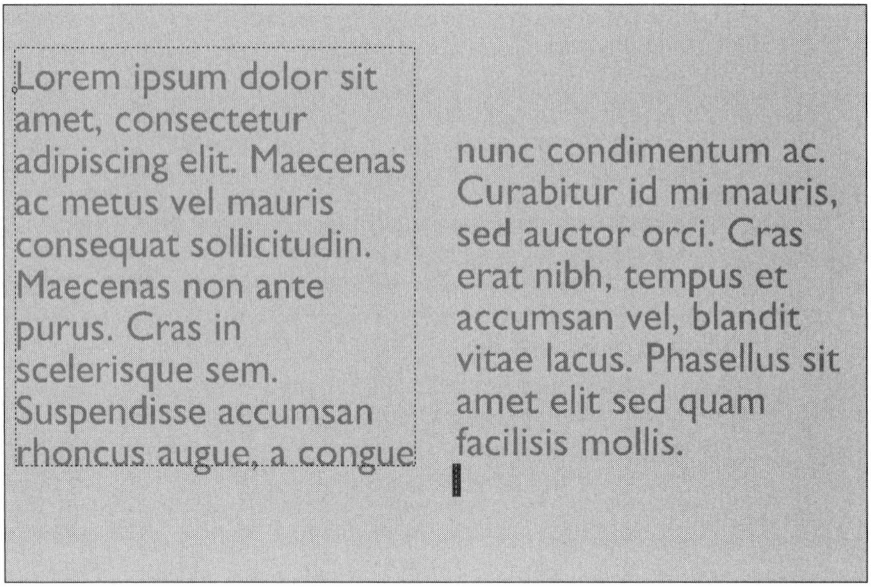

Figure 6-19:
Using text
frames to
get multi-
column text
layouts.

Controlling text appearance

The block of buttons in the Font panel control how the text appears in the selected text object:

- ✔ **Size:** This field allows you to adjust the font size on a scale from 0.010 to 10. Changing the font size value is generally a better way to change the size of your text rather than simply scaling the text object.

- ✔ **Shear:** Shearing is a quick-and-dirty way to fake italic on a font. Values between 0 and 1 tilt characters to the right, whereas values between –1 and 0 tilt them all to the left.

- ✔ **Object Font:** Using this field, you can actually define Blender objects as characters in a font. I cover this later in the "Changing fonts" section.

- ✔ **Text on Curve:** If you need your text to flow along the length of a curve object, use this datablock field to choose that particular curve object.

- ✔ **Underline Position:** Adjust this value to control the position of the underline, if enabled (Ctrl+U on highlighted text). This value has a range from –0.2 to 0.8.

- ✔ **Underline Thickness:** From this field, you can control the thickness of the actual underline, if enabled (Ctrl+U on highlighted text). You can set this value between 0.01 and 0.5.

- ✔ **Character:** The three check boxes under the Character label – Bold, Italic, and Underline – add those attributes to the selected text in your 3D View, if you've defined fonts for those font variations (see the "Changing fonts" section).

You can adjust the appearance of your text using still more controls in the Paragraph panel:

- ✔ **Spacing:** You can customize the amount of spacing between characters and lines in your text. To do so, you have the following three values available to adjust:

  - **Character:** The global distance between all characters in your text object, also known as *tracking*. This value has a range from 0 to 10.

  - **Word:** Globally defines the space between words in your text object. This field also has a range from 0 to 10.

  - **Line:** Line distance, also referred to as *leading*. This value defines the distance between lines of text in your text object and it also has a range from 0 to 10.

- ✔ **Offset:** These values offset the text object from its default position. X values less than zero shift it left and Y values less than zero shift down, whereas values greater than zero shift it right (X) or up (Y).

If you're familiar with typography, you may notice two things right off the bat. First, the terms used here are not the standard typography terminology, and second, the values are not in your typical percentage, point, pica, or pixel sizes for two primary reasons. First, Blender is a 3D program intended for 3D artists, many of whom may not be familiar with typography terms and sizes. The second reason dovetails with the first one, but it's a bit more on the practical side. Blender text objects are 3D objects that can be just about any size in virtual 3D space. Sizes like points, pixels, and picas don't really mean anything in 3D because there's not a frame of reference, like the physical size of a printed piece of paper.

Changing fonts

Another thing that's different about Blender's text objects is the way they handle fonts. If you're used to other programs, you may expect to see a drop-down menu that lists all the fonts installed on your computer with a nice preview of each. Unfortunately, Blender doesn't currently have that ability. Instead, what you need to do is left-click the Load button to the right of the Regular Font datablock in the Font panel of Object Data Properties. Blender then shows you a File Browser where you can track down the actual font file for the typeface that you want to use.

Here are the standard places you can find fonts on Windows, Mac, and Linux machines:

- ✔ **Windows:** `C:\Windows\Fonts`
- ✔ **Mac OS:** `/System/Library/Fonts` or `/Library/Fonts`
- ✔ **Linux:** `/usr/share/fonts`

After you load a font, it's available for you to use in that specific .blend file whenever you want it from the font drop-down list. You always have Blender's built-in font available as well.

Now you would think that after you have a font loaded, you should be good to go, right? Well, not quite. See, Blender's method of handling bold and italic in text is kind of unique. You actually load a separate font file for each one (hence the four separate Font datablocks: Regular, Bold, Italic, and Bold & Italic). Typically, you use these datablocks to load the bold and italic versions of the font file you choose in the Regular datablock. However, that's not a hard-and-fast requirement. You can actually use an entirely different font altogether. While the ability to choose different fonts in the Bold and Italic datablocks is perhaps a mild abuse of the terms, that ability does provide a pretty handy workaround. Technically speaking, Blender doesn't allow you to arbitrarily change fonts in the middle of a text object. However, using the different font datablocks, you can get around that problem by making your Bold or Italic font the other fonts you want to use. To choose a font file for any style of font is pretty straightforward:

1. **In the Font panel of your text object's Object Data Properties, left-click the Load button on the font datablock you want to change.**

   By default, the built-in font, Bfont, is chosen for all four datablocks.

2. **Navigate your hard drive using the File Browser and choose the font you want to use.**

3. **Use your chosen font in your text object.**

   As an example, say that you chose a new font for the Bold datablock. You can assign that font to characters in your text object with the following steps:

   a. **From Edit mode (Tab), highlight the text you want to change (Shift+← or Shift+→).**

   b. **Enable the Bold check box under the Character label in the Font panel of Object Data Properties.**

Figure 6-20 shows the results of using multiple fonts in a single text object

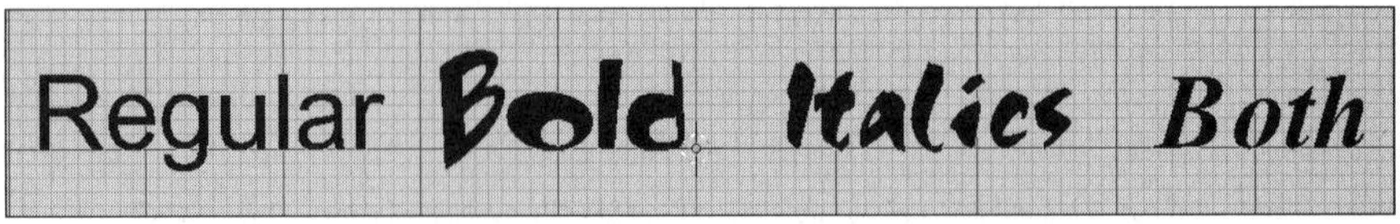

Figure 6-20:
Using the
Bold and
Italics fonts
to use
widely dif-
ferent fonts
in a single
text object.

You may find that while you're typing, you need certain special characters like the copyright symbol or the upside-down question mark for sentences written in Spanish. For these situations, you have three options:

✔ If the special character is common, you may find it in Text⇨Special Characters.

✔ You can memorize the hotkey combination for various commonly used special characters as listed in Blender's online documentation.

✔ If the character is rare or just not in the menu, but you have it in a text file outside of Blender, you can use the Text⇨Paste File to get that character into your text object.

Deforming text with a curve

Another really powerful thing you can do with Blender's text objects is have the text flow along the length of a curve. This way, you can get text that arcs over a doorway or wraps around a bowl or just looks all kinds of funky. The key to this feature is the Text on Curve field in the Font panel. To see how this feature works, use the steps in the following example:

1. **Create a text object (Shift+A⇨Text).**

   Feel free to populate it with whatever content you would like.

2. **Create a curve to dictate the text shape (Shift+A⇨Curve⇨Bézier).**

   This curve is your control. You're using a Bézier curve here, but a NURBS curve works fine as well. Also, I like to make my curve with the same origin location as my text object. Granted, that's just my preference, but it works nicely for keeping everything easily manageable.

3. **Select the text object and type or click the name of your control curve in the Text on Curve field.**

   Blam! The text should now follow the arc of the curve. If you select (right-click) the curve and tab into Edit mode, any change you make to it updates your text object live.

Figure 6-21 shows 3D text along a curve.

You should keep your curve as a 2D curve. Because the text is technically a special type of 2D curve, trying to get it to deform along a 3D curve won't work. For text to follow a 3D curve, you're going to need to convert the text into a mesh, as described in the next section.

Converting to curves and meshes

Of course, while Blender's text objects are pretty powerful, curves and meshes just do some things better. Fortunately, you don't have to model

your text by using meshes and curves unless you really, really want to.
Instead, you can convert your text object into a curve or a mesh by pressing Alt+C in Object mode and choosing Curve from Mesh/Text or Mesh from
Curve/Meta/Surf/Mesh. If you're curious as to some specific cases why you'd
want to do make this conversion, here are a few:

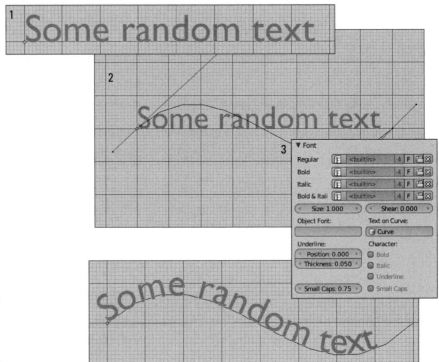

Figure 6-21:
Text on a
curve.

✔ Custom editing the characters for a logo or a specific shape (convert to
  a curve)

✔ Needing to share your `.blend` file, but the license of your font prevents
  you from legally packing it into the `.blend` (convert to a curve)

✔ Getting extruded text to follow a 3D curve (convert to a mesh)

✔ Rigging the letters to be animated with an armature (convert to a mesh
  or curve)

✔ Using the letters as obstacles in a fluid simulation (convert to a mesh)

✔ Using the letters to generate a particle system (convert to a mesh)

Using Alt+C also works on curve objects, surfaces, and meta objects to convert them to meshes. Just be aware that most of these conversions are permanent. You can't go back on them without using the undo function.

Chapter 7

Changing That Boring Gray Default Material

In This Chapter

▶ Understanding how Blender handles materials

▶ Taking advantage of Vertex painting

▶ Trying your hand at a practical example

As you work on your models in Blender, you're eventually going to get tired of that plastic gray material that all Blender objects have by default. Nothing against neutral colors — or plastic, for that matter — but the world is a vibrantly colorful place, and you may occasionally want to use these colors in your 3D scenes. To add colors to your scenes and models, you use materials and textures. In some ways, Blender's way of adding materials and textures to an object is one of the most confusing parts of the program, even with the new changes to Blender's user interface. It can be a pretty big challenge to wrap your brain around the full functionality of it.

This chapter is intended to give you the skills to know enough to be dangerous with Blender's materials. Hopefully, with a little practice, you can become lethal. Well, *lethal* might be the wrong word: I don't think I've ever heard of anyone killed by excessively sharp specular highlights. (Don't worry if you don't get the joke right now. After you finish this chapter, you'll realize how horrible a pun this is.)

Playing with Materials

By default, all newly added objects in Blender share a gray, plasticlike material. The easiest way to change the look of an object is to adjust its material properties. The controls are in the Material section of the Properties editor. Twelve panels are visible in Material Properties:

✔ **Context:** Like other sections of the Properties editor, the Material Properties starts with a context panel. This panel provides a list of material datablocks associated with your selected object and the means to define some basic attributes of those materials.

✔ **Preview:** The Preview panel displays an image of the material on a variety of preset objects: a plane, a sphere, a cube, Suzanne's head, hair strands, and a sphere on a sky background.

✔ **Diffuse:** The *diffuse color* is the main color of the object, or the primary hue that the material reflects to the camera. The controls in this panel allow you to set that color, as well as how it reflects light.

✔ **Specular:** One cool thing about working in computer graphics is that you have a say over things that you don't normally control in the real world. The *specular color,* or *spec,* is the color of highlights on your object. From the Specular panel you can adjust the specular color object, its intensity, and how it reflects light.

✔ **Shading:** The Shading panel gives you a set of broad controls to dictate how your object reflects light, regardless of the settings chosen in the Diffuse and Specular panels.

✔ **Transparency:** As advertised, this panel controls how transparency is handled on your material, if you choose to enable it by clicking the check box at the heading.

✔ **Mirror:** If you want your material to be reflective, you enable and configure that feature here. I go into reflection and transparency more in depth later in this chapter in the section aptly named "Reflection and transparency."

✔ **Subsurface Scattering:** Have you ever put your hand in front of a flashlight and seen the light shine through your hand with a slightly reddish glow? In computer graphics, that effect is called *subsurface scattering,* or *SSS* for short. The light is scattered beneath the surface of your skin. The settings in this panel give you control over SSS in your material, should you need it.

✔ **Strand:** If your material is destined to be used for hair particles (see Chapter 13), this panel gives you control over settings for that specific purpose.

✔ **Options:** The Options panel is a bit of a grab bag of check boxes for material controls that don't really fit in other panels. However, most of these check boxes have a big influence over how your final render looks (and more important, how long that render takes to process).

✔ **Shadow:** The settings in this panel control how your material treats shadows. In particular, you can dictate if (and how) the material receives shadows cast by other objects and if (and how) the material casts shadows itself.

✔ **Custom Properties:** All sections of the Properties editor allow you to create custom properties. They're used primarily by people who do more advanced work with Blender that involves scripting in python. This panel is where you add those properties.

Figure 7-1 shows the panels in Material Properties.

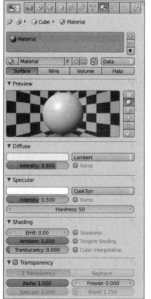

Figure 7-1:
The
Material
Properties.

Of these panels, the Context panel gives you the most high-level control over the material, defining which material gets assigned to the selected object and how the renderer recognizes the material. The first control element is a list box. This box shows all the materials associated with your object. By default, only one material should be here. Later in this chapter, I show how to use multiple materials on a single object.

Below the list box is a datablock field. From this datablock field, you can tie a material to the current active material slot in the list box. This datablock functions the same as any other datablock field, as explained in Chapter 4.

From left to right, here is a description of what each button in the datablock does.

✔ The Material button on the left gives you the ability to load an existing material that you've already created.

✔ The text field allows you to give your material a custom name. Simply left-click in the field and type the name you want to use. The name is automatically updated in the material list box.

Understanding how light reflects

To understand materials, it helps if you have an idea of how human sight works. Most *rendering engines*, or the code that converts your virtual 3D environment into a 2D picture, use eyesight as the basic model for how they work. In order to see, you need to have light. The light comes from one or more sources and bounces off of any object within its range. When the light hits these objects, they influence the direction that the light bounces and how much of the incoming light is absorbed versus reflected. When you look around, you're seeing light that is bounced off of these objects and into your eyes.

Most rendering engines, Blender's included, use a simplified version of this scenario. The following sentence sums up the biggest difference: *Unless otherwise stipulated, light bounces only once.* Professional photographers often have their flash aimed away from their subject and into an umbrella-shaped reflector that bounces light back to whatever they're shooting. The light from the flash has at least two bounces to get to the camera's lens; once off of the umbrella and once off of the subject. Because this fairly common meatspace scenario uses more than one light bounce, it's a bit difficult to set up something similar in Blender and expect it to work accurately (although it's gotten easier in recent releases of Blender). Instead, you're better off directly lighting your scenes, so then your materials themselves control that one bounce the light has off of them and into the 3D camera.

Exceptions to this rule do, of course, exist, as do ways to cheat around them. You can use techniques (particularly those including ray tracing) covered throughout this chapter and in Chapter 8, to implement those cheats.

✔ If your material is linked to more than one object, it has a numbered button next to it, representing the number of objects using this material. Left-clicking this button ensures that the datablock has only a single user — that is, it creates a copy of the material that is used only by the current active object.

✔ Enable the button with an F on it to give your material a *fake user*. Without a fake user, if you unlink a material from all objects, it has no users and won't be saved in your .blend file. Giving the material a fake user ensures that your material sticks around when you save. Fake users are great if you want to create a .blend file as a material library.

✔ Clicking the plus (+) button adds a new material datablock and assigns it to your active material slot.

✔ The X button disconnects the material datablock from the active material slot in the list.

To the right of the datablock control buttons is a Nodes button. This button activates the advanced node-based material editor. Because that's a more advanced topic, look to Blender's online documentation for more information.

The Link drop-down menu after the node button is a pretty unique control. Using these menu options requires recalling information about how .blend files are structured. Chapters 2 and 4 detail how .blend files are structured, but basically Blender objects are separate from the low-level data (mesh, curve, and so on). The objects link to this data. Now, here's how this information relates to materials. By default, Blender's materials link to the low-level data, as indicated by the Link drop-down menu in the Context panel being set to Data. However, you also have the option of linking the material to the object as well, as shown in the schematics of Figure 7-2.

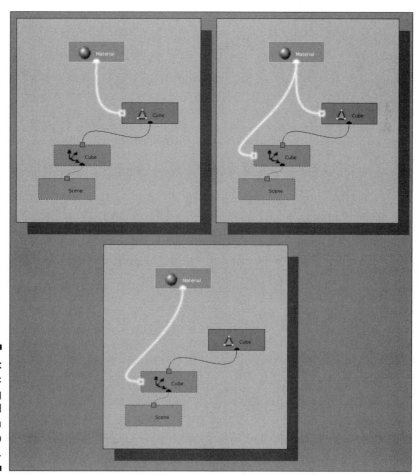

Figure 7-2:
A schematic showing a material linked to a mesh and to an object.

Why is having the ability to link a material to either the mesh or the object a useful option? Well, say that you have a bunch of objects that are linked duplicates (Alt+D), sharing the same mesh information. If the material is linked to the mesh, all your linked duplicates have the exact same material. If you want to have a different material for each duplicate, you can link the material to the object datablock rather than the mesh datablock. Figure 7-3 shows a set of linked duplicate Suzanne heads, each with a different material.

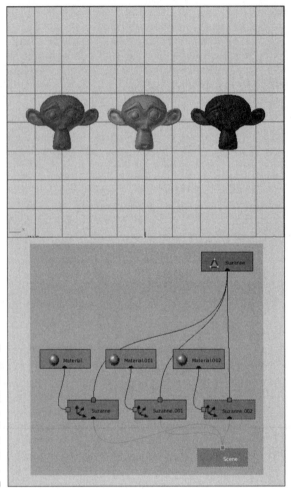

Changing colors

You may be wondering how you actually change the color of a material. The simplest way to is to left-click on the color swatch next to the type of color (diffuse or specular) you want to set. When you do, Blender's color picker pops up. Figure 7-4 shows what the color picker looks like.

The default color picker is a bit different from what you might find in other graphics applications. Left-click anywhere in the large color wheel to choose the color you want to use. Scroll your mouse wheel or use the vertical slider to the right of the color wheel to adjust brightness.

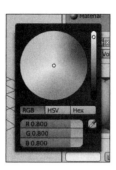

Figure 7-4:
Blender's
color picker.

 Picking absolute white with your mouse in this color picker is difficult. You can use the value sliders at the bottom of the picker, but the fastest way is to press 0 (or Numpad 0) on your keyboard and scroll your mouse wheel all the way up.

Another cool feature is that the color picker gives you a sampler. Left-click the Sample button below the value slider (it has an icon of an eye dropper), and your mouse pointer changes to a color dropper. The next place you left-click is sampled for color, making it your selected color. The cool thing is that you can sample any color in Blender's interface, including the buttons and icons, if you want to.

 When it comes to setting colors for materials, more often than not, I keep my spec color set to white. The only exception is that, on occasion, it makes more sense to set the specular color to a value that is slightly lighter than the diffuse color. This technique is sometimes used when faking a metallic look on materials. Of course, no hard-and-fast rule tells you when to go one way and when to go another in terms of the specular color. It's really a matter of experience and changing to what looks right in your final render.

 If you find Blender's current color picker to be a bit disorienting, you have the ability to choose other color pickers in the User Preferences editor under System.

Adjusting shader values

Ah, computer graphics: You have nearly complete control over how your materials look. Part of this control is how the diffuse and specular colors are dispersed across the surface of the object. You control both of these attributes independently with shader types. A *shader type* is a computer algorithm that defines how the color reacts in the material, and it's usually named after the computer scientist or mathematician who came up with it. So although the names may seem weird or arbitrary, the good news is that their names are pretty universal from one piece of 3D software to another.

Your shaders are set and controlled in the panel tied to the type of color you're adjusting. Both the Diffuse and Specular panels have a drop-down menu to the right of the color swatch where you can pick the shader you want to use. To change your diffuse shader type, left-click the drop-down menu at the upper right of the Diffuse panel. By default, its value is set to the Lambert shader, but you have the following options:

✔ **Lambert:** The only adjustable setting for this good, general-purpose shader is the Intensity slider. This slider controls how much light the material reflects. The default setting of 0.8 means that the material reflects 80 percent of the light and absorbs 20 percent.

✔ **Oren-Nayar:** The Oren-Nayar shader is similar to the Lambert shader, although it is slightly more realistic due to an additional Roughness slider that takes into account the imperfections on an object's surface.

✔ **Toon:** In sharp contrast to the previous two shaders, the Toon shader doesn't aim to be realistic. Instead, it tries to reproduce the hard-edged *cel shading* that's often seen in traditional hand-drawn animation.

✔ **Minnaert:** This shader is pretty slick. By default, it's set up to behave just like the standard Lambert shader. However, if you adjust its Darkness value to a number less than 1, the edges of an object with this material get lighter. Darkness values greater than 1 darken the parts of the object that point to the viewer. The Minnaert shader is a great way to fake a backlight on an object or give it a somewhat velvety look.

✔ **Fresnel:** Pronounced "FRAY-nel," this shader is also a nice one to use for metals and glassy materials. It's like the Minnaert shader, except instead of working relative to the viewer, the Fresnel shader works relative to the light source. Higher Fresnel values darken parts that point toward the light source and this multiplies by the Factor value.

Figure 7-5 shows Suzanne shaded with each of the different diffuse shaders. For simplicity, the specular intensity has been reduced to 0 in this figure.

Figure 7-5:
Suzanne with Lambert, Oren-Nayar, Toon, Minnaert, and Fresnel shaders.

You also have control over the way the specular highlight appears on your materials. You change this in the Specular panel the same way you change the diffuse shader: Left-click the drop-down menu next to the color swatch. All specular shaders share an Intensity value that controls the strength of the specular highlights. Higher values make the highlights brighter; lower values make them dimmer and can reduce the specularity altogether. As with the diffuse shaders, you have a choice of algorithms that control how the specular highlight appears:

- ✔ **CookTorr (Cook-Torrance):** The Cook-Torrance shader is Blender's default specular shader. In addition to the Intensity slider, this shader also has a setting to control Hardness. Higher Hardness values make the highlight smaller and more compact, whereas lower values spread the highlight over more of the object's surface. This shader is good for shiny plastic materials.

- ✔ **Phong:** This shader is nearly identical to the Cook-Torrance shader, although not quite as optimized. The edge of the specular highlight is softer, making it a bit nicer for less shiny plastics and organic materials.

- ✔ **Blinn:** The Blinn shader is a more refined shader that is generally more accurate than the Cook-Torrance or Phong shaders. In addition to the Intensity and Hardness values, this shader also has a IOR, or Index of Refraction, setting. This refraction isn't quite like you might expect. The IOR value, in this case, controls the softness of the highlight. This shader works well for getting materials that behave more like materials in the real world.

- ✔ **Toon:** Like the Toon diffuse shader, the Toon specular shader breaks the specular highlight into discrete bands of lightness to re-create the look of traditional cartoon coloring.

- ✔ **WardIso:** I like to use the WardIso, short for Ward Isotropic, shader along with the Minnaert and Fresnel diffuse shaders for metallic or shiny plastic materials. The Slope value is a mathematical variable in the shader algorithm, which controls the sharpness of the highlight's edge. Lower values are sharper and higher values are more dispersed.

Figure 7-6 shows Suzanne with the default Lambert diffuse shader and each of the different specular shaders.

Figure 7-6:
Suzanne
with Cook-
Torrance,
Phong,
Blinn,
Toon, and
WardIso
specular
shaders.

Reflection and transparency

A common challenge of 3D computer graphics is making your materials reflective and transparent. Fortunately, adding those properties to your materials in Blender isn't too difficult. The bulk of the work is done in two panels of Material Properties (see Figure 7-1): Mirror and Transparency.

Adding reflectivity to your material

Enable mirroring by left-clicking the Mirror check box and increasing the Reflectivity slider within the Mirror panel of Material Properties. An important thing to know about doing reflections this way is that it uses *ray tracing*. To create accurate reflections, Blender's renderer follows, or traces, a ray of light as it bounces off of objects and into the camera. To ensure its accuracy, the renderer follows thousands of these rays. This accuracy comes at the expense of using more processing power from your computer and has a high likelihood of lengthening the rendering process. Figure 7-7 shows an example image with high reflectivity.

Figure 7-7: An example image with high levels of ray traced reflectivity.

In order to properly see any ray traced results in your render, make sure that the Ray Tracing check box is enabled in Render Properties.

Ray traced reflectivity is also one of those exceptions to the "light only bounces once" rule. In order to get a reflection, you have to have at least two bounces. The light comes from the light source, bounces off of one object, and then off of your reflective object before it reaches the camera. You can actually define how many bounces the renderer recognizes by adjusting the Depth value in the Mirror panel. Of course, the higher the Depth value, the more bounces that Blender has to trace and therefore the longer your renders are likely to take.

Making your material transparent

In addition to reflectivity, you can also control an object's transparency. The main control for a 3D material's transparency is its *alpha* value. The alpha value in Blender runs on a scale from 0, for completely transparent, to 1, for completely opaque. You adjust this value with the slider in the Transparency panel, labeled Alpha.

You can adjust the alpha value even if you have the Transparency check box disabled. If you keep Transparency disabled, however, the preview panel shows a white-to-blue gradient over the preview object instead of the checkerboard pattern in the background. This gradient shows that as you reduce the alpha value, the more your object's material is replaced with your scene's sky color. The sky color is set in World Properties. Chapter 9 covers setting the sky color and other World Properties in greater detail.

Getting the object's material to show the sky color rather than what's actually behind it doesn't initially seem useful, but it's actually a really quick way to create a material that can make an object behave as a three-dimensional mask. Of course, you may not want a mask and instead you want to see the actual 3D environment through your object. Enable the Transparency check box to make the checkerboard background show up through the preview object.

By default, Blender uses *Z transparency* to get the rest of your scene's environment to show up through your object. However, if you're trying to re-create glass, you might realize that things don't look quite right. With real glass, you have refraction. The transparent material actually bends the light, warping what you see through it, like a magnifying glass. Regular Z transparency can't easily re-create this effect. In order to get that effect, you should use ray traced transparency instead.

You can activate ray traced transparency by left-clicking the Raytrace button in the Transparency panel. When you enable this button, it automatically disables the Z Transparency button. You can't have both of these settings active at the same time. In addition, initially, it doesn't look like much changed by enabling Raytrace. This is because the IOR value for ray traced transparency is set to 1.00. A value of 1.00 means that the material has the same IOR as the air around it and therefore doesn't bend light as it passes through it. However, increasing the IOR warps the checkerboard pattern seen through the object. Now, the cool thing about the IOR value is that it actually matches the physical IOR values of real-world materials. You could look up the IOR value of a specific material, like glass or jade, on a table online or in a physics book and use it to get an accurately transparent material.

Figure 7-8 shows the difference in results that you get with straight alpha transparency, Z transparency, and ray traced transparency.

Common values for reflectivity and transparency

When it comes to the ray tracing settings, both the Mirror and Transparency panels have a few values in common. The first ones you might notice are the Fresnel and Blend sliders. The Fresnel setting adjusts an effect that's similar to the Fresnel diffuse shader, but with a specific influence on reflectivity and transparency. For reflectivity, rather than decreasing the material's color value in the direction of the light source like the Fresnel diffuse shader, increasing this value reduces the reflectivity relative to the camera. The Blend slider acts like a multiplication factor for the Fresnel effect, with higher values intensifying the effect.

For transparency, it's a bit different. It's also relative to the camera view, but instead of clouding out the transparency in that direction, it actually increases the transparency, reducing the color in the direction of the camera. Another interesting thing about the Fresnel setting for ray traced transparency is that it also works on Z transparency, so you can take advantage of the Fresnel effect without having to fake it.

If you want Fresnel or Blend (or any other value for that matter) values to be consistent in both the Transparency and Mirror panels, you can use Blender's copy-and-paste feature. Hover your mouse cursor over the value you want to copy (*don't click!*) and press Ctrl+C. Then hover your mouse cursor over the value you paste (again, without clicking) and press Ctrl+V. Alternatively, you can copy and paste using the menu that appears when you right-click a value.

Another common setting between these ray traced effects are the Gloss settings. The default value of 1.00 makes the material perfectly reflective and transparent. Reducing this value in either panel blurs the reflection or makes the material more translucent than transparent. When changing the glossiness, the blurry reflection may look dirty or pixelated. This blurriness is because of how Blender handles glossiness. The glossiness is approximated based on the Samples value, which is located beneath the Gloss slider for both ray traced reflection and ray traced transparency. Increasing the number of samples makes the glossiness appear more accurate, but at the expense of longer render times. Figure 7-9 shows some of the cool effects that you can get by varying the Gloss value.

Figure 7-9:
Playing with the gloss value on an object with ray traced reflections and ray traced transparency.

Controlling how materials handle shadows

In the "Adjusting shader values" section earlier in this chapter, I cover how Blender gives you control over the way your materials reflect diffuse color and deal with specular highlights. You can also control how your material works with shadows. Most important, you can dictate the type of shadows the material can receive, as well as whether the material itself casts a shadow.

All these controls live in the Shadow panel of Material Properties. The following list describes the most important controls in this panel:

- **Receive:** Enabled by default, the Receive check box controls whether your material receives shadows cast by other objects.

- **Receive Transparent:** If your scene has other objects with transparent materials, you may want to enable the Receive Transparent check box. If you don't, the shadows cast from the transparent object appear as if they're cast from an opaque material. It's disabled by default for performance reasons; if your scene doesn't have transparent materials, there's no reason to waste computer resources trying to account for them.

- **Shadows Only:** I mention many times throughout this book that the beauty of computer graphics is that you can do things that are impossible in the real world. The Shadows Only check box is another example of that fact. Enable this check box, and your material is transparent *except* for where shadows are cast upon it.

✔ **Cast Only:** Occasionally, you run into a situation where you only need the shadow cast from your object, and you don't need to see the object at all. This situation — impossible in meatspace — is easy to make happen by enabling the Cast Only check box.

✔ **Cast Buffer Shadow:** The Cast Buffer Shadow — enabled by default — controls whether your material casts a shadow. If you run into a situation where you don't want your object casting a shadow, disable this check box.

Assigning multiple materials to different parts of a mesh

Using the same material across an entire object is great for objects that are the same uniform material, but what if you want to have multiple different materials on the same object? For that sort of situation, you want to use material slots. Basically, you create a *material slot,* sometimes referred to as a *material index,* by defining a set of object subcomponents — faces in meshes, individual characters in text, and control points in curves and surfaces — and assigning them to a material. You create material slots directly from the Context panel of Material Properties. However, you have to be in Edit mode.

For an idea of how this process works, say that you want to model a beach ball and give it the classic primary-colored panels. Use the following steps:

1. **Add a UV sphere mesh (Shift+A⇨Mesh⇨UV Sphere).**

   Using the Last Operator panel of the Tool Shelf or the F6 pop-up panel, edit the UV sphere to have 12 segments, 12 rings, and a radius of 1.00. You may also add a Subdivision Surface modifier (Ctrl+1) and set the faces to render as smooth (Tool Shelf⇨Shading⇨Smooth).

2. **Tab into Edit mode and switch to Face Select mode (Tab⇨Ctrl+Tab⇨ Face).**

3. **Add a new material using the material datablock.**

   Left-click the New button to add a new material or choose an existing material from the datablock drop-down menu. The list box at the top of Material Properties adds your new material to the list.

4. **Use the datablock text field to name your material.**

   For this example, name it White.

5. **Change the color to white by left-clicking the color swatch in the Diffuse panel.**

   The entire ball turns white. All the faces are currently assigned to this material slot.

6. **Use face loop select to select two adjacent vertical face loops (Alt+ right-click and Shift+Alt+right-click).**

7. **Add another new material slot.**

   This time, left-click the button with the plus (+) icon in the upper left of the materials list box. A new material slot appears in the list named White.001.

8. **Change the material name to Blue.**

9. **Change the color to blue by left-clicking the swatch in the Diffuse panel and choosing blue with the color picker.**

   After you change the color of this swatch, you might expect the faces that you have selected to automatically change to match this color. That's not quite how it works: Even though you have these faces selected, they're still assigned to the White material slot. Use the next step to remedy that situation.

10. **Assign the selected faces to the current material slot, Blue, by clicking the Assign button beneath the material list box.**

    The moment you left-click the Assign button, the selected faces all change to the blue color you picked in Step 9.

11. **Using the process in Steps 6 through 10, work your way around the sphere, creating and assigning colors for the other panels.**

    If you create a beach ball like the one in Figure 7-10, you should end up with four material slots, one for each color on the ball.

Figure 7-10: Creating a beach ball with a UV sphere and four material slots.

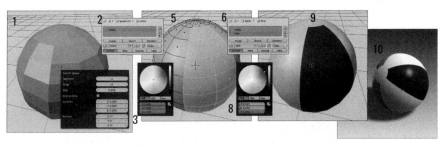

Material slots aren't limited to be used only by meshes. You can also use them on curves, surfaces, and text objects. The process is similar to meshes, with one main exception. Meshes, as shown in the preceding example, allow you to assign individual faces to different material slots. This exception isn't the case with curves, surfaces, and text objects, which assign material slots to discrete closed entities. So you can assign individual text characters and curves to a material slot. However, you can't set the material slot of an individual control point or a portion of a text character. Figure 7-11 shows material slots working on a curve, surface, and text object.

Figure 7-11:
Material
slots on
curves, sur-
faces, and
text objects.

Coloring Vertices with Vertex Paint

One downside to material slots is the fact that although they make defining multiple colors and materials on a single mesh easy, there's a very distinct line between materials. The color of one material doesn't smoothly transition into the next. For example, if you want to create a car with a paint job that's light blue near the ground that smoothly transitions to a bright yellow on its roof and hood, you can't effectively do this color graduation with material slots. However, with *vertex colors,* it's completely doable. This technique works only on mesh objects, but it's also a very effective way of quickly coloring a mesh without the hard-edged lines that material slots give you.

The way vertex colors works is pretty simple. You assign each vertex in your mesh a specific color. If the vertices that form a face have different colors, a gradient goes from each vertex to the others, where the color is most intense at the vertex and more blended with other colors the farther away it gets.

Of course, trying to go in and explicitly set the color for each and every vertex in a mesh can get really tedious on complex meshes. To alleviate this problem, Blender has a Vertex Paint mode. You activate Vertex Paint mode by selecting (right-clicking) the mesh object that you would like to paint in the 3D View and then pressing V. You can also use the mode drop-down menu in the 3D View's header. When you enter Vertex Paint mode, your mouse cursor changes to include a paint brush circle similar to the one you see when in Sculpt mode and the Tool Shelf updates with paint options. The Tool Shelf for painting is shown in Figure 7-12.

The largest function of the paint options in the Tool Shelf is in the Brush panel. Here you set the color you want to use and control how that color is applied to the selected object. You can choose the color you want by adjusting the embedded color picker.

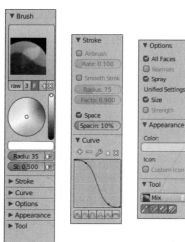

Figure 7-12:
The paint
options in
the Tool
Shelf while
in Vertex
Paint mode.

After you pick the color you want to use, left-click and drag your mouse over vertices in the 3D View. Those vertices take on the color you defined. To get an idea of where the vertices that you're painting actually exist on your mesh, you may want to have Blender overlay the object's wireframe in the 3D View. To do so, navigate to Object Properties and left-click the Wire check box in the Display panel. Blender adds the wireframe over the surface of the object, making it much clearer where each of the vertices of the mesh lie.

By default, the base vertex color for an object is a flat white. If you would rather start with a different base color, choose Paint⇨Set Vertex Colors (Shift+K) from the 3D View's header. Doing that sets all the vertices in your mesh to have the color you defined in the Vertex Paint color swatch.

In Vertex Paint mode, the buttons in the Tool panel of the Tool Shelf control how the paint color is applied to the vertices. The default setting of Mix simply blends the defined color with the color that the vertex already has assigned, according to whatever value is set by the Strength slider. Choosing the Add, Subtract, or Multiply options from the drop-down menu in the Tool panel takes the current color and respectively adds, subtracts, or multiplies that with the current vertex color under the brush in the 3D View. The Blur option is the only paint setting that doesn't use the selected color. It uses the vertices that are within the radius defined by the Radius slider and attempts to mix their colors, effectively blurring them. The Lighten and Darken options take the value of the color you chose and use that to control how much influence it has on the already existing colors. So if you have your color set to full white, painting with Darken enabled won't change the vertex colors at all. But using that color to paint with Lighten enabled makes it appear everywhere you work.

If you're familiar with Sculpt mode (see Chapter 5), you may be tempted to try to adjust the radius of your brush by using the F hotkey. Go ahead, try it;

it works! The same goes for using Shift+F to adjust the strength of your brush. You can also use the brush datablocks like you can with Sculpt mode to create your own savable custom brushes.

Occasionally when vertex painting, your mesh may have some faces on it that you don't want to receive any of the color you're currently painting. In this case, you want to define face selection masking by left-clicking the Painting Mask button in the 3D View's header. It has an icon of a cube with one face showing a checkerboard pattern, as shown in Figure 7-13.

Figure 7-13:
Enabling
the Painting
Mask
button.

When you enable the painting mask, you can select faces of your mesh by right-clicking. After you do, these faces are the only ones that are affected by your painting. This method is an excellent way of isolating a portion of your mesh for custom painting without changing the color of the faces around that area. By using a painting mask, you can actually get the hard-edged color changes that you get with material slots, should you want such a thing.

In order to have your vertex colors appear in your render, you need to enable the Vertex Color Paint check box in the Options panel of Material Properties.

Practical Example: Coloring the Eye

If you follow the practical example in Chapter 5, you should have a model of an eye that has the boring, plastic default gray material. If you haven't modeled that eye, don't worry; it's on the companion DVD for this book as well as the companion Web site. The purpose of this practical example is to make that eye look more like an actual eye and less like a gray ball.

Setting up a Materials screen

When working with materials in Blender, you find out very quickly that you often have to scroll the Properties editor or you frequently have to switch between different sections of the Properties editor. This fact is even more apparent when you start working with textures (see Chapter 8). What it comes down to is that the default screen layout is inadequate for working with materials. The best way to alleviate that problem is to create your own screen layout that shows you all the information you need all at once.

To start, I recommend that you set up this new screen from a fresh Blender scene, so either open Blender now or reload the startup file by pressing Ctrl+N. This way, after you set up this new screen, you can include it with your startup file and it will be available for you in all your future Blender sessions.

With your new scene loaded, go to the header at the top of the Blender window and use the Plus (+) button on the right of the screen datablock to add a new screen. When you do so, not much will appear to change, aside from the screen name now showing as Default.001. Left-click the text field in the screen datablock and change the name of this new screen to"Materials. Now you can actually edit the screen layout to suit your needs. I tend to like the layout shown in Figure 7-14.

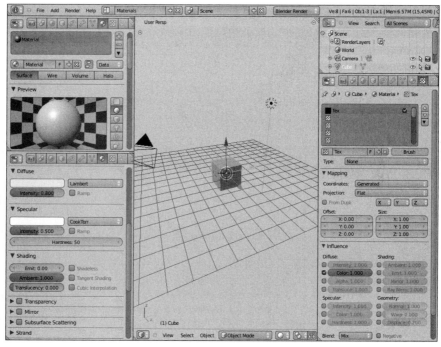

Figure 7-14:
A new
screen
layout
for work-
ing with
materials in
Blender.

To get this screen layout, use the following steps:

1. **Remove the Timeline at the bottom of the screen.**

   If you're not sure how to split and join areas in Blender, see Chapter 2.

2. **Vertically split the 3D View so that you have a narrow column on the left side of the window.**

3. **Change your new area to a Properties editor (Shift+F7).**

4. **Flip the header of your new Properties editor to the top of the area.**

   To do so, hover your mouse over the header and press F5 or right-click the header and choose Flip to Top.

5. **Set your new Properties editor to display Material Properties.**

6. **Split this new Properties editor horizontally, showing just enough space to see the material preview panel in the upper area.**

   This way, you can always see what your materials look like as you make adjustments in the lower Properties editor.

7. **Change the right-side Properties editor to show Texture Properties.**

   This step isn't really necessary at this point, but it will be useful down the road.

8. **Switch back to the Default screen layout (Ctrl+←⇨Ctrl+←) and save user settings to your startup file (Ctrl+U).**

   Now, whenever you start Blender, you have a Materials screen that you can jump to for editing materials on a model.

At this point, you can load the eye .blend file (F1) and begin working on its materials. One note: Because the eye model was created before you made your custom Materials screen, if you simply double-click the .blend file and load it outright, you won't see your Materials screen in the screens data-block. To get around this issue, look to the left region on the side of Blender's File Browser. Disable the Load UI check box near the bottom of that region. After you do that, you can double-click the eye .blend file you want to load. Now you should be able to look in the screens datablock and choose your custom Materials screen. Your Blender window should now appear something like the window shown in Figure 7-15.

The easy part: Material slots

Now to play with materials! Specifically speaking, you need to create two materials for the eye: one for the cornea/sclera around the eye and another for the eye interior.

Creating the cornea material

To create the cornea material:

1. **Left-click the New button in the material datablock of Material Properties and name this material cornea.**

   The cornea and sclera wrap around the eye, so the layer is transparent.

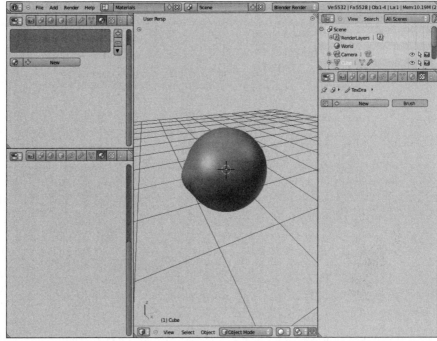

Figure 7-15:
The eye
model
loaded in
a custom
Materials
screen
layout.

2. **Enable the Transparency check box in Material Properties and reduce the Alpha setting down to 0.500.**

    The material preview updates, but the 3D View has no apparent effect.

3. **Go to Object Properties and enable the Transparency check box in the Display panel.**

    I like doing this in the right-hand Properties editor in the custom Materials screen created in the preceding section. Figure 7-16 highlights the controls for enabling transparency in the 3D View.

4. **Return to Material Properties and make the following adjustments to your cornea material:**

    - **Diffuse Shader:** Oren-Nayer

    - **Diffuse Roughness:** 0.300

    - **Specular Shader:** WardIso

    - **Transparency Fresnel:** 3.000

    - **Options⇨Traceable:** Disabled

    - **Shadow⇨Cast Buffer Shadows:** Disabled

    The last two settings are particularly useful because by disabling them, you prevent your cornea from casting a shadow upon the interior of the eye. If later, when you render a character with these eyes, the eyes render in all black, chances are good that you forgot to disable these material settings.

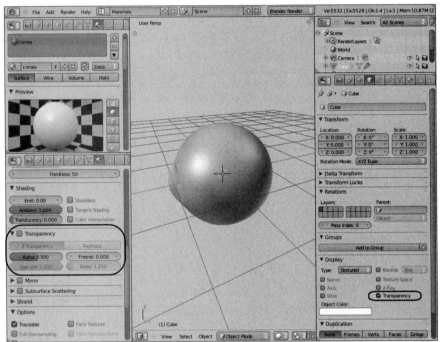

Figure 7-16:
Enabling transparency in the 3D View.

Building a base material for the eye interior

After the cornea material is complete, you can work on the interior elements. Currently, the entire eye is the same transparent material as the cornea; that's not likely what you want. In that case, you need to create a new material:

1. **Return to the top of Material Properties and add a new material slot by left-clicking the plus (+) button next to the material list box.**

   This step creates a duplicate of your cornea material, named cornea.001.

2. **Rename this material eye.**

   Your new material still has the same settings as the cornea material.

3. **Make the following adjustments to the settings in the Material Properties:**

   • **Diffuse Color:** White

   • **Diffuse Intensity:** 0.900

- **Diffuse Roughness:** 0.500
- **Specular Shader:** CookTorr
- **Transparency:** Disabled
- **Transparency Alpha:** 1.000
- **Transparency Fresnel:** 0.000
- **Options⇨Traceable:** Enabled
- **Shadow⇨Cast Buffer Shadows:** Enabled

At this point, you've created a base texture for the interior of the eye that looks something like the preview image shown in Figure 7-17.

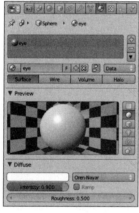

Figure 7-17: A base material for the eye's interior components.

Assigning the base material to interior faces

Of course, although you created a new material for the eye's interior, that material has not yet been assigned to any faces of your model.

1. **Tab into Edit mode and make sure that no faces are selected.**

   You can do so by pressing A until nothing is selected.

2. **Select all the linked faces for the cornea/sclera by hovering your mouse on the exterior faces of the mesh and pressing L.**

3. **Hide the selected faces (H) and then select all visible faces (A).**

4. **In the Context section of Material Properties, click the Assign button to assign the eye material to the selected faces.**

5. **Tab back into Object mode.**

   Your results should appear like the image in Figure 7-18.

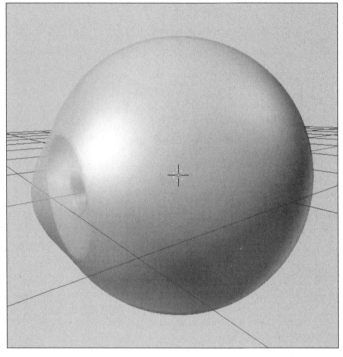

Creating a pupil

Now you need to create a material slot for the eye's pupil. Using the same basic steps described in the earlier section, "Building a base material for the eye interior," create a new material slot for your pupil.

1. **Left-click the plus (+) button next to the material list box in Material Properties.**

2. **Rename your new material pupil.**

3. **Make the following adjustments to Material Properties:**

    - **Diffuse Color:** Black

    - **Shading⇨Shadeless:** Enable

4. **Use the same basic steps described earlier in the "Assigning the base material to interior faces" section to assign your new pupil material to the central faces of the eye.**

    When you finish, your result should appear like Figure 7-19.

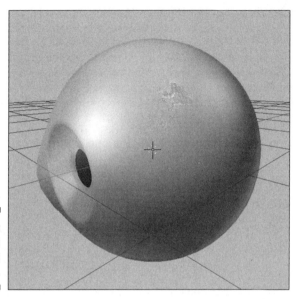

Figure 7-19:
The eye now has a pupil.

From here, you have two options. The easiest thing would be to create another material slot for the eye's iris. And if you're not too worried about detail, that could very easily be enough. However, if you want a bit more detail, you may want to use Blender's Vertex Paint feature to give you colors with more subtle variations than just straight material slots can get you.

Getting more detailed with Vertex Paint

In this section, you can get more detailed and subtle color results for the main body of the eye. Before you bolt face-first into Vertex Paint mode, you should first make sure that your painting gets rendered:

1. **Select the `eye` material in the list box at the top of Material Properties.**

2. **Enable the Vertex Color Paint check box in the Options panel.**

Now you're ready to start painting.

Painting the iris and the back of the eye

If you go to Vertex Paint mode (V) right now, the eye model changes into a solid white blob. This setup isn't a particularly nice way to paint your vertices. Not only can you not determine what parts of the eye you're looking at, you also only have access to painting the exterior cornea/sclera of the eye.

The interior parts of the eye model are completely obscured and inaccessible. Fortunately, there's a way around this issue. Left-click the Face Selection for Masking button in the 3D View's header. Upon doing so, you see a shaded version of your interior eye model with light wireframe lines drawn over the surface.

You may be wondering why the exterior faces of the eye model disappeared. Well, earlier in this practical example, you went into Edit mode, selected the external faces (L), and hid them (H). When you're in Vertex Paint mode and you enable the Face Selection Masking button, Blender shows only the faces that are visible in Edit mode. It's a pretty handy trick for Blender's various paint modes in the 3D View.

Another handy tip to keep in mind is that any faces you selected in Edit mode persist in Vertex Paint mode when you have the Face Selection Masking button enabled. Although most of Blender's selection tools (right-click, border select, circle select, lasso select) work in Vertex Paint mode with Face Selection Masking, some of the useful selection operations, like loop select (Alt+right-click), don't work. If you need to select a loop, you can quickly tab into Edit mode, do your loop selection, and tab back out to Vertex Paint mode.

In fact, to select the faces that make up the eye's iris, loop selecting is exactly what I recommend you do:

1. **From Vertex Paint mode with Face Selection Masking, tab to Edit mode.**

2. **Use Blender's loop select operation (Alt+right-click) to select the faces that make up the eye's iris.**

3. **Tab back into Vertex Paint mode and paint your iris using the vertex paint tools.**

   When you do your vertex painting, it affects only the currently selected faces.

4. **Tab back to Edit mode and invert your face selection (Ctrl+I).**

   You should have everything other than the iris selected. You may also want to deselect the faces of the pupil, but because they're assigned to another material, that's really not necessary.

5. **Tab back into Vertex Paint mode to paint red and pink tones around the back of the eye.**

When you finish, the result should look something like Figure 7-20.

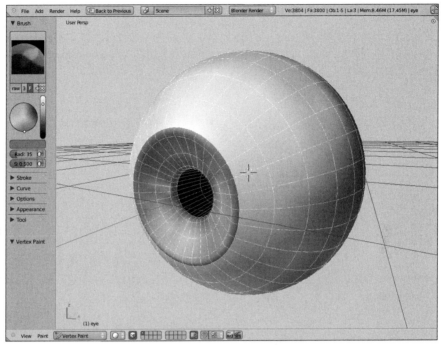

Figure 7-20:
Using
Vertex Paint
mode to
paint details
for the eye.

Seeing your vertex colors in the 3D View

If you pop back into Object mode, your freshly painted vertex colors may not appear on your model. Don't worry, though, they're definitely there. To see your colors in the 3D View, you need to adjust your display settings. The first thing you need to do is switch your 3D View to the Textured Viewport Shading mode (Alt+Z). By default, the results aren't particularly pleasant. The transparency of your cornea is no longer apparent, and the front of the eye is probably completely darkened.

This ugliness is actually caused by two things: your display settings for the 3D View and your light placement in your scene. To deal with the former, bring up the Properties region of the 3D View (N) and go down to the Display panel. This panel contains a drop-down menu labeled Shading. By default, this menu is set to Multitexture. Left-click the menu and choose GLSL. Assuming that you have a suitably modern video card, the results in your 3D View should already be improved. Of course, the front of the eye is still dark.

To deal with the darkness at the front of the eye, simply select the lamp in your scene, grab it (G), and move it so that it's in front of the eye. Moving the lamp should illuminate the iris and pupil of the eye model. If the eye is still too dark for you, you can duplicate the lamp (Shift+D) a couple times and move those duplicated lamps around your scene to more clearly light the scene. Chapter 9 has more detailed information about lighting in Blender. When you're satisfied, you can hit F12 and kick out a quick render to see what it looks like. Figure 7-21 shows an example of what the eye might look like in the 3D View.

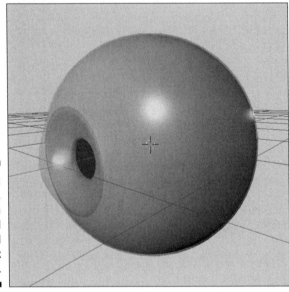

Figure 7-21:
The eye,
colored with
material
slots and
vertex
colors.

Chapter 8

Giving Models Texture

· ·

In This Chapter

▶ Working with textures

▶ Creating procedural textures

▶ Thinking about texture mapping

▶ Unwrapping a mesh to use image-based textures

▶ Trying your hand at texturing with an example

· ·

*I*f you want a more controlled way of adjusting the look of your object than what's described in Chapter 7, then using material settings alone won't get you there. You can use Vertex Paint (V), but if you're working on a model that you intend to animate, Vertex Paint can cause you to have many extraneous vertices just for color. Those vertices end up slowing down the processes of rigging, animating, and even rendering. Also, you may want to have material changes that are independent of the topology and edge flow of your mesh.

For those sorts of scenarios, you're going to want to use textures, which is the focus of this chapter. (Note: This chapter pairs well with Chapter 7.)

Adding Textures

Generally speaking, a *texture* is a kind of image that you stretch or tile over the surface of your object to give it more detail without adding more geometry. Not only can textures influence the color of your object, but they can also allow you to make additional adjustments, such as stipulating the specularity of some specific parts of the model. For example, on a human face, skin tends to be shinier across the nose and forehead, and a reduced specularity exists around the eyes. With textures, you can control these sorts of things.

You can add and edit textures to a material in Texture Properties, as shown in Figure 8-1.

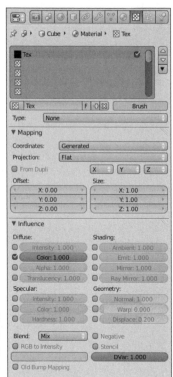

Figure 8-1:
The Texture
Properties.

Like Material Properties, Texture Properties has a Preview panel that displays the texture as you work on it. By default, the Preview panel is hidden because the initial texture type is None. You can change this type in the Context panel with the Type drop-down menu. The list box at the top of the Context panel is similar to the list box in Material Properties. With these Texture slots, you can control the textures applied to your material (which, in turn, is applied to your object). However, unlike the list box in Material Properties, you can't arbitrarily add and remove texture slots. You have exactly 18 slots to work with. Left-click any texture slot in the list to choose that slot as the one you want to work on. The texture slots that are populated with a texture display the name of that texture next to its icon. You can customize the name of the texture by left-clicking the texture datablock name field below the list box. This field is part of a set of datablock controls just like the ones used in Material Properties or Object Properties (see Chapter 7).

When you pick a specific texture type (other than None) by clicking the Type drop-down menu, a Preview panel appears in Texture Properties. By default, the Preview panel has a window that displays your current texture. However, if you left-click the Material button beneath the preview window, it's updated with the same preview panel you see in Material Properties. With this preview type, you can actively see how your texture is mapped to an object without the hassle of bouncing between Material Properties and Texture Properties. If you left-click the Both button, the preview splits to display the material preview on the left and the texture preview on the right. Figure 8-2 shows the three different views of the Preview panel.

Figure 8-2:
From left to right, the Preview panel in Texture Properties allows you to preview your texture, see how your texture is applied in your material, and see a split view of both.

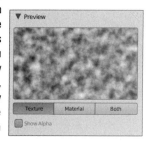 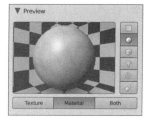 

Using Procedural Textures

Blender offers basically two kinds of textures: image-based textures and *procedural textures*. Unlike image-based textures, where you explicitly create and load an image as a texture, procedural textures are created in software with a specific pattern algorithm.

The advantage of procedural textures is that you can quickly add a level of detail to your objects without worrying about the unwrapping described later in this chapter in the section "Unwrapping a Mesh." The software handles mapping the texture to the mesh for you. Of course, procedurals can be a bit more difficult to control than image-based textures. For example, if you have a character with dark circles under his eyes, getting those circles to show up only where you want can be pretty tough, maybe even impossible. So the ideal use for procedural textures is as broad strokes where you don't need fine control. Procedural textures are great for creating a foundation or a base to start with, such as providing the rough texture of an orange rind's surface.

Besides the None texture type, Blender has 13 procedural texture types that you can work with, accessible through the Type drop-down menu in Texture Properties. In addition to these procedurals, you can also choose Image as a texture type. Figure 8-3 shows all available texture types.

Noise basis option

Roughly half of all the procedural textures share an option labeled Basis, short for *noise basis*. The noise basis is a specific type of pseudorandom pattern that influences the appearance of a procedural texture. Noise basis has two controls:

✔ **Basis:** The Basis menu allows you to choose one of several algorithms for generating noise. The available choices are shown in the figure.

✔ **Nabla value:** The Nabla value offers more advanced control of the sharpness or smoothness of the texture when it's applied to the material.

The types of noise basis fall roughly into three different kinds of noise:

✔ **Cell noise:** A blocky, pixelated type of noise, cell noise stands apart from the other noise basis types because it's the least

organic-looking. If you're interested in a very digital-looking texture, this type is the one to choose.

✔ **Voronoi family:** These noise types include Crackle, F2-F1, F4, F3, F2, and F1 and are all roughly based on the same algorithm. A primary attribute of Voronoi noise is a somewhat distinct partitioning throughout the texture with generally straight lines. This partitioning is most apparent in the Voronoi Crackle noise basis. These noise types are good for hammered metal, scales, veins, and that dry desert floor look.

✔ **Cloudy noise:** *Cloudy* is my own terminology, but it includes the Improved Perlin, Original Perlin, and Blender Original noise basis types. These types of noise tend to have a more organic feel to them and work well for generic bump textures and clouds or mist.

Figure 8-3: The available textures you can use that are built into Blender.

The following are brief descriptions of each type of procedural texture:

✔ **Blend texture:** The Blend texture is one of the unsung heroes in Blender's procedural texture arsenal. This texture may seem like a simple gradient, but with the right mapping, it's really quite versatile.

I use Blend textures for mixing two other textures together, creating simple toonlike outlines for meshes, and adjusting the color along the length of hair strands. You can see the real power of the Blend texture when you use it with a ramp that you define in the Colors panel.

✔ **Clouds texture:** The Clouds texture is a good general-purpose texture. You can treat the Clouds texture as a go-to texture for general bumps, smoke, and (of course) clouds.

✔ **Distorted Noise texture:** The Distorted Noise texture is pretty slick. Actually, strike that; this type of texture is best suited to very rough, complex surfaces. The way the Distorted Noise texture works is pretty cool, though. You use one procedural noise texture, specified by the Noise Distortion menu, to distort and influence the texture of your noise basis. With this combination, you can get some really unique textures.

✔ **Environment Map texture:** An *environment map* is a way of using a texture to fake reflections on your object. It works by taking the position of a given object and rendering an image in six directions around that object: up, down, left, right, forward, and back. These images are then mapped to the surface of your object. So, an environment map isn't exactly a procedural texture in the traditional sense, but because the environment images are taken automatically, I say it's part procedural and part image-based. Environment maps aren't as accurate as using ray traced reflection (see Chapter 7), but they can be quite a bit faster. So if you need a generically reflective surface that doesn't need to be accurate, environment maps are a handy tool that keeps your render times short. In the Environment Map panel, the Viewpoint Object field is set, by default, to be the object that you intend on mapping the texture to. However, sometimes you can get a better reflective effect by using the location of a different object, such as an Empty. Using an Empty as a Viewpoint Object is particularly useful when applying an environment map to an irregular surface.

When using environment maps, make sure that you do two things. First, choose the Reflection option from the Coordinates drop-down menu in the Mapping panel of Texture Properties. Second, enable the Environment Map check box in the Shading panel of Render Properties. Unless you do both of these things, your environment map won't work properly.

✔ **Magic texture:** At first glance, the Magic texture may seem to be completely useless — or at the very least, too weird to be useful. However, I've found quite a few cool uses for this eccentric little texture. If you treat the Magic texture as a bump map, it works well for creating a knit texture for blankets and other types of cloth. If you stretch the texture with your mapping controls, you can use it to re-create the thin filmy look that occurs when oil mixes with water. And, of course, you can use it to make a wacky wild-colored shirt.

✔ **Marble texture:** This texture has a lot of similarities with the Wood texture covered later in this section. However, the Marble texture is a lot more turbulent. You can use the Marble texture to create the look of polished marble, but the turbulent nature of the texture also lends itself nicely to be used as a fire texture and, to a lesser extent, the small ripples you get in ponds, lakes, and smaller pools of water.

✔ **Musgrave texture:** This procedural texture is extremely flexible and well suited for organic materials. You can use the Musgrave texture for rock cracks, generic noise, clouds, and even as a mask for rust patterns. As a matter of fact, with enough tweaking, you can probably get a Musgrave texture to look like nearly any other procedural texture. Of course, the trade-off is that this texture takes a bit longer to render than most of the other textures.

✔ **Noise texture:** Noise is the simplest procedural texture in Blender. (Well, the None texture type is probably simpler, but it's not very useful.) This texture has no custom controls of its own; it's simply raw noise, which means that you'll never get the same results twice using this texture. Each time you render, the noise pattern is different. This lack of predictability may be annoying if you're looking to do a bump map. However, if you're looking to have white noise on a TV screen, this texture is perfect.

✔ **Point Density texture:** The Point Density texture is used primarily with Blender's particle system to generate volumetric textures. These kinds of materials are well suited for creating smoke and clouds. (See Chapter 13 for more on Blender's particle system.)

✔ **Stucci texture:** Stucci is a nice organic texture that's most useful for creating bump maps. The Stucci texture is great for industrial and architectural materials like stucco, concrete, and asphalt. This texture is also handy if you just want to give your object's surface a little variety and roughen it up a bit.

✔ **Voronoi texture:** The Voronoi procedural texture doesn't have a noise basis because it's a more detailed control over the same algorithm that is used for the Voronoi noise basis options. It may be helpful to think of those basis options as presets, whereas this texture gives you full control over what you can do with the Voronoi algorithm. The Voronoi texture is pretty versatile, too. You can use it to create scales, veins, stained glass, textured metals, or colorful mosaics.

✔ **Voxel Data texture:** A *voxel*, short for *volumetric pixel*, is the three-dimensional equivalent to a pixel. The Voxel Data texture type is primarily used in Blender for smoke simulations, but you can also use it for other forms of volumetric data, such as the image slices provided by medical CT scans.

✔ **Wood texture:** The Wood texture is a bit of a misnomer. Sure, you *can* use it to create textures that are pretty close to what you see on cut planks of wood. However, the Wood texture has a lot more versatile uses. You can use the Wood texture to create nearly any sort of striped texture. I've actually even used it to fake the look of mini-blinds in a window.

Behold the power of the ramp!

A powerful and under-recognized tool in Blender is the *ramp*. A ramp is basically a gradient, and its editor interface is used in procedural textures, ramp materials, the material node editor, and even the node compositor. For materials, you can enable ramps by clicking the Ramp check box tab in the Diffuse and Specular panels of Material Properties. For procedural textures, the Ramp check box appears in the Colors panel. Ramps are a great way, for example, to adjust the color of the stripes in the Wood texture or determine which colors you want to use for your Blend texture. You can even use ramps to have a more controlled custom toon coloring than you can get with the diffuse or specular Toon shaders. The ramp editor works much like gradient editors in other programs. By default, it starts with a color positioned at either end of a *colorband* bar, and the color smoothly transitions from one side to the other. The color can be any value in the RGB spectrum, and, using the color picker, you also can control its transparency with the alpha value.

To change a color, first select it by either left-clicking its position in the colorband or adjusting the position value in the number field above the colorband. Color positions count up from left to right, starting at 0. So with the default arrangement, the transparent black color on the left is 0, and the white color on the right is 1. After you select the color, you can change its value by left-clicking the color swatch and using the color picker. To move the color position, you can left-click and drag it along the colorband, or you can adjust the Pos, or Position, value after you've selected it.

To add a new color position, left-click the Add button. A color position appears at the halfway point in the colorband. You can delete any position by selecting it and left-clicking the Delete button.

It may not seem like much, but mastering ramps and knowing when to use them makes your workflow for adding materials and textures much faster.

Understanding Texture Mapping

After you create your texture, be it procedural or image-based, you're going to have to relate that texture to your material and, by extension, the surface of your object. This process is called *mapping*. Mapping basically consists of relating a location on a texture to a location on the surface of an object. Mapping controls are located in Texture Properties in the Mapping and Influence panels, as shown in Figure 8-4.

The Mapping panel

The Mapping panel controls how the texture is mapped to the object, defining how the texture coordinates are projected on it. The most important button is the drop-down menu labeled Coordinates. The following list explains the types of coordinate mapping available:

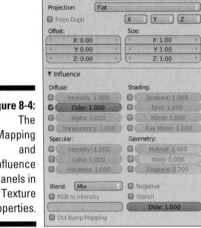

Figure 8-4:
The
Mapping
and
Influence
panels in
Texture
Properties.

✔ **Global:** Choosing this option uses the scene's coordinates to define the texture space. So if you have an animated object with a texture mapped this way, the texture will seem to be locked in place as the object moves across it. Global coordinates produce kind of a strange effect, but it's helpful in a few situations, such as faking shadows on a moving character.

✔ **Object:** This neat option allows you to use a different object's location as a means of placing a texture on your object. To tell Blender which object you want to use, pick or type its name in the Object field. For example, you can load an image texture of a logo and place that logo on a model of a car by using the location, size, and orientation of an Empty.

✔ **Generated:** This option is the default, and it generates texture coordinates based on the object's local coordinates. The Generated option works fine for most situations, especially when you're using procedural coordinates.

✔ **UV:** UV coordinates are probably the most precise way of mapping a texture to an object. NURBS surfaces have UV coordinates by default. For meshes, however, getting UV coordinates requires you to go through a process called unwrapping, covered later in this chapter in the "Unwrapping a Mesh" section.

✔ **Strand:** This option is useful only when your object has a particle system with the Strand render option enabled. As the name indicates, the Strand option is intended specifically for particle strands. When activated, the texture is mapped along the length of the strand.

✔ **Sticky (Camera coordinates):** Sticky coordinates are a way of getting a somewhat precise mapping based on the location and orientation of the camera.

✔ **Window:** This option is similar to the Global coordinates option, but instead of using the scene's global coordinates, it uses the coordinates from the finished render window. In other words, it uses the camera's coordinates. But unlike Sticky coordinates, which use the camera's coordinates just once, this option always uses them. So if the object is animated, the texture is not stuck to it. It remains in place.

✔ **Normal:** Choosing this option causes the texture to be mapped according to the normal vectors along the surface of the object. This option is helpful for effects that require textures to react to the viewing angle of the camera.

✔ **Reflection:** The Reflection option uses the direction of a reflection vector to map your texture to the object. Basically, you want to use this option with an environment map texture to get fake reflections when you don't need the accuracy of ray tracing.

✔ **Stress:** Stress maps are a pretty cool option that's intended for use with dynamic or simulated geometry. The *stress value* is the difference between the location of an original texture coordinate and location of the coordinate when rendered. As an example, say that you have a character with stretchy arms. You can use stress mapping as a mask to make the arms more translucent the more they stretch.

✔ **Tangent:** In some ways, this option is similar to Normal coordinates. However, instead of using the surface normal, it uses an optional tangent vector to map the texture coordinates. Notice that I wrote *optional* tangent vector. By default, no tangent vector is on the material, so choosing this option by itself doesn't do much to it. However, if you left-click the Tangent Shading check box in the Shading panel of Material Properties, you have a tangent vector for your texture to work with.

In addition to these map inputs, you can also control what's called the *texture projection*. Texture projection, along with the map input, controls how the texture is applied to the mesh for everything except UV textures. Because UV textures explicitly map a texture coordinate to a coordinate on the surface of your object, changing projection doesn't have an effect on anything.

Blender has four different types of projection:

✔ **Flat:** This type of projection is the easiest to visualize. Imagine that you have your texture loaded in a slide projector. When you point the projector at a wall, you get the best results. However, if you point the slide projector at a curved or uneven surface, you get a little bit of distortion. This behavior is basically what happens with Flat projection.

✔ **Cube:** Cube projection uses the same idea as Flat projection, but instead of having just one projector, imagine that you have one pointing at the front, left, and top of your object (and shining through to the other side). The texture appears on all six sides of the cube. Of course, when you try to project on a more curved surface, you still get some seams and distortion.

✔ **Tube:** Tube projection is where the slide projector metaphor kind of stops making sense. Imagine that you have the unique ability to project on a curved surface without the distortion — of course, pretty close to impossible in the real world, but pretty trivial in computer graphics. Using Tube projection is ideal for putting labels on bottles or applying other sorts of textures to tubular objects.

✔ **Sphere:** Spherical projection is best suited for spherical objects, such as planets and balls, and it's also the cleanest way to apply a texture to an arbitrary three-dimensional surface because it usually doesn't leave any noticeable seams like Cube projection does.

Figure 8-5 shows a set of primitive objects with Flat, Cube, Tube, and Sphere projection.

Figure 8-5: Projecting textures in different ways on the same set of 3D objects.

At the bottom of the Mapping panel are fields that give you finer control over how your texture is positioned on your object. The Offset values define an offset in the X, Y, and Z directions. And the Size values scale the texture in each of those directions.

The Offset and Size values aren't relative to the global or local coordinates in the 3D View. They're actually relative to the texture image itself. The X and Y values are horizontal and vertical, whereas the Z value is a depth value into the texture. The Z values don't have a lot of influence unless the texture is a procedural texture with a noise basis because many of those textures actually have 3D depth information.

The Influence panel

Not only do you control how a texture is mapped to an object, but you also control how that texture affects the material, thanks to the controls in the Influence panel.

Each Influence value is enabled using a check box to the left of each slider. After you enable a check box, you can adjust its slider to dictate the level of influence. Most sliders span both positive and negative values, typically from –1 to 1. Using this range, values greater than 0 enables the option and increases its effect, but negative values indicate that the texture's effect on the material is inverted.

You can use any combination of the following options:

- **Diffuse controls:** Use these values to dictate how your texture influences various attributes of your material's diffuse shader. You have four options:

  - **Intensity:** Influences the intensity value in the material's diffuse shader, controlling how much light the material reflects.

  - **Color:** Affects the material's diffuse color.

  - **Alpha:** Controls the transparency and opacity of the material.

  - **Translucency:** Affects the amount of translucency in the material.

- **Specular controls:** These controls are like the Diffuse values, but they relate specifically to the material's specularity. You have three options:

  - **Intensity:** Influences the strength in the material's specular shader.

  - **Color:** Affects the material's specular color.

  - **Hardness:** Affects the specular hardness values for the specular shaders that support it.

- **Shading controls:** The values here dictate how your textures influence corresponding values in the Shading panel of the Material Properties. You have four options:

  - **Ambient:** Affects the amount of ambient light the material gets.

  - **Emit:** Affects the material's emit value for radiosity.

  - **Mirror Color:** Affects the material's mirror color.

  - **Ray Mirror:** Influences the amount of ray traced reflection that the material has.

- **Geometry controls:** With the values in this section, your textures can actually deform geometric elements of your object, be they the face normals or the location of faces themselves. You have three options:

- **Normal:** Influences the direction of the surface normals on the material. Enabling this check box enables bump mapping. This option can give your object much more detail without the computational slowdown of additional geometry.

- **Warp:** This value actually controls how one texture in the list of textures affects the next one in the stack. Higher Warp values cause this texture to influence the coordinates of the next texture in the stack.

- **Displace:** This option is similar to the Normal option, except that it actually moves the geometry of the object based on the texture map. Whereas bump mapping only makes it look like geometry is added and moved around by tricking out the surface normal, displacement actually moves the geometry around. The downside to Blender's displacement is that you have to have the vertices already in place to move around. Blender won't create the vertices for you on the fly. You can use the Subdivision Surface modifier to get around this a bit, but creating your additional vertices with that tool definitely increases your render times.

Unwrapping a Mesh

The most precise type of mapping you can use is UV mapping. UV mapping also allows you to take advantage of other Blender features, such as Texture Paint mode and texture baking. With NURBS surfaces, you get UV coordinates for free as part of their structure. However, Blender is predominantly a mesh editor, and in order to get proper UV coordinates on your mesh objects, you must put those meshes through a process known as unwrapping.

To understand this process, think about a globe and a map of the world. The map of the world uses the latitude and longitude lines to relate a point on the three-dimensional surface of the globe to the two-dimensional surface of the map. In essence, the world map is an unwrapped texture on the globe, whereas the latitude and longitude lines are the UVs.

Marking seams on a mesh

You unwrap a mesh in Blender by selecting all vertices (A) and, while in Edit mode (Tab), either pressing U or choosing UV Mapping⇨Unwrap in the Tool Shelf. You then see a menu with a handful of options.

However, despite the menu's variety of options, unless your mesh is simple or a special case, you should use the first menu item, Unwrap. Blender has very powerful unwrapping tools, but to take full advantage of them, you need to first define some seams. Remember that you're basically trying to flatten a 3D surface to a 2D plane. In order to do so, you need to tell Blender where it can start pulling the mesh apart. This location on your mesh is a *seam*. If you were unwrapping a globe, you might choose the prime meridian as your seam. I like to think about seams for unwrapping in terms of stuffed animals, such as a teddy bear. The seam is where the bear is stitched together from flat pieces of cloth.

To add a seam to your mesh, use the following steps:

1. **Tab into Edit mode and switch to Edge Select mode (Tab⇨Ctrl+Tab⇨ Edges).**

   You can also add seams from Vertex Select mode, but I find that it's easier in Edge Select.

2. **Select the series of edges you want to make into a seam (right-click⇨ Shift+right-click).**

   Using edge loop selection (Alt+right-click) can really be helpful here. Everyone has their own tastes when it comes to defining seams, but a good general rule is to put the seams on parts of the mesh that are easier to hide (for example, behind the hairline on a character, the undercarriage of a car, and so on).

3. **Use the Edge Specials menu to make the seam (Ctrl+E⇨Mark Seam or, in the Tool Shelf, UV Mapping⇨Mark Seam).**

   Seams on your mesh are highlighted in orange. If you mistakenly make a seam with the wrong edges, you can remove the seam by selecting those edges (right-click) and pressing Ctrl+E⇨Clear Seam or choosing UV Mapping⇨Clear Seam in the Tool Shelf.

With your seams defined, you're ready to unwrap your mesh. In order to see what you're doing, though, you should make a couple changes to your screen layout. First, change the viewport shading of your 3D View to textured (Alt+Z). Then split off a new area and change it to be a UV/Image Editor (Shift+F10). Alternatively, you can switch to the default UV Editing screen that ships with Blender by clicking the screen datablock at the top of your Blender window. Your layout should look something like what is shown in Figure 8-6.

Adding a test grid

The next thing you need is an image for mapping to your mesh. Using a *test grid* — basically an image with a colored checkerboard pattern — is common practice when unwrapping. A test grid is helpful for trying to figure out where the texture is stretched on your mesh. To add a test grid, go to the UV/Image Editor and choose Image⇨New or press Alt+N. A set of buttons like the ones in Figure 8-7 appear. Name the image something sensible, such as Test Grid, and left-click the UV Test Grid check box. Leave the other settings at their defaults for now. The UV/Image Editor updates interactively.

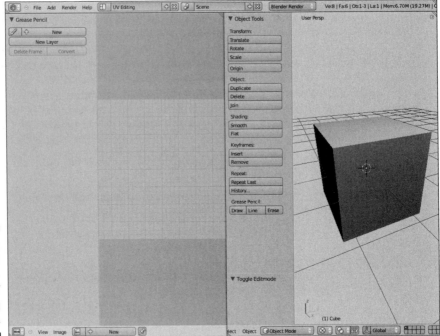

Figure 8-6:
A typical screen layout for UV unwrapping and editing.

Figure 8-7:
The New Image buttons for adding a test grid image.

TIP

You can unwrap your mesh without adding a test grid, but a test grid gives you a frame of reference to work from when unwrapping.

Also, note the height and width of the test grid image. The most obvious thing is that it's square; the height and width are equal. When you create the image, you can make it nonsquare, but UV texturing is optimized for square images, so it's in your best interest to keep it square.

Another tip that helps performance when working with UV textures is to make your texture size a *power of two* — a number that you get by continually multiplying 2 by itself. The default size is 1,024 pixels square, or 2^{10}. The next larger size is 2,048 (2^{11}) pixels, and the next size down would be 512 (2^9) pixels.

Generating and editing UV coordinates

All righty, after marking seams on your mesh and adding a test grid for reference, *now* you're ready to unwrap your mesh. From Edit mode, unwrapping is pretty simple:

1. **Select all vertices (A).**

   Remember that the A key is a toggle, so you may have to hit it twice to get everything selected.

2. **Unwrap the mesh (U⇨Unwrap).**

   Poof! Your mesh is now unwrapped! If you used a Suzanne to practice unwrapping, you may have something that looks like Figure 8-8.

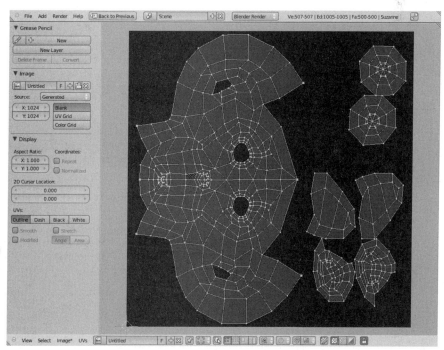

Figure 8-8:
An unwrapped Suzanne head.

From this point, you can edit your UV layout to arrange the pieces in a logical fashion and minimize *stretching*. You can tell a texture is stretched with your test grid. If any of the squares on the checkerboard look distorted or grotesquely nonsquare-shaped, stretching has taken place. If you don't see the test grid texture on your monkey, make sure that you're using Textured Viewport Shading (Alt+Z). The controls in the UV/Image Editor are very similar to working in the 3D View. The Grab (G), Rotate (R), and Scale (S) hotkeys all work as expected, as well as the various selection tools like Border select

(B), Circle select (C), and Edge Loop Selection (Alt+right-click). There's even a 2D cursor like the 3D cursor in the 3D View to help with snapping and providing a frame of reference for rotation and scaling.

If you're trying to fix stretching, you may notice that moving some vertices in your UV layout to fix stretching in one place distorts and causes stretching in another part. To help with this problem, Blender offers you two features: vertex pinning (P) and Live Unwrap (UVs⇨Live Unwrap). They actually work together. The workflow goes something like these steps:

1. **In the UV/Image Editor, select the vertices that you want to define as** *control vertices* **(right-click⇨Shift+right-click).**

   The control vertices are usually the vertices at the top and bottom of the center line and some corner vertices. I tend to prefer using vertices that are on the seam, but sometimes using internal vertices is also helpful.

2. **Pin these selected vertices (P).**

   The vertices now appear larger and are a bright red color. If you want to unpin a vertex, select it (right-click) and press Alt+P.

3. **Turn on Live Unwrap (UVs⇨Live Unwrap).**

   If a check mark appears to the left of this menu item, you know it's currently enabled.

4. **Select one or more pinned vertices and move them around (right-click⇨G).**

   As you edit these pinned vertices, all the other vertices in the UV layout automatically shift and adjust to compensate for this movement and help reduce stretching.

When using pinned vertices and Live Unwrap, selecting and moving unpinned vertices isn't normally going to be very helpful. The moment you select and move a pinned vertex, any manual changes you made to unpinned vertices are obliterated.

You can actually see the changes you make in the UV/Image Editor in real time if you left-click the Lock button (the last button with an icon of a lock) in the header of the UV/Image Editor. The Lock button is enabled by default. Of course, if your computer seems to be performing slowly with this option on, you can always disable it by left-clicking it.

Figure 8-9 shows the unwrapped Suzanne head from before, after a bit of editing and adjustment.

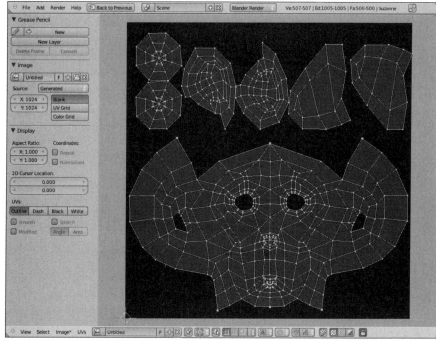

Figure 8-9:
An
unwrapped
and (mostly)
stretchless
Suzanne
head.

Painting Textures Directly on a Mesh

If you followed the earlier sections in this chapter, you have an unwrapped
mesh and a texture on it that doesn't stretch. Woohoo! But say that, for some
crazy reason, you don't want your object to have a checkerboard as a texture,
and you want to actually use this UV layout to paint a texture for your mesh.
You can either paint directly on the mesh from within Blender or export the UV
layout to paint in an external program like GIMP or Photoshop. I actually prefer
to use a combination of these methods. I normally paint directly on the mesh
in Blender to rough out the color scheme and perhaps create some bump
and specularity maps. Then I export that image along with an image of the UV
layout to get more detailed painting done in an external program.

After you have an unwrapped mesh, the starting point for painting textures
on it is Blender's Texture Paint mode. Activate Texture Paint mode by left-
clicking the mode button in the 3D View's header. From here, things are
pretty similar to Vertex Paint mode, with a few exceptions. The Tool Shelf
updates with an array of paint options, but the specific content of the Tool
Shelf has some differences from Vertex Paint. The Brush datablock is largely
the same, though with a few more preset brushes and a Jitter slider. There's
also a Texture panel in the Tool Shelf where you can actually define a texture
for your brush, so you're not just painting flat colors. You define the brush

texture in the Texture like you set up any other texture. Using Blender textures to paint UV textures gives your painting quite a bit more flexibility.

When you're in Texture Paint mode, start painting directly on your mesh by left-clicking and dragging your mouse cursor on it. If you have a test grid image already loaded on the image, you will begin painting directly on this image. In fact, if you still have the UV/Image Editor open, you can watch the test grid image get updated as you paint your mesh. And actually, you can paint directly on the UV image itself by enabling painting in the UV/Image Editor (Image⇨Image Painting). With Image Painting enabled in the UV/Image Editor, the Properties region in that editor has the same painting controls that are available in the Tool Shelf of the 3D View.

Because of this cool ability to paint in both the 3D View and the UV/Image Editor, when I paint textures in Blender, I like to have my screen laid out like Figure 8-10. I have the 3D View and UV/Image Editor both in Texture Paint mode. If I need to tweak a texture for my brush, I temporarily switch one of the areas to a Properties editor (Shift+F7) and make adjustments from Texture Properties. This layout and workflow is a pretty effective way to get work done.

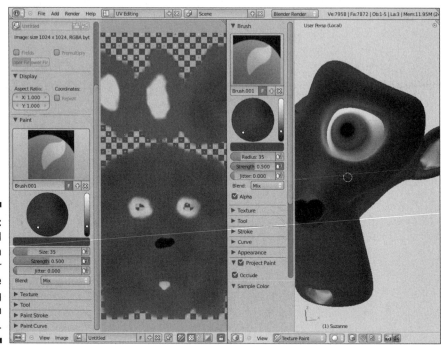

Figure 8-10:
A good screen layout for texture painting directly on your mesh.

Of course, despite the cool things that you can do with Blender's Texture Paint mode, you're better off doing some things in a full-blown 2D graphics program like GIMP or Photoshop. To work on your image in another program, you need to save the texture you already painted as an external image. You should also export your UV layout as an image so that you have a frame of reference to work from while painting.

To save your painted texture, go to the UV/Image Editor and choose Image⇨ Save As. A File Browser appears, allowing you to save the image to your hard drive in any format you like. I prefer to use PNG because it has small file sizes and lossless compression.

With your image saved, the next thing you probably want out of Blender for your 2D image editor is the UV layout of your object. To export the UV layout, you need to be in the UV/Image Editor while in Edit mode (Tab). Navigate to UVs⇨Export UV Face Layout. This brings up a File Browser where you can choose where to save your UV layout on your hard drive.

This UV export feature gives you the option to save in the familiar PNG format as well as two other formats: SVG and EPS. Both SVG (Scalable Vector Graphics) and EPS (Encapsulated PostScript) are vector image formats. If your UV layout is in a vector format, you can scale it to fit any image size you need without losing any resolution. So you can use the same UV layout file to paint both low-resolution and high-resolution textures.

Most graphics applications should be able to read SVG files just fine. If you run into a problem, though, I recommend opening the SVG in GIMP (`www.gimp.org`) or Inkscape (`www.inkscape.org`). Both applications are powerful open-source graphics programs, and they're included on this book's DVD. You can edit your UV texture directly in these programs, or you can use them to convert the SVG file to a raster format that your graphics application of choice recognizes, such as PNG or TIFF.

Baking Texture Maps from Your Mesh

Another benefit of unwrapping your mesh is *render baking*. Render baking is the process of creating a flat texture for your mesh that's based on what your mesh looks like when you render it. What good is that? Well, render baking is really useful to people who want to create models for use in video games. Because everything in a game has to run in real time, models can't usually have a lot of complicated lighting or highly detailed meshes with millions of vertices. To get around this limitation, you can fake some of these effects by using a texture. And rather than paint on shadows and detail by hand, you can let the computer do the work and use a high-resolution render instead.

Although this technique is used a lot in video games, render baking is also helpful when creating animated models for film or television. If you can create a model that looks really detailed but still has a relatively low vertex count, your rendering and animating process goes faster.

Another use of render baking is for texture painters. Sometimes it's helpful to have an ambient occlusion or shadow texture as a frame of reference to start painting a more detailed texture. A technique that I like to use is to first rough in colors with vertex painting (see Chapter 7). Then you can bake out those vertex colors to a texture, which can serve as a great starting point for a hand-painted texture.

So how do you create these baked textures? Well, the magic all happens in the Bake panel (see Figure 8-11) at the bottom of Render Properties.

Figure 8-11:
The Bake panel in Render Properties.

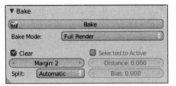

You have six different kinds of images that you can bake out:

- ✔ **Full Render:** This is the whole mess — textures, vertex colors, shadows, ambient occlusion, specular highlights — the works.

- ✔ **Ambient Occlusion:** *Ambient occlusion,* or AO, is an approximated form of *global illumination,* or the effect that happens from light bouncing off of everything. If you have AO enabled in World Properties, you can bake its results by choosing this option.

- ✔ **Shadow:** Any shadows that fall on this object are baked out as a texture.

- ✔ **Normals:** A normal map is similar to a bump map, but instead of just using a grayscale image to define height, normal maps can get even more detailed by using a full-color image to define height as well as direction. Artists who like to use Sculpt mode bake the normals from their sculpted mesh to a low-resolution version of the mesh to get details on the model without the additional geometry.

- ✔ **Textures:** This option takes all the textures you applied to the mesh, both image-based and procedural, and flattens them out to a single texture. This option is also what allows you to bake out vertex colors.

- ✔ **Displacement:** Baking displacement is similar to baking normals. The difference is that normal maps just redirect surface normals to provide the illusion of more geometry, whereas a displacement map can actually be used to move geometry around and create real depth on the surface of the object. Using displacement maps in Blender can be computationally expensive. However, a few third-party rendering engines have a nice way of handling displacement maps without the need to heavily subdivide your mesh.

After you have an unwrapped mesh, the steps to bake a new texture are pretty straightforward. Create a new image in the UV/Image Editor (Alt+N) at the size you want the texture to be and just choose the type of texture that you'd like to bake out from the Bake panel. Then left-click the Bake button and wait for the texture to be generated.

Using UV Textures

After you create a bunch of UV textures, either by painting them yourself or by baking them from the mesh, you need a way to bring them back into Blender and apply them to your mesh. This process is where Image textures in your Texture Properties come in. Figure 8-12 shows Texture Properties with image textures on two different texture slots, one for a color map and another for a bump map.

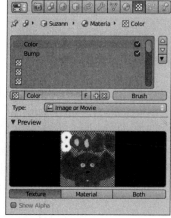

Figure 8-12:
Texture
Properties
with two
Image
textures
loaded.

The process for adding an Image texture is pretty similar to adding any of the procedural textures:

1. **Choose Image or Movie from the Type drop-down menu in Texture Properties.**

2. **In the Image panel, left-click the Open button.**

   A File Browser opens, and it's where you can find the image you want to load as a texture. Alternatively, if you already have an image loaded, you

can use this datablock to select that image by clicking the image datablock button on the left of the datablock field.

3. **Choose your image from the File Browser.**

4. **With the image loaded, choose Clip from the Extension drop-down
menu in the Image Mapping panel.**

This step isn't critical, but it's something I like to do. Basically, it prevents the image from tiling. Because I'm loading a UV texture, I don't
need it to tile.

5. **Choose UV as the type of Coordinates in the Mapping panel.**

This step tells the material to use your UV layout for texture coordinates
to properly place the texture. Even if the image isn't the original one you
painted in Texture Paint mode, as long as you painted the texture using
the UV layout as your reference, it should perfectly match your mesh.

6. **In the Influence panel, choose the material attributes you want the
texture to influence.**

If the texture is just a color map, left-click the Color check box. If it's a
bump map, left-click the Normal check box, and so on.

7. **Repeat Steps 1 through 6 for each texture channel that you want add a
UV image texture to.**

Practical Example: Unwrapping Your Eye and Painting a Detailed Texture

In the following example, you start with an eyeball model (see Chapter 5)
that you may have added basic materials to (see Chapter 7). (If you didn't do
those examples, you can find the file on the book's companion DVD.) While
the model looks pretty good, you can provide an additional splash of realism
to it. In particular, you can get a much more detailed iris, and you can add
some of the fine blood vessels around the white section of the eye.

Start this example by opening your eye .blend file or the one included in
this book's companion DVD in Blender and switch to the UV Editing screen
layout.

Marking seams and unwrapping

This example starts with marking your seams. Select your eye object and tab
into Edit mode. With this model, you don't really need to be concerned with
texturing the faces on the cornea/sclera. Because you don't have to worry
about texturing those faces, you also don't need to be overly concern with

unwrapping them. That being the case, if the faces for the cornea/sclera of your eye mesh are visible, make sure that no faces are selected and then select the faces that form the cornea by hovering your mouse over one of them and pressing L. Then hide those faces (H). Now you can focus on the part of the eye that really needs the detailed texture.

To make selection easier, you may want to enable the Limit Selection to Visible button in the 3D View's header.

To start marking your seams, set up your work environment in the following way:

1. **Switch to Edge Select mode (Ctrl+Tab).**

2. **Make sure that you're in solid viewport shading type (toggle with Z).**

3. **Toggle the 3D View to an orthographic view (Numpad 5) of the rear of your eye model (Ctrl+Numpad 1).**

Now, using Blender's selection tools, select edges around the pole on the back side of the eye, as shown on the right of Figure 8-13. The idea here is that you're only really concerned with how the front of the eye looks. Because the back of the eye is probably going to be all red anyway, stretched textures back there are much less of a concern.

Mark your selected edges as seams by using the UV Mapping⇨Mark Seam button in the Tool Shelf or by pressing Ctrl+E⇨Mark Seam in the 3D View. When you deselect all your edges by pressing A, your seams are clearly marked in red. Now, press A again to select all edges and then unwrap your eye mesh by either clicking the UV Mapping⇨Unwrap button in the Tool Shelf or by pressing U. In either case, choose the first item, Unwrap, from the menu that appears. Congratulations! You've unwrapped an eyeball. You result should look similar to the image in Figure 8-13.

Reducing texture stretching

After you unwrap your eye, it still looks pretty nasty. The UV layout is a kind of ugly star shape, and the edges are all uneven. Worse, the part that you want to detail the most — the iris and the area around it — takes up the least amount of space in your unwrap, so adding any real detail is difficult. You can see just how bad the situation is by generating a UV test grid image using the following steps:

1. **Create a new image by going to Image⇨New in the UV/Image Editor or by pressing Alt+N.**

2. **In the pop-up panel that appears, name your image test grid and enable the UV Test Grid check box prior to left-clicking OK.**

   Leave all other settings at their default values.

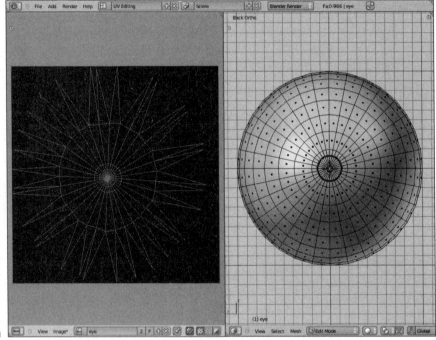

Figure 8-13:
On the right,
selecting
seams for
unwrapping
your eye-
ball. On the
left, your ini-
tial unwrap.

3. **In the 3D View, switch to textured viewport shading (Alt+Z).**

   If you don't see the test grid, you may still be using GLSL display in
   the 3D View. If this is the case, switch back to Multitexture by going
   to the Shading drop-down menu in the Display panel of the 3D View's
   Properties region (N).

The stretching in your UV layout is even more apparent if you go back to the
UV/Image Editor in its Properties region and change your test grid type from
UV Grid to Color Grid in the Image panel. Don't worry, though! All is not lost.
You just have to spend a few minutes in the UV/Image Editor.

First things first: Orienting your UVs so that they match the orientation of
your eye is a good idea. Just looking at the unwrap, it's hard to tell which way
is up. An easy way to take care of this problem is to go back to the 3D View
and use the following steps:

1. **Switch to Face Select mode (Ctrl+Tab) and deselect all faces (A).**

   All the edges and faces in the UV/Image Editor disappear. Don't panic!
   The edges and faces are still there; it's just that what's visible in the UV/
   Image Editor corresponds to the selected faces in the 3D View.

2. **Around the rear pole of the eye, select the four triangular faces
   around the vertical meridian.**

Your selection looks a bit like an hour glass. In the UV/Image Editor, the corresponding faces appear as two pairs of triangles pointing away from each other.

3. **In the UV/Image Editor, select the corner vertices where each pair of triangles connect and pin them by pressing P.**

   Those vertices are now marked in red.

4. **Enable Live Unwrap in the UV/Image Editor (UVs⇨Live Unwrap).**

5. **Return to the 3D View and select all faces (A⇨A).**

6. **In the UV/Image Editor, select your two pinned vertices and align them vertically.**

   You can do this step in two ways. Technically, the more correct way is to use weld/align operators (W⇨Align X) and then update the unwrap by pressing E. However, because you've enabled Blender's Live Unwrap, it's faster to scale the two vertices along the X-axis down to zero (S⇨X⇨0). Either way, the result is the same.

7. **Enable Constrain to Image Bounds (UVs⇨Constrain to Image Bounds), disable proportional editing (O), and select all vertices in the UV/ Image Editor (A⇨A).**

   These setup steps are all so that you can quickly maximize the amount of space your UV layout takes in its square.

8. **Scale your UVs so that they're as large as they can be without exceeding the size of the square that they're in.**

   If you enabled Constrain to Image Bounds in the last step, Blender automatically stops scaling when your UVs first hit the border of the square. You may have to grab (G) the UVs and move them around if they're not well centered.

9. **Unpin your vertices (Alt+P) and deselect all vertices (A).**

10. **Select the outermost loop of edges (Alt+right-click) and scale (S) that loop out so that it's as large as possible without overrunning the vertices at the tips of the outer triangles.**

    The next step is where the magic happens.

11. **Select all vertices and use Blender's Minimize Stretch feature (UVs⇨Minimize Stretch or Ctrl+V).**

    When you activate the Minimize Stretch feature, the vertices start moving out on their own in an effort to reduce the amount of stretching in the UVs. Eventually, your UV layout in the UV/Image Editor will start looking like the vertices aren't moving at all, which means that Blender has found the best solution that it can based on your initial layout.

12. **Press Enter to complete the operation.**

Figure 8-14 shows the results you should have at this point.

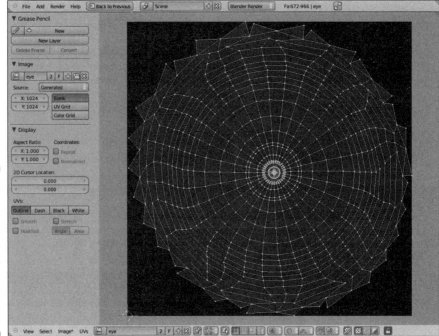

Figure 8-14:
UV coordi-
nates with
reduced
stretch-
ing thanks
to the
Minimize
Stretch
feature.

You still have a bit of noticeable stretching around the iris area. However, by going to the UV/Image Editor and enabling proportional editing (O), you can loop select (Alt+right-click) vertices around the iris and scale (S) them until you're satisfied. Don't worry so much about stretching as you get farther away from the iris. That part of the eyeball is rarely seen and generally has the same flat color anyway.

Baking vertex colors

After you have your eye unwrapped, you can get rolling with painting your textures. But why do by hand what Blender can do for you? Some people may call this part being lazy. I call it being efficient.

In the practical example in Chapter 7 (or in this example's start file from the companion DVD), Blender's Vertex Paint mode is used to paint in rough colors for your iris and the back of the eye. Why do the same work twice? You can use those vertex colors as the starting point for your more detailed image texture, thanks to render baking.

To bake your vertex colors to an image texture, use the following steps:

1. **While still in Edit mode, go to the UV/Image Editor and create a new image (Alt+N), named `eye`.**

   All the default settings should work just fine.

2. **Tab into Object mode and split your 3D View vertically.**

3. **Change the newly added area to a Properties editor (Shift+F7).**

4. **In Render Properties, expand the Bake panel at the bottom and set the Bake Mode drop-down menu to Textures.**

5. **Left-click the Bake button in the Bake panel of Render Properties.**

   You soon see the formerly black square in the UV/Image Editor update with the vertex colors that were applied to your eye model.

6. **Save your newly created image (F3).**

   You're saving for two reasons. First, saving your work is always a good idea. Second, now you can take your image texture and open it in any image editor, such as GIMP or Photoshop, and start painting details on top of your rough color.

Figure 8-15 shows the result of baking vertex colors to a texture.

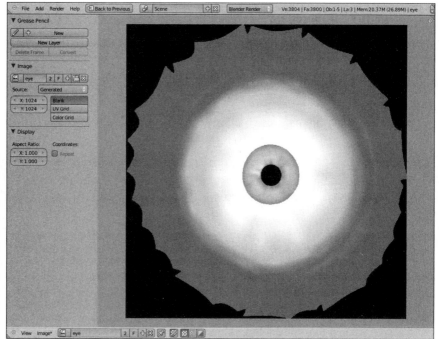

Figure 8-15:
After you bake your vertex colors to a texture, you can paint details on your eye in any painting program.

Assigning textures to your material

Before you get all crazy with going to other programs and painting your texture, it would be wise to disable the vertex colors on your eye mesh and apply your newly created image texture. To do so, switch back to the custom Materials layout (see Chapter 7). In the 3D View of this screen, make sure that you're using the textured viewport shading type (Alt+Z) and go to the 3D View's Properties region and confirm that the Display panel has GLSL as your active Shading method. At this point your 3D View looks *nearly* identical to the figure at the end of Chapter 7. However, your screen isn't identical; you have an image texture that you need to apply.

First, though, you need to disable your vertex colors by going to Material Properties and disabling the Vertex Color Paint check box in the Options panel. Now you're back to a boring gray interior for your eyeball. To apply your image texture, switch the right side Properties editor to Texture Properties and use the following steps:

1. **Create a new texture in the topmost texture slot and name it** `eyeball`.

   Create the new texture by left-clicking the New button in the texture datablock.

2. **Change the texture Type drop-down menu to the Image or Movie option.**

3. **In the Mapping panel, choose UV from the Coordinates drop-down menu.**

4. **In the Image panel, left-click the datablock button on the left and choose your eye image.**

5. **(Optional) In the Image Mapping panel at the bottom, change the Extension drop-down menu to Clip.**

   Although this step is optional, it's generally a good idea. Now your image texture is applied to your eye.

If you did these steps correctly right, your 3D View should look nearly identical to the vertex color results you had before disabling vertex colors on your model. The difference now, however, is that you can add even more detail. Woohoo!

Painting textures

You can paint your texture in an image-editing program like GIMP or Photoshop, but you may not have to. You can add a lot of detail within Blender using a combination of the UV/Image Editor and Texture Paint mode in the 3D View.

If you haven't already, switch back to the UV Editing screen layout and get rid of the Properties editor that you split in the previous section on baking. You don't need it; this part is all about painting.

Image painting in the UV/Image Editor

Probably the quickest and easiest way to start painting is to hop right into the UV/Image Editor and enable Image Painting mode (Image⇨Image Painting or left-click the paintbrush icon in the UV/Image Editor's header). The Properties region of the UV/Image Editor updates with a set of paint tools you can use.

For any kind of texture painting, I highly recommend that you use a pen-based drawing tablet like those made by Wacom. This tablet takes a little bit of time to get used to, but it's a much more natural drawing and digital painting experience.

After you enter Image Paint mode in the UV/Image Editor, you can start painting directly on your image texture. The really cool thing is that, as you paint, your model in the 3D View updates in real time. With this feature, you can start cleaning up your vertex colors, add little blood vessels to the eye, and produce a more detailed iris texture.

Using Texture Paint mode

On some models, however, the disconnect between painting on the image and seeing the result on the mesh is too disorienting. Predicting how the texture will ultimately lay on the mesh is sometimes too difficult. In these cases, painting directly in the 3D View is often easier. For painting in the 3D View, I prefer to use the Multitexture Shading style, which you can set from the 3D View's Properties region in the Display panel. Although you don't see the lighting results that you get when using GLSL, the texture colors are more vibrant and close to what you're actually painting.

When you switch into Texture Paint mode using the Modes drop-down menu in the 3D View's header, you may notice that, like when vertex painting in Chapter 7's example, your interior eye is obscured by the cornea/sclera faces. You need to hide those faces and use the Face Selection Masking feature. Fortunately, because this model has been vertex painted, those faces should still be hidden. You can quickly tell by enabling the Face Selection Masking button. If you're able to see the interior eye parts, then you're good to go. Press A a couple times to make sure that all the faces in the eye mesh are selected. Now you can paint directly on the eye, using the brush and paint tools available in the Tool Shelf. In fact, something I like to do is leave Image Painting mode active in the UV/Image Editor and Texture Paint active in the 3D View at the same time. Then you can switch between painting on the image and painting on the mesh, depending on what your specific needs are.

With a little bit of work, you can get a texture on your mesh like the shown in Figure 8-16.

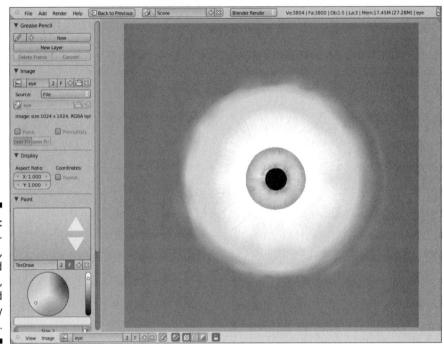

Figure 8-16: A completed, detailed eye texture, painted completely in Blender.

Chapter 9

Lighting and Environment

- -

In This Chapter

▶ Taking advantage of different types of lights in Blender

▶ Setting up effective lighting

▶ Changing the look of your scene with background images, colors, and ambient occlusion

- -

*I*n terms of getting the work you create in Blender out to a finalized still image or animation, having your scene's environment and lighting set up properly is incredibly important. It goes along hand in hand with setting up materials on your object (see Chapter 7) as well as the rendering process (see Chapter 14). Without light, the camera — and by extension, the renderer — can't see a thing. You could create the most awesome 3D model or animation in the world, but if it's poorly lit, it won't be turning any heads.

This chapter covers the types of lights available to you in Blender and details some of the best practices to use them in your scenes. In addition to lighting details, I go into setting up the environment in your scene with the settings in World Properties. In many ways, the topics covered in this chapter are what give your scenes that final polish, making them look really good.

Lighting a Scene

Lighting has an incredible amount of power to convey your scene to the viewer. Harsh, stark lighting can give you a dramatic film noir look. Low-angle lights with long shadows can give you a creepy horror movie feeling, whereas brighter high-angle lights can make things look like they are taking place during a beautiful summer day. Or, you can use a bluish light that projects a hard noise cloud texture and makes your scene feel like it's happening under water.

Equally important is setting up your environment. Depending on how you set it up, you can achieve a variety of looks. You can set your scene in an infinitely large white space, commonly known as *the white void* in film and television. Or, you can adjust your environment such that your scene takes place outside during the day or somewhere on the moon. When you combine good lighting and a few additional tricks, you can make your scene take place just about anywhere. Figure 9-1 shows a pretty simple scene with a few different environment and lighting schemes to illustrate this point.

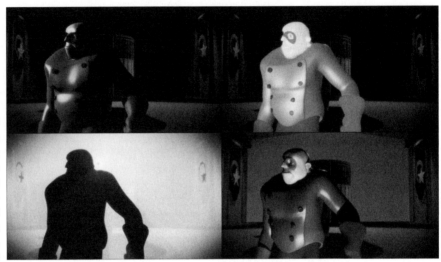

Figure 9-1: Different lighting configurations can drastically affect the look of a scene.

Understanding a basic three-point lighting setup

Before I get too deep into how you light a scene in Blender, you should understand some standard lighting setups and terminology. The cool thing is that most of this information isn't limited to use in 3D computer graphics. It's actually pretty standard in professional film, video, and still photography. In fact, quite a few photographers and directors like to use 3D graphics as a form of previsualization to test out lighting setups before arriving on set for the actual shoot. (And you thought you were just making pretty pictures on a computer screen! Ha!)

One of the most common ways to arrange lights is called *three-point lighting*. As the name implies, it involves the use of three different sets of lights. It's a common studio setup for interviews, and it's the starting point for nearly all other lighting arrangements. Figure 9-2 shows a top-down illustration of a typical three-point lighting setup.

The key light

Setting up a three-point lighting scheme starts with placing your subject at the center of the scene and aiming your camera at that subject. Then you set up your main light, the *key light*. The key light is usually the most powerful light in the scene. It's where your main shadows come from, as well as your brightest highlights. Typically, you want to set this light just to the left or just to the right of your camera, and you usually want it to be higher than your subject. This placement is to ensure that the shadows fall naturally, and you don't get that creepy flashlight-under-the-chin look that your friends used for telling scary stories around the campfire.

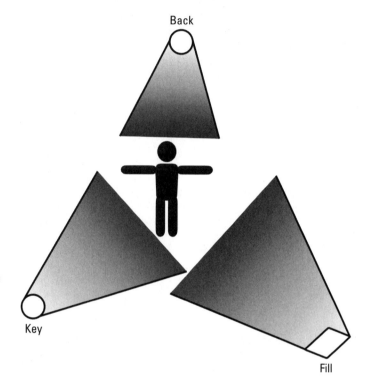

Back

Key

Fill

Figure 9-2:
A typical three-point lighting setup.

The fill light

After your key light is established, the next light you want to place is the *fill light*. The purpose of the fill light is to brighten up the dark parts of your subject. See, the key light is great for putting shadows on your subject, but without any other light, your shadows end up being stark black, obscuring your subject. Unless you're aiming for a dramatic lighting effect, this effect is not what you normally want. The fill light tends to be less powerful than the key, but you want it to have a wider, more diffuse throw. The *throw* is the radius of space that the light reaches. For example, a flashlight has a narrow throw, whereas fluorescent lights like the ones used in office buildings throw light wider. You want this wide throw on your fill because it reduces the amount of highlight generated by this light. Typically, you don't want highlights from your fill to compete with the highlights from your key. As far as placement goes, you normally want to place your fill on the opposite side of the camera from the key and roughly at the same height as your subject.

Here's a way to figure out a good place to position your fill light. Draw an imaginary line from your key light to your subject. Now, with your subject as the pivot point, rotate that line 90 degrees. When you do, the line points right where you should place the fill.

The back light

The last light in a three-point lighting configuration is the *back light* or *rim light*. This light shines at the back of your subject, creating a small edge of light around the profile. That sliver of light helps separate your subject from the background and serves as the nice little bit of polish that often separates a mediocre lighting setup from a really good one.

Now, I've sat through many long discussions about the best way to position a back light (yes, my friends are nerds, too). Some people like to place it directly opposite from the key light, which works well, but sometimes the rim effect competes with the key's highlights. Other people prefer placing it opposite to the camera, which, too, is a good way to go, but if the subject moves, you risk the possibility of blinding the audience. And yet another group of people recommend placing the back light opposite to the fill. This approach can create a nice rim of light that complements the key, but it also has the possibility of looking a bit unnatural. As you can see, everything is a tradeoff when it comes to lighting. In fact, the only really consistent thing that people agree on is that the light should generally point toward the subject. The bottom line is that the best course of action is to play around with your back light and see for yourself where you get the best results.

As for the power and throw, you typically want to use a back light that is less powerful than your key so things appear natural. The throw can vary because the highlights are all on the opposite side of your subject. I personally like to keep it narrow, but a wide throw can work nicely for large scenes.

That's basic three-point lighting for you. It works well in computer graphics as well as the "real world" and it's the starting point for most other lighting configurations. Lower the angle of your key to make your subject creepy. Remove or reduce the power of your fill and back lights to get more dramatic shadows. Place your key behind your subject to get a mysterious or romantic silhouette. And that's just the tip of the iceberg!

Knowing when to use which type of lamp

After you're familiar with the basic principles of three-point lighting, you can use that knowledge to light your scenes in Blender. To add a new light, use Shift+A⇨Lamp and you see the menu shown in Figure 9-3.

Figure 9-3:
Adding a
lamp in the
3D View.

The Lamp menu offers you the following types of lights to choose from:

- **Point:** This type of light is sometimes also referred to as an *omni light,* meaning that the light is located at a single point in space and emanates in all directions from that point. The default Blender scene has a single light of this type. The Point lamp is a good general-purpose light, but I prefer to use it as secondary illumination or as a fill light.

- **Sun:** The Sun lamp represents a single universal light that comes from a single direction. Because of this single source, the location of the Sun lamp in your scene doesn't really matter; only its orientation is relevant. This type of light is the only one that affects the look of the sky and is well suited as a key light for scenes set outdoors.

- **Spot:** In many ways, the Spot is the workhorse of CG lighting. It works quite a bit like a flashlight or a theater spotlight, and of all the light types, it gives you the most control over the nature of the shadows and where light lands. Because of this control, Spots are fantastic key lights.

- **Hemi:** A Hemi lamp is very similar to the Sun lamp in that it doesn't matter where you place the lamp in your scene. Its orientation is its most important aspect. However, because it's treated as a full hemisphere of light around the scene, lighting from a Hemi tends to be softer and flatter than the sun. Hemis are also the only Blender lights that cannot cast shadows. I like using them for fills and back lights. They're also handy for outdoor lighting.

- **Area:** Area lights are powerful lights that behave similar to Spots; however, the shadows tend to be softer and more accurate because they're based on having a grid of lights to work with. As a result, they work well for key lights, but because they tend to take more time to process, you should use them sparingly.

Figure 9-4 shows what each light type looks like in the 3D View.

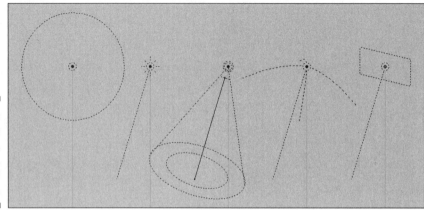

Figure 9-4:
From left to right, Point, Sun, Spot, Hemi, and Area lights.

Universal lamp options

When you've chosen a type of lamp and added it to the scene, the controls to modify these lamps are in Object Data Properties. When you have a lamp selected, the Object Data Properties button in the Properties editor features a lamp icon. With a couple of exceptions, all the lamps share a few of the same controls. Figure 9-5 highlights the options that are universal for nearly all lights.

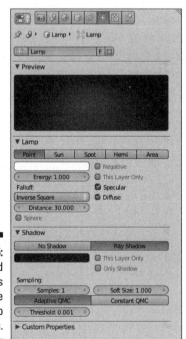

Figure 9-5:
Panels and options available for all lamp types.

One cool thing about Blender's lamps is that you can instantly change lamp types whenever you want. Simply select the lamp you want to work with and choose the type of lamp you would like it to be in the Lamp panel. This feature is great for quickly sorting out the type of light you want to use. You can test out different lighting schemes without cluttering the scene by having a bunch of extraneous lights that you have to move to other layers or hide.

The Energy value and color swatch control the strength and color of the lamp. I rarely set the Energy to a value greater than 1.000, but when you need it, it's handy to have the option. And, of course, to set the color for your lamp, left-click the color swatch and use Blender's color picker.

The Distance value is only available for the Point, Spot, and Area lamps. The value is in the units you define in Scene Properties and, if an object is farther away from the light than that distance, it receives no light. For each of the light types, an indicator defines the range of this value. For the Area lamp, it's a line pointing in the direction that the light is facing. For the Spot, it's the length of the cone. For the Point lamp, no indicator is on by default, but if you enable the Sphere check box in the Lamp panel, a dashed circle appears to indicate the distance of the Point lamp's throw. If you don't see this circle immediately, you may have to zoom out in the 3D View so that you can see it.

Be careful when enabling the Sphere check box on the Point lamp. It subtly changes how the light works. With Sphere enabled, light coming from the Point lamp starts to weaken, or *attenuate,* starting at the light's location, so by the time it gets to the Distance value, no light is available. However, if you have Sphere disabled, that attenuation doesn't start until you actually reach that Distance value, so you have a farther throw. Having Sphere enabled makes the light behave more like it would in meatspace, but it's often more convenient to keep it disabled. In either case, you can control how dramatically that attenuation occurs by using the Falloff drop-down menu. The default value of Inverse Square behaves the most like real-world lights.

With the exception of the Hemi lamp, each lamp has the option of using ray tracing to cast shadows. Ray traced shadows are enabled by left-clicking the Ray Shadow button in the Shadow panel, and it's the default behavior for new lights. Know, however, that using ray traced shadows can drastically increase your render times. The next section goes more deeply into some techniques for optimizing your lighting to try to deal with that. However, if you do want to use ray traced shadows, you should be aware of a few options:

- ✔ **Shadow color:** Left-click this swatch to get a color picker for selecting the color of your cast shadow. Of course, this isn't physically accurate. Real-world shadows are always black unless other lighting is present.

- ✔ **Samples:** This option dictates how many samples the ray traced shadow uses. Increasing this value increases the accuracy of the shadows at the expense of longer render times.

Adaptive QMC

Without getting too deep into all the crazy mathematical details, understanding QMC requires knowing a little bit more about how ray tracing works. In Chapter 7, I give a brief description of ray tracing that says it's done by tracing each and every vector of light bouncing from the light source(s) to the camera. This description is somewhat oversimplified. Tracing *every single vector* would take an incredibly excessive amount of time. In order to get around that, programmers decided to take a sampling of those vectors and approximate everything in between them. To choose which sample vectors to select, they first tried just randomly picking them. The problem, though, is that raw random selection doesn't give consistent or accurate results. Samples aren't necessarily where they're most useful. So to accommodate that, it was decided that samples could be random, but evenly dispersed. Evenly dispersed random sampling is basically constant QMC. Of course, the downside to constant QMC is that you still might be taking samples from parts of the scene that don't need very many. If you can stay random, but have more of the samples taken from busier parts of the scene, you might get better performance. This logic is behind adaptive QMC.

- ✔ **Soft Size:** This option controls how blurry the edge of your cast shadows are. The higher the value, the blurrier the shadow. However, with only one sample (the previous option), the shadows won't blur that much. Blurry shadows require more samples.

- ✔ **QMC Sampling Types:** You generally have the choice between Adaptive QMC and Constant QMC. QMC stands for Quasi-Monti Carlo and is an algorithm for taking random samples. Generally speaking, the Adaptive QMC setting gives you faster render times and better results.

- ✔ **Threshold:** This option is available only when you choose the Adaptive QMC sampling type. It basically helps the renderer decide which samples to use and which ones to ignore. A higher Threshold value shortens your render times, but may decrease accuracy.

Like with materials for objects, you can also apply textures to your lights and apply them to the lamp's color, its shadow's color, or both. This ability is a great way to use lighting to enhance the environment of your scene or to fake certain lighting effects that are typically only achievable with ray tracing. One specific example is caustic effects. If you have some free time, take a glass of water and shine light through it. Due to the refractive nature of the glass and the water, you usually see a strange light pattern on the table near or around the glass. That effect is an example of caustics and, if you don't need 100 percent accuracy, you can fake it with a Clouds texture on a Spot lamp.

On a larger scale, caustics are what make the cool moving patterns you can see on the bottom of a swimming pool. To add a texture to your selected lamp, use Texture Properties and use the same procedures covered for texturing materials as described in Chapter 8.

Light-specific options

As you can see in Figure 9-5, the Point lamp has options that are available on nearly every other lamp but doesn't have much in the way of unique controls. The same could actually be said of the Hemi lamp. In fact, it has even fewer controls because Hemis can't cast shadows. However, the remaining three lights have some interesting options that allow you to optimize their usage to meet your needs.

Options specific to Sun lamps

The Sun lamp is incredibly useful because it has the ability to behave more like the real sun. It's the only type of light that Blender has that influences the look of the sky and even provides some atmospheric effects. You control this lamp with the Sky & Atmosphere panel that appears when you set your lamp to be a Sun. By default, both the Sky and Atmosphere check boxes are disabled, but you can enable them with a left-click. Figure 9-6 shows the options as they pertain to the Sun light type.

When you enable the Sky check box, you can use the controls in its panel to determine how the Sun lamp influences the sky background. At the top of the panel is the Turbidity value. Keep Turbidity low for clear day skies and increase it for hazy, overcast skies. When you see the sky on a clear day — the real sky outside; you know, in the for-really-real world —that it's lighter near the horizon and darker as you look farther up. The Brightness and Size values under the Horizon label control this effect in Blender. The Brightness and Size values under the Sun label adjust your sun's visibility.

If you try to render your scene, you may not see the sun in your sky, even if you've placed the Sun lamp within your camera's view. Because the position of the Sun lamp is irrelevant and only its orientation is important, you have to rotate the lamp so that it points in the opposite direction of the camera's orientation.

When you enable the Atmosphere check box, you can control the sun's influence on how the air in your scene looks from a distance. These options are best suited where you have a wide outdoor shot of your scene's environment. There's really no good way to preview the effects of these values other than to do test renders. Here's a quick guideline to help understand what each one does:

- ✔ **Sun:** This value adjusts the influence of the Sun's intensity on the atmosphere. Increasing it makes objects in the distance bluer.

- ✔ **Distance:** This value controls the distance that the atmosphere has an influence. At low values, you see everything. Increasing this value, the light becomes yellower, and distant objects become more like silhouettes.

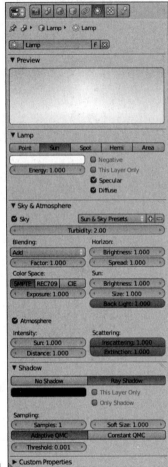

Figure 9-6:
Controls
for the Sun
lamps.

✔ **Inscattering:** Increasing this value makes the light appear to scatter more between the camera and the objects it's pointing at. Set this value to 1.0 for the most physically accurate results.

✔ **Extinction:** Lower numbers for this option reduce the amount of detail seen in your objects. This setting is similar to Distance, except it doesn't really matter how close objects are to the camera. Like Inscattering, you get the most physically accurate results with a value of 1.0.

Options specific to Spot lamps

When working with Spot lamps, you have the option of two different ways to cast shadows: ray tracing or buffers. The simplest way to know the difference between the two is to know that, generally speaking, ray traced shadows are more accurate whereas buffered shadows render faster.

What would a book on Blender be without some full-color images in it? Well, it'd be black and white, yes, but it would also be a bit lacking in showing how to use Blender; not to mention all the cool art that's been created with it. Have a look through here and enjoy the full-color glory.

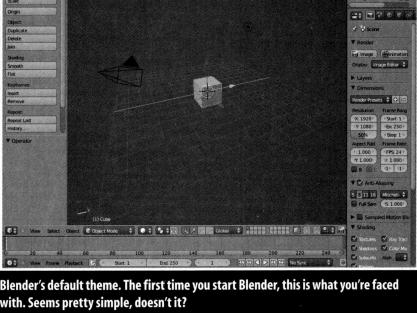

Blender's default theme. The first time you start Blender, this is what you're faced with. Seems pretty simple, doesn't it?

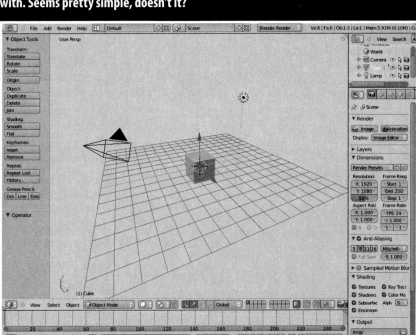

You can change Blender's theme to suit your tastes. This image features the custom theme I made to help make screenshots more readable in the black-and-white pages of this book.

A few frames from *Sintel*, the latest open movie project from the Blender Institute, codenamed Durian.

Keyboard reference for the hotkeys on the numeric keypad.

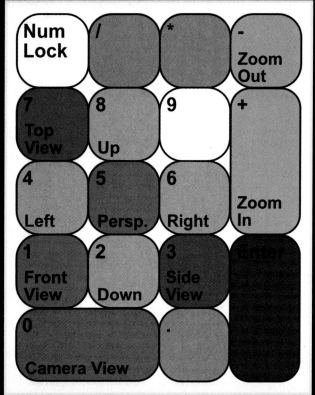

Num Lock	/	*	- Zoom Out
7 Top View	8 Up	9	+
4 Left	5 Persp.	6 Right	Zoom In
1 Front View	2 Down	3 Side View	Enter
0 Camera View	.		

A frame from *Big Buck Bunny*, the Peach open movie project from the Blender Institute.

A screen capture from *Yo Frankie!*, the Apricot project and the first open video game from the Blender Institute.

Claudio Andaur, known as malefico, is an incredible Argentinian Blender artist who runs Licuadora Studio in Buenos Aires and gained quite a bit of success. He created this image as part of his film, *Mercator*. This image is also on the cover of the book he coauthored with Tony Mullen, *Blender Studio Projects: Digital Movie-Making*, published by Sybex.

Claudio also created this fun little image. As an interesting side note, the appearance of pages in the book in this image is entirely faked using a texture bump map. See Chapter 8 for more information on texturing.

Another very cool image from Claudio Andaur. Let's hope the guy in this image doesn't look up. He'd get dizzy and fall!

Computer graphics isn't always about getting super-realistic images. Mark Cannon shows with this image that you can get some really cool nonphotorealistic images out of Blender, too. Do note that Mark did this with an experimental branch of Blender that uses a renderer called Freestyle. That branch is planned to be merged with the official version after Blender 2.6 is released.

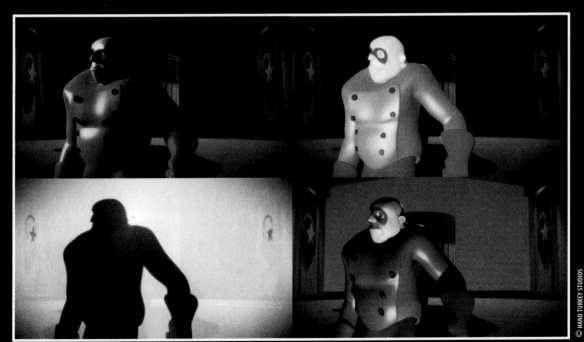

A color version of Figure 9-1, showing some of the different dramatic effects you can achieve by simply changing the lighting. This image was produced as part of a short animation called *Grey Justice: Puncher of Men* by my company, Hand Turkey Studios.

Sam Brubaker is a longtime Blender artist who won a Suzanne Award for animation while he was still in high school. (The Suzanne Awards are a part of the annual Blender Conference in Amsterdam.) In this image, Sam integrates heavy use of Blender's texture system and adds a splash of action with the fluid simulator.

Sam also uses Blender to create his Web comic, *Us the Robots*. This image is a still shot from that comic. Laugh!

Dolf Veenvliet, known as macouno in the Blender community, released this image, called *Sentry*, shortly after his time working at the Blender Institute on the Durian open movie project.

An incredible render from Mike Pan. Mike has been doing a lot of work in Blender's integrated game engine recently, but he still found the time to kick out this excellent image with Blender 2.5 while it was still very early in its development.

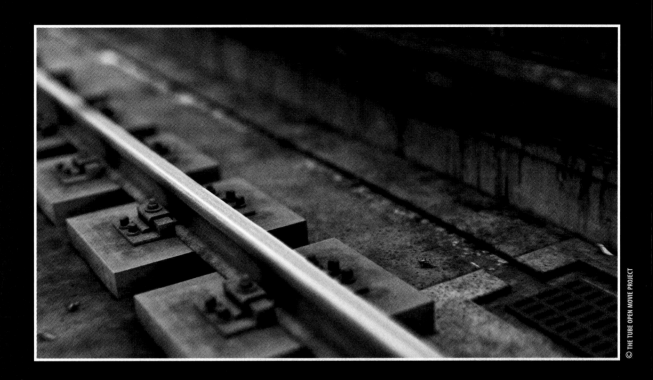

These two images are stills from a teaser for *Tube,* an animation currently in production by this book's Technical Editor, Bassam Kurdali. Bassam, also known as slikdigit, was also the director of the Blender Institute's first open movie project, *Elephants Dream*.

Blender is also being used by Morpho Animation Studio in Costa Rica to produce children's television shows and television commercials. These two images are stills from one of their shows, *Poison Squad*.

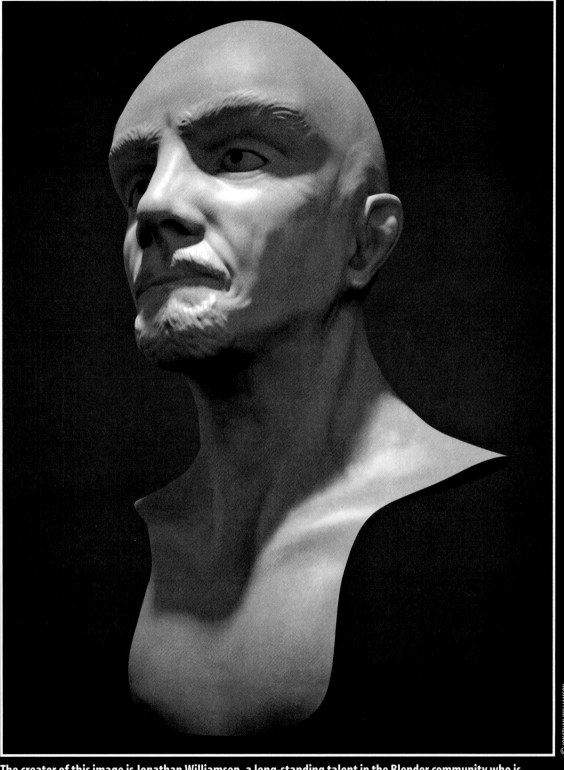

The creator of this image is Jonathan Williamson, a long-standing talent in the Blender community who is known for his clean, detailed models and the sickening speed at which he works. (He produced this image in a couple of hours.) Jonathan regularly posts high-quality tutorials on BlenderCookie.com. I highly recommend that you check them out.

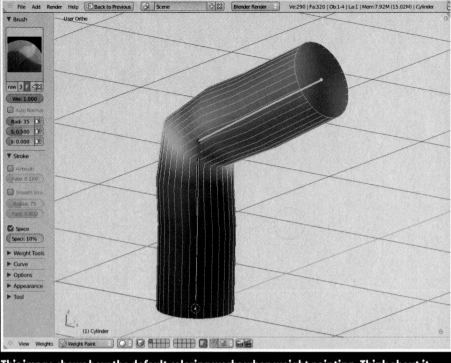

This image shows how the default coloring works when weight painting. Think about it like a thermal graph. Red is hot and the highest weight, whereas blue is cold and therefore represents no weight at all.

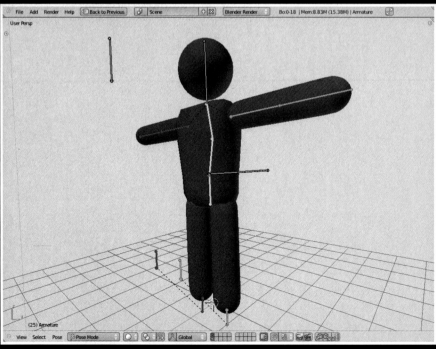

Stickman has colored bone groups!

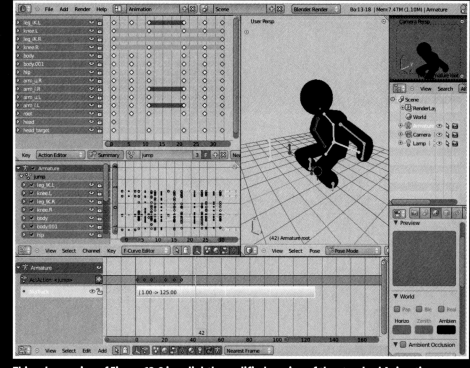

This color version of Figure 12-8 is a slightly modified version of the standard Animation screen that comes with Blender. In this example, the Timeline has been changed to an NLA Editor.

Sebastian König is an incredibly talented Blender artist out of Germany, as this image clearly shows. You can find out more about how Sebastian works by following his Blender tutorials at cmiVFX.com.

Another awesome image displaying the talents of Sebastian König. In particular, pay attention to the detail in the combing he did on the mammoth's fur. You can read more about Blender's particle-based hair system in Chapter 13.

Regardless of which type of shadows you cast (if you decide to cast shadows at all with this lamp), a handful of settings are available in the Spot Shape panel:

- ✔ **Size:** This setting controls the width of the Spot's throw, measured in degrees. So a value of 180 degrees is completely wide, whereas a value of 30 degrees gives you a narrower cone. Unless I'm doing something special, I like to start with my Spots with a Size value around 60 degrees.

- ✔ **Blend:** Blend controls the sharpness of the edges at the boundary where the Spot's cone of influence ends. Lower values give you a crisp edge, whereas higher values soften it, making the light appear more diffuse.

- ✔ **Halo:** Enabling this check box allows the renderer to show the full cone of light generated by the Spot. This is called *volumetric* light. You see this effect when you use a flashlight in a dusty room or when you want the "sunbeams from the sky" effect.

- ✔ **Intensity:** Specifically speaking, this value controls Halo Intensity. This value has no influence unless you enable the Halo check box. If Halo is enabled, increasing this value brightens the volumetric effect.

- ✔ **Square:** Enable this check box if you would prefer the Spot lamp to come from a square source rather than a round one.

- ✔ **Show Cone:** New to Blender, this feature is incredibly cool and useful. When you enable the Show Cone check box, Blender allows you to more clearly see the volume of the cone, making it much easier to see what objects are within your Spot lamp's influence area.

Using buffered shadows instead of ray traced ones, the options in the Shadow panel change. All the ray traced shadow controls are replaced with a different set of options because buffered shadows use an image-based process instead of ray tracing. You have more ways to control how the shadows look because you're no longer constrained by the limits of reality. Figure 9-7 shows the various settings for a Spot lamp with buffered shadows.

Trying to sort out all these controls can be daunting. However, the following values are the most important ones that you should know about:

- ✔ **Sample Buffers:** In essence, Sample Buffers are basically the same as the Samples values discussed elsewhere throughout this chapter, but they're specifically for helping render hair and fur more effectively. Higher values give better results, but at the cost of more system memory when rendering. Unless you're rendering hair or fine detail, keep this set to 1.

- ✔ **Size:** Buffered shadows is an image-based technique. The shadow buffer size is the resolution of the image used to create the shadows. Lower values work faster, but look more jagged.

Figure 9-7:
Controls for
a buffered
Spot lamp.

✔ **Samples:** Each sample is an offset copy of the shadow buffer. Soft
shadow edges come from mixing samples, so a higher value makes them
look better. Render time does increase with more samples, but because
buffered shadows are typically much faster than ray traced shadows, it's
okay to splurge a bit and allow yourself a few extra samples.

✔ **Soft:** Increasing this value makes your shadows softer and blurrier. To
use this setting effectively, make sure that you have a Samples value
greater than 1. And at the same time, you get the best results by not
setting the Soft value higher than double your Samples value. So at the
default Samples setting of 3, you should keep your Soft value below 6.

✔ **Bias:** This value offsets the shadow from where it connects to the
shadow-casting object. Occasionally, you may get some weird jaggies or
artifacts in your shadows. Increasing the Bias can help get rid of those
artifacts. If you do have to adjust the Bias, adjust it only as low as it can
go before you get artifacts in your renders. Otherwise, your shadows
will begin to look very unnatural. A good practice is to do a series of test

renders starting with a Bias value of 0.1 and working your way up until you no longer see artifacts.

✔ **Clip Start/Clip End:** Consider these values as a secondary control in addition to the Distance value in the Lamp panel. Objects that appear within these two values, indicated by a line on the Spot lamp in the 3D View, cast shadows, whereas objects outside of this range do not. Keeping the Clip values as close to your shadow-casting objects as possible gives you the most accurate results. If you don't want to adjust these values manually, enable the Autoclip check box to either value. Blender then automatically sets the Clip values to include objects within the Spot's cone.

✔ **Halo Step:** This value is in the Spot Shape panel and has an effect only if you have the Halo check box enabled. Adjusting it controls your *volumetric shadow*, or how much of the volumetric effect your object blocks. Higher values render faster, but are less accurate. Setting it to 1 gives you the best, albeit the slowest, results. However, setting it to 0 means that you have no volumetric shadow, so you have the volumetric cone, but your object won't block it at all.

Options specific to Area lamps

Area lamps are very similar to Spots, except Area lamps can use ray tracing only for creating shadows. The shadows are generally smoother and more accurate; however, they can increase your render time dramatically. Figure 9-8 shows the options and settings for Area lights.

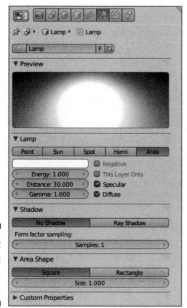

Figure 9-8:
The controls for Area lights.

The way an Area light works is pretty simple. Imagine that at the lamp's location, you don't have a single light, but instead you have a grid of lights, and you can control the width and height of this grid as well as the number of lights in it. As a result, you have even more control over your lamp's throw.

To control the dimensions of your Area lamp, use the Size value in the Area Shape panel. This size is measured in units chosen in Scene Properties and, by default, controls both the width and the height of the Area lamp. You control the number of lights in the Area lamp by adjusting the Samples value in the Shadow panel. Because the default shape of the lamp is a square, increasing the number of samples gives you the square of the sample value. So setting Samples to 3 creates 9 lights in the grid, and setting it to 5 creates 25 lights in the grid.

If you'd rather have a rectangular Area lamp, left-click the Rectangle button in the Area Shape panel. When you do, you can set the width (Size X) and height (Size Y) of your Area lamp. In addition, the Samples value in the Shadow panel changes to Samples X and Samples Y, giving you control over the number of horizontal and vertical lights you have on your Area light's grid. The total of lights you have in the grid is the value of Samples X multiplied by the value of Samples Y. Figure 9-9 shows an illustration of how the lights are arranged in square and rectangular Area lamps.

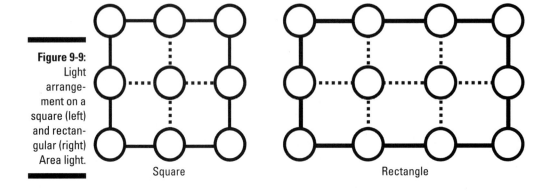

Figure 9-9:
Light arrangement on a square (left) and rectangular (right) Area light.

Square   Rectangle

When working with Area lights, remember that you actually have multiple lights arranged on the lamp's grid, which can make an Area light with an Energy of 1.0 excessively bright. So if you use an Area lamp, try a much lower Energy value. Depending on the number of samples in your Area lamp, you may want to start as low 0.050.

Lighting for Speedy Renders

Six additional controls for lamps exist. I like to refer to them as my "cheat buttons" because they're incredibly useful for achieving lighting effects that are difficult or impossible in the real world. The functions that these options control are really what makes lighting in 3D computer graphics so powerful. More often than not, if you use these controls effectively, they can speed up your render times without having a negative effect on the overall quality of your image. Figure 9-10 highlights these controls in the lamp Object Data Properties.

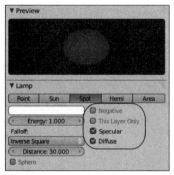

Figure 9-10: The cheat buttons in the Lamp panel.

Here are descriptions of each cheat button in the Lamp panel:

- ✔ **Negative:** What this check box enables is, in my opinion, one of the coolest capabilities in CG lighting: inverting the light's output. You can basically shine *darkness* on your scene, an impossibility in meatspace that opens the door to all sorts of interesting uses. If part of your scene is too bright or you want to have deeper shadows, don't play with adjusting the Energy of your lights or increasing the Samples for your shadows. Just shine some darkness on the area with a negative light!

- ✔ **This Layer Only:** Enabling this control makes the light illuminate only the objects that are on the same layer as the light. In real-world lighting, technicians do a lot of work to hide or mask out some lights, so they illuminate only certain parts of the scene. For example, you may want to brighten up the environment without making the lighting on your characters any brighter. Because you're in CG, you don't have to mask anything out: You just enable this check box and make sure that your characters aren't on the same layer as the light.

- ✔ **Specular:** In three-point lighting, you want to reduce the highlights produced by the fill so that they don't compete with the key's highlights. Meatspace lighting technicians often attempt to reduce the highlights by diffusing the fill as much as possible. In Blender, you don't have to go through the trouble. You can just turn off the lamp's specular highlights altogether by disabling this check box. Pretty sweet, huh?

- ✔ **Diffuse:** Sometimes when you're lighting, you want to have fine control of your highlights, but you don't want to change the basic illumination of the scene. If you turn off shadow casting for the light and disable this check box, you're basically left with a specular highlight that you can move around your subject at will. This feature isn't commonly used, but having it available has certainly made my life easier more than once.

The last two cheat buttons are in the Shadow panel, farther down Object Data Properties for lamps. The following describes each one:

- **This Layer Only:** This check box works like the corresponding checkbox in the Lamp panel, but only relates to shadows.

- **Only Shadow:** Enabling this option allows your lamp to cast shadows without adding more light to the scene. I sometimes use this option to reduce render times by using buffered Spots for shadows while using other lamps without shadows for main illumination.

Any object — even lamps — can exist on multiple layers. This ability dramatically increases the power of layer-only lamps and shadows. With the lamp selected, press M to reveal the layer selection pop-up. To place your lamp on more than one layer, Shift+left-click the layer buttons you want it on.

I often tell people that when it comes to computer graphics, if you're not cheating or faking something, you're probably doing it wrong. Even though you can get great results by using ray traced shadows everywhere with the highest number of samples, these results all come at the expense of high memory usage and lengthy render times. So your scene may look perfect, but if you're taking 16 hours to render every frame in an animation, you could be rendering for a month and not even have two seconds of it done.

A large part of being a CG artist is doing everything you can to reduce the amount of work that needs to be done by both you *and* the computer, while still creating high-quality images. You don't want to be old and gray by the time your first animation is complete. That's why CG artists worry so much about keeping their render times as short as possible and why they use features like these cheat buttons to cut corners where they can.

Working with three-point lighting in Blender

My preferred lighting rig in Blender usually starts with a three-point lighting setup. Here's what I normally start with:

- **Key:** A buffered Spot works well as the key light. Keep all settings at their default values except for the spot Size and Clip range. Set the Spot Size to 60 degrees and activate the Autoclip check boxes for the Clip Start and Clip End values.

✔ **Fill:** Typically, I start with a Hemi with an Energy of 0.5 and the Specular check box disabled in the Lamp panel.

✔ **Back:** Also a Hemi, but the Energy is usually between 0.75 and 1.0 to get a nice rim light. The lamp is behind the subject, so specularity doesn't matter as much, but just to make sure that it doesn't compete with the key's spec, I normally disable the specularity on this light as well. Don't get too picky with the location of the back light just yet. Back lighting in CG is a bit tricky; it's one of the rare situations where real-world lights have an easier time yielding the desired effect. For that reason, you end up tweaking the location of the back light a lot, so it's not critical that you get it right the first time in your initial setup.

This setup is good for studio lighting, and it works really well for scenes set indoors or for lighting isolated objects. I included this lighting rig on the book's companion DVD.

The only problem with using a Hemi as your back light is that Hemis don't cast shadows at all. This lack of shadows can be an issue, for example, if you're lighting a character who's speaking. If you use a Hemi as your back light, you find that the interior of the character's mouth is unnaturally lit because the Hemi doesn't allow the character's head to cast a shadow on the inside of the mouth. In this situation, you may be better off back lighting with a Point light or a wide-angled Spot.

Creating a fake Area light with buffered Spots

Using a buffered Spot as your key works nicely, but an Area light can usually give you softer shadows. However, Area lights can use ray tracing only for shadows, and you have somewhat limited control of the Area lamp's shape because it can be only a flat square or rectangle. To get around these limitations, you can get a bit creative with buffered Spots and use them to make your own Area light. To make your own custom Area light out of Spots, start with the three-point rig in the last section and then go through the following steps:

1. **Create a circle mesh (Shift+A⇨Mesh⇨Circle).**

2. **In the Last Operation panel of the Tool Shelf (F6), set the number of vertices to 8 and the radius to 2.0; also enable the Fill check box.**

3. **Add the Spot to your selection (Shift+right-click), making it the Active object.**

   Adding the circle object makes it selected by default, so all you should have to do is Shift+right-click the buffered Spot you're using as your key.

4. **Copy the location and rotation of the Spot to the circle object.**

To do so, open the 3D View's Properties region (N), right-click any of the Location values, and choose the Copy to Selected option from the menu that appears. Then do the same sequence on one of the Rotation values. The circle appears in the same place as the Spot with the same orientation.

5. **Make the circle your Active object (Shift+right-click).**

Both the Spot and the circle are still selected, but now the circle is active.

6. **Parent the Spot lamp to the circle (Ctrl+P⇨Make Parent).**

Now if you just have the circle selected and try to move it around, the Spot follows.

7. **Turn on Dupliverts for the circle (from Object Properties, Duplication⇨Verts).**

Dupliverts are a cool part of Blender. When you have an object parented to a mesh, activating Dupliverts on the mesh object places a copy of the child object at every vertex on the parent.

You now have an Area light created by buffered Spots arranged on a custom shape.

8. **Select your Spot and adjust its settings to taste.**

I typically use the following settings as my starting point:

- **Energy:** 0.200
- **Blend:** 1.000
- **Samples:** 8
- **Soft:** 16.00
- **Clip Start/Clip End:** These values may need to be manually adjusted to make sure that the shadow appears properly.

Figure 9-11 shows a circular Area light created with buffered spots.

Dealing with outdoor lighting

What if you have a large scene or your scene is set outdoors? The limited lighting cone of a single Spot or Area lamp makes it difficult to illuminate the whole scene in a believable way. For a large or outdoor scene, I usually bounce between one of two solutions. Both of them involve the Sun lamp.

The easiest solution to implement is to change the buffered Spot in the earlier three-point lighting setup into a Sun with ray traced shadows. You get shadows for all objects in your scene, and with the sky and atmosphere settings, you can get a really believable result. That said, lighting your scene this way brings two disadvantages. First, it uses ray tracing for your shadows, which can increase your render times if you're not careful. And second, because the Sun illuminates the same everywhere, you don't have as much control over individual shadows.

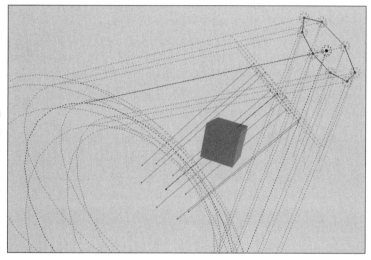

Figure 9-11:
Using
dupliverted
buffered
Spots to
create a
buffered
Area light.

In contrast to earlier versions of Blender, the ray tracing capability of the current version of Blender is dramatically faster. The ray tracing performance is so much better now that, in some cases, it may be faster to just go ahead and use ray traced shadows instead of fiddling with all the settings involved with Spot lamps. I know of a few projects (my own included) where, in the time I spent trying to get the perfect Spot light settings, I could have rendered my scene with ray tracing and just been done with it.

An alternative solution to using ray traced shadows from a Sun lamp is to keep the Sun for full scene lighting and atmosphere, but leave the shadow creation to the Spot light. To do so, begin with the previous basic three-point lighting rig and proceed with the following steps:

1. **Add a Sun lamp (Shift+A⇨Lamp⇨Sun).**

   I like to put the Sun at the center of the scene. (Press Shift+C to put the 3D cursor at the center before adding the Sun.)

2. **Add the buffered Spot to your selection (Shift+right-click).**

   The newly added Sun is selected by default. Shift+right-clicking the Spot also selects it and makes the Spot lamp the Active object.

3. **Copy the Spot light's rotation.**

   From the 3D View's Properties region, right-click one of the Rotation values and choose Copy to Selected. Now light from the Sun is coming from the same direction as the Spot. Location for the Sun is irrelevant.

4. **Make the Spot lamp a shadow-only lamp (from Object Data Properties, Shadow⇨Only Shadow).**

5. **Disable shadows on the Sun by selecting the Sun (right-click) and then disabling ray traced shadows by left-clicking the Ray Shadow button in the Shadow and Spot panel.**

   Done! If you have other objects in your scene that need shadows, make a linked duplicate (Alt+D) of your shadow-only spot and position the duplicate by grabbing (G) it to the correct location.

I include a version of this lighting rig on this book's companion DVD. Feel free to use it in your own scenes.

Setting Up the World

When you set up your scene for rendering, lighting is really only part of the equation. You must also consider your scene's environment. For example, are you outdoors or indoors? Is it daytime or nighttime? What color is the sky? Are there clouds? What does the background look like? You have to consider these factors when thinking about the final look of your image. Fortunately, nearly all the controls for setting up your environment are in World Properties, as shown in Figure 9-12.

Changing the sky to something other than dull gray

If you've worked in Blender for a while and gotten a few renders out, you might be pretty tired of that dull gray background color that the renderer uses by default. Here's where you change that color: Look in the World panel of World Properties. The leftmost color swatch sets the horizon color. You can adjust it by left-clicking the color swatch and using the color picker.

To the right of the horizon color is the *zenith* color. You may notice that trying to change this color doesn't seem to affect the background color at all. By default, Blender is set to use only the horizon color, so you end up with a solid color as the background. To change this default, left-click the Blend Sky check box in the World panel. When you do, the Preview shows a linear gradient that transitions from the horizon color at the bottom to the zenith color at the top. If I'm doing a render where I just want to see a model I've created, I often use this setup with my horizon color around 50 percent gray and my zenith color nearly black.

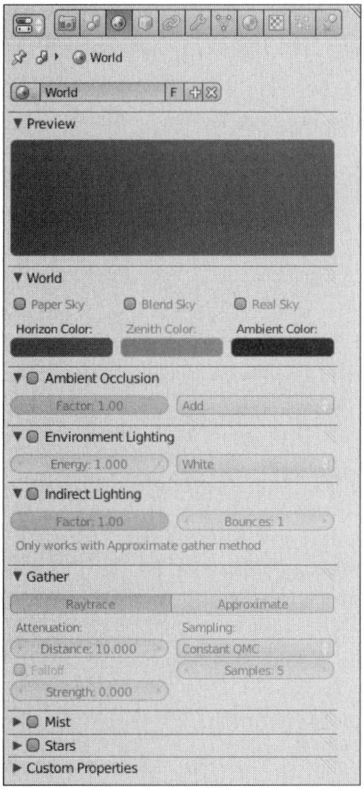

Figure 9-12:
World
Properties.

Of course, the next question you might have is, "Okay, so what do the other two check boxes in the World panel do?" I'm glad you asked. You can actually activate any combination of these check boxes. Here is a description of what each option does when enabled:

✔ **Paper Sky:** You typically use the Paper Sky setting with both Blend Sky and Real Sky also enabled. This setting keeps the horizon at the center of the camera, no matter where it's pointing. It also adjusts the gradient to make sure that the full zenith and horizon colors are visible.

✔ **Blend Sky:** Blend Sky enables a gradient going from the horizon to the zenith. When enabled by itself, the horizon is always at the bottom of the camera view and the zenith is at the top.

✔ **Real Sky:** Enabling Real Sky sets the horizon to the XY ground plane and the gradient to the zenith color along the global Z-axis. A bonus is that, because the horizon is locked to the XY ground plane, the gradient rotates with the camera, giving a much more realistic feeling to the background. I'm very fond of this setting, especially if I'm using a texture in the background.

Figure 9-13 shows a simple scene rendered with the various combinations of the Blend Sky check box enabled with the other two options so that you can get a better idea of what they do.

Figure 9-13: Ways to control the Blend gradi-ent and the horizon.

Blend

Blend + Real

Blend + Real +Paper

Understanding ambient occlusion

Take a look outside. Now, hopefully it's daytime, or this example isn't going to work, but notice how much everything seems to be illuminated. Even on a bright sunny day, the deepest shadows aren't completely black. The reason is that light from the sun is basically bouncing off of every surface many times, exposing nearly all objects to at least *some* amount of light. In com-puter graphics, this phenomenon is often referred to as *global illumination,* or GI, and it's pretty difficult to re-create efficiently. As you may have guessed, the biggest reason is the "light only bounces once" rule (see Chapter 7).

Another result of GI is that all this bounced light also makes subtle details, creases, cracks, and wrinkles more apparent. At first, this statement may seem like a paradox. After all, if light is bouncing off of everything, intuitively, it would make sense that everything should end up even brighter and seem flatter. However, remember that not only is the light bouncing off of every-thing, but it's also casting small shadows from all the weird angles that it bounces from. Those small shadows are what bring out those minor details.

The GI effect is most apparent outdoors on overcast days where the light is evenly diffused by cloud cover. However, you can even see it happening in well-lit rooms with a high number of light sources, such as an office building with rows and rows of fluorescent lights lining the ceiling. You can somewhat fake this effect by using a Hemi lamp, but the problem with Hemis is that they don't cast shadows, so you don't get that nice, added detail from GI.

The bad news is that Blender's internal renderer doesn't have "true" GI capa-bility. However, Blender does have a great way of approximating GI, thanks to *ambient occlusion* (AO). Often called *dirty GI* or *dirt shader*, AO finds the small details in your object and makes them more apparent by making the rest of the model brighter or making the details darker.

To enable AO, left-click the check box next to the Ambient Occlusion panel in World Properties. When you enable AO, Blender makes the settings in the Gather panel available. This panel gives you two ways of calculating AO: with ray tracing or as an approximation of the result. Figure 9-14 shows the Gather panel with the options for ray traced AO and approximate AO.

Figure 9-14:
The Gather
panel in
World
Properties
with ray
traced AO
options
(left) and
approximate
AO options
(right).

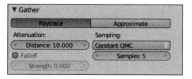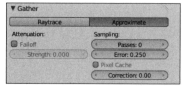

If you're going to use ray traced AO, make sure that you have the Ray Tracing check box enabled in the Render panel of Render Properties.

Most of the controls in the Ambient Occlusion and Gather panels are the same, regardless of whether you're using ray traced or approximate AO. Here's a description of the options available for both types of AO:

- ✔ **Ambient Color:** This color swatch in the World panel controls the source color for the diffuse energy used by AO. The Ambient color adds itself to the overall color of the scene. I don't normally advocate setting the Ambient color to anything other than black because it has a tendency to wash out the shading in the scene. However, when you enable AO and adjust the Ambient color, the shading isn't washed out as much, and you actually end up with a more believable image.

- ✔ **Factor:** The Factor value is the strength of the overall AO effect. The effect you choose from the Add/Multiply menu is multiplied by this value. Usually it's a good idea to keep this at 1.0, although I recommend that you play with it a bit to see how it affects your scene.

- ✔ **Add/Multiply:** With this drop-down menu in the Ambient Occlusion panel, you can control how AO creates shadows. Choosing Add brightens the rest of the object, making the details apparent by simply staying their own color. Choosing Multiply darkens the detailed areas while keeping the object's original shading.

✔ **Falloff:** This option in the Gather panel controls the size of the extra shadows that AO creates. When you enable the Falloff check box, you can use the Strength value field below it. Setting this value to higher numbers makes the shadows more subtle.

The other values for ray traced and approximate gathering are there for refining and optimizing how they work. If you read about ray traced lights earlier in this chapter in the "Universal lamp options" section, the settings for ray traced gathering are pretty familiar. I recommend using adaptive QMC because it typically yields faster results at good quality. I've even found that in a lot of situations, using ray traced gathering with adaptive QMC sampling is even faster than using approximate gathering. Using the other sampling types usually gives you a *noisier,* or more speckled, result.

When choosing between ray traced and approximate gathering, keep in mind a set of tradeoffs. As you might expect, ray traced gathering gives you more accurate results, but it often takes longer to process when you use a higher Samples value to reduce the noisiness of the AO shading. Approximate gathering works fast and doesn't suffer the noise problem that you get with ray traced gathering. Of course, some people actually prefer that noisy grain that ray traced gathering gives, and approximate gathering is a bit more error-prone in creating its shadows, especially where things touch. So it may take some additional time to set things up so that they look believable. You have to weigh out the advantages and disadvantages for yourself and see which method works best for your projects. Figure 9-15 shows the same scene rendered with both types of gathering, as well as without any AO at all.

Figure 9-15:
From left to right, with their render times: no AO, ray traced AO, and approximate AO.

No AO - 1.48 seconds   Retraced AO - 3.89 seconds   Approximate AO - 1.84 seconds

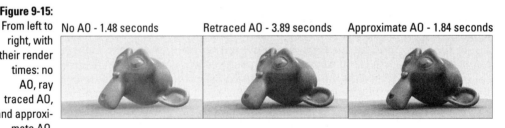

Adding mist and stars

Other panels in World Properties are Mist and Stars. The settings in these panels are somewhat primitive in terms of what they actually do, but they can be pretty handy in a pinch for creating nice atmospheric effects and quick backgrounds.

Mist

Blender's Mist works by decreasing the opacity of objects as they get farther away from the camera, mixing more with whatever the sky is. To use it, enable the Mist check box and expand its panel. From here, you can adjust the Start and Depth values. Start defines how far away from the camera the mist starts to take effect. Depth is the distance from the Start value that the mist effect is at 100 percent. Anything farther away from the camera doesn't show up in the final render.

These values are in the units you specify in Scene Properties, but it can be difficult to know intuitively where they actually fall in the scene, relative to your camera. Fortunately, you can see mist limits visually. Select the camera and switch to Object Data Properties. On the left side of the Display panel are four check boxes. Left-click the Mist check box. When you do, a line appears extending from your camera. If you switch back to World Properties and adjust the Start and Depth values, you can now see exactly where the mist region of influence is. Figure 9-16 shows a scene in the 3D View with a camera that has its mist limits visible.

Figure 9-16: A camera in the 3D View with its mist limits visible. To the right is a render of that scene.

The Falloff drop-down menu controls how the mist gets thicker from start to finish. Quadratic tends to be a more subtle effect, whereas Linear tends to make the mist thicker faster. If you want to limit the mist to a certain height, like when you see an early morning mist in a field, adjust the Height value. Like the other values, Height is set in your specified units and works relative to the XY ground plane. The Intensity value increases the mist's intensity. Be careful with this setting. Putting it too high hides your entire scene from you.

Stars

Blender's Stars feature is a quick way of adding starlike halos to your scene. You enable it by left-clicking the Stars check box in World Properties. Remember that Blender creates these stars in 3D space. They actually have a physical location and they aren't just a randomly generated speckled background. Descriptions of each option are as follows:

- ✔ **Size:** Size controls the average size of the stars in your scene. For realistic stars, use a relatively small Size value.

- ✔ **Min. Dist:** This value controls the minimum distance that stars can be from the camera. Unless you want stars to show up in front of some objects in your scene, this value should be larger than the distance between the camera and the farthest object away from it.

- ✔ **Colors:** Increasing this value colors the stars randomly. Setting this value to its maximum value makes your scene look a bit like a piñata exploded in space. However, lowering the value to 0.050 gives some subtle variety to your stars.

- ✔ **Separation:** The Separation value is the average distance between stars. Stars are randomly placed in the background, but this setting controls how dense the star field is.

Figure 9-17 shows a simple scene rendered with the Stars feature enabled.

Figure 9-17:
Mon-
keeeeyysss
innnnnnnnn
spaaaaace!

When using stars, enable Real Sky in the World panel. This way, if you animate your camera moving in the scene, the stars behave realistically.

Creating sky textures

Flat colors, gradients, and procedural stars are nice, but in some cases, you'd definitely rather have an image as your background. You can apply a texture to the World for your scene, like materials and lights.

In the new Blender interface, applying a texture is actually a little bit tricky to do. Like with texturing materials and lights, you use Texture Properties. What makes things a little complicated is that if you want to edit textures for your World, you need to first let Blender know the context in which you want to work. To do so, bring up Texture Properties and left-click the World button in the Context panel. The Texture Properties are the same familiar ones that I describe in Chapter 7. The primary difference is in the Influence panel, visible after you add a new texture.

The Influence panel gives you the ability to map the color of the texture to the blend, horizon color, and the upper and lower zenith colors. To use an image as your Sky texture, follow these steps:

1. **Left-click the New button in the texture datablock.**

   This button is located beneath the list box in Texture Properties.

2. **Change the texture Type to Image or Movie.**

3. **In the Image panel, left-click the Open button and use the File Browser to find the image you want to use.**

   You may want to enable thumbnail view from the File Browser's header.

4. **In the Influence panel, map the texture to the horizon color by enabling the check box next to the Horizon slider.**

5. **Back in World Properties, go to the Preview panel and enable the Real Sky check box.**

   This step ensures that the sky moves properly (or, more accurately, the sky stays still) as you move your camera in the scene.

6. **Switch back to Texture Properties and tweak the mapping and input settings to taste.**

   You may have to adjust the input coordinates as well as the texture size and offset. It's worth it to play around with these settings a bit to land on the look you want. When you're finished, you may have something that looks like Figure 9-18.

Figure 9-18:
A simple
scene
with a sky
texture, as
well as the
World and
Texture
Properties
that set
it up.

Part III
Get Animated!

The 5th Wave   By Rich Tennant

"You know, I've asked you a dozen times <u>not</u> to animate the torches on our Web page!"

In this part . . .

There's just *something* about making things move. Your work can take on a life of its own and communicate to an audience in a way that a single still image could never do. It has to do with your creations working in coordination with time. This part goes into the steps you need to go through to give your 3D objects the illusion of life. Not only is there technical information on the details of Blender's tools for rigging characters and creating animations, but the chapters in this part also cover some of the essential principles of animation that are applicable to all forms of animation.

The last chapter in this part goes into how to make Blender do the heavy lifting in animation. Integrated simulation tools allow you to do complex, physically accurate animations more quickly than you could by hand. Blender gives you this power.

Chapter 10

Animating Objects

I have to make a small admission: Animation is not easy. It's time consuming, frustrating, tedious work where you often spend days, sometimes even weeks, working on what ends up to be a few seconds of finished animation. An enormous amount of work goes into animation. However, there's something incredible about making an otherwise inanimate object move, tell a story, and communicate to an audience. Getting those moments when you have beautifully believable motion — life, in some ways — is a positively indescribable sensation. The process of animation truly has my heart more than any other aspect of computer graphics. It's simply my favorite thing to do. It's like playing with a sock puppet, except better because you don't have to worry about wondering whether or not it's been washed.

This chapter, as well as the following three chapters, go pretty heavily into the technical details of creating animations using Blender. Blender is a great tool for the job. Beyond what this book can provide you with, though, animation is about seeing, understanding, and re-creating motion. I highly recommend that you make it a point to get out and watch things. And not just animations: Go to a park and study how people move. Try to move like other people move so that you can understand how the weight shifts and how gravity and inertia compete with and accentuate that movement. Watch lots of movies and television and pay close attention to how people's facial expressions can convey what they're trying to say. If you get a chance, go to a theater and watch a play. Understanding how and why stage actors exaggerate their body language is incredibly useful information for an animator.

While you're doing that, think about how you can use the technical information in these chapters to re-create those feelings and that motion with your objects in Blender.

Working with Animation Curves

In Blender, the fundamental way for controlling and creating animation is with animation curves called *f-curves*. F-curve is short for *function curve,* and it describes the change, or *interpolation,* between two key moments in an animated sequence.

To understand interpolation better, flash back to your grade-school math class for a second. Remember when you had to do graphing, or take the equation for some sort of line or curve and draw it out on paper? By drawing that line, you were interpolating between points. Don't worry though; I'm not going to make you do any of that. That's what we have Blender for. In fact, the following example shows the basic process of animating in Blender and should help explain things more clearly:

1. **Start with Blender's default scene (Ctrl+N⇨Reload Start-Up File).**

2. **Select the default cube object and switch to the camera view (right-click, Numpad 0).**

3. **Split the 3D View vertically and change one of the new areas to the Graph Editor (Shift+F6).**

4. **In the 3D View, make sure that the default cube is selected and press I⇨Location.**

   This step sets an initial location keyframe for the cube. I give a more detailed description of keyframes later in the chapter in the "Inserting keys" section. The important thing to notice is that the left region of the Graph Editor is now updated and shows a short tiered list with the items Cube, CubeAction, and Location.

5. **Press the up arrow on your keyboard.**

   You move forward in time by 10 frames.

6. **Grab (G) the cube in the 3D View and move it to another location in the scene.**

7. **Press I⇨Location again in the 3D View.**

   A set of colored lines appears in the Graph Editor. These colored lines are f-curves. Each f-curve represents a single attribute, or *channel*, that's been animated. If you expand the Location block in the Graph Editor by left-clicking the triangle on the left side of its name, you can see the three location channels: X Location, Y Location, and Z Location. To see the actual curves a little bit better, move your mouse to the large graph section of the Graph Editor and press Home. Your Blender screen should look something like the one in Figure 10-1.

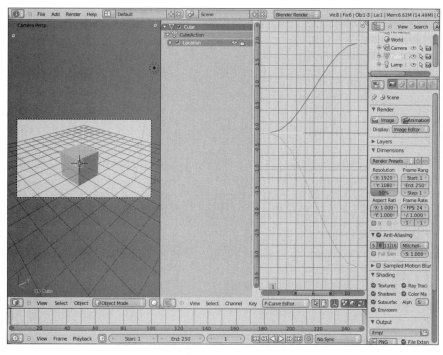

Figure 10-1:
Animating
the loca-
tion of the
default cube
object.

Congratulations! You just created your first animation in Blender. Here's
what you did: The largest part of the Graph Editor is a graph (go figure!).
Moving from left to right on this graph — its X-axis — is moving forward in
time. The vertical axis on this graph represents the value of whatever channel is being animated. So the curves that you created describe and control
the change in the cube's location in the X-, Y-, and Z-axes as you move forward in time. Blender creates the curves by interpolating between the control points, called *keys*, that you created.

You can see the result for yourself by playing back the animation. Keeping
your mouse cursor in the Graph Editor, press Alt+A. A green vertical line,
called the *timeline cursor,* moves from left to right in the graph. As the timeline
cursor moves, you should see your cube move from the starting point to the
ending point you defined in the 3D View. Press Esc to stop the playback. You
can watch the animation in a more controlled way by *scrubbing* in the Graph
Editor. To scrub, left-click in the graph area of the Graph Editor and drag your
mouse cursor left and right. The timeline cursor follows the location of your
mouse pointer, and you can watch the change happening in the 3D View.

Customizing your screen layout for animation

A screen layout in Blender is specifically set up for animation. You can choose it from the Screen Layout datablock at the top of the Blender window or by using the Ctrl+←⇨Ctrl+← hotkey combination.

This screen layout isn't too dissimilar from the Default layout, but it does have a few differences. In particular, the Outliner is larger, and on the left side of the screen, there's a Dopesheet and Graph Editor. A second 3D View is also placed above the Outliner. The Timeline from the Default layout is pretty much unchanged. (For a full reminder of what each editor does, refer to Chapter 1.)

You may be wondering, however, why this layout has three editors (the Timeline, Graph Editor, and Dopesheet) that allow you to adjust your position in time on your animation. The quick answer is that each editor gives you different kinds of control over your animation. For example, the Timeline gives you a central place to control the playback of your overall animation. This way, you can use the Graph Editor to focus on specific detailed animations and the Dopesheet for making sense of complex animation with a lot of animated attributes. Like the Graph Editor, you can scrub the Timeline and Dopesheet by left-clicking in it and dragging your mouse cursor left and right.

One change I usually like to make to this layout is in the secondary 3D View above the Outliner. I like to change the viewport shading in this editor to be Shaded (Z) or Textured (Alt+Z). The reason for this secondary view is so that you can use any perspective in the main 3D View but still retain an idea of what the camera sees. That way, you don't end up animating something that will never be on camera. The default Wireframe shading in this 3D View is good for fast playback, but it's usually too difficult to tell what's going on.

To that end, I also use a new feature that was added in Blender 2.5: Render Only display. Render Only sets the background color to the Horizon color that's set up in World Properties and hides anything that won't be rendered (3D grid, relationship lines, lamps, empties, and so on) from the 3D View, allowing you to get a truer understanding of what your final animation looks like. To activate this feature, reveal the Properties region (N) in this secondary 3D View and enable the Render Only check box in the Display panel.

The last change I make to this screen layout is in the main 3D View. I swap out the Translate manipulator for the Rotate manipulator and change its coordinate space to Normal (Alt+spacebar⇨Normal). I do this change because normally I can grab and scale with the G and S hotkeys pretty quickly, but precise rotation when animating is often faster and easier with the Rotate manipulator. Plus, this manipulator doesn't obstruct my view as much as the other ones do. Figure 10-2 shows my modestly modified Animation screen layout.

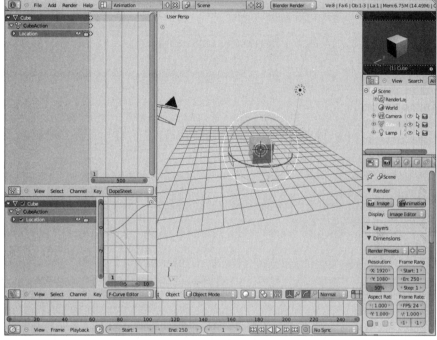

Figure 10-2:
The
Animation
screen
layout with
a few small
modifica-
tions to
make work-
ing more
pleasant.

Working in the Graph Editor

Working in the Graph Editor is very similar to working in the 3D View. The following describes the basic controls available in the Graph Editor:

- **Middle-click+drag** moves around your view of the graph.

- **Ctrl+middle-click+drag** allows you to interactively scale your view of the curve horizontally and vertically at the same time.

- **Scroll your mouse wheel** to zoom in and out.

- **Shift+scroll** moves the graph vertically.

- **Ctrl+scroll** moves the graph horizontally.

- **Right-click** selects individual f-curve control points.

- **Press A** to toggle selecting all or no control points.

- **Press B** for Border Select.

- **Left-click** a channel in the left region of the Graph Editor to select it.

- **Ctrl+left-click** allows you to arbitrarily add points to a selected f-curve in the graph. Anywhere you Ctrl+left-click in the graph, a new control point is added to the selected channel.

Inserting keys

Instead of Ctrl+left-clicking in the Graph Editor to add control points, you have another, more controlled option. Blender also uses a workflow that's a lot more like traditional hand-drawn animation. In traditional animation, a whole animated sequence is planned out ahead of time. Then an animator goes through and draws the primary poses of the character. These drawings are referred to as *keyframes* or *keys*. They're the poses that the character must make in order to most effectively convey the intended motion to the viewer. With the keys drawn, they're handed off to a second set of animators called the *inbetweeners*. These animators are responsible for drawing all the frames between each of the keys in order to get smooth motion.

Translating the workflow of traditional animation to how you do work in Blender, you should consider yourself the keyframe artist and Blender the inbetweener. In the quick animating example at the beginning of this section, you create a keyframe after you move the cube. By interpolating the curve between those keys, Blender creates the in-between frames. Some animation programs refer to creating these in-between frames as *tweening*.

To have a workflow that's even more similar to traditional animation, it's preferable to define your keyframes in the 3D View. Then you can use the Graph Editor to tweak the change from one keyframe to the next. And this workflow is exactly the way Blender is designed to animate. Start in the 3D View by pressing I to bring up the Insert Keyframe menu. Through this menu, you can create keyframes for the main animatable channels for an object. I describe the channels here in more detail:

- ✔ **Location:** Insert a key for the object's X, Y, and Z location.
- ✔ **Rotation:** Insert a key for the object's rotation in the X, Y, and Z axes.
- ✔ **Scaling:** Insert a key for the object's scale in the X, Y, and Z axes.
- ✔ **LocRot/LocScale/LocRotScale/RotScale:** Insert keyframes for various combinations of the previous three values.
- ✔ **Visual Location/Rotation/LocRot:** Insert keyframes for location, rotation, or both, but based on where the object is visually located in the scene. These options are explicitly made for use with constraints, which I cover later in this chapter in "Using Constraints Effectively."
- ✔ **Available:** If you already inserted keys for some of your object's channels, choosing this option adds a key for each of those preexisting curves in the Graph Editor. If no curves are already created, no keyframes are inserted.

When Blender sets keyframes for location, rotation, and scale, bear in mind which coordinate system the Graph Editor is using. Location is stored in global coordinates, whereas rotation and scale are stored in the object's local coordinate system.

Here's the basic workflow for animating in Blender:

1. **Insert an initial keyframe (I).**

   A keyframe appears at frame 1 in your animation. Assuming that you enter a Location keyframe, if you look at the Graph Editor, notice that Location channel is added and enabled.

2. **Move forward 10 frames (Up Arrow).**

   This puts you at frame 11. The Up Arrow and Down Arrow hotkeys move you 10 frames forward or backward in time, regardless of the editor your mouse cursor is in. To move forward or back one frame at a time, use the ← and → keys. Of course, you can also use the Timeline, Graph Editor, or Dopesheet to change what frame you are in.

3. **Grab your cube and move it to a different location in 3D space (G).**

4. **Insert a new keyframe (I).**

   Now you should have curves in the Graph Editor that describe the motion of the cube.

You can insert keys in an easier way using a feature called Autokey. Like its name indicates, Autokey automatically creates keys when you make changes in your scene. To enable the Autokey feature, look in the Timeline. Next to the playback controls in the Timeline's header is a button with a red circle on it, like the Record button on a DVR. Left-click it to activate Autokey. Now you can simply use tools in the 3D View like grab (G), rotate (R), and scale (S) as you move forward in time and keyframes are automatically inserted for you. Pretty sweet, huh?

A really cool addition that came in the 2.5 series of Blender is the concept of "[almost] everything animatable." You can animate nearly every setting or attribute within Blender (within reason). Want to animate the skin material of your character so that she turns red with anger? You can! Want to animate the Count attribute in an Array modifier to dynamically add links to a chain? You can! Want to animate whether your object appears in wireframe or solid shading in the 3D View? Ridiculous as it sounds, that, too, is possible!

So how do you do this miraculous act of animating any attribute? It's amazingly simple. In the Properties editor, nearly every text field, value field, color swatch, drop-down menu, check box, and radio button is considered a property and represents a channel that you can animate. Insert a keyframe for that channel by right-clicking one of those properties and choosing Insert Keyframes from the menu that appears. Figure 10-3 shows what this menu looks like.

After you insert a new keyframe for that property, its color changes to yellow, and a channel for that property is added in the Graph Editor. When you move forward or backward in time, the color of the control changes from yellow to green. This green color indicates that the property is animated, but you're not currently on one of its keys. Insert another keyframe for that property, and BAM! You have an animated property.

Figure 10-3:
Right-click
any prop-
erty in the
Properties
editor, and
you can
insert a key-
frame for it.

For an even faster way to insert keyframes on properties, hover your mouse over the control and just press I. This trick even works on the show/hide/ selectable icons (known as the *restrict columns*) in the Outliner. How's that for awesome?

Editing motion curves

After you know how to add keyframes to your scene, the next logical step is to tweak, edit, and modify those keyframes, as well as the interpolation between them, in the Graph Editor. The Graph Editor is similar to the 3D View, and you can select individual control points on f-curves by right-clicking or by using the B key for Border Select. Well, the similarities with the 3D View goes farther than that. Not only can you select those control points in the Graph Editor, but you can edit them like a 2D Bézier curve object in the 3D View. The only constraint is that f-curves can't cross themselves. Having a curve that describes motion in time do a loopty-loop doesn't make any sense.

For more detailed descriptions of the hotkeys and controls for editing Bézier curves in Blender, see Chapter 6. Selecting and moving control point handles, as well as the V hotkey for changing handle types all work as expected. However, because these curves are specially purposed for animation, you have a few additional controls over them. For example, you can control the type of interpolation between control points on a selected curve by pressing Shift+T or going to Key➪Interpolation Mode in the Graph Editor's header. You then see the options shown in Figure 10-4:

  ✔ **Constant:** This option is sometimes called a *step function* because a series of them look like stair steps. Basically, this interpolation type keeps the value of one control point until it gets to the next one, where it instantly changes. Many animators like to use this interpolation mode when blocking out their animations. This way, they can focus on getting their poses and timing right without the distraction of in-between frames.

✔ **Linear:** The interpolation from one control point to the next is a completely straight line. This option is similar to changing two control points to have Vector handles.

✔ **Bézier:** The default interpolation type, Bézier smoothly transitions from one control point to the next. In traditional animation, this smooth transition is referred to *easing in* and *easing out* of a keyframe.

Figure 10-4:
Changing the interpolation type on selected f-curve control points.

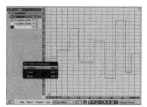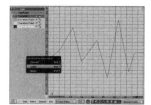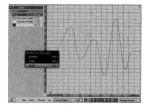

The interpolation mode options work only on the selected control points in the Graph Editor, so if you want to select all the control points in a single f-curve, select one of those control points and press L. Then you can apply your interpolation mode to the entire curve.

You can also change what a selected channel does before and after its first and last keyframes by changing the curve's *extrapolation mode.* You can change a curve's extrapolation mode by selecting an f-curve channel in the left region of the Graph Editor and then pressing Shift+E or navigating to Key⇨Extrapolation Mode in the Graph Editor's header. When you do, notice two possible choices:

✔ **Constant Extrapolation:** This setting is the default. The first and last control point values are maintained into infinity beyond those points.

✔ **Linear Extrapolation:** Instead of maintaining the same value in perpetuity before and after the first and last control points, this extrapolation mode takes the directions of the curve as it reaches those control points and continues to extend the curve in those directions.

Figure 10-5 shows the menu for the different type of extrapolation modes, as well as what each one looks like with a simple f-curve.

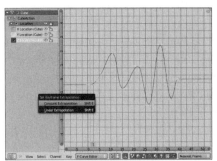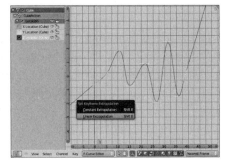

Figure 10-5:
The two
different
extrapola-
tion modes
you can
have on
f-curves.

If you have lots of animated objects in your scene, or just one object with a high number of animated properties, it may be helpful to hide extraneous curves from view so that you can focus on the ones you truly want to edit. To toggle a curve's visibility, left-click the check box next to its name in the channel region along the left side of the Graph Editor. If you want f-curves to be visible, but not editable, select a channel from the channel region and either left-click the lock icon or press Tab.

If you need explicit control over the placement of a curve or a control point, the Graph Editor has a Properties region like the 3D View. You bring it up the same way, too: Either press N or choose View⇨Properties. Within this region, you can enter the exact value that you'd like to set your selected control point or that control point's handles. Figure 10-6 shows the Properties region in the Graph Editor.

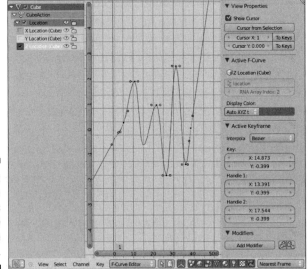

Figure 10-6:
The
Properties
region (N)
in the Graph
Editor.

Often, you run into the occasion where you need to edit all the control points in a single frame so that you can change the overall timing of your animation. You may be tempted to use Border Select (B) to select the strip of control points you want to move around. However, a cleaner and easier way is to select one of the control points on the frame you want to adjust and press K in the Graph Editor or choose Select⇨Columns on Selected Keys. All the other control points that are on the same frame as your initial selection are selected.

Table 10-1 covers the most common hotkeys and mouse actions used to control animation in the Graph Editor.

Table 10-1	Commonly Used Hotkeys and Mouse Actions for the Graph Editor		
Mouse Action	*Description*	*Hotkey*	*Description*
Left-click graph	Move time cursor	Alt+A	Playback animation
Left-click channel check box	Hide/Reveal channel	Shift+E	Extrapolation Mode
Left-click channel	Select channel	K	Select columns of selected control points
Right-click	Select control point	L	Select linked control points
Middle-click	Pan graph	O	Clean f-curves
Ctrl+middle-click	Scale graph	N	Properties region
Scroll	Zoom graph	Shift+S	Snap Menu
Shift+scroll	Pan graph vertically	Shift+T	Interpolation Type
Ctrl+scroll	Pan graph horizontally	Home	Fit curves to graph

Using Constraints Effectively

Occasionally, I get into conversations with people who assume that because there's a computer involved, good CG animation takes less time to make than traditional animation. In most cases, this assumption isn't true. High-quality work takes roughly the same amount of time, regardless of the tool. The time is just spent in different places. Whereas in traditional animation, a very large portion of the time is spent drawing the in-between frames, CG animation lets the computer handle that detail. However, traditional animators don't have to worry as much about optimizing for render times, tweaking and re-tweaking simulated effects, or modeling, texturing, and rigging characters.

That said, computer animation does give you the opportunity to cut corners in places and make your life as an animator much simpler. Constraints are one feature that fit this description perfectly. Literally speaking, a *constraint* is a limitation put on one object by another, allowing the unconstrained object to control the behavior of the constrained one.

With constraints, you can do quite a lot without doing much at all. Animation is hard work; it's worth it to be lazy whenever you can.

To see the actual constraints that you have available, go to Constraint Properties and left-click the Add Constraint button. Alternatively, you can press Shift+Ctrl+C in the 3D View. Either way, you see a menu similar to the one in Figure 10-7.

Figure 10-7:
The types of constraints available by default within Blender.

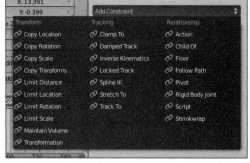

In Chapter 4, I present a mnemonic for remembering how the parenting operation relates to the active object (children first!). For constraints, the mnemonic is a little bit backward because the active object is actually the object you're constraining. Because a constraint, by definition, restricts an object in some way, that object basically becomes a kind of prisoner. So for constraints, I think, "Prisoners last." And there you have it, a handy mnemonic device for remembering selection order when parenting or constraining: children first (parenting) and prisoners last (constraining).

Because of limitations to this book's page count, I can't cover the function of each and every constraint in full detail. However, the remaining sections in this chapter covers features found in most constraints and some usage examples for more frequently used constraints.

The all-powerful Empty!

Of all the different types of objects available to you in Blender, none of them are as useful or versatile in animation as the humble Empty. An Empty isn't much — just a little set of axes that indicate a position, orientation, and size in 3D space. Empties don't even show up when you render. However, Empties are an ideal choice for use as control objects, and it's a phenomenal way to take advantage of constraints.

As a practical example of how useful Empties can be, consider that 3D modelers like to have a *turnaround* render of the model they create. Basically, a turnaround render is like taking the model, placing it on a turntable, and spinning it in front of the camera. It's a great way to show off all sides of the model. Now, for simple models, you can just select the model, rotate it in the global Z-axis, and you're done. However, what if the model consists of many objects, or for some reason everything is at a strange angle that looks odd when spun around the Z-axis? Selecting and rotating all those little objects can get time consuming and annoying. A better way of setting up a turnaround is with the following rig:

1. **Add an Empty (Shift+A⇨Empty).**

2. **Grab the Empty to somewhere at the center of the model (G).**

3. **Select the camera and position it so that the model is in the center of view (right-click, G).**

4. **Add the Empty to your selection (Shift+right-click).**

5. **Make the Empty the camera's parent (Ctrl+P⇨Object).**

6. **Select the Empty and insert a rotation keyframe (right-click, I⇨Rotation).**

7. **Move forward in time 50 frames**.

8. **Rotate the Empty 90 degrees in the Z-axis and insert a new rotation keyframe (R⇨Z⇨90, I⇨Rotation).**

   The camera obediently matches the Empty's rotation.

9. **Bring up the Graph Editor and set the extrapolation mode for the Z Rotation channel to linear extrapolation (Shift+F6, left-click, Shift+E⇨Linear Extrapolation).**

10. **Switch to the camera view and playback the animation (Numpad 0, Alt+A).**

    In the 3D View, you see your model spinning in front of your camera.

In this setup, the Empty behaves as the control for the camera. Imagine that a beam extends from the Empty's center to the camera's center and that rotating the Empty is the way to move that beam.

Adjusting the influence of a constraint

One of the most useful settings that's available to all constraints is at the bottom of each constraint block: the Influence slider. This slider works on a scale from 0 to 1, with 0 being the least amount of influence and 1 being the largest amount. With this slider, you have the capability of just partially being influenced by the target object's attributes. There's more to it, though.

You can animate any attribute in the Properties editor by right-clicking it and choosing Insert Keyframe, which means you can easily animate the influence of the constraint. If you key the Influence value of a constraint, a curve for that influence becomes visible in the Graph Editor.

Say that you're working on an animation that involves a character with telekinetic powers using his ability to make a ball fly to his hand. You can do that by animating the influence of a Copy Location constraint (see the "Copying the movement of another object" section) on the ball. The character's hand is the target, and you start with 0 influence. Then, when you want the ball to fly to his hand, you increase the influence to 1 and set a new keyframe. KERPLOW! Telekinetic character!

Using vertex groups in constraints

Many constraints have a Vertex Group field that appears after choosing a valid mesh object in the Target field. In the Vertex Group field, you can type or choose the name of a vertex group in the parent mesh. When you do, the constrained object is bound only to those specific vertices. (See Chapter 11 for details on how to create a vertex group.) After you assign those vertices to the group and choose your new vertex group from the Vertex Group field of your constraint, even the relationship line from the child object changes to point to the group of vertices you've made part of the group. Figure 10-8 shows a Suzanne head with a Child Of constraint bound to a vertex group consisting of a single vertex on a circle mesh.

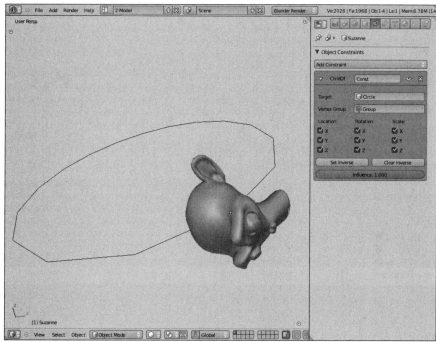

Copying the movement of another object

Using simple parenting is helpful in quite a few instances, but it's often not as flexible as you need it to be. You can't control or animate the parenting influence or use only the parent object's rotation without inheriting the location and scale as well. And you can't have movement of the parent object in the global X-axis influence the child's local X-axis location. More often than not, you need these sorts of refined controls rather than the somewhat ham-fisted Ctrl+P parenting.

To this end, a set of constraints provide you with just this sort of control: Copy Location, Copy Rotation, and Copy Scale. Figure 10-9 shows what each constraint looks like when added in Constraints Properties.

You can mix and match multiple constraints on a single object in a way that's very similar to the way you can add multiple modifiers to an object. So if you need both a Copy Location and a Copy Rotation constraint, just add both. After you add them, you can change which order they come in the stack to make sure that they suit your needs.

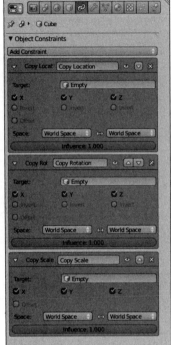

Figure 10-9:
The Copy
Location,
Copy
Rotation,
and Copy
Scale
constraint
controls.

Words and picture aren't always the best way of explaining how constraints work. It's often more to your benefit to see them in action. To that end, the DVD and Web site that accompany this book have a few example files that illustrate how these constraints work. It's worth it to load them up in Blender and play with them to really get a good sense for how these very powerful tools work.

Probably the most apparent thing about these Copy constraints is how similar their options are to one another. The most critical setting, however, is the object that you choose in the Target field. If you're using an Empty as your control object, this is where you choose that Empty or type its name. Unless you do so, the Constraint Name field at the top of the constraint block remains bright red and the constraint simply won't work.

Below the Target field are a series of six check boxes. The X, Y, and Z check boxes are already enabled, and beneath them are corresponding check boxes, each labeled Invert. By default, the Invert check boxes are disabled. These check boxes control which axis or axes the target object influences. If the axis check box is enabled and the Invert check box below it is also enabled, the target object has an inverted influence on the constrained object in that axis. Using the preceding Copy Location example, if you disable the X check box and then grab the Empty and move it in the X-axis (G⇨X), the cube remains perfectly still. However, enabling the X check box as well as the Invert check box beneath it causes the cube to translate in an opposite X direction when you move the target Empty.

Next up is the Offset check box, which is useful if you've already adjusted your object's location, rotation, or scale prior to adding the constraint. By default, this feature is off, so the constrained object mirrors the target object's behavior completely and exactly. With it enabled, though, the object adds the target object's transformation to the constrained object's already set location, rotation, or scale values. The best way to see this is to create a Copy Location constraint with the following steps:

1. **Start with the default scene (Ctrl+N).**

2. **Grab the default cube to a different location (G).**

3. **Add an Empty (Shift+A⇨Empty).**

4. **Add the cube to your current selection and put a Copy Location constraint on it (Shift+right-click, Shift+Ctrl+C⇨Copy Location).**

   The cube automatically snaps directly to the Empty's location.

5. **Left-click the Offset check box in the Copy Location constraint within Constraints Properties.**

   The cube goes back to its original position. Grabbing (G), the Empty influences the cube's location from there.

Putting limits on an object

Often when you animate objects, it's helpful to prevent objects from being moved, rotated, or scaled beyond a certain extent. Say that you're animating a character trapped inside a glass dome. As an animator, it's helpful if Blender forces you to keep that character within that space. Sure, you *could* just pay attention to where your character is and visually make sure that he doesn't accidentally go farther than he should be allowed, but why do the extra work if you can have Blender do it for you? Figure 10-10 shows the constraint options for most of the limiting constraints Blender offers you.

Here are descriptions of what each constraint does:

✓ **Limit Location/Rotation/Scale:** Unlike most of the other constraints, these three don't have a target object to constrain them. Instead, they're limitations on what the object can do within its own space. For any of them, you can define minimum and maximum limits in the X, Y, and Z axes. You enable limits by left-clicking their corresponding check boxes and define those limits in the value fields below each one.

The For Transform check box that's in each of these constraints can be pretty helpful when animating. To better understand what it does, go to the Properties region in the 3D View. If you have limits and For Transform is not enabled, the values in the Properties region change even after you reach the limits defined by the constraint. However, if you enable For Transform, the values in the Properties region are clipped to the limitations you defined with the constraint.

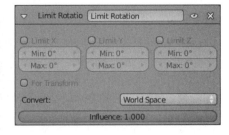

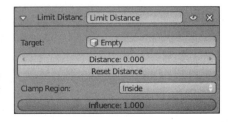

Figure 10-10:
The options
for the
limiting
constraints
that Blender
offers you.

✔ **Limit Distance:** This constraint is similar to the previous ones except it relates to the distance from the origin of a target object. The Clamp Region menu gives you three ways to use this distance:

- **Inside:** The constrained object can only move within the sphere of space defined by the Distance value.

- **Outside:** The constrained object can never enter the sphere of space defined by the Distance value.

- **On Surface:** The constrained object is always the same distance from the target object, no more and no less.

✔ **Floor:** The Floor constraint uses the origin of a target object to define a plane that the origin of the constrained object can't move beyond. So, technically, you can use this constraint to define more than a floor; you can also use it to define walls and a ceiling as well. Remember, though, that this constraint defines a plane. If your target object is an uneven surface, it doesn't use that object's geometry to define the limit of the constrained object, just its origin. Despite this limitation, this constraint is actually quite useful, especially if you enable the Use Rotation check box. This option allows the constrained object to recognize the rotation of the target object so that you can have an inclined floor, if you like.

When animating while using constraints, particularly limiting constraints, it's in your best interest to insert keyframes using Visual Location and Visual Rotation, as opposed to plain Location and Rotation. Using the visual keying types sets the keyframe to where the object is located visually, within the limits of the constraint, rather than how you actually transformed the object. For example, assume that you have a Floor constraint on an object that you're animating to fall from some height and land on a floor plane that's even with the XY grid. For the landing, you grab (G) the object and move your mouse cursor 4 units below the XY grid. Of course, because of the constraint, your object stops following the mouse when it hits the floor. Now, if you insert a regular Location keyframe here, the Z-axis location of the object is set to –4.0 even though the object can't go below 0. However, if you insert a Visual Location key, the object's Z-axis location is set to what you see it as: 0.

Tracking the motion of another object

Tracking constraints is another set of helpful constraints for animation. Their basic purpose is to make the constrained object point either directly at or in the general direction of the target object. Tracking constraints are useful for controlling the eye movement of characters or building mechanical rigs like pistons. Figure 10-11 shows the options for three of Blender's tracking constraints.

Figure 10-11:
Control
options for
Blender's
tracking
constraints.

Following are descriptions of each tracking constraint:

✔ **Track To:** Of these constraints, this one is the most straightforward. In other programs, this constraint may be referred to as the Look At constraint, and that's what it does. It forces the constrained object to point at the target object. The best way to see how this constraint works is to go through the following steps:

1. **Load the default scene (Ctrl+N).**

2. **Add a Track To constraint to the camera with the target object being the cube (right-click the cube, Shift+right-click the camera, Shift+Ctrl+C⇨Track To).**

3. **In the buttons next to the To label, left-click -Z.**

4. **In the Up drop-down menu, choose the Y-axis.**

Now, no matter where you move the camera, it always points at the cube's origin. By left-clicking the X, Y, and Z buttons next to the To label and choosing an axes from the Up drop-down menu, you can control how the constrained object points relative to the target.

✔ **Locked Track:** The Locked Track constraint is similar to the Track To constraint, with one large exception: It only allows the constrained object to rotate on a single axis, so the constrained object points in the general direction of the target, but not necessarily directly at it. A good way to think about the Locked Track constraint is to imagine that you're wearing a neck brace. With the brace on, you can't look up or down; you can rotate your head only left and right. So if a bird flies overhead, you can't look up to see it pass. All you can do is turn around and hope to see the bird flying away.

✔ **Stretch To:** This constraint isn't exactly a tracking constraint like Track To and Locked Track, but its behavior is similar. The Stretch To constraint makes the constrained object point toward the target object like the Track To constraint. However, this constraint also changes the constrained objects scale relative to its distance to the target, stretching that object toward the target. And the Stretch To constraint can even preserve the volume of the constrained object to make it seem like it's really stretching. This constraint is great for cartoony effects, as well as for controlling organic deformations, such as rubber balls and the human tongue. On a complex character rig, you can use the Stretch To constraint to help simulate muscle bulging.

Practical Example: Building and Animating a Simple Eye Rig

In this quick example, you build a simple rig for controlling eyes and ultimately animating them.

Before getting started, I should note that while the eye rig you have at the end of this section works well, I don't recommend that you use this exact rig in a full character without some modifications. The modifications aren't too drastic; mostly you need to replace the Empties in this rig with bones in an armature. I go over using bones in more detail in Chapter 11. In the meantime, work your way through this example, and you'll be much better prepared when you get into more complex rigs.

Creating your rig

If you worked through the practical examples in previous chapters of this book, you should have a nice, textured eyeball. If you haven't worked through those examples, that's okay, too. I provide an eye model for you to work with on this book's companion DVD and Web site.

Appending an eye

This practical example starts off a bit differently from the previous ones in this book. Instead of opening the existing model .blend and working directly in that file, you start this project from the default startup scene (Ctrl+N) and append your eye model. To do so, use the following steps:

1. **Open Blender or load Blender's default scene (Ctrl+N) and delete the default cube (X or Delete).**

   All that's left in your scene now is the camera and a Point light.

2. **Append the eye object from the .blend file where it lives (Shift+F1).**

   Blender's File Browser appears. When you left-click the .blend file, the File Browser allows you to drill down into the file. You're looking at the innards of your .blend file.

3. **Left-click the Object folder.**

   You see an object named eye. If you're working on a file from the practical examples in Chapters 5, 7, and 8, I'm assuming that you named your model. If you're using the model provided on the DVD or Web site, the eye object is definitely named.

4. **Double-click the eye object.**

   Blender brings up your eye in the 3D View.

At this point, your Blender screen should look like the screenshot in Figure 10-12.

Setting up your rig

After you have your eye model in-scene (see preceding section), you can set up the rig. I recommend that you do the next steps from the front orthographic view (Numpad 1, Numpad 5). First things first: Most characters have two eyes, so you're going to need two eyes:

1. **Select the eye object and grab it along the X-axis 1.5 units (G⇨X⇨1.5).**

   If you're using a different custom eye model, the number of units you move it may be different. The idea here is to offset the eye to the right of the Z-axis.

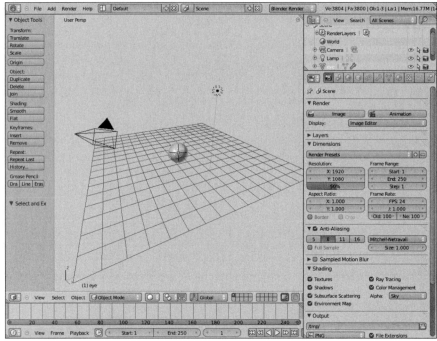

Figure 10-12:
Append
your eye
model into
a default
Blender
scene.

2. **Create a linked duplicate of the eye and move it along the X-axis -3.0 units (Alt+D⇨X⇨–3).**

   Again, your move in the X-axis may not be exactly –3.0. Just double the value you used in Step 1 and negate it.

3. **Select the left eye (on your right if you're looking at it from the front) and name it `eye.L`.**

   You can name it from the Item panel in the 3D View's Properties region or from Object Properties in the Properties editor.

4. **Select the right eye and name it `eye.R`.**

   Adding `.L` and `.R` as a suffix for left and right parts of a character is a good practice to get into.

Now you have a disembodied binocular character. Sweet! For the next step, you need to add the controls for your new eyes. For this step, you're going to use Empties — three of them, to be exact: one for each eye and one for overall control:

1. **Select `eye.L` and snap the 3D cursor to its origin (right-click, Shift+S⇨ Cursor to Selected).**

2. **Add an Empty and name it `eye_control.L` (Shift+A⇨Empty).**

3. **Select `eye.R` and snap the 3D cursor to its origin (right-click, Shift+S⇨Cursor to Selected).**

4. **Add an Empty and name it `eye_control.R` (Shift+A⇨Empty).**

5. **Select your new Empties.**

   The Empties may be obscured by your eye models, so you may find it easier to select them using the Outliner or by quickly toggling wireframe viewport shading (Z).

6. **Grab these Empties and move them forward along the Y-axis (G⇨Y).**

   Moving them about 6 units forward (G⇨Y⇨-6) should be enough.

7. **With the two Empties still selected, snap the 3D cursor to the location between them (Shift+S⇨Cursor to Selected).**

   Because both Empties are selected, the 3D cursor should snap right to the Y-axis.

8. **Add a new Empty and name it `eye_control` (Shift+A⇨Empty).**

9. **Scale the `eye_control` Empty to be twice the size of the other two Empties (S⇨2).**

At this point, all the elements for your simple rig are in place. Your setup should look like the screenshot in Figure 10-13.

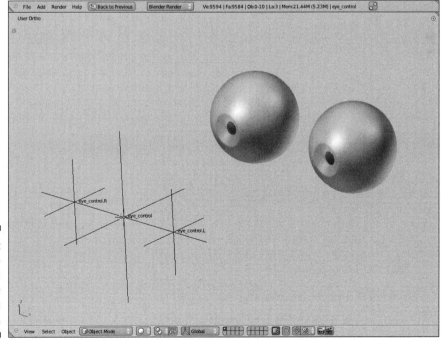

Figure 10-13:
All the elements for a simple eye rig are in place.

Applying constraints

All your pieces and parts are in place; the actors are all on stage, if you will. The next step is getting your Empties to control your eyes. To do this step, you need to set up a couple constraints. Specifically speaking, the workhorse of this rig is the Track To constraint. Use the following steps to apply that constraint to the left eye:

1. **Select the `eye_control.L` Empty and then add `eye.L` to your selection (right-click, Shift+right-click).**

   Remember: Prisoners last.

2. **Add a Track To constraint to `eye.L` (Shift+Ctrl+C⇨Track To).**

   Your eye flips around and faces away from the Empty. The next step fixes that issue.

3. **In Constraints Properties, left-click the –Y button next to the To label in the Track To constraint.**

   Your eye flips back to pointing in the correct direction.

The control for your left eye is now ready to go. Go ahead and play with it. Select `eye_control.L` and grab (G) it around your scene. Your eye should follow it around. Right-click or press Esc to stop grabbing the Empty and it should go back to its original position. From here, you have two options. You can either repeat the preceding steps used on `eye.L` and apply them to `eye.R`, or you can take advantage of a handy Blender add-on: the Copy Attributes Menu. This menu was a built-in feature in previous versions of Blender, brought into the current version of Blender as an add-on.

To enable the Copy Attributes Menu add-on, bring up the User Preferences editor (Ctrl+Alt+U) and go to the Add-Ons section. Left-click the check box to enable the add-on labeled 3D View: Copy Attributes Menu. After you enable this add-on, close the User Preferences editor and go back to the 3D View. Now you can use the following steps to copy the Track To constraint from `eye.L` to `eye.R`:

1. **Select `eye.R` and add `eye.L` to your selection (right-click, Shift+right-click).**

   Remember: Children first.

2. **Copy the Track To constraint from `eye.L` to `eye.R` (Ctrl+C⇨Copy Selected Constraints).**

   When you choose Copy Selected Constraints, Blender provides a menu.

3. **Left-click the TrackTo option and then left-click OK.**

   POW! Your `eye.R` object now has a Track To constraint with the exact same settings as `eye.L`.

Of course, a small problem is that `eye.R` is pointing to the wrong control Empty. Fortunately, this fix is easy. Select `eye.R`, go to its Track To constraint, left-click the Target field, and choose `eye_control.R` from the menu that appears. `eye.R` should now point to the proper control Empty.

Making it easier to control both eye targets at once

At this point, you're basically done with your rig. The only downside is that you have to select both `eye_control.L` and `eye_control.R` to control the direction of both eyes simultaneously. You can parent each of the Empties to the large `eye_control` Empty between them to solve this issue:

1. **Select eye_control.L and eye_control.R (right-click eye_control.L, Shift+right-click eye_control.R).**

2. **Add eye_control to your selection, making it the active object (Shift+right-click eye_control).**

3. **Make eye_control the parent of the other two Empties (Ctrl+P⇨ Object).**

4. **Select eye_control.L and eye_control.R and hide them from view (H).**

   This step isn't critical, but it does help prevent you from selecting those empties and moving them accidentally.

Your simple eye rig is now complete, and you can start animating your eyes. You can control regular eye movement by grabbing (G) the `eye_control` Empty and moving it around your scene. If you want to cross your character's eyes, you can scale (S) the control down. And if you want your character to look like a crazy person, try rotating (R) the `eye_control` Empty.

If you'd like, you can set up basic three-point lighting (see Chapter 9) and set your 3D View to use Textured viewport shading (Alt+Z) and GLSL display shading (N⇨Display⇨GLSL). And if having two disembodied eyes floating in the scene makes you too uncomfortable, you may want to add a sphere as a simple stand-in head.

Animating your eyes

After you have a basic rig created, you can start animating your eyes. Start by switching to the Animation screen layout (Ctrl+←⇨Ctrl+←) and make the modifications described earlier in the section "Customizing your screen layout for animation." You may also want to increase the size of the Graph Editor on the left of the screen as well. Then select the camera in the 3D View and adjust its location and orientation to frame your eyes to your taste. Your screen should look like Figure 10-14.

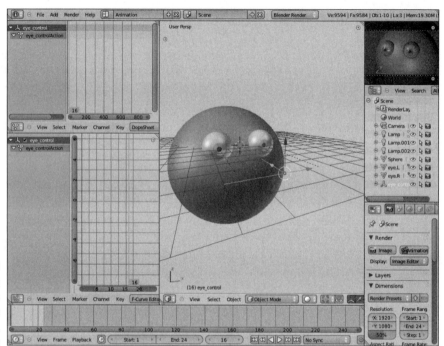

Figure 10-14:
Now you're
ready to
animate.

This specific example is a simple animation of a character rolling its eyes. As a quick test, roll your own eyes and try to figure out how long that action takes. Trying for myself, to get the right feel of the action, it feels like the action takes a full second. I've also noticed that my eyes seem to move faster at the end of the motion than at the beginning. Bearing all this information in mind, you can start animating:

1. **Select `eye_control` and grab it to the left of your character (right-click, G).**

2. **Insert a location keyframe (I⇨Location).**

   This keyframe is the starting point for your animation.

3. **Move forward in time to frame 24.**

   You can move forward by scrubbing in the Timeline or Graph Editor or by changing the Current Frame field in the Timeline's header. Blender's default behavior is to have motion happen at 24 frames per second (fps). This action takes 1 second to complete, which is why you go to frame 24.

4. **Move the `eye_control` Empty to the right of your character (G).**

5. **Insert another location keyframe (I⇨Location).**

You've now animated your character's eyes looking from left to right.

6. **Set the current frame as the end frame of your animation by hovering your mouse over the Timeline and pressing E or by using the Frame⇨Set End Frame menu item.**

You can test the timing of your animation by pressing Alt+A or left-clicking the play button in the Timeline. Press Esc or left-click the pause button to stop playback.

7. **Move to frame 16.**

Because I noticed that my eyes move faster at the end of the motion, I want this keyframe to be closer to the end of the action.

8. **Grab the `eye_control` Empty and move it up in the Z-axis so that it's above your character's head (G).**

9. **Insert another location keyframe (I⇨Location).**

When you play back your animation, your character should now be successfully rolling its eyes.

10. **Tweak your animation to taste using more keyframes or by editing the f-curves in the Graph Editor.**

See? Animation *can* be easy!

Chapter 11

Rigging: The Art of Building an Animatable Puppet

*W*hen it comes to character animation, a character is often a single seamless mesh. As a single seamless mesh, it's virtually impossible to animate that character with any detailed movement using the object animation techniques in Chapter 10. I mean, you can move the whole character mesh at once from one location to another, but you can't make the character smile or wiggle her toes or even bend her arms. You can break the mesh apart and use a complex set of parenting and constraints, but then you lose its nice seamlessness.

What you really want to do is find ways to animate specific parts of the mesh in a controlled way without tearing the mesh apart. To do so, you need to create a rig for your character. A *rig* is an underlying structure for your mesh that allows you to control how it moves. Rigs are an integral part of modern computer animation, and if done well, they make the life of an animator monumentally easier. Think about it like turning your 3D mesh into a remote-control puppet. This chapter explains the various tools and techniques used to create more complex rigs. Then you can create a rig for nearly any object in Blender and have a blast animating it.

Creating Shape Keys

Whether you have to animate a character or a tree or a basketball with any detail, it has to deform from its original shape to a new one. If you know what this new shape looks like, you can model it ahead of time.

As an example, say that you have a cartoony character — maybe the head of a certain monkey. You know that you're going to need her eyes to bulge out because all cartoon characters' eyes do this. To create this effect in Blender, you create a *shape key,* sometimes called a morph target or a blend shape in other programs. A rough outline of the process goes something like this (the next section in this chapter goes into more detail):

1. **Start with your original mesh.**

2. **Edit the vertices of the original mesh *without creating new geometry* to the new pose you want to use.**

    In the cartoony character example, you'd model the character's eyes all bulgy. (Yes, *bulgy* is a real word. I think.)

3. **Record this new arrangement of your vertices as a shape key to be used later when you animate.**

Creating new shapes

Assuming that you selected an object that supports shape keys (meshes, curves, surfaces, and lattices), you can start adding shape keys in the Shape Keys panel of Object Data Properties.

Figure 11-1 shows three different states for the Shape Keys panel. By default, this panel looks pretty innocent and empty with just a list box and a few buttons to the right of it. However, when you left-click the Plus (+) button, a *basis shape,* or the original shape that other shape keys relate to, is added to the list. Left-clicking the Plus (+) button a second time gives you an additional set of options that control the change from the basis shape to a new one, named Key 1.

Figure 11-1:
The three different sets of options that the Shape Keys panel can provide you.

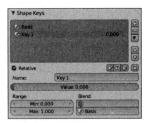

The best way to see how to create new shapes is to go through a practical example. Staying with the bug-eyed monkey theme, use Suzanne as your test subject, and follow these steps:

1. **Start with the default scene and delete the cube (Ctrl+N, right-click the cube, X).**

2. **Add Suzanne, give her a Subdivision Surface modifier, set her smooth, and rotate her 90 degrees around the X-axis (Shift+A⇨Mesh⇨Monkey, Ctrl+1, Tool Shelf⇨Shading⇨Smooth, R⇨X⇨90).**

3. **Change to the front view (Numpad 1).**

4. **Add a shape key (Object Data Properties⇨Shape Keys⇨Plus [+]).**

   Your basis shape is created. The other shapes that you create will be relative to this one.

5. **Add a second shape key (Object Data Properties⇨Shape Keys⇨Plus [+]) and rename it, if you want.**

   The Shape Keys panel looks like the last one in Figure 11-1. You've created `Key 1`. If you want, you can rename it by left-clicking its name field. I named mine `Eye Bulge`.

6. **Tab into Edit mode and change the mesh to have bulged eyes.**

   Make sure that your `Eye Bulge` shape key is active in the Shape Keys panel before making adjustments. As you modify the mode, be sure that you *do not add any extra vertices* to the mesh. You should define the shape by moving around the vertices you already have. A quick way to make Suzanne's eyes bulge is to move your mouse cursor over each eye and press L to select just the vertices there. Then with the Proportional Edit Tool (O) turned on, scale (S) the eyes.

7. **Tab back to Object mode.**

   Figure 11-2 illustrates this process.

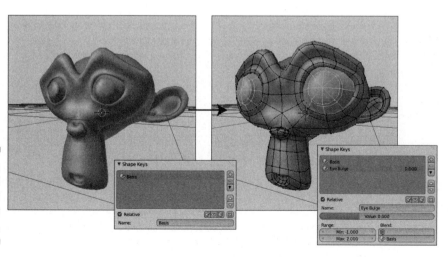

Figure 11-2:
Creating a
bug-eyed
shape key
for Suzanne.

This process creates two shape keys: Basis and Eye Bulge. Using the Value slider in the Shape Keys panel, you can smoothly transition from the Basis shape to the Eye Bulge shape. A value of 0 means that Eye Bulge has no influence and you just have the Basis, whereas a value of 1 means that you're fully at the Eye Bulge shape.

But here's where things get really cool. Notice the Min and Max values at the bottom of the panel, labeled Range. The Min is set to 0.000, and the Max is set to 1.000. Just for kicks, change the Max value to 2.000 and pull the slider all the way to the right. Your bulged eyes grow larger than your actual shape key made them. Now change the Min value to –1.000 and pull the slider to the left. Now Suzanne's eyes pinch in to a point smaller than the Basis pose. Figure 11-3 shows the results of these changes. Adjusting the Min and Max Range values is a great way to provide even more extreme shapes for your characters without having to do any additional shape key modeling. How's that for cool?

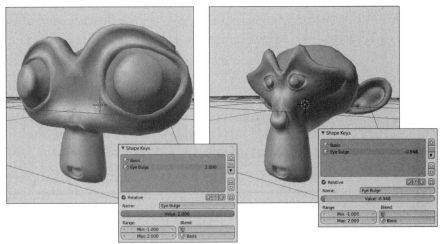

Figure 11-3: Suzanne with excessively bulged and pinched eyes, just by changing the minimum and maximum values for a single shape key.

Mixing shapes

From this point, you can create additional shape keys for the mesh. Say that you want to have a shape key of Suzanne's mouth getting bigger, like she's screaming because her eyes have gotten so huge. In that case, the first thing you want to do is switch back to the basis key by left-clicking the Basis key in the list box of the Shape Keys panel. Unless you're doing something special, you want to have most of your shapes based on the basis. Otherwise, you may end up accidentally overamplifying a shape key or nullifying it. When you're back at the Basis shape, the process is about the same as when creating your initial shapes:

1. **Add a new shape key (Object Data Properties➪Shape Keys➪Plus [+]).**

   Feel free to name this key whatever you want. I called mine Scream.

2. **Tab into Edit mode and model the mouth open with the existing vertices.**

   Make sure that you're not touching Suzanne's eyes. You're just editing the mouth to get bigger.

3. **Tab back into Object mode.**

   Figure 11-4 shows the results of this process.

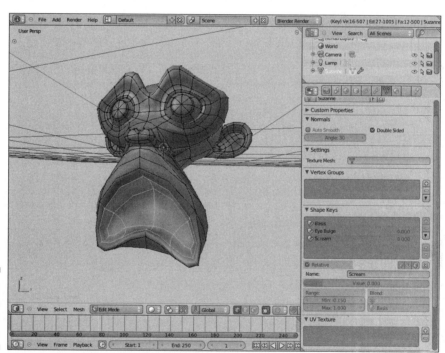

Figure 11-4: Creating a scream shape key.

After you have the Scream shape key created, you can freely mix it with the Eye Bulge shape key, or you can have Suzanne screaming with her regular, bulge-free eyes. The choice is yours. You have the flexibility here to mix and match your shape keys as it pleases you. And animating the mesh to use these keys is really easy.

One principle in this new version of Blender is the idea of "[almost] everything animatable," so animating shape keys is as easy as inserting keyframes on the Value slider in the Shape Keys panel. (Right-click the Value field➪Insert Keyframe or hover your mouse over that field and press I.)

With keys inserted, split off a Graph Editor from your 3D View. Now you can scrub the timeline cursor forward in time and watch Suzanne bulge and scream to your complete delight. As another nice little bonus, if you enable the Show Sliders feature in the Graph Editor (View⇨Show Sliders), you can see the numeric values for your shape keys' influences and even key them.

Knowing where shape keys are helpful

Now, you *could* do an entire animation using shape keys. But do I recommend it? No. You can control your meshes in other ways that may give you more natural movement for things like animating arms and legs.

That said, shape keys are the perfect choice for things that you can't do with these other means (or, at least, that are very difficult). One big one is facial animation. The way parts of the face wrinkle up and move around is pretty difficult to re-create without modeling those deformations. Furrowed brows, squinty eyes, natural-looking smiles, and *phonemes*, or mouth shapes for lip-syncing, are where shape keys shine. You can also team them up with other controls discussed throughout this chapter to achieve cool effects like cartoon stretchiness, muscle bulges, and morphing objects from one shape to another.

Adding Hooks

Shape keys work well for getting specific predefined deformations, but they can be pretty limiting if you want to have a little bit looser control over your mesh or if you're animating things that move in arcs. For these sorts of situations, you have another control mechanism: hooks. *Hooks* are a special kind of modifier that takes a set of vertices or control points and binds them to be controlled by another object, usually an Empty.

Creating new hooks

The workflow for adding a hook is pretty straightforward. You tab into Edit mode and select at least one vertex or control point. Then you press Ctrl+H⇨Hook to New Object. An Empty is created at a location that's the median point of all your selected vertices or control points. You also get a new modifier added to in Modifiers Properties, as shown in Figure 11-5.

Figure 11-5:
Control
options for
the Hook
modifier.

Tab back into Object mode and transform the hook. All the vertices or control points that you assigned to the hook move with it. And using the options in the Hook modifier, you can control how much influence the hook has over these vertices or control points. The following example gives you a clearer understanding of adding and modifying the influence of hooks:

1. **Start with the default scene in Blender (Ctrl+N).**

2. **Select the cube and tab into Edit mode.**

   All the cube's vertices are selected by default. If not, press A until the vertices are selected.

3. **Do a multisubdivide with four cuts (W⇨Subdivide, F6⇨Number of Cuts: 4).**

4. **Select one of the cube's corner vertices (right-click).**

5. **Press Ctrl+Numpad Plus (+) a few times to increase the vertex selection.**

6. **Add a new hook (Ctrl+H⇨Hook to New Empty).**

7. **Tab back into Object mode.**

   At this point, behavior is as expected. If you select and move the Empty, all the vertices that hooked to it move as if they're parented to it.

8. **Increase the Falloff value in the Hook modifier to 1.00 (Modifiers Properties⇨Hook-Empty⇨Falloff: 1.00).**

   Now when you select and transform the Empty, the way the vertices follow it is much smoother, kind of like when you're modeling with the Proportional Edit Tool (O). For additional kicks, do the next step.

9. **Add a Subdivision Surface modifier to the cube and have it drawn smooth (Ctrl+1, Tool Shelf⇨Shading⇨Smooth).**

   Now the transition is even smoother, as shown in Figure 11-6.

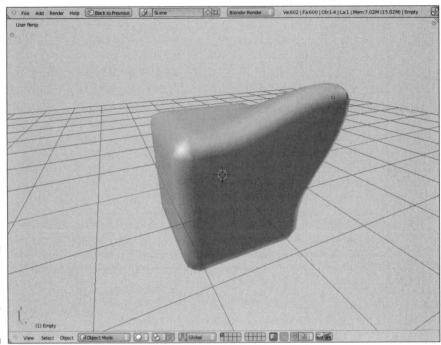

Figure 11-6:
A cube
smoothly
deformed by
a hook.

Knowing where hooks are helpful

The best use for hooks is for large organic deformations. Like shape keys, hooks are nice for creating muscle bulges and cartoony stretching. You can even use them along with shape keys. Because shape keys always use the same shape as the basis for deformation, adding a hook can bring a bit more variety. For example, in the bug-eyed Suzanne example from the "Creating Shape Keys" section, you can add a hook for one of the eyes to make it bulge asymmetrically. These touches give more *character* to your 3D characters.

Another great use for hooks is in animating curves. All the steps in the previous examples of this section work for curves and surfaces as well as meshes. If you have a curve that you're using as a character's tail, you can add a hook at each control point. Then you can animate that tail moving around.

Using Armatures: Skeletons in the Mesh

Shape keys and hooks are great ways to deform a mesh, but the problem with them is that both are lacking a good underlying structure. They're great for big, cartoony stretching and deformation, but for a more structured deformation, like an arm bending at the elbow joint, the motion that they produce is pretty unnatural looking. To solve this problem, 3D computer animation took a page from one of its meatspace contemporaries, stop-motion animation. *Stop-motion animation* involves small sculptures that typically feature a metal skeleton underneath them, referred to as an *armature*. The armature gives the model both structure and a mechanism for making and holding poses. Blender has the same structure and it, too, is called an armature. Armatures form the basis of nearly all Blender rigs.

To add an armature to your scene, go to the 3D View and press Shift+A⇨ Armature⇨Single Bone. As Figure 11-7 shows, adding an armature creates a single object with a weird shape called an octahedron. Continuing to use the skeleton analogy, that octahedron is referred to as a bone in the armature. The wide end of the bone is referred to as the bone's head or root, and its narrow end is referred to as the bone's tail or tip. Typically, a bone pivots at the head.

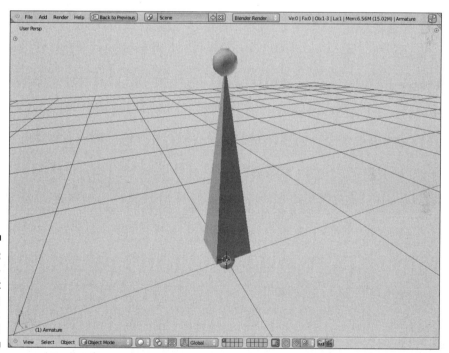

Figure 11-7:
An armature object with a single bone. Woohoo!

Editing armatures

You can take a rather inauspicious single bone armature and do something more interesting with it. Like nearly every other object in Blender, you can edit the armature in more detail by selecting it (right-click) and tabbing into Edit mode. In Edit mode, you can select the sphere at the bone's head, the sphere at the bone's tail, and the bone itself. (Selecting the bone body actually also selects both the head and tail spheres as well.)You can add a new bone to your armature in five ways:

- ✔ **Extrude:** Select either the head or tail of the bone and press E to extrude a new bone from that point. This method is the most common way to add new bones to an armature. If you add a bone by extruding from the tail, you get the additional benefit of having an instant parent-child relationship. The new bone is the child of the one you extruded it from. These bones are linked together, tail to head, and referred to as a bone *chain*. The Ctrl+left-click extrude shortcut for meshes and curves also works for bones.

- ✔ **Duplicate:** Select the body of the bone you want and press Shift+D to duplicate it and create a new bone with the same dimensions, parent relationships, and constraints.

- ✔ **Subdivide:** Select the body of the bone you want and press W⇨Subdivide. You see two bones in the space that the one you selected used to occupy. The cool thing about this option is that it keeps the new bone in the correct parent-child relationship of the bone chain. Also, you can use the Last Operations panel (F6) and do multiple subdivisions.

- ✔ **Adding:** Press Shift+A while still in Edit mode. A new bone is created with its head at the location of the 3D cursor.

- ✔ **Skeleton sketching:** This somewhat advanced feature is incredibly useful for some of the more complex rigging tasks. If you want to try out skeleton sketching, pop open the 3D View's Properties region, enable the Skeleton Sketching check box, and expand its panel at the bottom of the shelf. The fastest way to see what skeleton sketching does is to enable the Quick Sketching check box. Now, when you left-click and drag your mouse cursor in the 3D View, a red line appears in the view. By simply clicking in the screen, you can draw single straight lines. After you're done drawing, right-click, and Blender generates bones along the line you drew.

Armatures can get very complex very quickly, so you should name your bones as you add them. Let me say that again: *Name your bones as you add them.* The fastest way to name your bones is from the Item panel in the 3D View's Properties region (N) and edit the names of your bones the same way you edit names of other Blender objects. Left-click the name in the Bone field and type the name of a bone that makes sense. Alternatively, you can go to Bone Properties and change the name of your bone from the text field at the top. As an example, if you have a two-bone chain to control a character's arm, you may name one bone `arm_upper` and the other `arm_lower`.

Unfortunately, both these techniques can be really slow if you're trying to name a lot of bones at once (because maybe, ahem, you forgot to name your bones as you were adding them). For this hopefully rare case, the Outliner is the best tool for the job. Expand the Armature object to reveal the hierarchy of bones within it. Ctrl+left-click the name of any bone (or any object, for that matter), and you can rename it right there. Figure 11-8 shows the three places where you can name your bones.

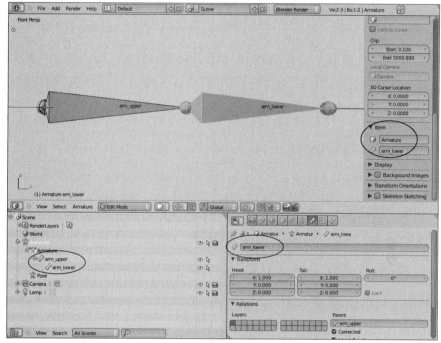

Figure 11-8:
Three different ways to name your bones.

Blender has a pretty cool way of understanding _symmetric rigs,_ or rigs that have a left side that's identical to the right. For these cases, use a `.L` and `.R` suffix on your bone names. So in the previous example, if you're rigging a character with two arms, the bones in the left arm would be named `arm_upper.L` and `arm_lower.L`. The right arm bones would be named `arm_upper.R` and `arm_lower.R`. This naming convention gives you a couple of advantages, but the one that's most apparent when modeling your rig is the X-Axis Mirror feature.

To understand how symmetric rigs and X-axis mirroring work better, create a new armature at the origin (Shift+S⇨Cursor to Center, Shift+A⇨Armature⇨ Single Bone) and follow these steps:

1. **Tab into Edit mode on your armature and change to front view (Numpad 1).**

2. **Select the tail of the single bone and extrude a bone to the right (E).**

3. **Name this bone Bone.R.**

4. **Select the tail of the main, or _root,_ bone again and extrude another new bone, but this time to the left (E).**

5. **Name this bone Bone.L.**

6. **In Tool Shelf (T), enable the X-Axis Mirror check box.**

7. **Select the tail of `Bone.R` and grab it to move it around (G).**

   Now, wherever you move the tail of this bone, the tail of `Bone.L` matches that movement on the other side of the X-axis. You can even extrude (E) a new bone, and a new bone is extruded on both sides of the axis. In this way, X-axis mirroring can speed up the rigging process immensely.

When editing bones, it's a good idea to make visible the mesh for which your rig is intended. This way, you get your proportions correct. A good general rule for placing bones is to think about where the character's real anatomical bones would be located and then use that as a guideline.

Parenting bones

One important thing that makes armatures helpful is the notion of how its bones relate to one another. The most important of these relationships is the parent-child relationships between bones. The same hotkeys for parenting and unparenting objects also work with bones, but with a couple additional features. To illustrate the additional features when parenting bones, start a new scene (Ctrl+N), delete the default cube (X), add a new armature object (Shift+A⇨Armature⇨Single Bone), and then tab into Edit mode. Then follow these steps:

1. **Select the single bone created, duplicate it, and place it somewhere in space (right-click, Shift+D).**

2. **Add the original bone to your selection (Shift+right-click).**

3. **Press Ctrl+P to make the original bone the parent of the duplicate.**

   You're given two options:

   • **Connected:** This option moves the head of the child bone to the same location as the tail of the parent, creating a bone chain as if you'd created the second bone by extruding it from the first.

   • **Keep Offset:** Choosing this option leaves the child bone in place and draws a dashed relationship line between the two bones. They're not connected, but one still has an influence on the other.

4. **After you create the parent relationship, select the child bone.**

5. **Clear the parent relationship by pressing Alt+P.**

   You have another pair of options:

   • **Clear Parent:** This option removes any sort of parent-child relationship this bone has. If the bone was connected to the parent bone, it's now disconnected, and you can move it around freely.

   • **Disconnect Bone:** This option doesn't actually clear the parent relationship. Instead, if your bones are connected, choosing this option maintains the parent-child relationship, but the child bone can move independently of the parent's tip. The bone behaves as if you made the parent by using the Keep Offset option.

Figure 11-9 shows how two bones in an armature can be related.

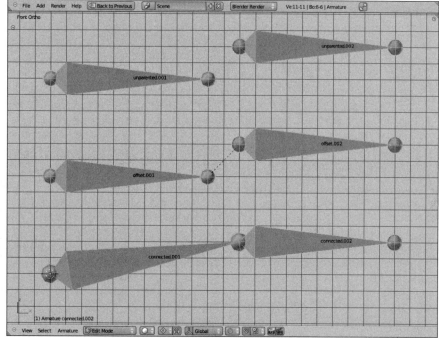

Figure 11-9:
Bones that are unparented, with an offset parent, and parented with a connection.

Even with bones parented — connected or otherwise — if you rotate the parent bone, the child doesn't rotate with it as you might expect in a typical parent-child relationship. That's because you're still in Edit mode, which is designed mostly for building and modifying the armature's structure. The parent-child relationship actually works in a special mode for armatures called Pose mode. You access this mode by pressing Ctrl+Tab. When you're in Pose mode, if you select individual bones and rotate them, their children rotate with them, as you might expect. From there, you can swap back out to Object mode by pressing Ctrl+Tab again, or you can jump back into Edit mode by just pressing Tab. Chapter 12 has more on working in Pose mode.

Armature properties

When working with armatures, the Properties editor has some sections specific to armatures with options and controls that are incredibly helpful. Select your armature (right-click) and have a look at the Properties editor. In particular, note that the Object Data Properties show an icon of a figure, and you see two additional sets of properties: Bone Properties and Bone Constraints Properties. Figure 11-10 shows the contents of these panels.

Figure 11-10:
Armature
properties.

As you may have guessed, Object Data Properties provide options for the Armature overall, while Bone Properties provide options for the currently selected bone. Looking first at the Bone Properties, some options and controls are immediately helpful. The text field at the top lets you rename your bone. The Transform panel gives you precise numeric control over the location of the head and tail of the selected bone, as well as its *roll angle,* or the orientation of the octahedron between the head and the tail. These controls are exactly the same as the transform controls in the 3D View's Properties region.

In the Relations panel, you can define how the selected bone relates to other bones in the armature. In particular, the Parent field displays the selected bone's current parent, if it has one, and allows you to choose another existing bone as its parent. If you have a parent defined here, the Connected check box beneath it allows you to tell Blender whether it's connected to its parent.

On the left side of the Relations panel are a series of buttons, known as *bone layers,* which look like the layers buttons in the 3D View's header. Just as you can place objects on layers in Object mode, Blender's armatures have a special set of layers to themselves. The reason is that character rigs can get pretty involved. Using bone layers is a good way to keep the rig logical and organized. Left-click a layer button to assign the bone to it. If you'd like the bone to live on more than one layer, you can Shift+left-click the buttons for those layers.

The options in the various armature-related sections of the Properties editor change a bit between Edit mode (Tab), Object mode, and Pose mode (Ctrl+Tab). What I cover is available in Edit mode and Pose mode.

Two other important sets of controls are in Bone Properties. The first is the Deform panel. Simply put, the check box for this panel is a toggle that tells Blender whether the selected bone can be mapped to the geometry of your mesh. If it is mapped, or *weighted,* to the mesh, then that bone is considered a *deformer.* Deformers should have the Deform check box in Bone Properties enabled. Besides deformers, you can also have bones whose purpose is to control the behavior of the deformer bones. These bones are often referred to as *control* bones. To prevent the control bones from inadvertently influencing your mesh's geometry, you want to make sure that the Deform check box is disabled in Bone Properties.

Back in Object Data Properties, two sets of layer buttons appear in the Skeleton panel. These buttons correspond to the bone layers in Bone Properties. The layer buttons under the Layers label control which layers the armature is actually displaying in the 3D View. The layer buttons under the Protected Layers label have an effect only if you're linking your rig into a separate scene file. That topic is a bit more advanced than what this book covers, so I leave it at that for now.

One option I like to enable in this panel is the Quaternion check box. This option is more relevant after you begin animating with your rig, but enabling it makes the armature deform the mesh assigned to it a lot more cleanly than if it's disabled. Occasionally, enabling the Quaternion check box can cause deformation artifacts in your character mesh, but that is usually pretty rare.

The Display panel contains a set of buttons for controlling how bones in the armature are displayed:

✔ **Bone types:** You can enable only one of these four buttons at any point in time. Note, however, that even though the bone type may not be drawn in the 3D View, its influences are still valid. That is, even if you're displaying Stick bones, they still control the same vertices within the range of the Envelope bones. Figure 11-11 shows examples of each of these bone types.

• **Octahedral:** The default bone type, the octahedral shape is great for building a rig because it shows which way a bone points as well as its roll angle.

• **Stick:** This type draws the bones as a thin stick. I like to animate with my bones in this type so that they stay out of my way.

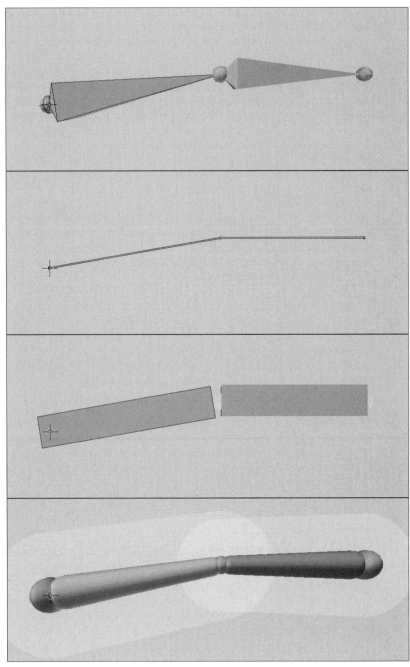

Figure 11-11:
The different types of bones in Blender from top to bottom: octahedral, stick, b-bone, and envelope.

- **B-Bone:** B-bones are drawn as boxes. The interesting thing, though, is that b-bones can be dynamically subdivided and treated as simple Bézier curves. To increase a bone's subdivisions, select the bone and switch to the Deform panel in Bone Properties. In this panel, increase the Segments value, which makes the deformation from one bone to the next much smoother. The chain on the cover of this book was rigged using b-bones. Even if you don't display the b-bone type, Blender still pays attention to the Segments value. So if your character deforms in an unexpected way, you may want to check the Segments value in Bone Properties.

- **Envelope:** This type draws the bones with a scalable sphere at each end and a tube for the bone body. Vertices on your mesh that are within the influence area of these bones will have their locations influenced by them. Ctrl+Alt+S increases the bone's range.

✔ **Extra display options:** You can enable all, one, or none of these controls in any combination you desire.

- **Names:** This control displays the name of each bone in the 3D View. Names can make selecting bones and defining constraints much easier.

- **Axes:** This control displays the center axis of the bones. The Axes check box is helpful for understanding the bones' true roll angle.

- **Shapes:** To help communicate a bone's purpose to the animator, you can display any bone in Blender as any object in your scene. While in Pose mode, select a bone and go to the Display panel in Bone Properties. There, you can define the object you want as your bone shape by choosing it from the Custom Shape field. With the Shapes check box enabled in Object Data Properties, the bone is displayed as your chosen object while in Pose mode.

- **Colors:** To help organize bones in an armature for an animator, you can actually define custom colors for bones by using bone groups (see the section "Making the rig more user friendly"). Set all facial controls to blue, or the left side of the armature in red. Enable this check box so that you can make use of those colors.

- **X-Ray:** The X-Ray check box in this panel does the same thing that the X-Ray check box in Object Properties does. It allows you to see the bone in the 3D View, even if it's technically inside or behind another object. Enabling this feature makes your bones much easier to select when rigging or animating.

- **Delay Refresh:** Rigs by themselves can be very complex. After they have a mesh assigned to them, the system becomes even more complex — sometimes to the point that slower computers can't keep up and perform with any reasonable response. In this type of scenario, enabling this check box may be beneficial because it prevents Blender from trying to calculate how your mesh deforms while you modify a pose on your rig, delaying that calculation until after you finish grabbing, scaling, or rotating a bone.

Putting skin on your skeleton

Armatures and bones are pretty interesting, but they do you no good if they don't actually deform your mesh. When you create your own rig, and Ctrl+Tab to Pose mode, you can grab, rotate, and scale bones, but the moving bones have no influence whatsoever on your mesh. What you need to do is bind the vertices of the mesh to specific bones in your armature. This binding process is commonly referred to as *skinning*. Blender has two primary ways of skinning: envelopes and vertex groups.

Quick-and-dirty skinning with envelopes

Envelopes are the quickest way to get a mesh's vertices to be controlled by the armature. You don't have to create anything extra: It's just a simple parenting operation that seals the deal. To use envelopes to control your mesh, use the following steps:

1. **In Object mode or Pose mode, select the mesh (right-click) and then add the armature to your selection (Shift+right-click).**

2. **Make the armature the parent of the mesh (Ctrl+P).**

   Choose Armature Deform from the menu that appears. Upon completion, your mesh is a child of the armature object, and it also now has an Armature modifier applied. The modifier is what allows the armature to deform your mesh. Without the modifier, it's just a simple parenting.

   When you Ctrl+Tab into Pose mode on your armature, the mesh is now under its influence.

3. **Go to Object Data Properties and enable the Envelope bone type.**

   This step reveals exactly where the influence of your envelopes lies.

4. **If some part of your mesh isn't under the influence of an envelope, tab into Edit mode and edit its size and influence.**

   (Actually, if you just want to edit the influence, you can do so directly with the Ctrl+Alt+S hotkey combination.)

Figure 11-12 illustrates envelopes in action.

Envelopes are great for quickly roughing out a rig and testing it on your mesh, but for detailed deformations, they aren't ideal. Where the influence of multiple envelopes overlap can be particularly problematic, and there's a good tendency for envelope-based rigs to have characters pinch a bit at their joints. For these cases, a more detailed approach is necessary.

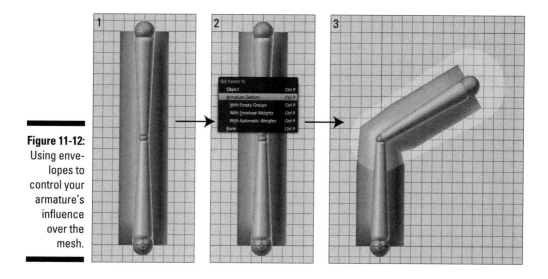

Figure 11-12:
Using enve-
lopes to
control your
armature's
influence
over the
mesh.

That said, using envelopes in your armature does give you one distinct control that you can't have with armatures otherwise. You can actually use an armature with envelopes to control the deformation of curves and surfaces. So long as a control point is within the influence space of a bone's envelope, you can modify it and therefore animate it with the armature.

Assigning weights to vertices

So if envelopes are the imprecise way of controlling your mesh, what's the precise way? The answer is vertex groups. A *vertex group* is basically what it sounds like — a set of vertices that have been assigned to a named group.

In many ways, a vertex group is a lot like a material slot (see Chapter 7). Besides the fact that vertex groups don't deal with materials, vertex groups have a couple of distinctions that set them apart from material slots. First of all, vertex groups aren't mutually exclusive. Any vertex may belong to any number of vertex groups that you define.

The other distinction is that you can give a vertex a *weight*, or a numerical value that indicates how much that particular vertex is influenced or dedicated to the vertex group. A weight of 1.0 means that the vertex is fully dedicated to that group, whereas a weight of 0 means that although the vertex is technically part of the group, it may as well not be.

One thing to note: Vertex groups need to have the exact name of the bones that control them. So if you have a bone called `pelvis`, you need a corresponding vertex group with the same name. The vertices assigned to that group then have their position influenced by the location, rotation, and scale of the pelvis bone, tempered by the vertices' individual weights.

To adjust the assignments and weights of vertices in their respective vertex groups, you can use the Vertex Groups panel in Object Data Properties for your selected mesh. You create a new group with the Plus (+) button to the right of the list box. To select the vertices that you want to assign to the group, you need to tab into Edit mode. With the vertices selected in Edit mode, you can adjust the value in the Weight slider and then assign them to the vertex group by left-clicking the Assign button.

If you don't see the Assign button or Weight slider in the Vertex Groups panel, then you're not in Edit mode. Tab into Edit mode and those controls should appear for you.

Something to note about vertex weights is that, when used for armatures, they are *normalized* to 1.000. That is, a vertex can be a member of two vertex groups and have a weight of 1.000 for both. In these cases, Blender adjusts the weights internally so that they add up to 1.000. So in my example, that double-grouped vertex behaves like it has a weight of 0.500 on both groups.

Of course, on a complex armature, this process of creating vertex groups and painstakingly assigning weights to each vertex can get excessively tedious. Fortunately, Blender has a couple tools to make things less painful. First of all, you don't have to create all the vertex groups by yourself. Refer to the preceding section on the process of skinning with envelopes. By parenting the mesh to the armature there, you're presented with a few options. For using envelopes only, you choose Ctrl+P⇨Armature Deform. However, the other options give you a lot of power when you use vertex groups:

- ✔ **Object:** This option is just a simple parenting operation. Your whole mesh becomes a child of the armature object, just as if you'd parented it to another mesh. No modifier is applied to your mesh at all.

- ✔ **Armature Deform:** As in the envelope skinning example of the preceding section, this option doesn't create any vertex groups, thereby ensuring that the mesh is only influenced by the bone envelopes.

  - • **With Empty Groups:** This option creates vertex groups for you using the names of all the bones with the Deform check box enabled in Bone Properties. However, it doesn't automatically assign any vertices to any of those groups. Use this option if you want to manually assign weights. Without assigning any weights, the default behavior is to be controlled only by bone envelopes.

  - • **With Envelope Weights:** This option is a bit of a compromise. It first creates the vertex groups based on the bones with their Deform option turned on. Then it looks at the influence area of the bone envelope and uses that to assign vertices to each vertex group, with their weights varied accordingly. The advantage of this option is that it gets you weighted vertices. The downside, though, is that if the influence area of your envelopes isn't set up well, the weight assignment can look messy.

- **With Automatic Weights:** This is my favorite option to use. It works like the With Envelope Weights option, but instead of using the influence area of the bone envelopes to determine weights, it uses a more complex process that generally results in better vertex assignments and weights.

✔ **Bone:** This is a simple parenting operation like the Object option. No Armature modifier is applied to your mesh. The only difference here is that rather than parent your mesh to the whole armature object, this option allows you to parent your object to a single bone.

Regardless of which option you choose, you'll probably still have to go in and manually tweak the weights of the vertices in each vertex group. Trying to do those tweaks just from the Vertex Groups panel can be pretty painful. Fortunately, there is Weight Paint mode. This mode is almost exactly like Vertex Paint mode (see Chapter 7), except that rather than painting color on the mesh, you're painting the weight assignment to a specified vertex group.

To access Weight Paint mode, select the mesh (right-click) and press Ctrl+Tab. Alternatively, you can choose Weight Paint mode from the Mode menu in the 3D View's header. Even if you don't intend to paint weights, Weight Paint mode is a great way to see how the weights were assigned by Blender if you used the automatic method.

The way that weights are visualized is kind of like a thermal map where red is the hottest value and blue is the coldest value. Extending this logic to work with bone weights, vertices that are painted red have a weight of 1.0, whereas vertices painted blue are either not assigned to the vertex group or have a weight of zero. The 50 percent weight color is bright green.

If the thermal map color styling isn't your thing (as can be the case if you're colorblind), you can define your own weight paint color range using the ramp editor in the bottom right of the System section of Blender's User Preferences (Ctrl+Alt+U). When in Weight Paint mode, you get a bunch of painting panels in the Tool Shelf, as shown in Figure 11-13. With a few minor exceptions, these controls are identical to the ones used in Vertex Paint mode.

When weight painting, it's often useful to enable the Wire check box in the Display panel of Object Properties. Enabling this check box overlays the mesh's wireframe on it. Seeing the wireframe is especially helpful when weight painting because it helps you see where the actual vertices on the mesh are. That way, you're not just painting in empty space where no vertices exist. The only slight hiccup is if you're painting *planar vertices,* or vertices that all share the same plane. In this particular case, Blender tries to simplify the wireframe overlay. While that simplification may be nice in general, it can be problematic when painting. To get around that obstacle, enable the All Edges check box in the Display panel in the 3D View's Properties region (N).

Figure 11-13:
The painting panels in the Tool Shelf when Weight Paint mode is activated.

A handy feature in the Tool Shelf while weight painting is the X-Mirror check box in the Options panel. X-Mirror can literally cut your weight painting time in half. When you enable this check box, Blender takes advantage of the left/right naming convention discussed earlier in the "Editing armatures" section of this chapter. So if you're tweaking the vertex weights on the left leg, Blender automatically updates the weights for the corresponding bone on the right leg so that they match. If that ain't cool, I don't know what is.

The actual process of weight painting is nearly identical to using vertex paint. However, you need to pay attention to one more thing with weight painting: the need to tell Blender which vertex group you're painting. You can do so in two ways. The slow way, you already know: Select the group from the list box in the Vertex Groups panel in your mesh's Object Data Properties.

Of course, the kind Blender developers have provided a faster way: Select (right-click) the bone that you want to paint weights for, and Blender automatically activates the corresponding vertex group and allows you to paint. As an added bonus, you can test your weights on the fly by grabbing, rotating, or scaling the selected bone while you're still in Weight Paint mode.

Because weight paint relies so much on color, I highly recommend you look at the full-color version of a simple mesh in Weight Paint mode in this book's color insert.

If you choose to use vertex groups, you have something else to decide. Have a look at the Armature modifier on your mesh. Under the Bind To label are two check boxes: Vertex Groups and Bone Envelopes. With both enabled, the mesh is influenced by both vertex groups, as well as the bone envelopes from your armature. This double influence can be useful in some instances, but I tend to prefer to work with just one or the other. And if I create vertex groups and assign weights to vertices, I generally disable the Bone Envelopes check box. Your rigging needs may be different, but this setup works for me because this way I know that the only reason a vertex is deforming improperly is that I didn't assign its weight properly. I don't have to concern myself with the influence of the bone's envelope.

Practical Example: Rigging Stickman

As you may have guessed, rigging is a pretty intensive process. You need to be technically minded and creative at the same time. The best riggers I've ever met are the sort of people who fit this description and have an eye for the big picture. These sorts of people enjoy playing Minesweeper, finding pleasure in solving the integrated relationships in each part of that game.

Well, regardless of whether you're one of these people, the best way to understand the full process of rigging is to actually create a rig of your own. The examples throughout the rest of this section are done with a simple stick figure character that I like to use for creating quick animations that test body language and timing. I love animating with stick figures, even in 3D. Ninety percent of an animated character's personality comes through in his body language. Animating with stick figures allows you to focus on that essential step and keeps you from getting distracted with secondary details.

This stick figure, in both rigged and unrigged versions, is included with the DVD that accompanies this book so that you have a finished reference, as well as a file, to practice with. Of course, if you have a character already modeled and want to rig it, that's great. You can use the techniques here for nearly anything you want to build a rig for.

Building Stickman's centerline

If you load the `stickman.blend` file from the DVD, the first thing you might notice is his pose. He's standing up with his arms out to his sides. This stance is referred to as a *T pose* because the character looks like the letter T. This pose is probably the most common one that modelers use when they create their characters, and it's the most preferred pose for riggers. Some modelers may also model with the arms at the sides, or sometimes they have the arms somewhere halfway between the T pose and having arms at the side. There are valid reasons people give for any of these poses, but ultimately it really comes down to personal preference.

Time to get an armature in this mesh. A good way to start is to create the centerline bones first: the body bones, the head, and the hipbone. To create these bones, use the following steps:

1. **Add your armature and start with the first body bone (Shift+A⇨ Armature⇨Single Bone).**

2. **Enable X-Ray viewing for the armature (Object Data Properties⇨ Display⇨X-Ray).**

   This step ensures that you can always see the bones of your armature.

3. **Tab into Edit mode and move this bone up in the Z-axis until it's around Stickman's waistline (G⇨Z).**

4. **Select the tail of this bone and move it up in the Z-axis until it's at the top of the torso (right-click, G⇨Z).**

5. **Subdivide this bone into two bones (W⇨Subdivide).**

6. **Name the bottom bone body.1 and the top bone body.2.**

7. **Select the joint between the two bones and move it back in the Y-axis a little bit (right-click, G⇨Y).**

   This step helps the bones match the natural curvature of the spine.

8. **Select the tail of body.2 and extrude it up in the Z-axis to the top of Stickman's head (right-click, E⇨Z).**

9. **Name this bone head.**

10. **Select the head of body.1 and extrude it down in the Z-axis to the bottom of Stickman's pelvis (right-click, E⇨Z).**

11. **Name this bone hip.**

    You have something that looks like Figure 11-14.

Adding Stickman's appendages

The next step is to create bones for the arms and the legs. You do so by creating bones for half of the rig and then letting Blender do the rest of the work for you by mirroring the bones. First things first, though — you have to create one-half of the rig:

1. **Switch to the front view, select the head bone, and duplicate it, putting its root at Stickman's left shoulder joint (Numpad 1, right-click, Shift⇨D).**

   Note that by working this way, the new bone is an offset child of the body.2 bone.

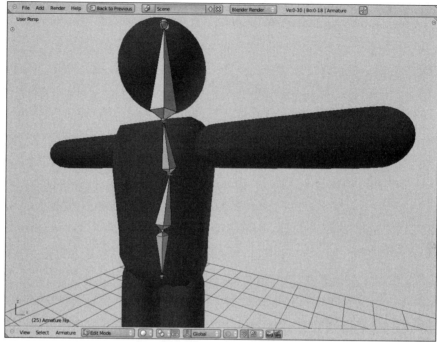

Figure 11-14:
Stickman
has an
armature
for his
centerline.

2. **Name this new bone `arm_upper.L`.**

3. **Select the tail of `arm_upper.L` and move it to Stickman's elbow.**

   It may help to press Ctrl to guarantee that the bone is perfectly horizontal (right-click, G➪Ctrl).

4. **Extrude this tail to create a new bone along the X-axis that extends to Stickman's hand (E➪X).**

5. **Name this new bone `arm_lower.L`.**

6. **From the front view, select the hipbone and duplicate it, placing the new bone's head at the top of Stickman's left leg (Numpad 1, right-click, Shift+D).**

7. **Select this new bone's tail and move it along the Z-axis to Stickman's feet (right-click, G➪Z).**

8. **Select this bone and subdivide it into two bones (right-click, W➪Subdivide).**

9. **Name the top bone `leg_upper.L` and the bottom bone `leg_lower.L`.**

10. **Select the joint between these bones and move it forward in the Y-axis a little bit (right-click, G➪Y).**

    This step gives the knee a little bit of bend, which helps deformation when adding constraints.

11. Parent `leg_upper.L` to hip (right-click `leg_upper.L`, Shift+right-click hip, Ctrl+P⇨Keep Offset).

You now have something that looks like Figure 11-15.

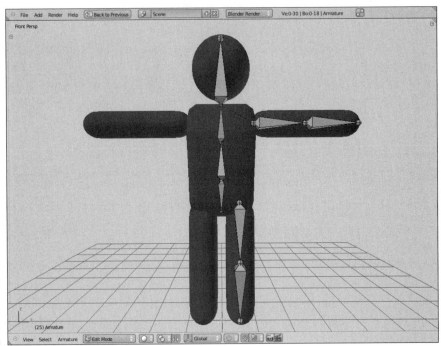

Now for the really cool part of letting Blender do the work for you. You want to select all the bones that aren't on the centerline, duplicate them, and mirror them along the X-axis. Here are the specific hotkeys and steps:

1. **Select both arm bones and both leg bones using Border Select (B).**

2. **Duplicate the selected bones and immediately press Esc (Shift+D, Esc).**

   The newly created bones appear in the exact same location as their originators.

3. **Have Blender automatically give these new bones the `.R` suffix to indicate that they're on the right side (W⇨Flip Names).**

   All your bones are properly named now, but half of them are still in the wrong part of the rig. The next step is where the magic lies.

4. **Enable X-Axis Mirror in the Tool Shelf (Tool Shelf⇨Armature Options⇨ X-Axis Mirror).**

5. **Select all bones (A⇨A).**

6. **Grab your bones and immediately escape out of it (G⇨Esc).**

   Pow! Instantly, your bones pop to their correct places and your rig now looks like what's in Figure 11-16.

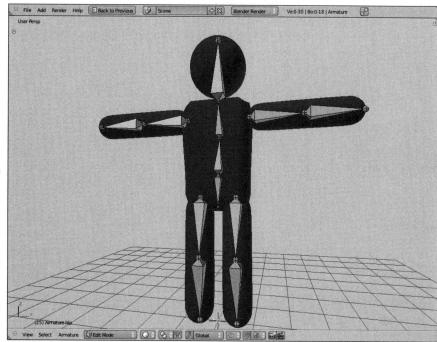

Figure 11-16: Stickman with a skeleton in him. He's almost rigged, but he still needs some controls.

As an astute reader, you may find yourself wondering why you didn't use Blender's Mirror operator (Ctrl+M) to flip Stickman's arms and legs to the correct side of his body. Unfortunately, sometimes the Mirror operation messes up the roll angle of bones in the rig. Letting the X-Axis Mirror feature handle things for you gives you a better chance of having correct roll angles on both sides of your character's rig.

Taking advantage of parenting and constraints

What you currently have in place is the basic structure of the rig's armature. The primary function of these bones is to deform the character mesh. Technically, you *could* animate with just these bones after you skin them to the mesh. However, you can (and should) add some additional bones to the armature to make it easier to animate. They work by taking advantage of the parenting set up by the bone chains and combining them with some reasonable constraints.

For example, you currently have a structured skeleton in place, but what happens if you Ctrl+Tab into Pose mode and grab the body.1 bone and move it (G)? Because the entire upper body is directly or indirectly a child of this bone, the upper torso, arms, and head move with the body.1 bone. Unfortunately, the lower half of the body doesn't share this relationship, so as Figure 11-17 shows, you end up tearing Stickman's skeleton in half. Ouch!

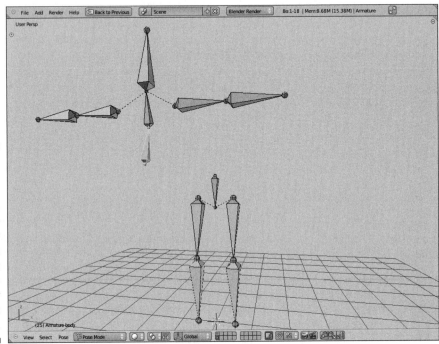

Figure 11-17:
There's nothing relating the upper body to the lower body, so you can accidentally tear Stickman in half.

To compensate, you need a bone — called a *root bone* — that both the hip and body.1 bones relate to, binding the upper half of the body to the lower half. Moving this bone should move the entire armature. Adding a root bone to the rig is pretty simple:

1. **Tab into Edit mode on the armature and switch to the side view (Numpad 3).**

2. **Select the head of either the body.1 or hip bones (right-click).**

   Both heads are located in the same place, so it doesn't really matter which one you select.

3. **Extrude a new bone along the Y-axis (E⇨Y) and name it root.**

   Move in the positive Y direction, toward the back of Stickman.

4. **Parent the body.1 and hip bones to the root bone (right-click body.1, Shift+right-click hip, Shift+right-click root, Ctrl+P⇨Keep Offset).**

   This parent relationship means that you can move the entire armature by just selecting and moving the root bone. Before creating this parent relationship, some people may choose to switch the direction of the root bone (W⇨Switch Direction) so that they can have the root bone's tip actually connected to the heads of body.1 and hip. It's all a matter of taste, but I prefer not to. Because bones naturally rotate around their head, it's more useful to me to keep the head of the root bone in the center of the character. In my opinion, using this setup helps make bending at the waist look more natural.

5. **Select the root bone and disable the Deform check box in its Bone Properties.**

   This bone is intended purely to control the other bones. You don't want any of the mesh's vertices assigned to it. Your Stickman rig now looks something like Figure 11-18.

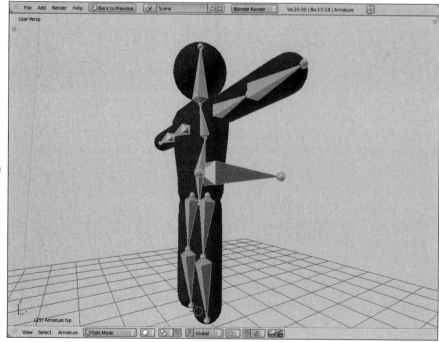

Figure 11-18:
Adding a root bone to the rig prevents the top of the body from unnecessarily leaving the bottom.

Another convenient control bone that you may want to add is a head control. Sure, you can rotate the head bone as you want, but using a bone as the head's (or eyes') target is often easier. That way, when you want the character to look at something, you just move the target bone to that something's location. An added benefit is that by building your rig this way, you can successfully create complex moves, such as keeping the character looking at an object as he walks by it. To add a head control to your rig, you use a Track To constraint:

1. **Tab into Edit mode and select the head bone (Tab, right-click).**

2. **Duplicate the head bone and move it in the Y-axis (Shift+D⇨Y) and name it head_target.**

   The idea is that you want the control bone to be far enough in front of the face so that you can have some control without getting in the way of the rest of the rig. I moved mine about 3 units out.

3. **Clear the parent relationship on the head_target bone (Alt+P⇨Clear Parent).**

   Because the head_target bone came into being by duplicating the head bone, it inherited the parent relationship to the body.2 bone. You don't want this relationship because you want to be able to move the head target independently of the rest of the rig.

4. **Ctrl+Tab into Pose mode, select the head_target bone, and then also select the head bone (right-click, Shift+right-click).**

5. **Add a Track To constraint to the head bone (Shift+Ctrl+C⇨Track To).**

   This step automatically adds a Track To constraint to the head bone's Bone Constraints Properties and makes the bone a nice shade of green. Chances are good that the head bone also rotates toward head_target and points directly at it — not the behavior you want. You need to change the alignment axes that the constraint works on.

6. **In the Track To constraint, change the To axis to -Z and the Up axis to Y.**

   This step fixes the head bone so that it points in the proper direction. Now when you grab (G) the head_target bone and move it around, the head bone always points at it.

7. **Select the head_target bone and disable the Deform check box in its Bone Properties.**

   Like the root bone, this bone isn't intended to deform the mesh, so disabling the Deform button ensures that it doesn't. Figure 11-19 shows what your rig looks like now.

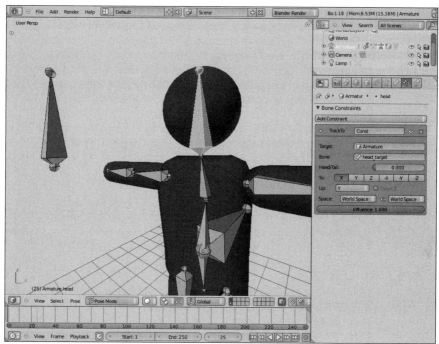

Figure 11-19:
The
Stickman
rig, now
with head
control!

Your Stickman is mostly functional now. However, another constraint is a staple of nearly all character rigs and is monumentally helpful to animators. It's called an *inverse kinematics*, or IK, constraint. The next section goes into what this constraint does, how it works, and how to give your rig its benefits.

Comparing inverse kinematics and forward kinematics

When it comes to animating characters in 3D with an armature, you have two ways to move limbs around: *inverse kinematics* and *forward kinematics*, or *IK* and *FK*. Kinematic is just a fancy way of saying motion. By default, your rig is set up to use FK. Say that you have a bone chain, and you want to place the tip of the last bone to a specific location in 3D space. In order to do so, you have to rotate the first bone in the chain, and then the next, and then the next, and so on until you can get that last bone's tip properly placed. You're working your way *forward* along the bone chain. Because of the parenting relationships between the bones, you can currently use FK with your Stickman rig.

That's FK. It gets the job done, but it can be awfully difficult and tedious to try to get the tip of that last bone exactly where you want it. It would be nice if you could just grab that tip, put it in place, and let the computer figure out how all the other bones have to bend to compensate. This method of letting the computer figure things out for you, basically, is the essence of IK. You move the tip of the last bone in the chain, and Blender works *backward* along the chain to get the other bones properly placed.

To see what IK is like, select your Stickman armature and Ctrl+Tab into Pose mode. Now, select the body.2 bone and press G to grab and move it. Notice that all the bone does is rotate; it doesn't actually change its location. Now go to Pose Options panel in the Tool Shelf and left-click the Auto IK check box. Auto IK isn't a real IK constraint, but it will help you understand how IK works. Grab (G) and move the body.2 bone. Notice that, now, this bone moves around, and the body.1 bone rotates to compensate for the locations that you try to put body.2. Selecting the head bone or one of the arm_lower bones results in similar behavior. Click around and play with Auto IK on your rig. It's pretty cool. When you're done, disable the Auto IK check box.

IK is really awesome stuff and it's very powerful, but it's not the ultimate solution for animating. See, one of the core principles of animation is that natural movement happens in arcs. Generally speaking, arcing movement is more believable and, well, natural looking. Things that move in a straight line tend to look stiff and robotic. Think about how a person's arms swing when walking. It doesn't necessarily matter exactly where the hand is. The entire arm rotates and swings back and forth. That is FK movement. If you're animating, you can easily re-create that motion by keying the rotation of the upper arm bone at the extreme ends of the action.

In contrast, IK movement tends to happen in a straight line. You're just keying the tip of the chain, so that tip moves directly from one location to the next and the bones along the chain rotate to compensate. To re-create a swinging arm in IK, you need *at least* three keyframes: one at each extreme and one in the middle to keep the hand from going in a straight line. And even then, the elbow might flip the wrong direction, or you might need even more intermediary keys to try to get that smooth arc that you get automatically with FK.

Where IK shines is when the tip of the bone chain needs to be precisely positioned. A perfect example is feet. When a person walks, the feet must touch the ground. Trying to achieve this effect with just FK usually ends up with feet that look floaty and not locked into place as the character moves. Another example is if the character is holding on to something and doesn't want to let go of it, like the edge of a cliff. You want to keep the hand in place and let the elbow bend naturally. In instances like these, IK is really helpful. The biggest use, though, is for foot and leg rigs on characters. And to that end, you're going to use the following steps to add IK controls to the Stickman rig:

1. **Tab into Edit mode on the armature and select the tip of the `leg_lower.L` bone.**

   You can actually select either the left or right bone. Because you should still have X-Axis Mirror enabled, whatever you do on one side also happens on the other. If X-Axis Mirror isn't enabled, go ahead and re-enable it.

2. **Extrude a new bone in the Z-axis (E⇨Z).**

   You don't have to extrude the new bone very far — just enough to know it's there.

3. **Name this bone `leg_IK.L` and make sure that the mirrored bone is named `leg_IK.R`.**

4. **Clear the parent-child relationship between `leg_IK.L` and `leg_lower.L` (Alt+P⇨Clear Parent).**

5. **Ctrl+Tab into Pose mode, select `leg_IK.L`, and add `leg_lower.L` to the selection (right-click, Shift+right-click).**

6. **Add an IK constraint (Shift+I⇨To Active Bone).**

   You can also use the Shift+Ctrl+C⇨Inverse Kinematics hotkey. Both provide the same results: an IK constraint in `leg_lower.L`'s Bone Constraints Properties.

7. **Go to the Bone Constrains panel and change the Chain Length value to 2.**

   By default, the IK bone chain goes all the way back to the head of the hipbone. You actually want it to have an influence only up to the head of the upper leg bone.

8. **Perform Steps 5 through 7 on `leg_IK.R` and `leg_lower.R`.**

   Sadly, X-Axis Mirror works only in Edit mode, so you have to add your IK constraints on both sides on your own.

9. **Select the `leg_IK.L` and `leg_IK.R` bones and disable the Deform check box in each of their Bone Properties.**

   Like the `root` and `head_target` bones, these control bones should not be used for skinning. At this point, you have a basic IK rig on your character's feet. The rig looks something like Figure 11-20.

Test your rig by selecting the `root` and moving it around, particularly up and down the Z-axis. The leg bones in your Stickman rig should bend all by themselves to compensate for the location of the root bone relative to the IK bones. You can also select each of the `leg_IK` bones and move them around to control the bending of each leg independent of the other.

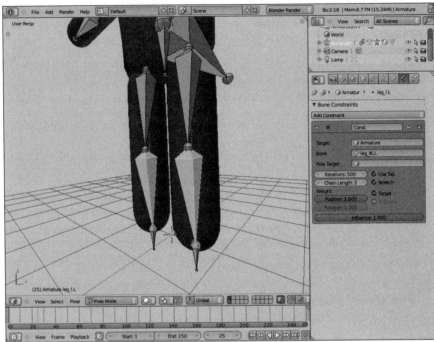

In doing so, however, you may notice that on some occasions, the legs don't quite know how to bend. They may randomly flip backward or roll out in odd angles. Aside from slightly bending the rig at the knees when you created the leg bones, you haven't provided the legs with much of a clue as to *how* exactly they should bend. Fortunately, the solution is pretty simple. It's called a *pole target*. To define a pole target, you need to create two more bones, one for each leg:

1. **Tab into Edit mode on Stickman's armature and select `leg_IK.L`.**

   Again, because X-Axis Mirror is enabled and you're in Edit mode, choosing either `leg_IK` bone works fine.

2. **Switch to side view, duplicate the bone, and move the new bone to somewhere in front of the knee (Numpad 3, Shift+D).**

3. **Name this bone `knee.L` and make sure that the mirrored bone is named `knee.R`.**

4. **Switch the direction of `knee.L` (W⇨Switch Direction).**

   This step isn't essential. I just like to have my floating bones pointing up.

5. **Parent `knee.L` to `leg_IK.L` (right-click `knee.L`, right-click `leg_IK.L`, Ctrl+P⇨Keep Offset).**

6. **Ctrl+Tab into Pose mode.**

7. **Select `leg_lower.L` and in its IK constraint panel (Bone Constraints Properties), choose your armature object in the Pole Target field and `knee.L` in the Bone field that appears.**

   This step defines `knee.L` as the pole target for the left leg's IK chain. However, the knee joint for the left leg may instantly pop to the side, bending the leg in all kinds of weird ways. The next step compensates for that problem.

8. **Still in `leg_lower.L`'s IK constraint panel, adjust the Pole Offset value to 90 degrees°.**

   This step causes the leg's knee joint to properly point at the `knee.L` bone. If it doesn't, try adjusting the Pole Offset value until it looks correct. Usually this value is 0, 90, –90, or 180. The default behavior is to point `leg_lower.L`'s local X-axis toward the pole. If the local X-axis isn't forward, adjusting the offset compensates.

9. **Perform Steps 7 and 8 on `leg_lower.R`.**

   At this point, you have a fully configured IK rig for both of Stickman's legs. You're nearly ready to animate him. For reference, your rig looks like the one in Figure 11-21.

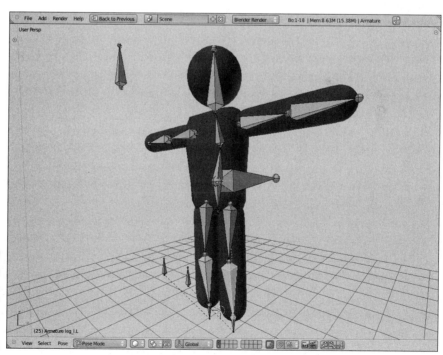

Figure 11-21:
A completely working Stickman rig.

At this point, skinning the Stickman mesh to your armature should be pretty safe. Using the automatic weights method gives you the best results, so select the mesh (right-click), select the armature (Shift+right-click), and press Ctrl+P⇨With Automatic Weights. Now when you move around and pose your rig, the Stickman mesh obediently follows in kind.

To ensure that your deformations look good, go to Object Data Properties and look at the Skeleton panel. Disable Envelopes and enable Quaternion, which should keep the mesh from pinching unnaturally at Stickman's joints.

Making the rig more user friendly

You have a great basic rig that you can start animating with immediately. However, you can make a few tweaks that make this rig even more usable.

You can change the way the bones display in the 3D View. Now that you're done with the bulk of rigging, knowing which end of a bone is the head or the tail is a bit less important. Go to the Display panel in Object Data Properties and change the bone type from Octahedral to Stick. Stick bones are the least obtrusive bones that are immediately available to you. Now you can see more of your mesh while you're animating without as much clutter and geometry in the way. Figure 11-22 shows the Stickman rig with stick bones.

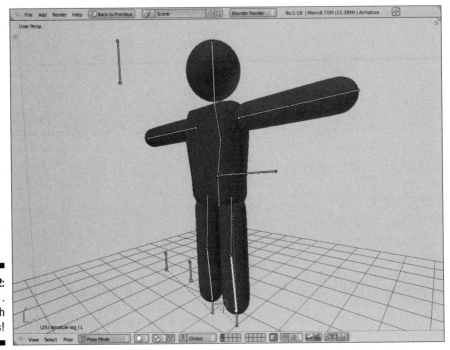

Figure 11-22: Stickman . . . rigged with sticks!

Another feature in Blender that is quite helpful for organizing your rigs is the ability to create bone groups. To do so, select the bones you want to group together and press Ctrl+G. When you do, you get four options:

- ✔ **Add Bone Group:** Choosing this option adds a new bone group, but does not include any bones in that group.

- ✔ **Remove Bone Group:** Choosing this option removes the group that is currently selected in the list box within the Bone Groups panel of Object Data Properties. This option doesn't remove the bones, just the group that they're associated with.

- ✔ **Add Selected to Bone Group:** Choosing this option adds your selected bones to the active group in the list box within the Bone Groups panel of Object Data Properties.

- ✔ **Remove Selected from Bone Groups:** If the bones you have selected are part of any groups, choosing this option removes them from all bone groups.

You can rename your bone groups in the Bone Groups panel of Object Data Properties. I used the bone groups feature to create groups for my main bone chains: left arm, right arm, left leg, right leg, and body. I left root, head, and `head_target` groupless. Create your own groups as you see fit.

Beyond organization, using bone groups offers an additional benefit. You can define custom bone colors based on the bone groups you have. The controls are also in the Bone Groups panel. Make sure that the Colors check box is enabled within the Display panel and then, in the Bone Groups panel, left-click the Color Set drop-down menu and choose a theme color set from the menu that appears. I used this feature to make all my left-side bones green and my right-side bones red. It's a good visual trick to let you or another animator quickly identify which bones are being used. Figure 11-23 shows what the Bone Groups panel looks like.

Figure 11-23:
The Bone Groups panel with controls for bone groups and bone colors for those groups.

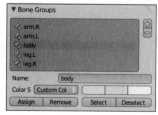

Besides groups, another organizational tool for making your rig more usable are bone layers. Bone groups make visualizing and selecting your bones easy. However, bone layers are a faster, more reasonable way of showing and hiding the bones in your rig.

As an example, have a look at Stickman's legs. They're entirely controlled by the IK and knee bones. Because you can see the Stickman mesh, you really don't need to see these leg bones. In some ways, they just get in the way of seeing your character's acting. In that case, moving the bones to a different layer and hiding that layer makes plenty of sense. Use Shift+right-click, Border Select (B), or press L with your mouse over the leg bones to select the entire leg chain and then press M to move them to a different layer. I moved the bones to the first layer in the second block of layers.

Now, if you ever want to see those bones, just go to the Armature panel and enable the layer there. In the meantime, though, as Figure 11-24 shows, your Stickman rig is much cleaner, and now you're *really* ready to start animating.

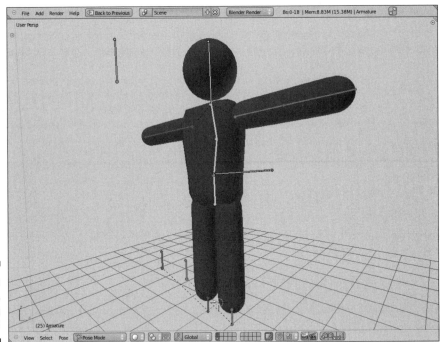

Figure 11-24:
Stickman, reporting for duty!

Chapter 12

Animating Object Deformations

In This Chapter

▶ Becoming familiar with the Dopesheet

▶ Using armatures for animations

▶ Animating quickly with the Non-Linear Animation Editor

*L*ooking at the title of this chapter, you may find yourself wondering how this chapter is different from Chapter 10. Both chapters cover animation, but this chapter covers the cool things you can do in Blender if you're animating with a fully rigged mesh. Chapter 10 covers what is often referred to as *object animation* — that is, animating the attributes of a single object.

With an animation rig, you have more bits and pieces to manage, keep track of, and control. Managing all that additional complexity can be daunting if you have the Outliner and the Graph Editor to work with. Fortunately, Blender offers a few more features that help make rigged *character animation* easier to wrap your head around.

Working with the Dopesheet

So you have a rigged character that you want to animate. Awesome! Change your screen layout to the Animation layout (Ctrl+←⇨Ctrl+←). After that, the first thing that you're probably going to want to do is change the primary 3D View to solid viewport shading (Z), change the Translate manipulator to the Rotate manipulator, and set it to Normal orientation (Alt+spacebar⇨Normal). You should switch to Normal orientation because when you're animating with an armature, most of the time, you're animating bone rotations. By setting the Rotation manipulator to the Normal coordinate space, you can have quick, controlled transformation of bone rotations without having the 3D manipulator get in your way too much.

The next thing you need to pay attention to is the Dopesheet. As nice as seeing the Graph Editor may be, seeing all the f-curves for each object and each bone in your scene can quickly get overwhelming. The Timeline shows keys for multiple objects in a simplified way, but you don't have a good way to see which key belongs to which object, and the Timeline provides no tools for actually editing these keyframes. You need a different editor — one that gives you a big picture of the keyframes for multiple objects and bones in your animation. And, perhaps more important, this editor allows you to edit the timing of bones, objects, and properties individually. The Dopesheet, (Shift+F12), shown in Figure 12-1, fills those needs.

Figure 12-1:
The
Dopesheet.

In traditional animation, the *dope sheet* was the entire animation planned out, frame by frame on paper, prior to a single pencil line being drawn by the animator. In computer animation, it's taken on a slightly different meaning and purpose, but the core notion of being able to see your entire animation all at once is still there. When you have elements in your scene animated, the Dopesheet shows a channel for each keyed bone, object, and property.

When it comes to editing the overall timing of a character's performance, the Dopesheet is really *the* tool for the job.

Like selecting in other parts of Blender, you can select individual keyframes by right-clicking the diamond-shaped keyframe indicator. You can select multiple keyframes in a variety of ways. You can use the familiar Shift+right-click or Border Select (B) functions. However, another way to select keyframes is incredibly helpful. If you have a Dopesheet open and a few keyframes set, right-click any keyframe to select it. Now, with that key selected, press K. This action selects any other key in the armature that's on the same frame as your selected key. This selection method is called a *column key selection,* and it's also available in the Graph Editor. You can get similar functionality with the time cursor. If you place your time cursor on a column of keys and press Ctrl+K, that column of keys is selected, rather than the column with your original selected keys.

Initially, you may not think that column key selection is all that useful. However, if you think about the process used for animating — especially cartoon-style animation — it starts making more sense. The workflow for animation usually goes from one pose to the next. At each pose that you key, multiple bones are all keyed at the same time, forming a column in the Dopesheet. In fact, unless you're doing some kind of frantic, shaky animations, it's a pretty good practice to make sure that you have nice columns in your Dopesheet. Uneven columns tend to indicate that your timing may be off on a specific part of the rig. Of course, this suggestion is a guideline more than a hard-and-fast rule.

After they're selected, you can manipulate keyframes with grabbing (G) and scaling (S). When performing these actions, there's something you should pay attention to. First of all, when you scale selected keyframes, the scale is relative to the position of the time cursor in the Dopesheet. So if you want to increase the length of your animation by stretching out the keyframes, put your time cursor at frame 1 before scaling. If you place your time cursor in the middle or at the end, the keys at the beginning of your animation are arranged so that they take place before your animation starts — typically what you don't want, so be careful.

By default, the Dopesheet has Nearest Frame snapping enabled. So when grabbing (G) or scaling (S), your keys snap to the frame to which they are closest. If you disable snapping from the snaps drop-down menu in the Dopesheet's header by changing it to No Auto-Snap, Blender stops this behavior and allows you to place keys between frames. However, you normally don't want this behavior. If you do have keys located in between frames, you can quickly fix that with the Snap Keys feature. Select the keys you want to fix in the Dopesheet and press Shift+S.

You have four options in this menu:

- ✔ **Current Frame:** This option snaps selected keys to the location of the time cursor in the Dopesheet.

- ✔ **Nearest Frame:** Choosing this option takes the selected keys and shifts them to the even frame number that's closest to them.

- ✔ **Nearest Second:** Like the Nearest Frame operation, but this option snaps the selected keys to the nearest frame that's at the start of a second in time.

- ✔ **Nearest Marker:** Blender's Dopesheet allows you to place reminders on the timeline referred to as *markers*. You can add a new marker at the location of the timeline cursor by pressing M in the Dopesheet with your mouse cursor near the bottom of the graph area. If you have one or more of these markers on your timeline, choosing this option snaps selected keyframes to the marker that's nearest to it.

Generally, though, it's best practice to use Blender's auto-snap feature that's enabled by default. You can change the auto-snap method by left-clicking the drop-down menu on the far right of the Dopesheet's header. This menu has almost all the same options as the preceding list. The only difference is the Time Step option, which snap keys to one-frame increments from their initial locations rather than to exact frames.

Animating with Armatures

If you're already used to object animation, using armatures to animate using the Dopesheet extends naturally from that base. When I animate, I like to use the following process:

1. **Plan the animation.**

   I can't emphasize this point enough:. Know what you're going to animate and have an idea about the timing of the motion. *Act out the action.* If you can, sketch out a few quick thumbnail drawings of the sequence. Even stick-figure drawings can be really helpful for determining poses and figuring out how things are going to look.

2. **Set your Timeline at frame 1 and create the starting pose for your character by manipulating its rig.**

3. **Select all visible bones (A) and Insert a LocRot keyframe for *everything* (I⇨LocRot).**

   Granted, there's a good chance that most of the bones can't be grabbed, but only rotated, so setting a location keyframe for them is kind of moot. However, setting a keyframe for all the bones is faster than going through and figuring out which bones can be keyed for just rotation and which bones can be keyed for both rotation and location.

4. **Move the timeline cursor forward to roughly when you think the next major pose should happen.**

5. **Create your character's second pose.**

   If the next pose is a *hold*, or a pose where the character doesn't change position, you can duplicate the keys of the previous pose by selecting them in the Dopesheet and pressing Shift+D.

6. **Select all visible bones (A) and Insert an Available keyframe (I⇨ Available).**

7. **Continue with Steps 4 through 6 until you complete the last major pose for your character.**

8. **Using the Dopesheet, play back the animation, paying close attention to timing.**

   At this point, hopefully your poses are acceptably refined, so you should pay even *more* attention to timing than to the accuracy of the poses.

9. **Go through the keys set in the Dopesheet and tweak the timing of the poses so that they look natural.**

10. **Continuing to tweak, go back and start adding secondary poses and keyframes for secondary motion between your major poses.**

11. **Continue on this course, refining the timing and detail more and more with each pass.**

One luxury of computer animation is the ability to continually go back and tweak things, make changes, and improve the animation. You can take advantage of this process by training yourself to work in passes. Animate your character's biggest, most pronounced motion first. Make sure that you have the timing down. Then move to the next pass, working on slightly more detailed parts of the performance. For example, animate your character's arm and hand bones before you get into the nitty-gritty details of animating the fingers. The biggest reason to work this way is time. It's much easier to go in and fix the timing on a big action if you do it earlier. Otherwise, you run into situations where you find yourself shuffling around a bunch of detail keys after you find out that your character doesn't get from Point A to Point B in the right amount of time.

Don't be afraid to break out a stopwatch and act out the action to find out exactly how long it takes to perform and what the action feels like. If you're fortunate enough to have friends, have them act out the action for you while you time it or even record it to video. Animation is all about timing.

Principles of animation worth remembering

As you create your animations, try to pull from a variety of sources to really capture the essence of some action, motion, or character expression. My first and most emphatic recommendation is to keep your eyes open. Watch everything around you that moves. Study objects and try to get an idea of how their structure facilitates motion. Then think about how you would re-create that item.

Of course, merely gawking at everything in the world isn't the only thing you should do (and you should be prepared for the fact that people will probably look at you funny). Studying early animation is also a good idea. Most of the principles that those wonderfully talented pioneers developed for animation are still relevant and applicable to computer animation. In fact, you should remember the classic 12 basic principles of animation that were established by some of the original Disney animators. These principles are a bit of divergence, but if your aim is to create good animation, you should know about them and try to use them in even the most simple of animations:

- **Squash and stretch:** This one is all about deformation. Because of weight, anything that moves gets deformed somehow. A tennis ball squashes to an oval shape when it's hit. Rope under tension gets stretched. Cartoon characters hit all believable and unbelievable ranges of this when they're animated, but it's valuable, albeit toned down, even in realistic animation.

- **Anticipation:** The basic idea here is that before every action in one direction, a buildup in the opposite direction occurs first. A character that's going to jump bends her knees and moves down first to build up the energy to jump up.

✔ **Staging:** The idea of staging is to keep the frame simple. The purpose of animation is to communicate an idea or a movement or an emotion with moving images. You want to convey this idea as clearly as possible with the way you arrange your shots and the characters in those shots.

✔ **Straight-ahead action versus pose-to-pose action:** These are the two primary methods of animating. The process that I discuss near the beginning of this chapter is more of a pose-to-pose technique. Pose-to-pose can be clearer, but it may be a bit cartoony. Straight-ahead action is generally more fluid and realistic, but the action may be less clear. Most modern animators use a hybrid approach, blocking in the initial poses and then working straight-ahead between them.

✔ **Follow through and overlapping action:** The idea here is to make sure that your animations adhere — or seem to adhere — to the laws of physics. If you have movement in one direction, the inertia of that motion requires you to animate the follow-through even if you're changing direction.

✔ **Ease in and ease out:** Ease in and ease out, sometimes known as "slow in, slow out," means that natural movement does not stop and start abruptly. It flows smoothly, accelerating and decelerating. By using Bézier curves in the Graph Editor, you actually get this principle for free.

✔ **Arcs:** Along the same lines as the previous two principles, most natural movement happens in arcs. So if your character is changing direction or moving something, you typically want that to happen in some sort of curved, arc motion. Straight lines are generally stiff and robotic (and therefore good for machinery and robots), but they're also very useful for powerful actions like punching.

✔ **Secondary action:** These actions are those additional touches that make characters more real to the audience. Clothing that shifts with character movement, jiggling fat or loose skin, and blinking eyes are just a few actions that can breathe life into an otherwise stiff, empty puppet.

✔ **Timing:** Timing is, in my opinion, one of the most important of the 12 principles. Everything happens according to time. If the timing is off, it throws off the effect for the whole animation. I'm not just talking about controlling the timing of actions to appear believable. I also mean *story-based timing* — knowing exactly the right time to make a character give a sad facial expression that impacts the audience the most.

✔ **Exaggeration:** Exaggeration makes animation fun. You can do anything with animation, and you're nearly duty-bound to take advantage of that fact. Otherwise, you may as well just work in video or film with for-real people.

✔ **Solid drawing:** Solid drawing refers to the actual skill of being able to draw. Computer animators *can* get away with not being experts at drawing, but it's to your benefit to make the effort. Drawing is an extension of seeing. When you draw, you turn on a part of your brain that studies how things look relative to each another. Being able to see the world with these eyes can make all the difference in re-creating believable motion.

✔ **Appeal:** This one is easy. Make things that are awesome. If you're going to animate something that is boring, what's the point? It needs to be interesting for you to make, and it's nice if it's also interesting for other people to watch.

Those are the basic principles of animation, but not a single one of them is carved in stone. You can effectively break every one of them and still pull off some incredible animation. That said, more often than not, it's in the best interest of your work and your sanity that you at least start within these principles and then find ways where you can break them in the best way possible.

Making sense of quaternions (or, "Why are there four rotation curves?!")

Even though the bulk of your time animating with armatures is spent working with the Dopesheet, you still may frequently need to tweak things in the Graph Editor. If you do go to the Graph Editor and view the f-curves for a bone with the intention of tweaking rotation, you may run into a particularly jarring shock. The X Rotation, Y Rotation, and Z Rotation channels that you would expect for rotation aren't there: They've been replaced with *four* channels to control rotation, called *quaternions*. Figure 12-2 shows a set of quaternions in the Graph Editor, describing the rotation of some bone.

Figure 12-2:
Quaternions in action! They're nearly incomprehensible!

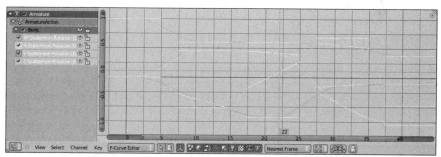

Quaternions are a different way of defining rotations in 3D space, and they're quite a bit different from the standard X, Y, and Z or *Euler* (pronounced "oiler") rotations. They're used in the rotation of bones because Euler rotations can get into a nasty situation referred to as *gimbal lock*, which involves being mathematically unable to compensate for or adjust a rotation because you only have three axes to define it. Having that happen in an armature is unacceptable. Fortunately, quaternions don't suffer from gimbal lock.

However, they do suffer from another affliction: They have virtually no intuitive relationship to rotation that nonmathematicians can understand.

To make a long story short, if you're using quaternion rotations, it may be easier for you to tweak a rotation by adding additional keyframes to the rotation. If you're not fond of mathematics, you may very well go crazy trying to figure out how they relate to your bone's rotation.

In the 2.5 series of Blender, there was an overhaul of the animation system. Part of this overhaul was the introduction of the ability to control the rotation mode of any bone in an armature. To do so, select a bone and bring up its Bone Properties. At the bottom of the Transform panel is a drop-down menu labeled Rotation Mode. By default, its set to Quaternion (WXYZ), and in most cases, you want to use this setting. However, in a couple cases where you're sure that you won't run into gimbal lock problems (like, for example, if you rigged a bone to define the rotation of a wheel), it may be more helpful to use a different rotation mode like XYZ Euler or Axis Angle.

Copying mirrored poses

One of the beauties of working in computer animation is the ability to take advantage of the computer's ability to calculate and process things so that you don't have to. In the animation world, animators love to find ways that the computer can do more work. Granted, you can (and should) always temper the computer's work with your own artistic eye, but there's nothing wrong with doing half the work and letting the computer do the other, boring, tedious, and repetitive half.

With the auspicious goal of getting the computer to do the work for you, Blender has three incredible little buttons, shown in Figure 12-3, located at the far-right end of the 3D View's header. They are visible only when you have an armature in Pose mode. With these buttons, you can copy and paste poses from and to the armature.

Figure 12-3:
Pose Copy and Paste buttons in the 3D View's header.

From left to right, the buttons are Pose Copy, Pose Paste, and Pose Mirror Paste. Here's how to use them:

1. **Select all bones (A).**

   You can actually get away with just selecting a few bones, but selecting all the bones actually illustrates my point a little better.

2. **Left-click the Copy Pose button.**

   The armature's pose loads into the computer's memory.

3. **Move to a different location in the timeline where you'd like your character to resume this pose.**

4. **Paste the pose back to the character.**

   In pasting, you have two options:

   - **Paste Pose:** This option takes the coordinates of all the bones you selected when copying the pose and applies those poses back to your character exactly as you copied them.

   - **Mirror Paste:** This option does the same thing as the regular Paste Pose, except it takes advantage of Blender's built-in left/right naming convention (see Chapter 11 for more details) and pastes the mirrored version of the pose to your character. Mirror Paste is really handy if you're doing something like creating a walk cycle. You can create a left-foot-forward pose and then use Mirror Paste to instantly create a right-food-forward pose. Figure 12-4 shows a character posed one way and then mirror pasted to pose the other.

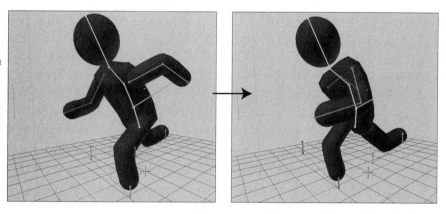

Figure 12-4:
All you have to do is put one foot forward, and Blender handles the other for you.

Note that after you paste the pose, you need to insert a keyframe for that pose at that location. Otherwise, the next time you scrub the timeline, the pose won't be there, and you'll have to copy and paste it all over again.

Seeing the big picture with ghosting

Traditional animation has a process called *onionskinning,* which consists of drawing on relatively thin paper and working on a table with a light in it. With this setup, the animator can stack his drawings on top of each other and get an overall sense of the motion in the animation. Blender has a similar feature for rigs; it's called *ghosting.* The controls for ghosting are in the Ghost panel of your armature's Object Data Properties.

To get the best sense of what the ghost feature does, increase the Range value in this panel to its maximum value of 30 ghosts. Now, for short animations or noncomplicated movement, having ghosting enabled may not be all that useful. However, the ghost feature is great for the more common forms of animation that are a bit longer and more complex. Having Ghost turned on is a great way to get a sense of where your character's coming from and where he's going. Think of ghosting as a way of having three-dimensional onionskinning, and it's certainly useful. Figure 12-5 shows a character jumping up and down, visualized with armature ghosting.

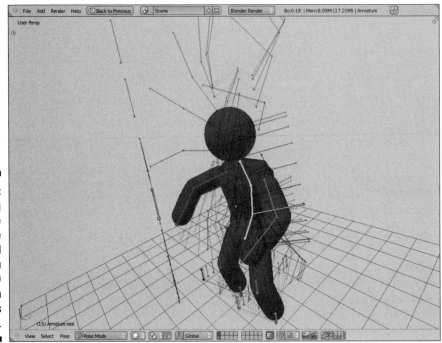

Figure 12-5: Increasing the Range value in the Ghost panel allows you to see a 3D onionskin of your rig's motion.

Visualizing motion with paths

One of the fundamental principles of animation is having arcs for movement. Smooth arcs are favorable for believable, natural-looking animated movement. To that end, Blender has a nice feature that makes it easier to analyze your animation and figure out whether you have acceptable arcs in your character's movement. This feature is called Motion Paths and is also available in Object Data Properties for your armature, within the Motion Paths panel.

This feature isn't like ghosts, where you just increase the range and they display instantly. Motion paths may take a second to generate. In order to generate them, first select the bone or bones that you want to visualize and then left-click the Calculate Paths button on the bottom-left side of the Motion Paths panel. You can use the settings above the Calculate Paths and Clear Paths buttons to create the motion path visualization. An added bonus to this feature is the ability to show the location of the keys along the path as a bright dot by enabling the Keyframes check box. If you want, you can also show the numerical frame numbers along the curves by enabling the Frame Numbers feature in the same panel. Figure 12-6 shows the same jump animation, but this time with motion paths enabled.

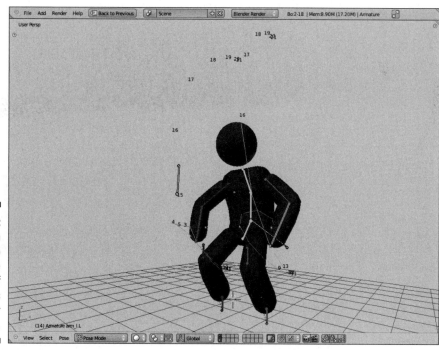

Figure 12-6:
Motion paths help visualize the motion of bones in your armature.

One thing to note is that, although it might be nice, you can't currently change or edit the motion path directly. The path can reflect only the motion created by your keyframes. So if you notice that the curve isn't as smooth as you might like, you need to go back into the Dopesheet and Graph Editor and tweak the motion a bit there. Then when you recalculate the motion paths, hopefully you should have a cleaner result.

Doing Nonlinear Animation

Animation is hard work, really hard work. So any time you can cut down the amount of work you have to do without detracting from the quality of the final animation, it's a good thing. Computer animation has given you another cool way to effectively and efficiently cut corners: *nonlinear animation*. Nonlinear animation, or NLA, is a way of animating that you can really do only with computers. The process of animating is typically very linear and straightforward (see preceding section). You may animate in passes, but you're still generally working forward in time with the full start-to-finish of your animation already planned out.

What if you didn't have to work this way? What if you could animate little chunks of character motion and then mix and match as you like? Imagine mixing a simple hand-waving motion with a simple jumping animation so that your character is both jumping and waving his arm? This is the basic concept behind nonlinear animation. Nonlinear animation takes many of the same principles used in nonlinear video editing and applies them to 3D computer animation. The idea is that you create a library of simple motions or poses and then combine them any way you like to create much more complex animated sequences. Using a library of motions is useful for background characters in larger productions and is also very handy for video game developers. Instead of trying to pull a specific set of frames from a single unified timeline, video game developers can now just make a call to one or more of these library animations and let the computer do the rest of the work.

In Blender, the basic building blocks for this library are Actions. *Actions* are collections of f-curves, and they are really cool because they have their own datablock. You can create multiple actions within a single .blend file, share the actions between armatures, and basically build up a library of movements.

To create a new action, first change the Dopesheet from the default DopeSheet editing context to the Action Editor context from the drop-down menu in the header. Then you can use the Action datablock, also in the header of the Dopesheet, to add a new action, as highlighted in Figure 12-7. This datablock widget is just like the one used for materials, textures, and even objects in other parts of Blender's interface. Create a new action by left-clicking the plus (+) icon on the right side of the datablock. After adding a new action, you can (and should) give it a custom name.

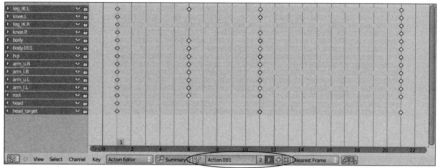

Figure 12-7:
Using the
Action data-
block in the
Dopesheet
to create a
new action
for your
armature.

With the new action created, you can create another core animation and start
building up your character's action library. Animate waving each arm, a walk
cycle, various facial expressions, a standing idle animation, and any other
simple action that comes to mind. Ultimately, your library will be populated
enough that you'll want to start mixing and matching them together. To do
this, you're going to want to use the NLA Editor. Add the NLA Editor to the
Animation screen layout with the following steps:

1. **In the Animation screen layout, left-click the seam at the top of the
   Timeline and drag it up, making more room for that editor.**

   Because the NLA Editor is covering the entire animation, it makes sense
   to forsake the Timeline and use the NLA Editor exclusively. But if you'd
   still like to use the Timeline, you can split it off of another area.

2. **Change the Timeline to a NLA Editor.**

   Your screen layout may look something like Figure 12-8.

The NLA is a very cool feature of Blender, but don't rely on it too much for animation. Blender has had the NLA Editor for a long time, but it could still use
some refinement to be a truly effective tool. The good news is that the NLA is
still being developed, and while it's likely to go through design iterations in
future releases of Blender, the principles that I explain here should still apply.

Mixing actions to create complex animation

When you have an action loaded in the Dopesheet's Action Editor, you
should notice a bright orange bar in the NLA Editor. This orange bar is a
track, and you can populate it with one or more actions.

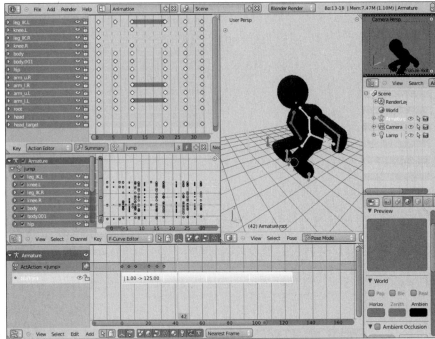

Figure 12-8:
An anima-
tion screen
layout with
the NLA
Editor added
to it.

To add one of your other actions to the NLA Editor:

1. **Activate the track by left-clicking the snowflake-looking icon in the channel region on the left of the NLA.**

   The track expands, and you should see your current action as a bright yellow strip.

2. **Add a new strip in the graph area of the NLA Editor (Shift+A).**

   You see a menu of all the actions you created.

3. **Choose the action you'd like to add to the NLA Editor.**

   The action is placed in the NLA Editor as a *strip,* and its start position is wherever the time cursor is located.

4. **Continue to add actions to the NLA.**

   Of course, unless you make the last frame of one Action strip match the pose at the head of the next frame, the animation looks pretty erratic.

The way to smooth out the animation is with the Properties region (N) in the NLA Editor. Figure 12-9 shows the Properties region of the NLA Editor. To make the transition from one strip to the next smoother, either make sure that the Auto Blend In/Out check box in the Active Strip panel for each strip is enabled (it should be by default) and let them overlap a bit or manually set the Blend In and Blend Out values in this panel.

Figure 12-9:
Using the
Properties
region in the
NLA Editor.

Taking advantage of looped animation

Another benefit of using the NLA is the ability to easily loop any action strip and rescale its timing. You can loop and rescale the timing in the NLA Editor from within the Properties region. In the Action Clip panel under the Playback Settings label are a pair of values: Scale and Repeat. The very first of these options is Scale. By default, this option is set to 1.0. However, you can increase or decrease this value as much as you like to adjust the timing on your action, speeding it up or slowing it down as necessary.

Below the Scale value is Repeat. Like Scale, the default value is Repeat, and you can increase or decrease the value to taste. As you do, you should see the strip increase in length proportional to the increase of the Repeat value. Now, to have an effective looping animation, it's definitely in your best interest to make the first and last poses in the action identical. The easiest way to do so is to use the copy and paste pose buttons in the 3D View:

1. **In the Dopesheet, select (right-click) the action strip you want to loop from the Actions datablock.**

2. **While still in the Dopesheet, move the time cursor to the first pose in the action (left-click and drag).**

3. **In the 3D View, select all bones (A) and left-click the Copy Pose button in the header.**

4. **Back in the Dopesheet, move the time cursor to some place after the last keyframe.**

5. **In the 3D View, left-click the Paste Pose button in the header.**

6. **Insert a new keyframe (I⇨Available).**

When you get to this step, all the bones should still be selected, so you don't need to reselect anything.

When you return to the NLA Editor, the action strip should automatically be longer to account for the additional frame at the end. Furthermore, the action strip should also loop seamlessly upon playback (Alt+A).

Figure 12-10 shows the NLA Editor with looped strips that have varied scales.

Figure 12-10:
Action
strips in the
NLA Editor,
looped and
rescaled.

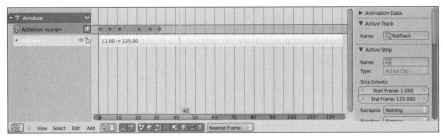

Be careful when changing the scale of Action strips. More often than not, changing the scale results in a keyframe being placed at what's called a *fractional frame* or *intraframe*, a spot on the timeline that isn't a nicely rounded frame number. Fractional frames aren't necessarily a bad thing, but animations do tend to look a little bit better if the keyframes fall on full frames so that the audience has the chance to "read" the pose.

Many of these animation concepts, especially ones involving the NLA, are much easier to grasp if you can see them in motion. After all, this is animation, the art of motion. Have a look at the .blend files that accompany this book to get a stronger notion of how these things work together.

Chapter 13

Letting Blender Do the Work for You

In This Chapter

▶ Playing with particles

▶ Simulating physics with soft body and rigid body dynamics

▶ Working with cloth simulation

▶ Creating fluid animations with Blender's fluid simulator

*W*hen animating, some actions are difficult or very time consuming to get right, such as explosions, fire, hair, cloth, and physics-related actions like moving fluids and bouncing objects. In order to get these actions to look right, one solution is to let the computer do the work and create a simulation of that action taking place. You use variables like gravity and mass to define the environment, and the computer calculates how the objects in the scene behave based on the values you set. Using the computer is a great way to get nearly accurate motion without the need to key everything by hand. That said, don't make the mistake of thinking simulations always give you a huge time savings in animation. This assumption isn't necessarily true, as some highly detailed simulations can take hours, or even days, to complete. Instead, think of simulations as a way to more reliably animate detailed, physically accurate motion better than you might be able to do by hand alone.

This chapter only scratches the surface of what you can do with the simulation tools in Blender, so you should certainly look at additional resources, such as Blender's official online documentation, the wide variety of online tutorials from the community, as well as Tony Mullen's *Bounce, Tumble, and Splash!* (published by Wiley) book on physics simulation in Blender 2.4 to get a full understanding of how each feature works. But hopefully, this chapter gives you an idea of the possibilities you have at hand.

Using Particles in Blender

Blender has had an integrated particle system from its early beginnings. Over the years, though, it has grown and matured into a much more powerful system for creating particle-based effects like hair, flock/swarm behavior, and explosions. And the particle system gets more and more powerful with every release.

The controls for Blender's particle systems live in Particle Properties, as shown in Figure 13-1. Initially, this section looks pretty barren, with just a single list box. However, if you have a Mesh object selected and click the Plus (+) button to the right of the list box, a whole explosion of additional panels for controlling particle behavior appear. Adding a particle system in Particle Properties also adds a Particle System modifier to your object. Technically, you can create your new particle system from Modifiers Properties as well, but it's usually much easier to do it from Particle Properties.

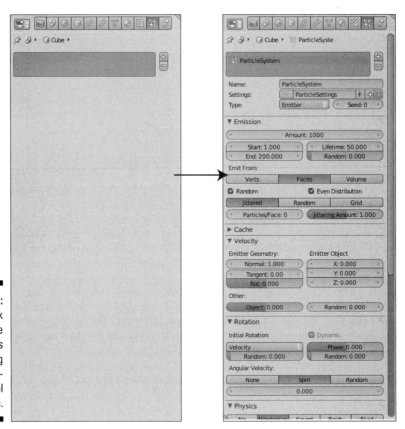

Figure 13-1:
Left-click the Particle Properties icon to bring up the particle control panels.

Knowing what particle systems are good for

Particle systems have a handful of good uses. Each use involves large numbers of individual objects that share some general behavior. Consequently, particle systems are ideal for groups of objects that move according to physics, such as fireworks or tennis balls being continuously shot at a wall. Particle systems are also good for simulating hair and fur. If the path along which an individual particle travels were to be considered a strand, you could use groups of these particle strands to make hair. This technique is exactly what Blender does.

There's also one other use for particle systems: simple flocking or crowd simulation. Say that you want to have a swarm of gnats constantly buzzing around your character's head. A particle system is a great way to pull off that effect. In Figure 13-1, a whole mess of configuration panels appear in the Particle Properties. Figure 13-2 boils these panels down and shows the most used and useful panels in this section of the Properties editor.

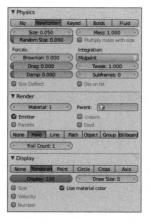
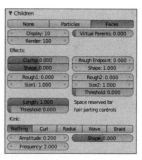

Figure 13-2: The most useful panels in the Particle Properties.

After you create your first particle system, the context panel at the top of Particle Properties gives you the broadest controls, allowing you to name your particle system or choose a different set of settings from the Particle Settings datablock. Objects in Blender can have more than one particle system and can even share the same particle system settings between objects. Beneath the Settings datablock is a Type drop-down menu that offers you two types of particle system behaviors to work with: Emitter and Hair. In most instances, you'll probably use the Emitter type. Hair particle systems are the way to create manageable hair and fur in Blender.

If you choose Emitter, the Emission panel has some of the most important settings for controlling how many particles you have and how long they exist in your scene. Here's a brief explanation for each value:

- ✔ **Amount:** As the name implies, this value is the total number of particles created by the system. After the particle system generates this number of particles, it stops. You can get additional particles in more than one way, but the most straightforward way is to increase this value.

- ✔ **Start:** This frame is where particles start being emitted from the source object. By default, this value is set to frame 1, but if you don't want to have your particles start until later in your animation, you can increase the value in this field. You can also set this value to be negative.

- ✔ **End:** This frame is where Blender stops emitting particles from the source object. By default, it's set to frame 200. With the default values for Amount and Start (1000 and 1.0, respectively), Blender creates five particles in each new frame in the animation up to frame 200 and then stops generating particles.

- ✔ **Lifetime:** The Lifetime value controls how long an individual particle exists in your scene. With the default value of 50.0, a particle born on frame 7 disappears from the scene when you reach frame 57. If you find that you need your particles in the scene longer, increase this value.

- ✔ **Random:** This value pertains specifically to the Lifetime of the particle. At its default of 0.0, it doesn't change anything; particles live for the exact length of time stipulated by the Lifetime value and disappear, or *die,* at the end of that time. However, if you increase the Random value, it introduces a variation to the Lifetime option, so all the particles born on one frame disappear at different times, giving a more natural effect.

You can associate any particle type (Emitter or Hair) with one of five varieties of physics simulation models stipulated in the Physics panel: None, Newtonian, Keyed, Boids, and Fluid. Very rarely do you have a need to use None as an option, but it's good to have. Typically, the default Newtonian setting is the most useful option because it tends to simulate real-world physical attributes, such as gravity, mass, and velocity. Occasionally, though, you may want to have more explicit control over your particles, such as when you're shaping the hair on a character. This is where Keyed physics come into play. You can use the *emitter object* of one particle system to control the angle and direction of another one. The Boids option tells your particles to have flocking or swarming behavior, and you get a set of settings and panels to control that behavior. The last option, Fluid, is a physics-based choice similar to the Newtonian option, but particles have greater cohesive and adhesive properties that make them behave like part of a fluid system.

To create a basic particle system, use the following steps:

1. **Add a mesh to work as your particle emitter (Shift+A⇨Mesh⇨Grid).**

   In this example, I use a simple grid, but really any mesh works. The key thing to remember is that, by default, particles are emitted from the faces of your mesh and move away from the face in the direction of that face's normal.

2. **Navigate to Particle Properties and add a new particle system.**

   After you click the Plus (+) button next to the particles list box, all the options available to particles become visible. If you try to play back the animation now (Alt+A), you see particles dropping from your grid.

3. **Decide what type of physics you would like to have controlling your particles.**

   Newtonian physics are usually the most common type of particle system used, but I'm also pretty fond of the Boids behavior for emitter particle systems. It just looks cool, and they're a lot of fun!

4. **Adjust the velocity settings to control particle behavior.**

   You change this setting from the Velocity panel in Particle properties. For Newtonian physics, you can give your particles some sort of initial velocity. I tend to adjust the Normal velocity first because it gives the most immediate results. Values above 0 go in the direction of each face's normals, whereas values below zero go in the opposite direction. Boid particles don't require an initial velocity, but the settings do adjust how each Boid particle interacts with its neighboring particles.

5. **Play back the animation to watch the particles move (Alt+A).**

   If you followed the tip in Step 2, you could be playing your particle animation already. If not, press Alt+A and see what your settings make the particles do. If your particles start behaving in erratic or unexpected ways, it's a good idea to make sure that your time cursor in the Timeline is at or before the frame you entered for the Start value in the Emission panel when you start the animation playback. Watch how your particles move and behave. You can now either tweak the particle movement during playback, or if it's more comfortable for you, press Esc to stop the playback and adjust your settings before playing the animation again. I usually use a combination of live adjustments and this back-and-forth tweaking to refine my particle system's behavior.

Figure 13-3 shows the preceding process. Bear in mind that these steps show a very basic particle system setup, and you're just barely scratching the surface of what's possible. I definitely recommend that you take some time to play with each of the settings and figure out what they do, as well as read some of the more in-depth documentation on particles in Blender's online documentation.

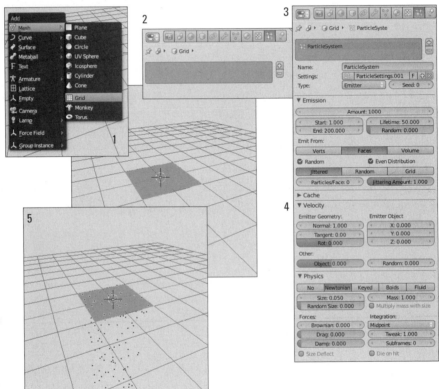

Figure 13-3: Creating a basic particle system.

Using force fields and collisions

After you create a basic particle system, you can have a little bit of fun with it, controlling the behavior of your particles. You control this behavior by using forces and deflectors. A *force field* is a controlling influence on the overall behavior of the particles, such as wind, vortices, and magnetism. In contrast, you can define collision objects, or *deflectors,* for your particles to collide with and impede their progress. Generally speaking, forces are defined using specialized empties, whereas deflectors are created with meshes.

All the controls for forces and deflectors live in Physics Properties, accessed by left-clicking the last button in the Properties editor's header. Its icon looks a bit like a blue check mark with a white circle at the end of it; it's really a visualization of a bouncing white ball. For particle force fields, left-click the Force Fields button, and a Force Fields panel appears. If you need collision settings, left-click the Collision button, and the Collision panel appears.

You typically use these panels to add force and collision behaviors to objects that are already in your scene. You select an object and then, from Physics Properties, add force field and collision properties to that object. For force fields, however, you can add them in a slightly faster way: from Blender's Add menu. If you press Shift+A⇨Force Field, you get a whole list of forces that you can add to your scene. Then you can just adjust the settings for your chosen force from the Force Fields panel in Physics Properties.

Now, I could go through each and every option available for force fields exhaustively, but things usually make more sense if you have an example to work with. That being the case, use the following steps to create a particle system that creates particles influenced by a wind force that causes them to collide with a wall and then bounce off of it:

1. **Create a simple particle system.**

   If you need a refresher, use the steps in the preceding section to create a basic emitter particle system with Newtonian physics.

2. **Add a Wind force field (Shift+A⇨Force Field⇨Wind).**

   Notice that the Wind force field object looks like an Empty with circles arranged along its local Z-axis. This visual cue lets you know the strength and direction of your wind force. Increasing the Strength value in the Force Fields panel spaces out four circles to help show how much wind you're creating. Play back the animation (Alt+A) to see how your wind is affecting the movements of the particles. While playing your animation, if you rotate your Wind object or adjust its force field settings, the particles are affected in real time. Neat, huh?

3. **Add a plane (Shift+A⇨Mesh⇨Plane).**

   This plane is your deflector. Grab the plane (G) and move it so that it's in the path of the particles pushed by your wind force. Rotate (R) the plane to make sure that the particles actually run into it head-on.

4. **Make the plane a Collision object.**

Add a Collision panel in Physics Properties. Whammo! You made a deflector! If you play back the animation (Alt+A), your particles should be blown by your wind force into your plane, which they should bounce off of rather than shoot straight through.

Figure 13-4 shows the results of this step-by-step process. And like the section preceding this one, you're just seeing the tip of the iceberg in terms of what's possible with forces and deflectors. You can use all sorts of cool forces and settings to get some very unique behavior out of your particle systems.

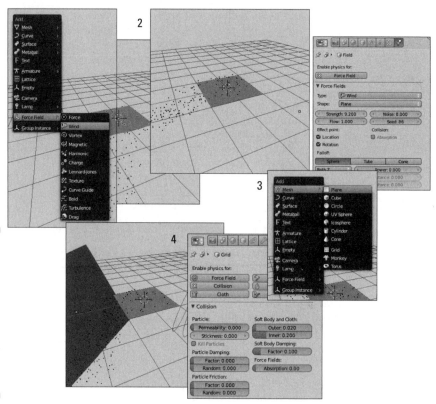

Figure 13-4: Creating a wind force that blows your particles into a plane, which they bounce off of.

Using particles for hair and fur

It would be remiss of me to cover particles and not say anything about Blender's hair and fur system. Blender uses particles to create hair and fur for your characters. As you may have guessed, you choose Hair as the type of particle system you want from the context panel at the top of Particle Properties. From there, the setup is roughly the same as using a regular emitter system with Newtonian physics, but with two notable differences.

The first difference is that Hair particles are, in some ways, easier to edit than emitter particles because you can use Blender's Particle mode to customize and comb your particle hair. When you start combing in Particle mode, Blender freezes the particle settings that you already set, and you can tweak and customize the hair from there. Figure 13-5 shows a screenshot of an object with particle hair being combed in Particle mode.

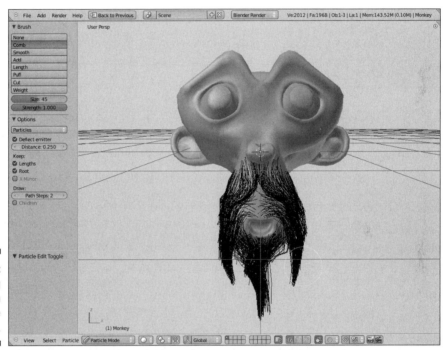

Figure 13-5:
Combing
hair in
Particle
mode.

 If you decide that you don't like the results you created in Particle mode, you can always reset your hair particles to their positions defined by the settings in Particle Properties. To reset your hair particles, left-click the Free Edit button in the context panel of Particle Properties. If you haven't edited your hair in Particle mode, this button isn't visible. But after you start combing, the button appears so that you can easily reset everything.

You switch to Particle mode using the Mode menu in the 3D View's header. With your emitter object selected, left-click the drop-down menu and choose

Particle Mode. When you're in Particle mode, you have the ability to directly edit particle hair, including combing, cutting, growing, and smoothing it out. To see these controls, look to the Tool Shelf (T). Particle Mode gives you a circular brush like the one used in Sculpting and Vertex Paint modes. You can adjust the brush's size and strength using the sliders from the Tool Shelf or by pressing F and Shift+F, respectively.

The other thing that differs in the setup of hair particles is the use of *child particles*. Creating and displaying hair particles can take up a lot of computing power, and when animating, you don't necessarily want to be waiting on Blender to draw all your character's fur in the 3D View. To deal with this problem, you have two solutions, and the results are best when they're used together. The first thing is to reduce the number of viewable particles in the 3D View using the Display slider in the Display panel of Particle Properties. The Display slider changes the percentage of particles being displayed in the 3D View. When you make this change, fewer particles show up in the 3D View, but all of them appear when you render. You get the best of both worlds.

Of course, for characters with a lot of hair, just reducing the displayable particles may not be enough. In this case, child particles are useful. In the Children panel of Particle Properties, left-click the Faces button. Additional particle strands grow from the faces of your emitter, with their locations determined by the particles around them. The Children panel has two amount values on the left column: Display and Render. The Display value dictates how many particles are seen in the 3D View. For speed while animating, I often set this value to 0. The Render value controls the number of child particles that each parent particle has at render time.

With the particle system properly generating your hairs, the only thing you have to worry about now is controlling how Blender renders this hair. Here's a quick-and-dirty rundown of the steps I go through to get the hair to render nicely (I include a reference file on the DVD that comes with this book):

1. **Enable the Strand render check box in the Render panel of Particle Properties.**

   This step tells Blender's rendering engine to render the particles as strands.

   Another helpful option in this panel is the Emitter check box near the top. Enabling this option makes the emitter visible, a helpful feature if you're using your actual character mesh to generate the hair.

2. **In Material Properties, enable Transparency and verify that Z Transparency is being used; set your Alpha value in the Transparency panel to 0.**

If you're using the Hair strands preview type in the Preview panel (I recommend doing so), you may notice that your hair is virtually non-existent because of the 0 Alpha value. Don't worry: This setting makes sense in the next couple of steps.

3. **In Texture Properties, add a new Blend texture and use the Ramp editor in the Colors panel to control the color and transparency along the length of the hair.**

   The most important thing here is that the right-hand side of the ramp represents the tip of your hair strand and should therefore be completely transparent. All other color positions in it should be opaque.

4. **In the Mapping panel, choose Strand/Particle from the Coordinates drop-down menu.**

5. **In the Influence panel, enable Color and Alpha.**

   The Preview panel should show hair strands that use your ramp gradient along the length of each strand, feathered out to semitransparent tips.

6. **Back in Material Properties, go to the Strand panel and check the settings.**

   A couple fields are worth mentioning:

   - Make sure that the Tangent Shading check box is enabled. This gives the hair a nice shiny effect.

   - Enable the Blender Units check box. By default, Blender's hair strands are measured in pixels. Using pixels works fine except in situations where you have a hairy object move toward or away from the camera. Enabling this check box makes the hair size relative to your scene's units (set in Scene Properties) rather than the size of your final render.

   - Because you're using the Blender Units option for hair size, you need to reduce the sizes for the Root and Tip of the hair strands. I usually use something like 0.02 and 0.01, respectively. You may need a few test renders to get it just right for your object.

   - The other sliders control the shape and shading of the strands; you can adjust these to taste with a few test renders.

Giving Objects Some Jiggle and Bounce

Have you ever sat and watched what happens when a beach ball gets hit or bounces off of the ground? Or seen what happens when someone places a plate of gelatin on a table? Or observed how a person's hair moves when they shake their head? When these things move and collide with other objects, they have a bit of internal jiggle that can be difficult to reproduce correctly with regular animation tools. This jiggling is the basis for what is referred to as *soft body dynamics.*

You can simulate soft body dynamics in Blender from Physics Properties. Left-click the Soft Body button, and a Soft Body panel appears. In that panel, you can make adjustments and tweak the behavior of your soft body simulation.

Like with particle systems, adding soft body dynamics to an object from Physics Properties also adds a Soft Body modifier to your object. You can verify this addition by looking in Modifiers Properties.

What follows is a simple step-by-step process for creating a simple soft body simulation with the default cube object:

1. **Select the cube with a right-click and grab it up in the Z-axis so that it floats above the 3D grid (G⇨Z).**

   You want to give the cube some height to fall from. It doesn't have to be very high; 3 to 5 units should be enough.

2. **Create a Plane mesh as a ground plane (Shift+A⇨Mesh⇨Plane) and scale it larger so that you have something for the cube to hit (S).**

   This plane is the surface for your jiggly cube to bounce off of. It may be helpful to put your 3D cursor at the origin (Shift+S⇨Cursor to Center) before adding the plane.

3. **Add a Collision panel in Physics Properties to give your plane collision properties.**

   Doing so makes Blender understand that the plane is an obstacle for your falling cube.

4. **Right-click the cube to select it.**

5. **Make a Soft Body panel in Physics Properties.**

   That's all you really have to do to enable soft body physics on your 3D objects. However, in order to get the cube to properly act according to gravity, there's one more step. Notice that adding soft body properties to your cube reveals a bunch of new panels to Physics Properties.

6. **Disable the Soft Body Goal check box next to its panel.**

   This step disables the default goal behavior of soft bodies. When Soft Body Goal is enabled, you can define a group of vertices in the object to be unaffected by the soft body simulation. A scenario where you may want to have Soft Body Goal enabled would be a character with loose skin, like the jowls of a large dog. You may want the dog's snout to be completely controlled by your armature animation, but have the jowls that hang off to be influenced by soft body simulation. Because in this case with the cube you want the entire object to be affected by the simulation, it's best just to turn it off.

7. **Play back the animation (Alt+A) to watch the cube fall, hit the ground plane, and jiggle as it lands again.**

   Pretty cool, huh? Figure 13-6 shows this process being completed. As with particles, it's a good practice to make sure that you're at the start frame of your animation before playing back your simulation.

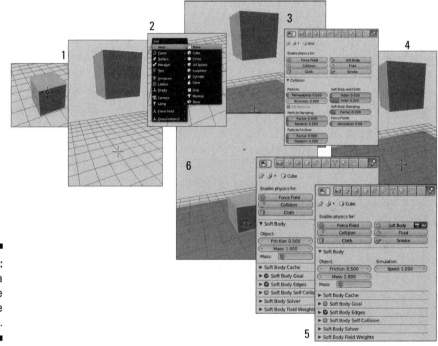

Figure 13-6: Dropping a jiggly cube into the scene.

Now, I have to admit that I cheated a bit in the preceding example by using a cube. If you were to try those steps with another type of mesh, like a UV Sphere or Suzanne, the mesh would collapse and look like it instantly deflated when it hit the ground plane. In order to get around this issue, you need to adjust one more setting. In the Soft Body Edges panel on the left column of values is a setting labeled Bending with a default value of 0.00. This value sets the bending stiffness of your object. With a setting of zero, you have no stiffness, so the mesh collapses. However, if you change this setting to a higher value, such as 3.0 or 5.0, the falling mesh retains its shape a little bit better when it collides with the ground plane. You can also enable the Stiff Quads check box in this panel to get your mesh to retain its shape even better, but be careful: This setting slows down the soft body calculation substantially.

Dropping Objects in a Scene with Rigid Body Dynamics

Not everything that reacts to physics has the internal jiggle and bounce that soft bodies have. Say, for example, that you have to animate a stack of heavy steel girders falling down at a construction site. For that animation, you don't want to have a soft body simulation. I mean, you could technically get the correct behavior with really stiff settings in the Soft Body Edges panel, but that's a bit of a kludge. You'd be better off with *rigid body dynamics*. As their name implies, *rigid bodies* don't get warped by collisions the way that soft bodies do. They either hold their form when they collide, or they break.

Unlike the other physical simulation, the controls for rigid bodies aren't in the Physics Properties. Not yet, at least; there are plans to integrate the rigid body simulation tools with the other physics tools in a future release of Blender. In the meantime, however, the way to get rigid body dynamics in Blender is to use the integrated game engine. That's right. Blender has a game engine built right into it!

If you used earlier versions of Blender, you may have already looked around Blender's interface and tried to find the game engine settings and controls. With the changes that came in Blender 2.5, the game engine is now treated like a separate render engine. To make Blender's game engine settings available, use the drop-down menu to the right of the Scene datablock at the top of the Blender window. By default, it's set to Blender Render, or Blender's internal renderer. Left-click this menu and choose Blender Game. Now you can use the following steps to get a simple rigid body simulation with the default cube:

1. **Select the cube by right-clicking and grab it up in the Z-axis by a few units (G⇨Z).**

   Like the soft body simulation, 3 to 5 units should be fine.

2. **Create a mesh plane to act as the ground (Shift+A⇨Mesh⇨Plane) and scale it larger so that you have something for the cube to hit (S).**

3. **In World Properties, make sure that the Physics Engine is set to Bullet, and Gravity is set at 9.80.**

   Bullet is the name for the main physics suite built into Blender's game engine.

4. **Right-click the cube to select it and bring up Physics Properties in the Properties editor.**

   Because you're now using the game engine as your renderer, your Physics Properties now house the controls for how objects behave in Blender's integrated game engine.

5. **Left-click the Physics Type drop-down menu and choose Rigid Body.**

   This step automatically enables the Actor check box, making the cube recognized as a moving object in the game engine. By choosing Rigid Body from the Physics Type drop-down menu, you tell the game engine that the cube is going to have simulated movement, and that the rigid body dynamics simulator will control the motion. This step also reveals some more controls for customizing the physical behavior of your object.

6. **Enable the Collision Bounds check box.**

   Activating the Collision Bounds check box enables the game engine to understand that the cube has boundaries that need to be recognized for collisions. Because you're using a cube, the default setting of Box works fine in this example. For more complex meshes, you may prefer to use the Convex Hull or Triangle Mesh options from the Bounds drop-down menu.

7. **Test the simulation by pressing P to start the game engine.**

   At this point, you have a valid rigid body simulation. You can stop the game engine at any time by pressing Esc. If you'd like, you can rotate (R) the cube to an odd angle and rerun the simulation to see how that affects the cube's motion. However, even though you have a valid simulation now, at this point, you can't see the simulation when you play back using Alt+A. This is because the simulation is only happening in the game engine. To get the simulation to play back in regular Blender, you have to feed the simulation data to Blender's animation system. You can do so with the next steps, called *baking* the simulation.

8. **Enable recording game physics to Blender's animation system.**

   Go to the main header and enable the Record Animation option (Game⇨Record Animation).

9. **Start the game engine (P) to run the simulation.**

   When the simulation is complete, press Esc to get back into the regular interface.

The simulation is now baked to f-curves, as you can see that the f-curves have been baked when you select the cube (right-click) and look in the Timeline. A yellow line should appear at each frame to indicate that a keyframe is stored there. For a more detailed view, change the Timeline to a Graph Editor (Shift+F6) and make it larger so that you can see what's going on. When you play back the animation (Alt+A), the results of the simulation should appear just fine, though perhaps not in real time. Figure 13-7 shows a breakdown of the preceding steps.

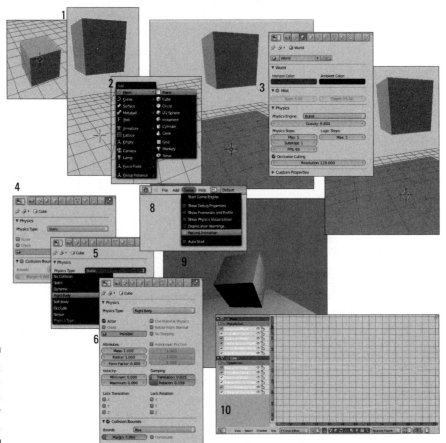

Figure 13-7:
Creating a simple rigid body simulation.

To render your baked simulation to a movie file, you need to switch back to using Blender's internal renderer (rather than the game engine) using the drop-down menu in the main header.

Simulating Cloth

Cloth simulation and soft body simulation are very similar in Blender, despite a few key differences. Both soft bodies and cloth work on open as well as closed meshes — that is, the mesh could be flat like a plane or more of a shell like a cube or sphere. However, soft bodies tend to work better on closed meshes, whereas cloth is better suited for open ones.

Also, the cloth simulator tends to work better with *self collisions*. Think about the fabric of a flowing dress. In the real world, if you bunch up part of a dress, it's technically colliding with itself. In computer simulations, you want to re-create that effect; otherwise, the fold of one part of the dress breaks through the fold of another part, giving you a completely unrealistic result. The cloth simulator handles these situations much better than the soft body simulator.

Revisiting the simple default cube, here's a quick walk-through on getting some cloth to drape across it:

1. **Create a mesh Grid (Shift+A⇨Mesh⇨Grid) and grab it along the Z-axis (G⇨Z) so that it's above the default cube.**

2. **Scale the Grid so it's larger than the Cube (S).**

   It doesn't have to be too high; just a couple of units should be plenty.

3. **Apply Set Smooth to these vertices (Tool Shelf⇨Shading⇨Smooth).**

4. **Apply a Subdivision Surfaces modifier to the plane (Ctrl+1).**

   The simulator now has even more vertices to work with. Of course, adding subdivisions causes the simulation to take longer, but this amount should be fine. It's important that you do this before adding cloth properties to your mesh. Like many other simulators, cloth is added in Blender as a modifier, and the order in the modifier stack is important.

5. **In Physics Properties, left-click the Cloth button to enable the cloth simulator.**

   The default preset for the cloth simulator is Cotton. That preset should work fine here, but feel free to play and change to something else.

6. **In the Cloth Collision panel, enable the Self Collision check box.**

   This step ensures that the simulator does everything it can to prevent the cloth from intersecting with itself.

   At this point, your cloth simulation is all set up for the plane. However, if you were to play the animation with Alt+A right now, the plane would drop right through the cube. You want the cube to behave as an obstacle, so follow the next steps.

7. **Select the cube object (right-click) and left-click the Collision button in Physics Properties.**

   Collision properties appear for your cube. Your simulation is set up.

8. **Press Alt+A to watch the cloth simulate.**

   Figure 13-8 shows what the results of this process should look like. It's a good idea to set your time cursor at the start of your animation in the Timeline before playing back the simulation.

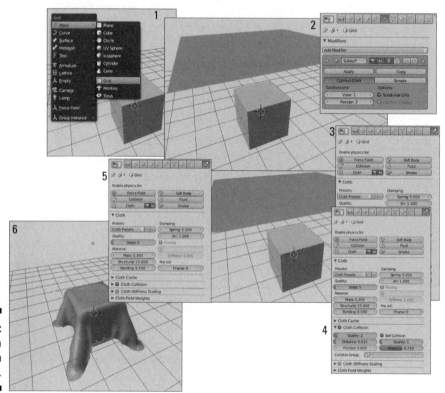

Figure 13-8: Creating a simple cloth simulation.

Splashing Fluids in Your Scene

In my opinion, one of the most remarkable features in Blender is its integrated fluid simulator. This thing is just really cool and a ton of fun to play with, to boot.

Before running head-long into fluid simulation-land, however, you should know a few things that are different about the fluid simulator. Like most of the other physics simulation controls, the main controls for the fluid simulator are in Physics Properties. However, unlike particle, cloth, and soft body simulations, which can technically work in an infinite amount of space, the fluid simulator requires a *domain*, or world, for the simulation to take place.

Another difference is that the fluid simulator actually creates a separate mesh for each and every frame of animation that it simulates. Because of the detail involved in a fluid, these meshes can get to be quite large and take up a lot of memory. To account for that size, the fluid simulator actually saves these meshes to your hard drive in .bobj.gz files. The other simulation systems also save data to your hard drive, but because fluid simulation data can take up an enormous amount of hard drive space, you need to tell Blender where to save these files. Because these files can get pretty large, it's a good idea to confirm that you have plenty of hard drive space available for storing your simulation.

The fluid simulator has all the other features of the other physics simulators. It recognizes gravity, understands static and animated collisions, and has a wide array of available controls.

Use these steps to create a simple fluid simulation:

1. **Right-click the default cube and scale (S) it larger.**

   This cube serves as your simulation's domain. The domain can actually be any size, but I definitely recommend that you use a cube or box shape as the domain. Other meshes just use their width and height, or *bounding box*. In this example, I scaled the default cube by 5 units.

2. **In Physics Properties, left-click the Fluid button and choose Domain from the Type drop-down menu.**

   Now the fluid simulator recognizes your cube as the domain for the simulation. Figure 13-9 shows the Fluid panel with the Domain option.

3. **Set the location where simulation meshes are saved.**

   Use the text field at the bottom of the Fluid panel. By default, Blender sends the .bobj.gz files to the /tmp directory. However, I recommend you create your own folder somewhere else on your hard drive, especially if you're using Windows and don't have a /tmp directory. Left-click the folder icon to navigate to that location with the File Browser.

4. **Decide at which resolution you would like to bake the simulation.**

   These values are set with the Final and Preview values under the Resolution label. The Final resolution setting is the value that is used when you render. Typically, it's a higher number than the Preview resolution, which is usually used in the 3D View. For the Preview value, you want a smaller number so that you can get your timing correct. The defaults should work fine for this example, although higher values would look better. Be careful, though, depending on the type of machine you're using: Values greater than 150 may try to use more RAM than your computer has, bringing the simulation time to a crawl.

Figure 13-9:
The Fluid panel with options for a domain object.

5. **Determine the time that you want to simulate the fluid's behavior.**

The Start and End values under the Time label in the Fluid panel are the time of the simulation, measured in seconds. By default, the simulator starts at 0.000 and runs until 4.000 seconds. An important thing to realize here is that this time is scaled across the full number of frames in your animation, as noted in the Timeline or the Dimensions panel of Render Properties. If you're using Blender's default frame rate of 24 fps and length of 250 frames, your simulation will be in slow motion, showing 4 seconds of fluid simulation over a span of roughly 10.4 seconds. For this test, I set the End time in the Fluid simulator to 3.000 seconds and the duration of the animation to be 72 frames long.

6. **Create a mesh to act as the fluid in your simulation (Shift+A⇨Mesh⇨ Icosphere).**

   I typically like to use an icosphere, but any mesh will work. To give yourself some more room, you may also want to move this mesh up the Z-axis (G⇨Z) to somewhere near the top of the domain cube so that you have some room for the fluid to fall.

7. **In Physics Properties, left-click the Fluid button and choose Inflow Type from the drop-down menu.**

   Your icosphere is set as the source for the fluids entering the domain. Choosing Inflow means that the mesh constantly produces more and more fluid as the simulation goes on. If you prefer to have a single fluid object with a fixed volume, choose Fluid rather than Inflow. Figure 13-10 shows the Fluid panel with the Inflow fluid type chosen.

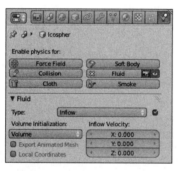

Figure 13-10: The Fluid panel with options for an inflow object.

8. **(Optional) Give the Inflow object an initial velocity in the negative Z direction.**

   This step is optional because the fluid simulator *does* recognize the Gravity setting in Scene Properties. Adding an initial force in the negative Z direction here just gives it a little extra push. The value doesn't have to be large: –0.10 should work just fine. You want to make this value negative so that it pushes the fluid down. This initial velocity is added to the force already set by gravity. At this point, your simulation is configured.

9. **Select the domain cube (right-click) and bake the simulation.**

   Left-click the large Bake button in the Fluid panel. I know that this sounds odd — "Baking fluids? Really? Won't it boil?" — but that's the terminology used. You're running the simulation for each frame and "baking" that frame's simulation result to a mesh that's saved on your hard drive. If you look at it in that way, it *kind* of makes sense.

10. **Watch the progress of the fluid simulation.**

    Depending on how powerful your computer is, this baking process can be pretty time consuming. I once had a 4-second fluid simulation that took 36 hours to bake. (Granted, it was at a high resolution, and I had a lot of crazy Inflow objects and complex moving obstacles, so it was entirely my own fault.) Just know that the more complexity you add to your simulation and the higher the resolution, the more time it's going to take. As the progress bar at the top of the screen shows your simulation processing, you can interactively follow progress in the 3D View. Remember that Blender has a nonblocking interface, so you can actually scrub the timeline, use the ←/→ hotkeys, and even play back the animation (Alt+A) while Blender is still baking. How's that for cool?

11. **Play back the finished simulation with Alt+A.**

    One thing to note here is that your mesh looks faceted. You can easily fix this issue by left-clicking the Smooth button beneath the Shading label in the Tool Shelf.

And, *POW!* You have water pouring into your scene! Using these same basic steps, you can add obstacles to the scene that can move the water around as you see fit.

Knowing when to use the right type of fluids

Blender's particle system also offers a way to do fluid simulation by choosing the Fluid physics type from the Physics panel in Particle Properties. And because that choice is available, you may find yourself wondering why you'd use this mesh-based method when that one is available. The short answer is that it all depends on what you're trying to do. For example, the particle-based fluid technique is useful if you need your fluids to interact with Blender's other simulators (force fields, cloth, and so on) or if you're simulating large-scale fluids that don't quite fit in the constraints of a 10-meter cube. The particle-based method is not so great, however, for detailed small-scale fluid simulations or if you need to use materials with ray traced transparency or shadows. The particle-based technique doesn't currently generate meshes where you can apply those materials (though that will likely change in future releases of Blender). For those situations, the fluid simulation technique covered in this section is more useful.

Part IV
Sharing Your Work with the World

The 5th Wave   By Rich Tennant

It started out as a wrap-around porch, but then Stuart took a one-day class on 3D modeling with Blender, and, well, it just sort of "took shape"...

In this part . . .

So you've created something awesome. Well, as great as that is, it's always more fun to show it to other people. You can get feedback and critiques for improvement, and you can get accolades and awards for your excellent work. In order to do that, you want to get your Blender scenes out as still images and your animations out as video files. The chapters in this part don't just focus on rendering your 3D scene: They also cover the integrated node compositor and video sequencer. These tools are fantastic for quick fixes, adjustments, and visual effects such as mixing your animation with live video.

Chapter 14

Exporting and Rendering Scenes

. . . .

In This Chapter

▶ Exporting to other programs

▶ Rendering still images and animations

. . . .

*W*orking in Blender is great, but eventually, you'll want to make the things you create viewable in programs other than Blender. You may want to have a still image of a scene, or a movie of your character falling down a flight of stairs, or you may want to export the geometry and textures of a model for use in a video game. In these situations, you want to export or render.

Exporting to External Formats

Exporting takes your 3D data from Blender and restructures it so that other 3D programs can understand it. There are two primary reasons why you'd might want to export to a 3D file format other than Blender's `.blend` format. The most common is to do additional editing in another program. For example, if you're working as a modeler on a large project, chances are good that whoever hired you, unfortunately, is not using Blender, so you'll probably need to save it in a format that fits into their pipeline and is understood by their tools.

The other reason for exporting is for video games. Many games have a public specification of the format they use for loading 3D data. Blender can export in many of these formats, allowing you to create custom characters and sets.

With only a few exceptions, all of Blender's exporters are scripts written in the Python programming language. Although all the export scripts that ship with Blender support the basic specifications in their respective formats, they may not support all the features. For example, many of the exporters have difficulty getting armature or animation information out of Blender. So keep this limitation in mind and, as many open source programmers like to say, "Your mileage may vary."

To export to a different format, choose File⇨Export and choose the format that you would like to use. A File Browser then appears so you can tell Blender where to save your new file. The left region of the File Browser contains options that are specific to the exporter you chose. Figure 14-1 shows the Export menu with a list of the available file types.

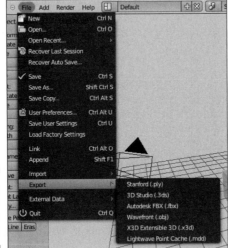

Figure 14-1: File⇨ Export⇨ Wheeeeeee!

If you're familiar with earlier versions of Blender, you may note that the export list appears strangely sparse. Many exporters in the new release of Blender are implemented as add-ons, most of which are disabled by default. If you're looking for a specific exporter and you don't see it in the File⇨Export menu, go to the Add-ons section of User Preferences (Ctrl+Alt+U) and find the add-on that provides the exporter you need. If the add-on is there, enable it, and the exporter should immediately be available in File⇨Export. To make the exporter to always available, left-click the Save as Default button at the bottom of User Preferences.

Rendering a Scene

More often than exporting, though, you probably want to render your scenes. *Rendering* is the process of taking your 3D data and creating one or more 2D pictures from the perspective of a camera. The 2D result can then be seen by nearly anyone using image viewers or movie players.

Rendering is very much like taking a photograph or a movie in meatspace. If you don't have a camera, you can't take a picture. Likewise in Blender, if there's no camera in your scene, Blender doesn't know what to render, so make sure that you have a camera in there.

Creating a still image

Rendering single images, or *stills,* in Blender is remarkably easy. Blender actually offers three different ways to do it. The fastest way is to simply press the F12 hotkey. Alternatively, you can click the Image button in the Render panel of Render Properties or choose Render⇨Render Image from the menu at the top of each of the screen layouts that ship with Blender.

Viewing your rendered images in Blender

Any way you decide to do it, Blender uses its integrated UV/Image Editor to display the rendered output. If you don't have a UV/Image Editor already open in your screen layout, Blender takes the largest area in your screen layout and changes it to the UV/Image Editor while rendering. Of course, some people would prefer a different behavior for displaying renders. Fortunately, available options allow you to change that behavior. The control is a drop-down menu in the Render panel of Render Properties, labeled Display. By default, it's set to Image Editor.

Figure 14-2 shows the Render panel and the three different options you have for where to send your renders. I like to use the default Image Editor setting or Full Screen. Choosing Full Screen does the same thing as the Image Editor option, except it also maximizes the UV/Image Editor to the entire Blender window. If you choose the New Window option, Blender creates a completely new window, populated only with a UV/Image Editor that displays your image. For any of these render options, you can quickly toggle between your regular Blender screen and the render screen by pressing F11.

Figure 14-2:
To view your renders, choose to use Full Screen, Image Editor, or Render Window.

Another cool feature that works regardless of which way you like to see your renders are the render buffer slots. When you have your render output onscreen in the UV/Image Editor, hover your mouse cursor in that editor and press J. Upon doing so, Blender switches to a different image buffer. The first time, it may seem odd because you see a blank UV/Image Editor. However, bounce back to your scene (F11) and make a small change. Then render again (F12). Now when you press Alt+J on your render, it pops back to your previous render. Press J, and you're back at your current render. Press J again, and you're in a third, blank, render slot. Blender offers you the ability to swap between up to eight render slots. Using these render slots, you can quickly compare the differences between different renders, cycling forward and backward through the slots by using J and Alt+J, respectively. Render slots are a great way to see whether you like the changes you've made to your scene.

Picking an image format

Now, you have your image rendered, but you still haven't saved it anywhere on your hard drive, so it's available for sharing with other people. This, too, is easy, but before you save, you may want to change the file type for your image. This is done in the Output panel of Render Properties, as shown in Figure 14-3.

Figure 14-3:
Output
panel in
Render
Properties.

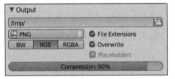

When you save with Blender's File Browser, you also can choose the file type for your image from a drop-down menu in the region on the left side. However, the Output panel in Render Properties gives you a few more options for controlling your saved file. The primary control for choosing the format of your file in the Output panel is a file type drop-down menu. By default, Blender saves renders as PNG images. If you want to render to a different image format, such as PNG, Targa, TIFF, or OpenEXR, left-click this drop-down menu and choose your desired file type. Depending on the file type you choose, the options at the bottom of the Output panel change. For example, with the PNG file type, the Compression slider is available for controlling the level of compression in the image.

The BW/RGB/RGBA buttons below the file type drop-down are always visible, and they're pretty important for both animations and stills. They control whether Blender, after rendering, saves a black and white (grayscale) image, a full color image, or a color image with an alpha channel for transparency.

Typically, you use one of the latter two. RGB is the most common and is supported by all formats, creating a full color image. On occasions, however, you'll want to render with transparency.

As an example, say that you've made a really cool building model, and you want to add your building to a photo of some city skyline. You need everything that's not your building, including the background of your image, to be rendered as transparent. An alpha channel defines that transparency. The *alpha channel* is basically a grayscale image that defines what is and is not transparent. Totally white pixels are opaque, and totally black pixels are transparent. Gray pixels are semitransparent.

Not all image formats support an alpha channel, such as the JPEG and BMP formats. If you choose one of these file types and have RGBA set, Blender just omits the alpha information when saving. If you want to make sure that your alpha channel is preserved, though, choose one of the following formats: PNG, Targa, TIFF, or OpenEXR.

Setting dimensions for your renders

The Dimensions panel close to the top of Render Properties gives you control over the size of your final render. The X and Y values under the Resolution label set the width and height of your image in pixels. The X and Y values under the Aspect Ratio label are for determining the horizontal and vertical aspect ratio of your image. The ability to adjust aspect ratio is for certain circumstances where you want to render your image with rectangular pixels rather than square ones. Typically, rectangular pixels are necessary only for television formats, so unless you know exactly what you're doing or if you're using a preset, I recommend setting these to the same value. I use 1.000 most of the time.

Speaking of presets, Blender offers a number of rendering presets for you to use. These presets are available from a drop-down menu at the top of the Dimensions panel. Choosing any one of them changes settings throughout Render Properties to get the render to properly match that preset. Using presets is a great timesaver when you know, for example, that you have to render to high-definition video specifications, but you can't remember the right resolution, aspect ratio, and frame-rate values.

Whenever you change the resolution or aspect ratio values in the Dimensions panel, you need to render your scene again (F12) to get it to appear in the right size. If you're just changing your output file type, you don't need to rerender.

Saving your still image

After you've adjusted all your settings, rendered, and chosen your output file format, you have just one thing left to do: Save your still. Saving is quick and painless. From the UV/Image Editor, press F3 or choose Image⇨Save As, and

Blender brings up a File Browser. Here, you can dictate where on your computer you want to save your render. That's it!

Remember, if you're rendering a still image, it's *not* saved anywhere on your hard drive unless you explicitly save it by pressing F3 or navigating to Image↪ Save As in the UV/Image Editor. I can't tell you how much time I spent rendering images that I forgot to save when I first started using Blender. Hopefully, you can benefit from my mistake.

Creating a finished animation

For rendering animations, the steps are similar to rendering stills (see preceding section), but you have a few more considerations. The largest consideration deals with the file type you choose. If, for example, you choose a still image format like JPEG, PNG, or OpenEXR, Blender creates an individual image for each frame in your animation. However, if you choose any of the movie options like AVI, QuickTime, or MPEG, Blender creates a single movie file that contains all the frames in the animation, as well as any sound you use for the animation. Note that Macintosh and most Windows users have the QuickTime option available, but Linux users do not.

Depending on the movie format you choose, an Encoding panel appears in Render Properties in which you have a second set of choices that enables you to pick the *codec,* or compression format, you want to use. QuickTime has its own interface, dependent on whether you're on a Windows computer or a Macintosh, whereas the other movie options work from the Encoding panel. Figure 14-4 shows the options in this panel.

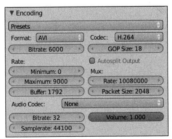

Figure 14-4: The Encoding panel in Render Properties.

The Encoding panel lets you choose which codec you would like to use, and it also offers you the ability to tweak how the actual video gets compressed. More often than not, though, the default settings tend to work pretty well.

Like in the Dimensions panel, a presets drop-down menu appears at the top of the Encoding panel for commonly used configuration. Using this menu automatically enables the proper settings to render for outputs such as DV, DVD, and VCD.

The Audio Codec drop-down menu lower down the panel gives you similar control over the sound that Blender renders (if the file type supports audio), but arguably the most important thing to remember is to make sure that the Audio Codec drop-down isn't set to None if you want audio to be included with your rendered movie file. The PCM option gives you the best results, but also yields the largest file sizes.

Make sure that you test your files if you want other people to be able to view them. I can't tell you how many times I've rendered a movie file that plays just fine on my Linux machine, but won't even open on a Windows or Macintosh machine. It's kind of ugly and makes everyone look bad. So make sure that you try to view the file on as many machines as possible before sharing it with the world.

The other consideration to make when saving an animation is where on your hard drive you intend to store it. Enter this information on the first field of the Output panel. By default, Blender saves your animations to the /tmp directory on your computer. However, you may not have a /tmp directory, or you explicitly may want to save the animation to a different folder on your hard drive. Left-click the file folder icon to the right of this text field and use the File Browser to navigate where you want to save your animation.

So, to render animation, the steps are pretty similar to rendering a still:

1. **Set up your render resolution from the Dimensions panel and your file type from the Output panel.**

   If you've been working on your animation, hopefully you've set it all up already. Although changing the output resolution (the width and height) of the image after you animate isn't too bad, changing to other frame rates after the fact can get to be a pain. The frame rate is set with the FPS value in the second block of buttons of the Dimensions panel.

2. **Confirm the start and end frames from the Frame Range values in the Dimensions panel.**

   You probably already made this setting while animating, but double-check these start and end frames to make sure that they're correct.

3. **Verify where you want to save your file in the Output panel.**

4. **Animate by pressing Ctrl+F12.**

   Also, you can press the Animation button in the Render panel or choose Render⇨Render Animation. Your animation immediately starts being created. Now go get a cup of coffee. Rendering an animation can take quite some time.

Unlike rendering a still image, which does not save anything to your hard drive until you press F3, rendering an animation automatically saves your renders wherever you stipulate in the Output panel.

Creating a sequence of still images for editing or compositing

In a couple of situations, rendering out a sequence of still images rather than a single movie file makes a lot of sense. One of the biggest reasons for rendering a sequence of stills is for *compositing*, or combining multiple images together. When you do compositing, you often rely on having an alpha channel that makes everything transparent except for your rendered subject. Most video formats simply don't support an alpha channel, so to accommodate this shortcoming, you render out a sequence of still images in a format that does support alpha, such as PNG.

Another reason that you may want to have a still image sequence rather than a movie file is for *editing,* or sequencing multiple video and animation clips. To get smaller file sizes, many video codecs throw out large chunks of image data from one frame to the next. The result is a small file that plays well, but is pretty difficult to edit because in editing, you may want to cut on a frame that doesn't have very much image data at all. Using a sequence of still images guarantees that all image data for each and every frame is completely there for smooth editing. Chapter 15 covers both compositing and editing in more detail.

The third reason you may want to render a sequence of still images is largely practical. When rendering to a movie format, what happens if you decide to stop the render and change a small part of it? Or what happens if Blender crashes in the middle of rendering? Or if an army of angry squirrels invade your office and shut down your computer midrender? Well, you have to restart the whole render process from the start frame. Starting over, of course, is painful, especially if you have to wait multiple minutes for each frame in your sequence to render. If you render by using a sequence of still images, those images are saved the second that they're created. If your render process gets stopped for any reason, you don't have to start rendering again from the beginning. You can adjust the Start value in the Dimensions panel of Render Properties to pick up where you left off and resume the render process.

If you choose to save a sequence of still images, you should create a specific folder just for these render files. You're going to create a *lot* of files. If the animation is 250 frames long and you render to still images, you're going to get 250 individual images saved to your hard drive.

Chapter 15

Compositing and Editing

*I*n live-action film and video, the term *post-production* usually includes nearly anything associated with animation. Nearly every animator or effects specialist has groaned upon hearing a director or producer say the line, "We'll fix it in post." Fortunately, in animation, post-production is more specific, focusing on editing and compositing.

This chapter is a quick guide to editing and compositing, using Blender's Video Sequence Editor and Node Compositor. Understand that these topics are large enough for a book of their own, so the content of this chapter isn't comprehensive. That said, you can find enough solid information here and in Blender's online documentation (`wiki.blender.org`) to figure it out. I explain Blender's interface for these tools, as well as some fundamental concepts, including nonlinear editing and node systems. With this understanding, these tools can help turn your work from "Hey, that's cool" to "Whoa!"

Comparing Editing to Compositing

Editing is the process of taking rendered footage — animation, film, or video — and adjusting how various shots appear in sequence. You typically edit using a *nonlinear editor* (NLE). An NLE, like Apple's Final Cut Pro or Adobe Premiere, differs from older *linear* tape-to-tape editing systems that required editors to work sequentially. With an NLE, you can easily edit the beginning of a sequence without worrying too much about it messing up the timing at the end. Blender has basic NLE functions with its Video Sequence Editor.

Compositing is the process of mixing animations, videos, and still images into a single image or video. It's the way that credits show up over footage at the beginning of a movie, or how an animated character is made to appear like she is interacting with a real-world environment. Blender has an integrated compositor that you can use to do these sorts of effects, as well as simply enhance your scene with effects such as blur, glow, and color correction.

Working with the Video Sequence Editor

The default Video Editing screen layout in Blender is accessible through the Screens datablock in the header or by pressing Ctrl+← three times from the Default screen layout. The large editor across the middle of the layout is a Video Sequence Editor (VSE) in Sequencer view. In this view, you can add and modify sequences, called *strips,* in time. The numbers across the bottom of the Sequencer correspond to time in the VSE in seconds. The numbers to the left are labels for each of the tracks, or *channels,* that the strips live in. The upper left area is a Graph Editor, used in this case for tweaking the influence or timing of individual strips' properties. To the right of the Graph Editor is a VSE in Preview view. When you're editing, the footage under the time cursor appears here. At the bottom is a Timeline, which, at first, may seem odd. However, as when animating, the benefit of having the Timeline around all the time is that you can use the Sequencer to edit a specific portion of your production, while still having the ability to scrub the full piece. The playback controls are also handy to have onscreen.

As with the Animation layout (see Chapter 10), I like to make a few tweaks to the Video Editing layout. When I first start editing in Blender's VSE, I'm usually more concerned with importing image sequences and movie clips than I am with tweaking the timing of edits. So one of the first changes I make is swapping the Graph Editor for a File Browser with files set to display thumbnails. This way, you can easily drag and drop footage from the File Browser directly onto the Sequencer. You may also note that you're missing the Properties editor. While you're in the process of editing, the Properties editor isn't critical to have open, but it's useful when you're doing your initial setup. For that reason, I often split the Sequencer and make a narrow strip on the right a Properties editor (Shift+F7). Figure 15-1 shows my modified Video Editing layout.

The settings in the Dimensions panel amid the Render Properties are important for editing in Blender because that's where you set the frame rate, measured in frames per second (fps), and resolution for the project. If you're editing footage that runs at a different frame rate or resolution than the one that is set here, that footage is adjusted to fit. So if your project is at standard HD settings (24 fps and 1920 x 1080 pixels in size), but you import an animation rendered at 50 fps and at a size of 640 x 480 pixels, the footage appears stretched and in slow motion.

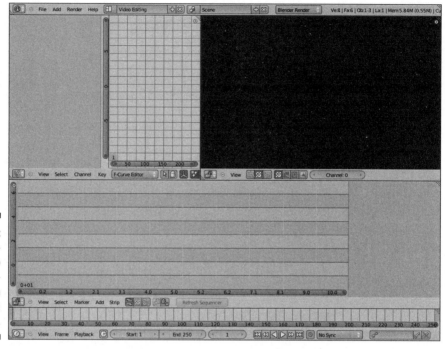

Figure 15-1:
A custom-
ized Video
Editing lay-
out for when
you start a
project.

Besides your Render Properties, the Properties region of the Sequencer is
relevant to your editing process. Because the default layout doesn't have
any strips loaded, this region appears as a blank section on the right side of
the Sequencer. However, if you have a strip in the Sequencer and you have it
selected, this region is populated and appears like the image in Figure 15-2.

Figure 15-2:
The
Sequencer's
Properties
region
gives you
controls on
a selected
strip.

As you may guess, the Properties region has the most relevant options for
working in the VSE. Five panels are available: Edit Strip, Strip Input, Effect
Strip, Filter, and Proxy. For most strip types, the Edit Strip, Strip Input, and
Filter panels are available. The Effect Strip and Proxy panels are available

only for certain types of strips. For example, audio strips can't have proxies, so that panel doesn't show up when you select a strip of that type.

Following are descriptions for the most commonly used panels:

- ✔ **Edit Strip:** The buttons in this panel pertain to where a selected strip appears in the VSE and how it interacts with other strips. You can name individual strips, control how a strip blends with lower channels, mute or lock a strip, set the strip's start frame, and change the strip's channel.

- ✔ **Strip Input:** The buttons in this panel allow you to crop and move the strip around the frame, as well as control which portion of the strip shows up in the Sequencer. When you have an audio strip selected, this panel has a few different controls and is labeled Sound.

- ✔ **Effect Strip:** This panel only appears for certain effect strips that have editable attributes. I give more detail on some effects that use this panel in the section "Adding effects," later in this chapter. The Timeline at the bottom of the screen controls how Blender plays your sequence. However, the most relevant button for the VSE is the Sync drop-down menu. To ensure that your audio plays back in sync with your video while editing, make sure that this drop-down menu is either set to AV-sync or Frame Dropping. Of the two, I tend to get better performance when I choose the latter. Nothing is worse than doing a ton of work to get something edited only to find out that none of the audio lines up with the visuals after you render. Figure 15-3 shows the options in the Sync drop-down menu of the Timeline.

Figure 15-3:
Choose Frame Dropping or AV-sync to ensure that your audio plays back in sync with your video.

Before I get heavily into using the VSE, let me first say that Blender's VSE is *not* a complete replacement for a traditional NLE. Although it is a very powerful tool, the VSE is best suited for animators who want to create a quick edit of their work. Professional video editors may have trouble because VSE is missing a number of expected features, such as a listing of available footage, sometimes called a *clip library* or *bin*. You can use the File Browser in thumbnail view to partially emulate the behavior of a bin, but it's still not quite the same. That said, all three of the open movie projects — *Elephants Dream*, *Big Buck Bunny*, and *Sintel* — were successfully edited using Blender's VSE. I find the VSE more than sufficient for quite a few of my own projects, so you ultimately have to decide for yourself.

Adding and editing strips

If you want to use the VSE to edit footage, you have to bring that footage into Blender. If you're using the modified Video Editing screen layout I describe in the preceding section in this chapter, you can use the File Browser and navigate to where your footage is. Then you can just drag and drop that file from the File Browser directly into the Sequencer. The ability to drag and drop from the File Browser is one of the handy new features added in the Blender 2.5 overhaul. Alternatively, you can add a strip by hovering your mouse cursor in the Sequencer and pressing Shift+A (just like adding objects in the 3D View). Figure 15-4 shows the menu of options that appears.

Figure 15-4:
The Add
Sequence
Strip menu.

Generally speaking, you can import five primary kinds of strips: scenes, movies, still images, audio, and effects. These strips are represented by the following options in the menu:

✔ **Scene:** Scene strips are an extremely cool feature unique to Blender. When you select this option, a secondary menu pops up that allows you to select a scene from the .blend file you're working in. If you use a single .blend file with multiple scenes in it, you can edit those scenes together to a final output sequence without ever rendering out those scenes first! This handy feature allows you to create a complete and complex animation entirely within a single file. Scene strips are also a great way to use Blender for overlaying graphics, like titles, on video.

✔ **Movie:** When you select this option, the File Browser that comes up allows you to select a video file in one of the many formats Blender supports. On files with both audio and video, Blender loads the audio along with the video file as separate strips in the sequencer.

✔ **Image:** Selecting this option brings up a File Browser that allows you to select one or more images in any of the formats that Blender recognizes. If you select just one image, the VSE displays a strip for that one image that you can arbitrarily resize in time. If you select multiple images, the VSE interprets them as a sequence and places them all in the same strip with a fixed length that matches the number of images you selected.

✔ **Sound:** This option gives you a File Browser for loading an audio file into the VSE. When importing audio, you definitely want to import sound files in WAV format, which gives you the best quality sound. Although Blender supports other audio formats like MP3, they're often compressed and sometimes sound bad when played.

✔ **Effect Strip:** This option pops out a secondary, somewhat lengthy, menu of options. These strips are used mostly for effects and transitions. I cover them in more depth in the next section.

When you load a strip, it's brought into the VSE under your mouse cursor. Table 15-1 shows helpful mouse actions for working efficiently in the VSE.

Table 15-1	Helpful Mouse Actions in the VSE
Mouse Action	*Description*
Right-click	Select strip to modify. Right-clicking the arrow at either end of the strip selects that end of the strip and allows you to trim or extend the strip from that point.
Shift+right-click	Select multiple strips.
Middle-click	Pan the VSE workspace.
Ctrl+middle-click	Zoom height and width of the VSE workspace.
Scroll wheel	Zoom the width in and out of the VSE workspace.
Left-click	Move the time cursor in the VSE. Left-clicking and dragging scrubs the time cursor, allowing you to view and hear the contents of the Sequencer as fast or slow as you move your mouse.

One thing you may notice is that quite a few of the controls are very similar to those present in other parts of Blender, such as the 3D View and Graph Editor. This similarity is also true when it comes to the hotkeys that the VSE recognizes, although a few differences are worth mentioning. Table 15-2 lists some the most common hotkeys used for editing.

Table 15-2	Common Features/Hotkeys in the VSE	
Hotkey	*Menu Access*	*Description*
G	Strip⇨Grab/Move	Grabs a selection to move elsewhere in the VSE.
E	Strip⇨Grab/Extend from frame	Grabs a selection and extends one end of it relative to the position of the time cursor.
B		Border select, for selecting multiple strips.
Shift+D	Strip⇨Duplicate	Duplicates the selected strip(s).
X	Strip⇨Erase Strips	Deletes the selected strip(s).
Shift+K	Strip⇨Cut (hard) at Current Frame	Splits a strip at the location of the time cursor. Similar to the razor tool in other NLEs.
M	Strip⇨Make Meta Strip	Combines selected strips into a single "meta" strip.
Alt+M	Strip⇨UnMeta Strip	Splits a selected meta strip back to its original individual strips.
Tab		Tabs into a meta strip to allow modification of the strips within it.
H	Strip⇨Mute Strips	Hides a strip from being played.
Alt+H	Strip⇨Unmute Strips	Unhides a strip.
Shift+L	Strip⇨Lock Strips	Prevents selected strips from being moved or edited.
Shift+Alt+L	Strip⇨Unlock Strips	Allows editing on selected strips.
Alt+A		Plays the animation starting from the location of the time cursor.

Editing in the Sequencer is pretty straightforward. If you have two strips stacked in two channels, one above the other, when the timeline cursor gets to them, the strip that's in the higher channel takes priority. By default, that strip simply overrides, or *replaces*, any of the strips below it. You can, however, change this behavior in the Edit Strip panel of the Sequencer's Properties region. The drop-down menu labeled Blend controls the *blend mode* of the selected strip. You can see that the default setting is Replace, but if you left-click this button, you get a short list of modes similar to the layer blending options you see in a program like Photoshop or GIMP. Besides Replace, the ones I use the most are Alpha Over and Add.

The Graph Editor is useful for animating all kinds of values in Blender, and it's quite useful for strips in the Sequencer. One of the primary animated values for strips is the Opacity slider in the Edit Strip panel. This slider controls the influence factor that the strip has on the rest of the sequence. For example, on an image strip — say, of a solid black image — you can use the Graph Editor to animate the overall opacity of that strip. Values less than 1.0 make the image more transparent, thereby giving you a nice way to create a controlled fade to black. The same principle works for sound strips, using the Volume slider in the Sound panel of the Sequencer's Properties region. A value of 1.0 is the sound clip's original loudness and it gradually fades away the lower you get. Values greater than 1.0 amplify the sound to a level greater than the original volume.

By combining the Graph Editor with Blending modes, you can create some very cool results. Say that you have a logo graphic with an alpha channel defining the background as transparent, and you want to make the logo flicker as if it's being seen through poor television reception. To make the logo flicker, follow these steps:

1. **Add a logo image to the Sequencer (Shift+A⇨Image).**

2. **Make sure that the logo's strip is selected (right-click) and, in the Edit Strip panel, change the strip's blend mode to Alpha Over.**

3. **Insert a keyframe for the strip's opacity (right-click Opacity in the Edit Strip panel and choose Insert Keyframe).**

4. **In the Graph Editor, tweak the Opacity f-curve so that it randomly bounces many times between 1.0 and 0.0 (Ctrl+left-click).**

   After tweaking the curve to your taste, you should now have your flickering logo effect.

Adding effects

Pressing Shift+A in the VSE provides you with quite a few options other than importing audio and video elements. A large portion of these options are effects, and many typically require that you select two strips that are stacked on top of each other in the VSE. When necessary, I point out which effects these are.

Pay close attention to the order in which you select your strips because it often has a dramatic influence on how the effect is applied. The second strip you select is the *active strip* and the primary controller of the effect.

Here's a list of the available options:

- **Add/Subtract/Multiply:** These effects are the same as the blend mode settings in the Edit Strip panel of the Properties region. Unless you really need some special control, I recommend using those blend modes rather than adding these as effects sequences. It works just as well and keeps your Sequencer from getting too cluttered. Using these effects requires that you select two strips before pressing Shift+A and adding any of them. As an example of how to use them, select the strip you want to start with and then Shift+right-click the strip you want to transition to. Next press Shift+A⇨Effect Strip⇨Add. A new red strip is created that's the length of the overlap between your two selected strips. On playback (Alt+A), the bright parts of the upper strip amplify the overlaying bright parts of the lower strip.

- **Alpha Over/Alpha Under/Over Drop:** These effect strips control how one strip's alpha channel relates to another. They're also available as Blending modes, and I suggest that you apply these effects that way in most cases. One example of a time where it makes sense to use these as strips is if you need to stack more than one of these effects together or if you need to use an f-curve to individually control the effect. Otherwise, stick with the blend mode.

- **Cross/Gamma Cross:** These effects are *crossfades* or *dissolves* between overlapping strips. The Cross effect also works in audio to smoothly transition from one sound to another. Gamma Cross works the same as Cross, but takes the additional step of correcting the color in the transition for a smoother dissolve.

- **Plugin:** Some people in the Blender community have written plug-ins for the VSE. Choosing this option opens a File Browser so that you can select the plug-in on your hard drive and load it into Blender. Please note that as of this writing, the plug-ins for the VSE weren't working. Hopefully, the kind Blender developers have fixed the problem by the time this book hits shelves.

- **Wipe:** Wipe is a transition effect like Cross and Gamma Cross. It transitions from one strip to another like a sliding door, à la the *Star Wars* movies. This effect also uses the Effect Strip panel in the Properties region to let you choose the type of wipe you want, including single, double, iris, and clock wipe. Also, you can adjust the blurriness of the wiping edge and the direction the wipe moves.

✔ **Glow:** The Glow effect works on a single strip. It takes a given image and makes the bright points in it glow a bit brighter. Ever wonder how some 3D renders get that glowing, almost ethereal quality? Glow is one way to do it. The Effect Strip panel in the Properties region lets you adjust the amount of glow you have and the quality of that glow.

✔ **Transform:** This effect provides very basic controls for the location, scale, and rotation of a strip. The effect works on a single strip, and you can find its controls on the Effect Strip panel of the Properties region. You can use f-curves on this effect strip to animate the transform values.

✔ **Color:** This handy little option creates an infinitely sized color strip. You can use this effect to do fades or set a solid background color for scenes.

✔ **Speed Control:** With the Speed Control effect, you can adjust the playback speed of individual strips. In the Effect Strip panel of the Properties region, you can choose to influence the Global Speed (1.0 is regular speed; setting it to 0.50 makes the strip play half as fast; setting it to 2.0 makes it play twice as fast). You can also have more custom control using the Graph Editor.

✔ **Multicam Selector:** If you're using Scene strips in the Sequencer and you have multiple cameras in your scene, you can use this effect strip to dictate which camera you're using from that scene. As with most things in Blender, you can animate that camera choice, allowing you to easily do camera switching in your scene.

Rendering from the Video Sequence Editor

To render your complete edited sequence from the VSE, the steps are largely identical to the ones outlined for creating a finished animation in Chapter 14. Actually, you must do only one additional thing.

In the Render Properties, have a look in the Post Processing panel. Make sure that the Sequencer check box is enabled. Activating this check box lets Blender know that you want to use the strips in the Sequencer for your final output rather than anything that's in front of the 3D camera. If you don't enable this check box, Blender just renders whatever the camera sees, which may be just the default cube that starts with Blender, or whatever else you might place in front of the 3D camera.

Working with the Node-Based Compositor

Compositing is the process of mixing multiple visual assets to create a single image or sequence of images. By this definition, you may notice that *technically* Blender's VSE qualifies as a sort of compositor because you can stack strips over each other in channels and blend them together with effects and transitions. Although this statement is true, the VSE is nowhere near as powerful as the Node Compositor is for mixing videos, images, and other graphics together.

As designed, the VSE is intended for working with multiple shots, scenes, images, or clips of video. It's also meant to play back in real time (or as near to that as possible). In contrast, the Compositor is intended for working with a single shot, and it's most certainly not meant for working in real time. There is a little bit of overlap in the functionality of these two parts of Blender, but depending on the task at hand, one is more suitable than the other.

What makes the Node Compositor so powerful? Well, it's in the name: *nodes*. One of the best ways to understand the power of nodes is to imagine an assembly line. In an assembly line, each step in the process depends on the step immediately preceding it and feeds directly into the following step. This methodology is similar to the layer-based approach used in many image manipulation programs like Photoshop and GIMP. Each layer has exactly one input from the previous layer and one output to the following one. Figure 15-5 illustrates this idea.

Figure 15-5:
An assembly line approach, like the layers in GIMP or Photoshop.

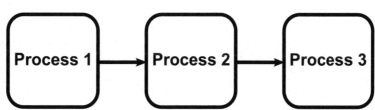

That approach works well, but you can enhance the assembly line a bit. Say that some steps produce parts that can go to more than one subsequent step, and that other steps can take parts from two or more earlier steps and make something new. And take it a bit farther by saying that you can duplicate groups of these steps and integrate them easily to other parts of the line.

You then have an assembly *network* like that depicted in Figure 15-6. This network like approach is what you can do with nodes.

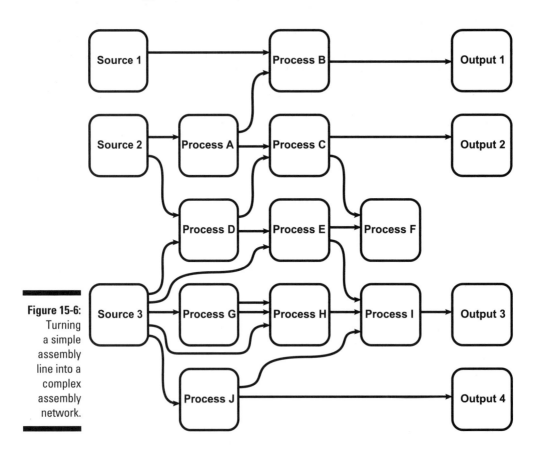

Figure 15-6:
Turning
a simple
assembly
line into a
complex
assembly
network.

Understanding the benefits of rendering in passes

Before taking full advantages of nodes, it's worthwhile to take a quick moment and understand what it means to render *in passes*. Assume for a moment that you animated a character walking into a room and falling down. The room is pretty detailed, so it takes a fairly long time for your computer to render each frame. However, because the camera doesn't move, you can really render the room just once. So if you render your character with a transparent background, you can superimpose the character on just the still image of the room, effectively cutting your render time in half (or less)!

That's the basics of rendering in passes. The preceding example had two passes, one for the room and one for the character. However, you can have many more passes with more detailed content. For example, if you want to, you can have a render pass that consists of just the shadows in the image. You can take that pass and adjust it to make all the shadows slightly blue. Or you can isolate a character while she's walking through a gray, blurry scene.

Another thing to understand for compositing 3D scenes is the concept of Z-depth. Basically, *Z-depth* is the representation of the distance that an object is from the camera, along the camera's local Z-axis. Z-depth is used quite often in compositing. The compositor can use this Z-depth to make an object look like it fits in a scene even though it was never rendered with it.

To do render passes in Blender, you use *render layers*. It's important to make a distinction here between Blender's regular layer system and render layers. Although render layers do use Blender's layer system, they are separate things. Basically, you can decide arbitrarily which Blender layers you'd like to include or exclude from any of the render layers you create. All the controls for render layers are in the Layers panel in Render Properties. Figure 15-7 shows the Layers panel

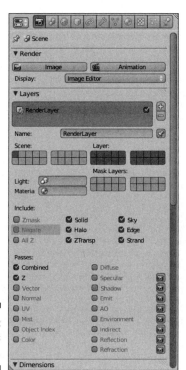

Figure 15-7:
The Layers
panel.

At the top of the Layers panel is a list box containing all the render layers in your scene. By default, there's only one, named 1 RenderLayer. Beneath the list box is a text field where you can enter or change the name for a selected render layer. The next section features three blocks of Blender layers. The first block of these layers shows the scene layers; the ones that are going to be sent actively to the renderer.

The next set of Blender layer buttons determine which Blender layers actually belong in this render layer. For example, if you're creating a render layer for background characters and you have all your background characters on layers 3 and 4, you Shift+left-click those layers in this block.

The third set of Blender layer buttons are mask layers. The objects in these layers explicitly block what's rendered in this render layer, effectively masking them out. You typically use these layer buttons for more advanced compositing scenarios.

The series of check boxes that fill the majority of the Layers panel are where the real magic and power of render layers lie. The first set of check boxes specify which *pipeline products* to deliver, or include (hence the label), to the renderer as input. These pipeline products refer to major renderable elements of this render layer that are seen by the renderer. If you disable Halo, for example, no halo materials are sent to the renderer. Basically, they're omitted. You can use these check boxes in complex scenes to turn off pipeline features you don't need in an effort to shorten your render times.

Here is a brief description of some of the more useful pipeline features:

- ✓ **Solid:** This feature is for solid faces. Basically, if you disable this option, the only things that render are lights, halo materials, and particles. Any solid-surfaced object doesn't appear.

- ✓ **ZTransp:** This name is short for *Z-transparency*. If you have an object that has a Z-transparent material, enabling this button ensures that the material gets rendered.

- ✓ **Strand:** *Strands* are static particles rendered in place. They're often used to approximate the look of hair or grass. Keeping this option enabled ensures that your characters aren't bald and that their front lawns aren't lifeless deserts.

- ✓ **All Z:** The simplest way to explain this option is with an example. Say that you have a scene with a wall between your character and the camera. The character is on one render layer, and the wall is on another. If you're on the character's render layer and you enable this option, the character is masked from the render layer and doesn't appear. With All Z off, the character shows up on its render layer.

Underneath the Include check boxes is a set of options that control which passes are sent to the render layer. These passes are most useful when used in the Node Compositor because essentially they make compositing so interesting and fun. Here are some of the most useful passes:

- ✔ **Combined:** The Combined pass is the fully mixed, rendered image as it comes from the renderer before getting any processing.

- ✔ **Z:** This pass is a mapping of the Z-depth information for each object in front of the camera. It is useful for masking as well as effects like *depth of field,* where a short range of the viewable range is in focus and everything else is blurry.

- ✔ **Vector:** This pass includes speed information for objects moving before the camera (meaning that either the objects or the camera is animated). This data is particularly useful for the Vector Blur node, which gives animations a decent motion blur effect.

- ✔ **Normal:** The information in this pass relates to the angle that the geometry in the scene has, relative to the camera. You can use the Normal pass for additional bump mapping as well as completely altering the lighting in the scene without rerendering.

- ✔ **UV:** The UV pass is pretty clever because it sends the UV mapping data from the 3D objects to the compositor. Basically, this pass gives you the ability to completely change the textures on an object or character without the need to rerender any part of the scene. Often, you want to use this pass along with the Object Index pass to specify on which object you want to change the texture.

- ✔ **Object Index:** This pass carries index numbers for individual objects, if you set them. The Object Index pass allows very fine control over which nodes get applied to which objects. This pass is similar to plain masking, but somewhat more powerful because it makes isolating a single object or group of objects so much easier.

- ✔ **Color:** The color pass delivers the colors from the render, completely shadeless, without highlights or shadows. This pass can be helpful for amplifying or subduing colors in a shot.

- ✔ **Specular:** The specularity pass delivers an image with the specular highlights that appear in the render.

- ✔ **Shadow:** This pass contains all the cast shadows in the render, both from ray traced shadows as well as buffered shadows. In my example from earlier in this section about taking the shadows from the render and adjusting them (such as giving them a bluish hue), you'd use this pass.

- ✔ **AO:** This pass includes any ambient occlusion data generated by the renderer. If you use this pass, it's a good idea to double-check to see whether you're using approximate or ray traced AO in the Ambient Occlusion panel of World Properties. If you're using ray traced AO, verify that ray tracing is enabled in Render Properties.

Working with nodes

After you set up your render layers the way you like, you're ready to work in the Node Compositor. As with the VSE, Blender ships with a default screen layout for compositing, appropriately named Compositing. You can access the Compositing layout from the Screens datablock at the top of the window or by pressing Ctrl+← once from the Default screen layout. By default, Blender puts you in the Node Editor for compositing, which is exactly where you want to be. The other node editors are for materials and textures and are for more advanced work.

By itself, the Node Editor looks pretty stark and boring, like a lame 2D version of the 3D View. However, left-click the Use Nodes check box in the header, and you see a screen layout that looks similar to the one shown in Figure 15-8.

Figure 15-8:
Starting
with nodes
in the
Composite
Node Editor.

Blender starts by presenting you with two nodes, one input and one output. You can quickly tell which is which by looking at the location of the connection points on each node. The left node labeled Render Layers has connection points on the right side of it. The location of these connection points means that it can serve only as an input to other nodes and can't receive any additional data, so it's an input node. It adds information to the node network. In contrast, the node on the right, labeled Composite, is an output node because it has no connection points on its right edge, meaning it can't feed information to other nodes. Essentially, it's the end of the line, the result. In fact, when you render by using the Node Compositor, the Composite node is the final output that gets displayed when Blender renders.

Setting up a backdrop

I personally prefer to see the progress of my node network as I'm working, without having to constantly refer back to another editor for the results of my work. Fortunately, Blender can facilitate this workflow with another sort of output node: the Viewer node.

To add a new node, position your mouse cursor in the Node Editor and press Shift+A. You see a variety of options. For now, navigate to Output⇨Viewer to create a new output node labeled Viewer.

If the Render Layer input node was selected when you added the Viewer node, Blender automatically creates a connection, also called a *noodle,* between the two nodes. Noodles are drawn between the circular connection points, or *sockets,* on each node. If the noodle wasn't created for you, you can add it by left-clicking the yellow Image socket on the Render Layer node and dragging your mouse cursor to the corresponding yellow socket on the Viewer node.

However, making this connection doesn't seem to do much. You need to take three more steps:

1. **Left-click the Backdrop check box in the Node Editor's header.**

   A black box loads in the background of the compositor. (Don't worry; it's supposed to happen, I promise.)

2. **Go to the Post Processing panel in Render Properties and ensure that the Compositing check box is enabled.**

3. **Render the scene by left-clicking the Image button in the Render panel or pressing F12.**

   When the render is complete and you return to the Blender interface by pressing F11, the empty black box has been magically replaced with the results of your render. Now anything that feeds into this Viewer node is instantly displayed in the background of the compositor.

This setup is the way I typically like to work when compositing. In fact, I often take it one step farther and press Shift+spacebar to maximize the Node Editor to the full window size. This way, you can take full advantage of your entire screen while compositing.

If you find that the backdrop gets in your way, you can disable it by left-clicking the Backdrop check box in the Node Editor's header, or you can move it around in the compositor by Alt+middle-clicking in the editor and dragging the image around. Also, you can get more space by middle-clicking in the compositor and dragging the entire node network around, or by using your scroll wheel to zoom in and out on the nodes. As of the Blender 2.5 series, you also have the ability to scale the backdrop image by using the V (zoom out) and Alt+V (zoom in) hotkeys. Table 15-3 shows most of the frequently used mouse actions in the Node Editor.

Table 15-3   Commonly Used Mouse Actions in the Node Editor

Mouse Action	Description
Right-click	Select a node.
Shift+right-click	Select multiple nodes.
Middle-click	Pan compositor work area.
Alt+middle-click	Move backdrop image.
Ctrl+middle-click	Zoom compositor work area.
Scroll wheel	Zoom compositor work area.
Left-click (on a node)	Select a node. Click and drag to move the node around.
Left-click (on a socket)	Attach or detach a noodle to/from the socket you click on. Click and drag to the socket you want to connect to.
Left-click+drag the bottom right corner of a node	Resize the node.
Left-click+drag in the compositor workspace	Create a box. Any noodles in the box's area are deleted, leaving just nodes. Think of it as cutting noodles.
Ctrl+left-click+drag in the compositor workspace	Lasso select.
Shift+Ctrl+left-click a node	Connect the active Viewer node to the output of the clicked node. Continuous Shift+Ctrl+left-clicks iterate through the multiple outputs of the node.

Identifying parts of a node

At the top of each node are four icons: the triangle on the left and the Plus (+), "equal," and sphere icons on the right. Following is a description of what each button (shown in Figure 15-9) does:

- ✔ **Triangle:** Expands and collapses the node, essentially hiding the information in it from view.

- ✔ **Plus (+):** Hides and shows sockets that have no connections. This button is useful for simplifying the display of your node network. However, a word of warning: You can easily forget that you have hidden sockets on your node and go a little crazy wondering where they ran off to.

- ✔ **Equal:** This button really isn't an equal symbol. If you zoom in closely, the icon is revealed to be a small slider and value widgets from Blender's interface. If you left-click this button, you toggle the visibility of editable values in the selected node. Any values that you set manually are hidden from view.

- ✔ **Sphere:** View window expand/collapse. This icon is available only on nodes that have an image window, such as a render layer node, any output node, or texture node.

Figure 15-9:
Each node has icons at the top that control how you see it in the compositor.

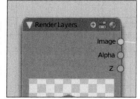

Navigating the node compositor

For the most part, editing nodes in Blender conforms to the same user interface behavior that's in the rest of the program. You select nodes by right-clicking, you can grab and move nodes by pressing G, and you can border select multiple nodes by pressing B. Of course, a few differences pertain specifically to the Node Editor. Table 15-4 shows the most common hotkeys used in Node Editor.

Table 15-4	Commonly Used Hotkeys in the Node Editor	
Hotkey	*Menu Access*	*Description*
Shift+A	Add	Open toolbox menu.
G	Node⇨Translate	Grab a node and move it.
B	Select⇨Border Select	Border select.
X	Node⇨Delete	Delete node(s).
Shift+D	Node⇨Duplicate	Duplicate node(s).
Ctrl+G	Node⇨Make Group	Creates a group out of the selected nodes.
Alt+G	Node⇨Ungroup	Ungroups the selected group.
Tab	Node⇨Edit Group	Expands the node group so you can edit individual nodes within it.
H	Node⇨Hide/Unhide	Toggles the selected nodes between expanded and collapsed views.
V	View⇨Backdrop Zoom Out	Zooms out (scales down) the backdrop image.
Alt+V	View⇨Backdrop Zoom In	Zooms in (scales up) the backdrop image.

When connecting nodes, pay attention to the colors of the sockets. The sockets on each node come in one of three different colors, and each one has a specific meaning for the type of information that is either sent or expected from the node. The colors and their meanings are as follows:

✔ **Yellow:** Color information. Specifically, this socket relates to color in the output image, across the entire red/green/blue/alpha (RGBA) scale. Color information is the primary type of data that should go to output nodes.

✔ **Gray:** Numeric values. Whereas the yellow sockets technically get four values for each pixel in the image — one for each red, green, blue, and alpha — this socket gets or receives a single value for each pixel. You can visualize these values as a grayscale image. These sockets are used mostly for masks. For example, the level of transparency in an image, or its alpha channel, can be represented by a grayscale image, with white for opaque and black for transparent (and gray for semitransparent).

✔ **Blue:** Geometry data. These sockets are pretty special. They send and receive information that pertains to the 3D data in the scene, such as speed, UV coordinates, and normals. Visualizing these values in a two-dimensional image is pretty difficult; it usually ends up looking like something seen through the eyes of the alien in *Predator*.

Grouping nodes together

As Table 15-4 shows, you can also group nodes together. The ability to make a group of nodes is actually one of the really powerful features of the Node Editor. You can border select a complex section of your node network and press Ctrl+G to quickly make a group out of it. Grouping nodes has a few really nice benefits. First of all, grouping can simplify the look of your node network so that it's not a huge mess of noodles (spaghetti!). More than simplification, though, node groups are a great organizational tool. Because you can name groups like any other node, you can group sections of your network that serve a specific purpose. For example, you can have a blurry background group and a color-corrected character group.

But wait, there's more! (Do I sound like a car salesman yet?) When you create a group, it's added automatically to the Group menu when you go to add a new node (Shift+A⇨Group). To understand the benefit of being able to add groups, imagine that you created a really cool network that gives foreground elements a totally sweet glow effect. If you make a group out of that network, you can now instantly apply that glow to other parts of your scene or scenes in other .blend files. Go ahead: Try it and tell me that's not cool — you can't do it!

When working with nodes, it's a good idea to have the network flow from the left to the right. Wherever possible, you want to avoid creating situations where you feed a node's output back to one of the nodes that gives it input. This feedback loop is called a cyclic connection. If you've ever heard the painfully loud feedback noise that happens when you place a microphone too close to a speaker, you have an idea of why a cyclic connection is a bad idea.

Discovering the nodes available to you

Blender has quite an extensive list of nodes that you can add to your network. In fact, it seems like with every release of Blender, more and more incredible node types are added to the compositor. Many nodes have a *Fac,* or factor, value that you can usually either set with a value from another node or explicitly set by typing. Values less than 1 make the node have less influence, while values greater than 1 make the node have more influence than usual over the image.

Input

The input nodes are one of the two most important node types in the Node Compositor. If your node network doesn't have any inputs, you don't have a composite. Figure 15-10 shows each of these nodes side by side.

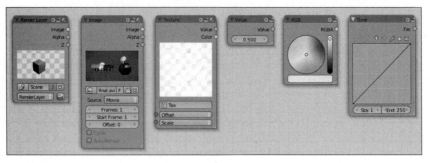

Figure 15-10:
Input nodes:
Render
Layer,
Image,
Texture,
Value, RGB,
and Time.

✔ **Render Layer:** This node feeds input from a scene into the compositor. The drop-down menu at the bottom of the node allows you to pick any of the render layers you created in any scene. Notice also the button with the camera icon that is to the right of this menu. Left-click this button to render just this layer. This handy feature allows you to update a portion of your node network without needing to rerender all the layers in the network.

✔ **Image:** The name for this node is a bit oversimplistic because it can actually load more than just a single still image. The Image node allows you to bring any sort of image data into the compositor, including sequences of images and movie files, and allows you to control when the sequence starts, how long it is, and whether to loop it continuously.

✔ **Texture:** The Texture node is unique as an input node in that it's the only one that can actually receive input data as well. Through this node, you can take any texture that you built in Blender and add it to your node network. This node is particularly useful with UV data because it can actually let you change the textures on objects in your image without rerendering.

✔ **Value:** This fairly simple input node allows you to feed any scalar (numerical) value to other nodes.

✔ **RGB:** With the RGB node, you can feed any solid color to any other node in the compositor. This node is a good, quick way to adjust the hue of an image or provide a simple colored background.

✔ **Time:** This node is probably one of the most powerful, yet misunderstood, nodes in Blender. In the past, the Node Compositor was not tied to the Graph Editor, making it difficult to animate attributes of individual nodes. The Time node was a way around this obstacle. Fortunately, as of Blender 2.5 and the ability to animate nearly everything, the Time node is less of an absolute necessity in the compositor. You can key node values just like any other value in Blender. However, the Time node is still useful.

Output

Input nodes are one of the two most important node types in Blender. As you may have guessed, the Output nodes are the other important node types, for a similar reason. If you don't have an output node, Blender doesn't know what to save when it renders. The following are the two most-used Output nodes:

✔ **Composite:** Blender recognizes the Composite node as the final output from the Node Compositor. When you set up your output files for animation in Render Properties, or when you press F3 to save a render, it's the information from this node that Blender saves out.

✔ **Viewer:** The Viewer node is similar to the Composite node, but it's not necessarily for final output. Viewer nodes are great for spot-checking sections of your node network and making sure that things are going the way you want them to. Also, output from these nodes is seen in the compositor's backdrop, if you enable it.

Color

The Color nodes have an enormous influence over the look of the final output. These nodes directly affect how colors appear, mix, and balance in an image. And because an image is basically just a bunch of colors arranged in a specific pattern, you can understand why these nodes have so much control. Figure 15-11 shows some of the most commonly used Color nodes. Following are descriptions of each node type:

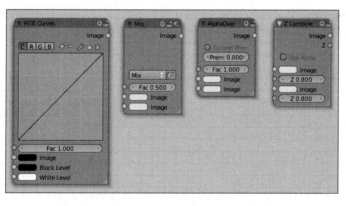

Figure 15-11:
Color nodes: RGB Curves, Mix, AlphaOver, and Z Combine.

✔ **RGB Curves:** Arguably one of the most powerful color nodes, the RGB Curves node takes image data and allows you to use curves to adjust the combined color, or any of the red, green, or blue channels in the image individually. Left-clicking the C, R, G, and B buttons on the upper left changes between combined, red, green, and blue color channels, respectively. With this node, you can do anything that the Hue Saturation Value, Bright/Contrast, and Invert nodes can do, but with more control.

✔ **Mix:** I personally use this node quite a bit. The Mix node has 16 different blending modes to allow you to control how to combine two input images. If you've used image editing software like GIMP or Photoshop, these blending modes should be pretty familiar to you. One thing to remember in this node — and it's something I used to constantly get backwards — is that the upper image input socket is the background image, whereas the lower image input socket is the foreground image.

✔ **AlphaOver:** This node is very similar to the Mix node, except it deals exclusively with combining images using their alpha channels. The lower socket is the foreground, and the upper socket is the background image. The other thing to note with this node is the Convert Premul check box. Basically, if you see weird white or black edges around parts of your foreground elements, left-clicking this button usually fixes them.

✔ **Z Combine:** Like the Mix and AlphaOver nodes, the Z Combine node mixes two sets of image data together. However, instead of using color information or alpha channels, this node can use Z-depth information.

Vector

Vector nodes use 3D data from your scene to influence the look of your final 2D image. The usage of these nodes tends to be a bit advanced, but they allow you to do things like change the lighting in a scene or even change the speed that objects move through the scene . . . all without rerendering! If you render to an image format that understands render passes, like the very cool OpenEXR format (more on this topic in the next section), and you include vector and normal passes, these nodes can be a huge timesaver.

Filter

Filter nodes can *drastically* change the look of an image and are probably the No. 1 way to fake any effect in an image. These nodes actually process the pixels in an image and can do things like put thick black lines around an object, give the image a variety of customized blurs, or make bright parts of the image glow. Figure 15-12 shows some of the most useful Filter nodes:

Figure 15-12: Blur, Vector Blur, Defocus, and Glare nodes.

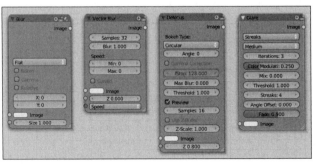

✓ **Blur:** As its name implies, this node applies a uniform blur across the entire input image. The first button gives you a drop-down menu to select the type of blur you want to use. I typically like to use Gauss for most of my effects. When you first apply this node, you may not think that anything is happening. Change the values in the X and Y buttons to adjust the blur size on a scale from 0 to 256, or 0.0 to 1.0, depending on whether you enable the Relative check box.

✓ **Vector Blur:** This node is the fastest way to get motion blur out of Blender. The Vector Blur node takes speed information from the Vector pass (enable Vector in the Layers panel of Render Properties) and uses it to fake the motion blur effect. One check box I recommend you enable in this node, especially if you're doing character animation, is the Curved check box. This option gives objects that are moving in an arc a more natural, curved motion blur. This node is specifically for use with 3D data coming from Blender. It can't add motion blur to just any footage.

✓ **Defocus:** Blender's Defocus node is the way to fake the *depth of field,* or DOF, effect you get with a real camera. If you've seen a photo where something in the middle of the picture is in focus, but objects in the foreground and background are blurry, it's called a *shallow DOF,* and it looks pretty sweet. You can get an idea where the camera's focal point is by selecting the camera in your scene and turning on Limits for the camera in its Object Data Properties. Then when you adjust the DOF Dist value, you can see the focal point as a yellow cross.

✓ **Glare:** This node is a really quick way to give the bright parts in your render just a little extra bit of kick. The Fog Glow and Streaks options in the first drop-down menu are what I tend to use the most. Of all the values, this node gives you to play with, probably the most influential one is Threshold. Setting the threshold to values between 0.0 and 1.0 tends to work best for me, but results vary from one image to the next.

Converter

These handy little utility nodes have a variety of purposes, including converting one set of data to another and ripping apart or recombining elements from a rendered image. The Color Ramp and ID Mask nodes in particular get used quite a bit. The Color Ramp node is great for helping visualizing or revisualizing numerical values on a scale. For example, the only way to get a good sense of what the Z-depth of an image looks like is to map Z values along a manageable scale and then feed that to a white-to-black color ramp, as shown in Figure 15-13.

The ID Mask node is handy because it allows you to isolate an object even more specifically than with layers and render layers. Assume that you want to apply the Glare node to a ball that your character is holding. If the scene is complex enough, it doesn't really make a lot of sense to give that ball a layer all by itself. So you can give the object a Pass Index value in the Relations panel of Object Properties. Then by using the ID Mask node, you can isolate just that ball and make it all shiny.

Figure 15-13:
Visualizing
a scene's
Z-depth
using a
ColorRamp.

Matte

The Matte nodes are specifically tailored for using color information from an image as a way of isolating certain parts of it. Matting is referred to as *keying* because you pick the main color, or *key color,* to represent transparency. Keying is the fundamental basis for those cool *bluescreen* or *greenscreen* effects used in movies. The filmmaker shoots the action over a blue or green screen (blue is used for analog film, whereas green is typically used for digital footage), and a compositor removes the blue or green and replaces it with other footage or something built in 3D.

Distort

The Distort nodes typically do general-purpose image manipulation operations like Translate, Rotate, Scale, Flip, or Crop.

Want to do that spinning newspaper effect you see in old movies? Wire an image of a newspaper and the Time node to the Rotate and Flip nodes, and you've got it! However, three special Distort nodes are worth talking more about: Displace, Map UV, and Lens Distortion. Figure 15-14 shows each of these nodes.

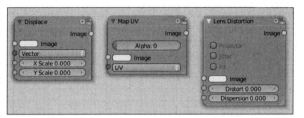

Figure 15-14:
Distort
nodes:
Displace,
Map UV,
and Lens
Distortion.

✔ **Displace:** This node is great for doing quick-and-dirty image distortions, such as generating heat waves in the desert, faking refraction, or making an object appear to push through the image on the screen. The key is the Vector input socket. If you feed a grayscale image to this socket, it uses those values to shift pixels in the image. Connecting a color image, normals, or vectors shifts the image around with a more three-dimensional effect, thereby giving you things like the heat wave effect.

✔ **Map UV:** In this entire chapter, I talk about how one cool thing that the Node Compositor can do is change textures on objects after you've already rendered them. Well, the Map UV node gets you that awesome functionality. To use this node, you need to enable the UV pass on your render layer. Feed that pass to this node, along with the new texture you want to use, and BAM! Your new texture is ready to be mixed back with the image. To make sure that you're changing the texture on the right object, combine the Map UV node with the ID Mask node before mixing.

✔ **Lens Distortion:** Sometimes you want to introduce the effects that some special (or, in some cases, poor) lenses have on the final image. The Lens Distortion node produces those effects for you. You can get everything from a wide fisheye lens look to that strange effect when an old projector isn't calibrated properly and the colors are misaligned.

Group

When you press Ctrl+G to create a node group, that group is placed in this menu. When you group a set of nodes, you instantly have the ability to apply that network to other parts of your composition. Also, grouping gives you the ability to share node networks between .blend files. When you append or link a node group from another file, it shows up in this menu. There's more on grouping in this chapter in the section "Grouping nodes together."

Whenever you have the opportunity, name *everything* you create. Unique names are especially important for groups because they're automatically added to the Group menu. Using names that make sense makes choosing the right node group a lot easier. You can always rename node groups from the Properties region of the Node Editor (N).

Rendering from the Node Compositor

If you're using the Node Compositor, you already know all the basic steps for getting a rendered image out of it. Of course, if you skipped straight to this section, here's the quick version: Make sure that the Compositing check box in the Post Processing panel of Render Properties is enabled.

That said, you need to know one other thing about rendering from the Compositor. Say that you're working on a larger production and want to save your render passes to an external file format so that either you or another compositor can work on it later without rerendering the whole scene. You'd have to save your renders to a file format that understands render layers and render passes. That format is the venerable OpenEXR file format, developed and gifted to the world by the cool people at Industrial Light & Magic.

Now I know what you're thinking, "Using this format is as easy as setting up my render layers and then choosing OpenEXR from the menu in the Output panel of Render Properties." You're actually two-thirds correct. You do set up your render layers and you do go to the Output panel. *However*, choosing OpenEXR saves only the final composite output (not the layers or passes) in an OpenEXR file (extension .exr). In order to get layers and passes, you should instead choose MultiLayer. With this format, you get an OpenEXR file that has all the layer and pass information stored with it.

Pay close attention to your hard drive space when you choose to render to OpenEXR with all your layers and passes embedded. Keeping all your render layers and passes is a great way to tweak and make adjustments after rendering. However, the file size for each individual .exr file can be *huge*. Whereas an HD frame in PNG format may be only a couple hundred kilobytes, an OpenEXR file on the same single frame with all the passes enabled may be well over 100 *megabytes* — yes, megabytes. And if your animation has a length in minutes, that 100 megabytes per frame starts taking up space quickly. So make sure that you do test saves to get a good benchmark for the file size and see that you have enough hard drive space to store all those frames.

Part V
The Part of Tens

The 5th Wave   By Rich Tennant

"I found these two in the computer lab morphing faculty members into farm animals."

In this part . . .

This is the (more) fun part of the book. These chapters are quick lists to help make you a better Blender user. Blender is a dense program, stuffed full of features. What's more, it's *constantly* changing and getting stuffed with more new features and enhancements. As a result, it's not difficult to forget things or get stumped with strange issues. The chapters here give you ways to deal with these issues. It's an incredible world, and it's great to have you as a part of it!

Chapter 16

Ten Problems for New Users in Blender (And Ways Around Them)

The community forums and Web pages for Blender are brimming with questions from new users. Many of them are the same question, or derivatives of the same question. The purpose of this chapter is to identify some of the most common ones and give you solutions to them so that you don't have to dig through these Web sites (unless you really, really want to).

Auto Saves and Session Recovery Don't Work

The problem of auto saves and session recovering not working is mostly unique to users of Microsoft Windows, but even if you're on another operating system, it's worth it to double-check. This problem happens because your Temp directory is improperly set to a folder that doesn't exist on your computer. If this path isn't set properly, your auto saves and Blender's session recovery (File⇨Recover Last Session) don't work. The Recover Last Session feature is particularly important to have for those cases where you close Blender without saving your project. It's amazing how many people have lost hours of work because Blender crashed (it happens sometimes!), or they accidentally closed Blender without saving. Blender won't warn you if your file hasn't been saved, so *don't be that person!*

By default, Blender sets the Temp path at /tmp, a directory that doesn't exist in Windows. Two solutions to this problem exist:

✔ Create the /tmp directory. In Windows, you'd create C:\tmp. After you create this directory, all auto saves and recoverable sessions are stored there.

✔ Change the Temp path in the File section of User Preferences (Ctrl+Alt+U) to a directory of your choice that already exists. Many people like to use C:\Windows\Temp.

Get into the habit of quitting Blender by pressing Ctrl+Q or choosing File⇨ Quit rather than clicking the window's close button (the X in the corner). In Windows, closing by pressing the X doesn't get you a quit.blend, the file that the Recover Last Session operation uses.

Blender's Interface Is Weird or Glitchy

Blender uses OpenGL, an accelerated 3D programming library, for its entire interface. Because of the extensive use of OpenGL, Blender often uses parts of the library that other programs may never touch. Depending what video card you have in your computer, the drivers for that card may not effectively implement these little-used library features that Blender needs.

On some machines, Blender may run very slow, or you may see weird screen glitches around the mouse pointer or menus. The first thing to check is the drivers for your video card. Go to the Web site for the manufacturer of your video card to see whether any updates are available.

You may want to turn off any fancy effects that your operating system adds, such as transparent windows, shadows on the mouse cursor, or 3D desktop effects. Because all these little bits of eye candy tend to be hardware accelerated, they may be conflicting with Blender a bit. At the very least, turning them off usually makes your computer use fewer resources like processor power and memory, thereby making more of those resources available to Blender. If you're using an nVidia video card, make sure that the Flipping check box in your OpenGL settings isn't enabled and that full-screen anti-aliasing is disabled.

Within Blender itself, go to the System section in User Preferences (Ctrl+Alt+U) and find the Window Draw Method drop-down menu in the center column. The default setting is Automatic, which normally works pretty well. However, on some Intel-based and ATI-based video cards, you may have better luck manually changing this menu to Overlap or Overlap Flip. Play with the different options here to see which one works best for you. Blender updates immediately when you make the change, so you don't need to restart anything.

A Notorious Black Stripe Appears on Models

Often when modeling, you run into a situation where a strange black crease goes along some edges. The stripe is usually most apparent when modeling with the Subdivision Surface modifier turned on. What's happening here is that the normals for one of the faces adjoining this edge are facing the wrong direction.

 Usually, the quickest way to fix this problem is to have Blender recalculate the normals for the model and attempt to have them all face outside. To do so, go into Edit mode, select all, and press Ctrl+N. Typically, pressing Ctrl+N alleviates all issues. If it doesn't, however, you may have to go in and manually flip the normals yourself. Manual flipping of normals is easiest to do from Face Select mode with face normals visible. To make face normals visible, enable the Face check box under the Normals label turned on in the Mesh Display panel of the Properties region of the 3D View (N). With that set, a cyan line points out from the face in the direction of the normal. Now you can see which normals are facing the wrong way. From there, select the offending faces and press W⇨Flip Normals or left-click the Normals⇨Flip Direction button in the Tool Shelf.

If that still doesn't solve your problem, it could mean that you have multiple vertices in the same place, or you have faces inside your mesh. You can fix multiple vertices by pressing W⇨Remove Doubles. Internal faces are harder to auto-detect, but if you view your mesh in Wireframe viewport shading (Z), it may be more apparent.

Objects Go Missing

Occasionally, you might run into a problem where not everything shows up in your 3D View, even though you're positive you didn't delete anything. The first thing to do is to make sure that nothing is hidden. Pressing H in Blender hides whatever you've selected, and it's easy to accidentally hit it when you're actually trying to press G and grab an object. Fortunately, you can unhide all hidden objects pretty quickly by pressing Alt+H. You can also look in the restrict columns on the right side of the Outliner. If your object is hidden, the first icon — the eye icon — appears closed. Left-clicking the eye icon unhides it. The camera icon on the far right controls whether your object is visible when rendering.

If you're sure that nothing is hidden, next try to make all layers visible and check to be sure that you didn't inadvertently move your object to a different layer. You do so by pressing the Tilde (~) key. You may also want to press Home in the 3D View to bring all objects into view.

One last thing to check is whether you're in Local View, the view that isolates all objects except for a few that you select. The hotkey that toggles this view is Numpad Slash (/), and it can be pretty easy to accidentally hit it when using the numeric keypad to change views. One quick way to tell whether you're in Local View is to look at the header for the 3D View. If no layer buttons are where they're supposed to be, you may be in Local View. In the upper left corner of the 3D View, text also tells you how you're viewing your scene. If you're in Local View, (Local) appears as the last part of that text.

If none of these things work, there actually *is* the chance that you deleted your object by accident. Fortunately, if you haven't closed your file, you can recover from this mistake as well. See, when you delete an object in Blender, it doesn't actually get completely deleted until you close the file or open a new file, so it still exists in Blender's internal database for this file.

I'm writing the next few steps under the assumption that your object was a Mesh, but the same technique works for curves, text, and other types of objects. To recover a deleted object, use the following steps:

1. **Create a dummy object that's the same type as the one you're trying to recover.**

   For meshes, use any of the options in Shift+A⇨Mesh.

2. **Bring up that object's Object Data Properties and look in the Context panel at the top; in the datablock, left-click the button on the left side.**

   You see a list of all the objects in the scene that share the current selected object's type. Anything you delete has an empty circle to the left of it. Figure 16-1 shows what this screen might look like.

3. **If your deleted object is in this list, select it and the dummy object you added in the first step is instantly replaced with the mesh for your deleted object.**

   Neat, huh?

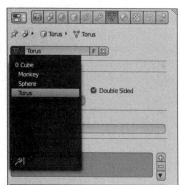

Figure 16-1: Deleted objects in the datablock at the top of Object Data properties.

Edge Loop Select Doesn't Work

The issue of Edge Loop Select not working happens the most on Linux machines that use the Gnome desktop environment. The Blender hotkey for doing a loop selection in Edit mode is Alt+right-click. Unfortunately, in Gnome and a few other window managers, this key sequence pops up a menu for controlling the window.

You can fix this issue in two ways. The easiest one is to use Shift+Alt+right-click. You typically use this combination to select multiple loops, but if nothing is selected, it works exactly the same as the Alt+right-click combination.

Of course, that's a bit of a kludge. A better solution is to modify the window manager's settings and bind the function that it ties to the Alt key to another key, like the infamous "super" or Windows key that most modern keyboards have. Fortunately, this process is very simple. From the Gnome taskbar, choose System⇨Preferences⇨Windows. You see a dialog box that allows you to change the movement key from Alt to Ctrl or Super. I recommend that you change the movement key to super because Blender also makes extensive use of the Ctrl key as well.

A Background Image Disappears

When using a photographic or drawn reference to base your models on, it's a common practice to load the reference image in the background of the 3D View (see Chapter 5). However, when working this way, you may orbit your view to do a spot-check and then when you return to side (or front or top or camera and so on) view, the background image may disappear, even though the Background Images panel in the 3D View's Properties region says it's still there.

The answer here is that you're viewing the scene through Perspective view rather than the Orthographic one. Blender doesn't show the background reference image in Perspective view. Switch back to Orthographic by pressing Numpad 5. It makes sense to use Orthographic for reference images because a Perspective view introduces distortion and scaling to the way the scene is viewed, so it wouldn't be a good idea to model from reference in this type of view even if you could. The Orthographic view is much more effective at getting a model to match a reference image.

Zooming Has Its Limits

When working in Perspective view, you may notice that occasionally you can't zoom in on your scene as much as you'd like. This limitation is because you're zooming toward a center point, and you're very near it. You can take advantage of four workarounds:

- ✔ **Place the 3D cursor at the location you'd like to zoom to and press Ctrl+Numpad Dot (.).** This workaround centers the view on the 3D cursor and gives you a clearer target to zoom in on.

- ✔ **Select the object that you want to zoom in on and press Numpad Dot (.).** This workaround centers the view on that object's center point so that you can now use that as your zoom target.

- ✔ **Try popping quickly into Orthographic view by pressing Numpad 5.** Because Orthographic view has no perspective distortion, the way it zooms is somewhat different, which may give you a better angle.

- ✔ **Enable the Auto Depth check box in the Interface section of User Preferences (Ctrl+Alt+U).** Enabling this option tells Blender to dynamically change the point you're zooming in and avoid this problem altogether.

Lost Simulation Data

As mentioned in Chapter 13, Blender saves some simulation data to your hard drive. Unfortunately, if that simulation data isn't where Blender expects it to be, your simulation doesn't show up in your `.blend` file. Generally, lost simulation data happens for one of three reasons:

- ✔ **You work on more than one computer.** If you work in Blender on more than one machine and only copy the `.blend` file between the two, the simulation data isn't where it needs to be on the second computer. You need to copy that simulation data to the same place relative to your `.blend` file on the second computer for it to show up properly.

- ✔ **You accidentally changed or deleted the path to the simulation data.** This reason isn't common, but it does happen. Fortunately, the fix is simple for fluid simulations. Select the domain object for your fluid simulation and go to Physics Properties. In the Fluid panel, the path to your simulation data is the last field. Enter the proper path here or left-click the folder icon to the right of the field and find the proper directory with the File Browser.

- ✔ **You're using the `/tmp` directory for your simulations.** Initially, using `/tmp` doesn't seem like that big of a deal. However, on some operating systems, the `/tmp` directory is periodically purged, deleting everything in it. If that directory gets purged, your simulation won't show up and your only option is to rebake it.

  Using `/tmp` all the time also has another nasty side effect: Different `.blend` files overwrite the simulation data that's in there. So you may run into a situation where you open one `.blend` with a fluid simulation only to see the simulation results from another file. Again, the only solution in this case is to rebake your simulation. This time, however, set the path somewhere else so this doesn't happen again.

Blender Doesn't Create Faces As Expected

So you're modeling along and having a good old time creating your next awesome creature. At some point along the way, though, you select four vertices with the intent of creating a quad, or four-sided face, between them. Only instead of creating your nice quad when pressing F, Blender gives you two triangles, and they look all twisted. This distortion occurs because the vertices are not *coplanar*, or all in the same plane in 3D space. Or Blender might give you an error that says "The selected vertices form a concave quad." A concave face is when a vertex is placed within the triangular shape formed by the other three vertices, as shown in Figure 16-2.

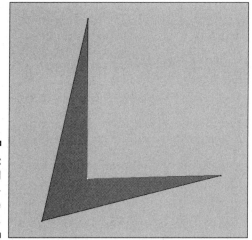

Figure 16-2:
You should avoid creating concave faces.

In either case, the solution is to move the offending vertex until the quad you want to form is convex and roughly coplanar. You can do so by manually moving the vertices around, or you can repeatedly use the Smooth operation (W⇨Smooth). This practice is pretty common in Blender. In fact, the very cool Bassam Kurdali, director of *Elephants Dream,* found himself pressing the Smooth button so often that he actually made his own custom version of Blender that binds the T key to the Smooth operation so that he wouldn't have to move his mouse as much! Fortunately, with features added in the 2.5 series like Repeat Last (Shift+R) and the ability to assign custom hotkeys, you don't necessarily have to go to those lengths, but it's great to know that the option is available.

Disorientation in the 3D View

Blender's 3D View allows you to see any part of your scene from just about every possible angle. However, many new users and users migrating from other 3D software packages find that they very easily become disoriented. Models flip upside down, and they find the whole thing very difficult to control.

The reason for this disorientation is because, by default, Blender uses an orbiting style in the 3D View known as Trackball. It's extremely flexible; when I'm modeling, I personally enjoy having the freedom that the Trackball style provides for orbiting my view to any arbitrary, off-the-wall angle. However, if you're not used to this behavior, I admit that it can be frustrating to use.

Fortunately, Blender offers a Turntable orbit style that's much more like the orbiting style featured in other 3D software, and it's often less disorienting for new users. To switch to the Turntable orbit style, go to Blender's User Preferences (Ctrl+Alt+U) and look in the Input section. On the left side, under the label of Orbit Style, is a pair of buttons. By default, the Trackball button should be activated. Left-click the Turntable button to switch orbit styles. If you find that you prefer the Turntable style over Trackball, left-click the Save As Default button at the bottom of User Preferences and that setting will persist each time you start Blender.

Chapter 17

Ten Tips for Working More Effectively in Blender

. . . .

In This Chapter

▶ Saving time with good work habits

▶ Planning and having fun

. . . .

*W*orking in Blender is a ton of fun, but you can adopt a few good work habits to make the experience even more enjoyable. These good habits let you work faster without sacrificing the quality of your work. In this chapter, I detail ten of my best suggestions for working more efficiently and effectively in Blender.

Use Tooltips and Integrated Search

Blender is a dense program, and users often forget what a button does or discover a new menu. If you don't know what a button in Blender does, hover your mouse pointer over it. More often than not, a helpful tooltip pops up to concisely describe what the button does. And even if the tooltip isn't completely clear, you have a better idea of what to search for to get help.

And speaking of searching, one of the side effects of the event system refactor that was completed during the development of Blender 2.5 is the addition of fully integrated search. Using the search hotkey (spacebar) in a particular editor, you can type the name of the feature or tool you're looking for, and Blender shows you a list of operations that may match within the context of the editor that you're working in.

Look at Models from Different Views

If you work in an environment modeling and animating by using just one 3D View, you should definitely make it a point to periodically orbit around your scene and look at it from a bunch of different angles. Double-checking is particularly important when modeling because it's very easy to get a model that looks perfect from the front, but really distorted and goofy-shaped from one side.

Split off another 3D View if you need it or use the numeric keypad hotkeys to quickly do spot-checks from different angles. If you're coming from a background in 3DStudio Max or CAD applications, you may want to use the Quad View in the 3D window to see multiple views at the same time by going to View⇨Toggle Quad View or using the Ctrl+Alt+Q hotkey.

Lock a Camera to an Animated Character

When animating a character, you frequently run into a case where you're trying to animate a secondary detail on the character as he's moving. For these situations, I like to create a new camera and parent it to the character. This way, the camera goes anywhere the character does. I find this approach helpful for facial animation on a moving character. To lock a camera to your animated character, use the following steps:

1. **Add a new camera (Shift+A⇨Camera) and put it in front of your character's face.**

2. **With the camera still selected, add the head bone of your character to the selection (Shift+right-click).**

3. **Press Ctrl+P⇨Bone to parent the camera to the bone.**

   Now, wherever the head goes and whichever direction it turns, the camera is always looking at your character's face.

4. **Whenever you want to work on the facial animation for your character, select this camera (right-click) and switch to its view by pressing Ctrl+Numpad 0.**

Don't Forget about Add-Ons

One of the neat things that was brought into Blender during the 2.5 development series were *add-ons*. Add-ons are a set of trusted Python scripts written to extend Blender's capabilities. They can be as small as a little script that adds a new menu or as large as a wizard that generates a landscape for you. By default, although these scripts ship with Blender, many are disabled by default. It's worth your time to go through the Add-Ons section of the User Preferences editor (File⇨User Preferences or Ctrl+Alt+U) to see what's available.

If you find an add-on that you know you frequently use (like the Dynamic Spacebar Menu add-on or a specific importer or exporter), enable the add-on and include it on your startup by clicking the Save As Default button at the bottom of the User Preferences editor.

Name Everything

Every time you add something to your scene in Blender, give it a name that makes sense. It's a very disorienting feeling when you open a .blend file that you haven't worked on in a while and you see that your characters are Cube.001, Cube.012, and Sphere.007, and that really cool skin material you made is called Material.015.

On small, one-shot projects, ambiguous names may not be so bad, but properly naming material makes finding it later that much easier. And on larger projects, good organization is even more valuable. Not only is it smart to name everything in your .blend file, but it's also a good idea to have a good structure for your projects. For most of my projects, I have a separate directory for the project. Within that directory, I create subdirectories for my libraries of models, materials, textures, and finished renders. For animations, my renders directory is broken down even farther into each shot.

Use Layers Effectively

Although only 20 layers are available, Blender's layering system is very versatile and used for a variety of purposes. Objects can live on more than one layer, lights can be made to only illuminate the layers they're on, and you can use layers to animate the visibility of objects in your scene. As such, keeping some form of organization in mind is in your best interest.

One thing I like to do is place all my models on the top row of layers (layers 1–10) and all other objects, such as lights, cameras, and armatures, on the bottom row (layers 11–20).

Also keep high-priority objects, such as characters and animated things, on the left-most layers, while keeping static objects like backgrounds on the right-most layers.

Specifically for character animation, when I put my character in one layer, I place his rig in the layer directly below it. I like to stick to this little convention, which is certainly a help for me when I want to quickly make sense of a `.blend` file that I haven't opened in a long time.

Of course, this organizational style may not work for you, but you should definitely make it a point to create *some* conventions that you can remember and reuse.

Do Low-Resolution Test Renders

When you're finalizing the look of a model, you often have to make a quick change to the model and render (F12) it to see what it looks like. If you're not careful, you could spend more time waiting for those little test renders than you do actually working on your model.

When you're just doing test previews, these tips can reduce the render time:

- ✔ **Turn off anti-aliasing.** *Aliasing* is that jaggy stair-stepping that happens around some edges in your renders. *Anti-aliasing* is the process of trying to smooth those jaggies out. The way anti-aliasing works in Blender is by using a technique known as *oversampling,* where it renders the same section multiple times and averages out the results to make those edges smoother. Having anti-aliasing enabled is great for final renders, but can really eat up time when you just want to do a quick test. Disable anti-aliasing by left-clicking its check box in the Render Properties.

- ✔ **Render at reduced size.** Most of the time, when you're doing a test, you don't really have to see what the full-size final image will look like. This generalization is especially true if the final render is for print or film, where the final resolution can be greater than 4,000 pixels wide. Of course, you could manually enter a smaller size in the Dimensions section of the Render Properties, but Blender offers a faster way. If you look in the Render Properties, you see a slider under the X and Y resolution values. Adjust this slider to make Blender render your image at that percentage of the final size, thereby reducing the render time for your test preview.

- ✔ **Turn off computationally intensive features if you don't need them.** Features like ambient occlusion (AO), ray tracing, and environmental lighting look great in a final render, but if you're just looking at the form of a model, they aren't necessarily needed for a test. You can turn off ray tracing in the Shading section of the Render Properties. Turning off AO or environmental lighting requires you to go to the World Properties and disable it there.

✔ **Render just the layers you need.** If you're working on just one model in a scene and only want to do a test render for that model, disable the layers for other objects in the scene. As long as you have the object and lights in the scene, your test render will be helpful, accurate, and most important, speedy.

✔ **Use the Border Render feature.** If you're only interested in doing a test render on a particular part of your scene, switch to the camera view (Numpad 0) and use Border Render by pressing Shift+B and using your mouse cursor to draw a box around the part of the shot you're interested in. When you finish doing tests, you can take this border off by left-clicking the Border check box in the Dimensions section of the Render Properties, or you can press Shift+B and draw a box anywhere outside of the camera's view area.

✔ **If you're animating, use OpenGL previews.** In the header of the 3D View, the last button has an icon of a film clapper. Clicking that icon will render your animation, using the same engine that creates the real-time display in the 3D View. In other software, a render that comes from the 3D View is referred to as a playblast. It allows you to see the action and timing of your animation without waiting for all the fancy render settings to kick in. As an additional bonus, I recommend going into the Display section of the Properties region in the 3D View (View⇨Properties or press N) and click the Only Render check box before creating your play-blast. The Only Render feature hides the extra, nonrendered objects (such as rigs, lights, and the grid plane) in your scene so that you can get a clear playblast without bothersome obstructions.

Mind Your Mouse

When you're using Blender's hotkeys to transform objects, where you place your mouse cursor before performing the operation can be pretty important. Although the importance of your mouse cursor's location has reduced a bit with the new continuous mouse feature, cursor placement can still be an issue, particularly for rotating and scaling.

For rotating, it's a good practice to keep your mouse distant from the object's origin. Doing so gives you more control over how you rotate. If your mouse cursor is too close to the center, you can have your object spinning in all kinds of unpredictable ways.

The same is true for scaling, but it's more dependent on whether you're scaling up or down. If you're scaling up, it makes sense to bring your mouse cursor a bit closer to the selection's origin so that you have more control. If you're scaling down, start with your mouse cursor farther away from the selection's origin and, as with rotation, you have more control of how small your object can get.

For grabbing, it's a bit less important, but I generally like to have my mouse somewhere near my object's origin.

Use Grease Pencil to Plan

Blender's Grease Pencil feature allows you to write or draw simple lines in 3D space. While this feature may seem a bit strange at first, it's actually incredibly useful. As an individual, you can use Grease Pencil to quickly sketch out ideas prior to modeling them in Blender. If you're working with a group of people, Grease Pencil allows you to include notes in the 3D View to facilitate collaboration. You can sketch a pose that a character should go into or draw an arc that the surface of a model should follow and pass those notes back to the original artist. You can even do rough 2D animation with this handy little feature!

To use Grease Pencil, simply hold down D while left-clicking and dragging your mouse cursor around the 3D View. The default color for Grease Pencil strokes is black, but you can adjust it, as well as other attributes from Grease Pencil section of the Properties region (N).

Have Fun, but Take Breaks

Don't be afraid to just play with Blender. If you ever find yourself wondering "What does this button do?" just press it and find out. Now, if you're working on something important, you should probably save first, but definitely make it a point to experiment and try things out. By this kind of playing, not only can you figure out how to use new parts of Blender, but you can also find new ways of using existing features in cool ways that might not have been intended.

Working in 3D can be incredibly serious fun, but it can also be addictive. But too much computer time can ultimately hurt the quality of your work. try to step away from the computer for a bit to rest your eyes, get some food, stretch your legs, or even talk to another human being.

Chapter 18

Ten Excellent Community Resources

In This Chapter

▶ Discovering Web sites that are valuable sources of information and help in Blender

▶ Finding a place for real-time communication with other Blenderheads

*T*he true strength of Blender is in its community. It's strong, organized, passionate, and perhaps even a little bit crazy. People use Blender for a variety of reasons, from producing animated films and video games to creating scientific and architectural visualizations. The following community resources give you a good idea of just how diverse and motivated this group is.

Blender.org

The official Blender Web site, Blender.org is *the* place to go for nearly anything Blender related. Most obviously, this Web site is the one to visit when you want to download the latest stable version of Blender. Not only that, but you can also track new developments in the Blender Foundation and Blender Institute, including new features being coded into Blender.

Another item of interest is the official Blender User Manual online. This "live" manual is in wiki format, so it's constantly being updated as changes are made to Blender.

You can also use this site to find Blender trainers who have been certified by the Blender Foundation or go to the Gallery to sit back and enjoy some of the best artwork created by the many skilled artists in the community.

BlenderArtists.org

If you had any questions about how active the Blender community is, you would only have visit www.blenderartists.org once to quell those doubts. The primary community Web site for Blender artists, this site is the main place to go for English-speaking Blender users.

BlenderArtists.org (or BA.org, as many affectionately refer to it) has some news and a gallery, but the main life of the site can be found on its forums. Here you can see artists of all skill levels sharing their work, learning new features, offering tips, participating in contests, and engaging in idle chitchat.

 A particularly cool thing on the BA.org forums is the Weekend Challenge. Late Thursday night (GMT), a theme is posted. Participants have until the same time Monday evening to model and render a scene to fit that theme. At the end of the weekend, the community votes on a winner, and that winner gets to pick the theme for the next Weekend Challenge. This is a great way to find out just how good you really are, and it's a lot of fun, too!

BlenderNation

If any new developments with Blender occur or anything interesting happens within the Blender community, BlenderNation, the main news site for anything Blender-related, reports on it. BlenderNation (www.blendernation.com) covers events, reviews books, and presents tutorials.

In particular, this Web site is a great way to see what kind of professional work is being done with Blender. (Many working professionals don't always have time to be active on the forums at BA.org.) BlenderNation also reports on topics that, although perhaps not directly related to Blender, may be of interest to Blender users (such as news on open source software or events in the larger computer graphics industry).

BlenderBasics.com

This Web site is the official *Blender For Dummies* Web site that I maintain in relation to this book. Not only can you find all the sample files available on the DVD included with this book (in case you lose yours), but I also periodically post video tutorials, additional files, and errata updates here. The Web site is maintained in blog format and organized by the chapters of the book. This means that you can quickly use it to look up information related to a specific chapter, or you can check the blog for the latest and greatest updates and information as I post it for you.

BlenderNewbies

A very handy blog-style Web site for new Blender users, `http://blender newbies.blogspot.com` reports on some Blender community news, but its real value is in the regular tutorials that get posted.

BlenderCookie.com

A regularly updated and high-quality site loaded with education material for Blender, BlenderCookie was one of the first sites to provide video tutorials and documentation for Blender's new interface. BlenderCookie continues to provide high-quality examples and tutorials for anyone interested in advancing their CG skills with Blender. The vast majority of materials on this Web site are freely available, although some tutorials offer the ability to purchase supplementary files and source files for a small fee.

Blendswap

At this online repository of a variety of 3D models created in Blender, models are contributed by the community and organized by category. Associated with each model is a license that clearly shows what you have permission to do with it. Blendswap played an instrumental part in some of the weekend modeling sprints for the most recent open movie project from the Blender Institute, *Sintel*.

Blenderart Magazine

Focusing on creating artwork with Blender, Blenderart is a very well-designed free online magazine in PDF format that is released on (roughly) a bimonthly schedule. Some of the best artists in the community have written for this magazine, and it's a great place to pick up new tricks.

Graphicall.org

When you really start getting into Blender, it can become highly addictive. One of the huge benefits of Blender being open source is the sheer amount of access you have to developers and, by extension, development versions of Blender.

Graphicall.org is a Web site set up by Blenderheads to provide everyone with periodic builds from the development source tree. Builds are created for each of the major platforms Blender supports, and they're uploaded to the site with incredibly high frequency. There are automated daily builds, and some users even upload builds more than once in a single day. This way, regular users can play with new features while they're being developed and, hopefully, contribute to the process by creating bug reports and providing feedback to developers. This level of access is unheard of for regular users of any of the proprietary 3D packages, and it's one of those things that you get with Blender precisely because it's open source.

Blender IRC Channels on freenode.net

The ultimate place to go for instant discussion and feedback from other Blender users is the Blender IRC channels on freenode.net. IRC is Internet Relay Chat, one of the oldest protocols on the Internet. Using a chat program (called a *client*) like mIRC or Chatzilla or even the open source IM program, Pidgin, you can log into the freenode server. If you don't want to install anything, you can use a Web interface at http://webchat.freenode.net. Simply choose a nickname and join one of the many channels devoted to Blender.

In particular, the following channels may be most interesting to you:

- ✔ **#blender:** Kind of the obvious de facto official Blender channel. You can often get quick help here, but sometimes the channel is populated with people who only know as much about Blender as you do.

- ✔ **#blenderchat:** For general discussion, critique, and occasional help in Blender. This is probably the most active Blender channel on freenode and is a great place to interact directly with other Blender users.

- ✔ **#blenderQA:** As the name suggests, for getting your Blender questions answered. This is usually a pretty good place to go if you're having problems and need help quickly.

- ✔ **#smc:** Speed Modeling Contest. Visit this channel to really challenge yourself. Artists here organize challenges where everyone is given an object to model and a time limit (usually 30 minutes to an hour) to create that model and render it.

- ✔ **#blendercoders:** For people involved with actually writing the code that makes Blender. Although discussions here might be a bit technical for new users (and even some experienced ones!), it's a good place to find out the latest information on Blender's development. Also, if you think you've found a bug or error in Blender, this is a good, quick way to talk with a developer and find out if the error is real or if you're just doing something incorrectly.

Appendix

About the DVD

In This Appendix

▶ Exploring system requirements

▶ Using the DVD with Windows, Linux, and Mac

▶ Discovering what you'll find on the DVD

▶ Troubleshooting any issues

*W*hat would a book about Blender be without a disc full of goodies on it? Well, hopefully the world will never know. The DVD that comes with this book is packed not only with copies of Blender for Linux, Windows, and Macintosh platforms, but also a multitude of other programs that you can use to round out your open-source creative toolbox. I also include example files for each chapter. I wanted to make sure that every megabyte of the DVD has something worthwhile on it. This appendix goes though the content of the disk and explains how to get at it.

System Requirements

Make sure that your computer meets the minimum system requirements shown in the following list. If your computer doesn't match up to most of these requirements, you may have problems using the software and files on the DVD. For the latest and greatest information, please refer to the ReadMe file located at the root of the DVD.

- A PC running Microsoft Windows or Linux with kernel 2.4 or later.

- A Macintosh running Apple OS X Tiger or later.

- A video card that supports accelerated OpenGL graphics. Most modern cards support OpenGL graphics, but you should double-check yours.

- A DVD drive.

If you need more information on the basics, check out these books published by Wiley: *PCs For Dummies* by Dan Gookin; *Macs For Dummies* by Edward C. Baig; *iMacs For Dummies* by Mark L. Chambers; *Windows XP For Dummies* and *Windows Vista For Dummies,* both by Andy Rathbone.

Using the DVD

To install the items from the DVD to your hard drive, follow these steps.

1. **Insert the DVD into your computer's DVD drive.**

   The license agreement appears.

   Note to Windows users: The interface won't launch if you have autorun disabled. In that case, choose Start⇨Run. (For Windows Vista, choose Start⇨All Programs⇨Accessories⇨Run.) In the dialog box that appears, type *D:\Start.exe*. (Replace *D* with the proper letter if your DVD drive uses a different letter. If you don't know the letter, see how your DVD drive is listed under My Computer.) Click OK.

   Note for Mac Users: When the DVD icon appears on your desktop, double-click the icon to open the DVD and double-click the Start icon.

   Note for Linux Users: The specifics of mounting and using DVDs vary greatly between different distributions of Linux. Please see the manual or Help information for your specific system if you experience trouble using this DVD. You may also note that all the software on this DVD is released under the GNU GPL and therefore it's a good possibility that your Linux distribution already includes the program in its online repositories. If you're using Linux, it's recommended that you check these online repositories for the latest, most stable version of these programs.

2. **If required, read through the license agreement and then click the Accept button if you want to use the DVD.**

   The DVD interface appears. The interface allows you to browse the contents and install the programs with just a click of a button (or two).

What You'll Find on the DVD

The following list is arranged by category and provides a summary of the software and other goodies you'll find on the DVD. If you need help with installing the items provided on the DVD, refer to the installation instructions in the preceding section.

For each program listed, I provide the program platform (Linux, Windows, or Mac). All programs on this DVD are *GNU software,* meaning the software is governed by its own license, which is included inside the folder of GNU software on the disc. There are no restrictions on distribution of GNU software other than the fact that source code must be made available. I provide links to the Web site of each piece of GNU software if you're interested in getting the source code.

- ✔ **Author-created material:** *For all operating systems.* All the examples provided in this book are located in the `Author` directory on the DVD and work on any machine that can run Blender. I used these `.blend` files to create many of the figures in this book. For a few chapters, I also include video tutorials that you can use as aids while you work. To play back the tutorials, I recommend you use VLC, also included on the DVD. The structure of the examples directory is

```
Author/Chapter01
Author/Chapter02
```

- ✔ **Blender:** *GNU software.For Linux, Windows, and Mac OS.* You can't have a DVD accompanying a book on Blender without including a copy of Blender itself. That would just be crazy! On the DVD is a copy of the latest official release of Blender (as of this writing) for each of the major operating systems, including Windows, Macintosh, and Linux. If you're using a different operating system or if you just want to see whether there's a newer version, head on over to `www.blender.org` to get a copy of Blender there.

- ✔ **GIMP:** *GNU software. For Linux, Windows, and Mac OS.* When building your 3D creations, you may find yourself in need of a tool that can do 2D image editing. You may need to adjust the colors on a final render, distort your render in an interesting way, or paint custom textures with a more advanced brush and layer system. A tool that can meet all these needs is GIMP (GNU Image Manipulation Program).

  Included on the DVD are versions for Windows and Mac OS X. If you're a Linux user, I recommend that you look to your distribution's package-management tool for installing the latest version of GIMP from its online repository. You can find more information on GIMP at its official Web site, `www.gimp.org`.

- ✔ **Inkscape:** *GNU software. For Linux, Windows, and Mac OS.* Blender's curves are great in 3D, but if you're working in 2D and you need to use curves to create a scalable image or logo, they're not always the best tool for the job. For that kind of task, Inkscape is the program you want to use. And the cool thing is that Inkscape uses the SVG (Scalable Vector Graphics) file format, for which Blender has a good-quality importer. That way, your logo can be brought into Blender and 3D-ified in only a few steps.

As with GIMP, I include Windows and Mac versions of Inkscape on the DVD. For the Linux version, I suggest using your distribution's package manager. Inkscape is available on all the major ones. You can find out more about Inkscape on its official Web site at `www.inkscape.org`.

✔ **MakeHuman:** *GNU software. For Linux, Windows, and Mac OS.* Modeling in 3D is difficult and time consuming. It can be even more so if you're trying to create a realistic human model. Fortunately, you have MakeHuman. MakeHuman was originally born as a plug-in for Blender and has since matured into a fully featured tool for generating believable human models for your own projects.

I include the most recent stable version of MakeHuman on the DVD, Version 0.9.1 RC1, for Linux, Windows, and Mac OS. However, if you feel adventurous, head on over to `www.makehuman.org` to download the current development version and see all the improvements.

✔ **MyPaint:** *GNU software. For Linux, Windows, and Mac OS.* While GIMP is a great image-editing application with some painting features included, it's not primarily designed as a digital painting program. Its brushes don't always behave like those in more traditional media (pencils, pens, paints, and so on). To fill in this gap, I include MyPaint. With MyPaint, you can more easily paint and draw in a way that looks and feels more like traditional media. MyPaint is one of the first tools I reach for when I want to make a concept sketch or paint a texture or background matte.

The DVD includes versions for Linux and Windows (Mac OS folks, to install on your machines, you need to use macports). You can find out more about using MyPaint at `http://mypaint.intilinux.com`.

✔ **Pencil:** *GNU software. For Linux, Windows, and Mac OS.* Pencil is an excellent little program for creating hand-drawn animations on a computer. If you've read through this book, you know that animating in 3D can be a time-consuming process with a large number of steps between concept and completion. For that very reason, it's often nice to create rough test animations to make sure that your timing works. Pencil is a tool that you can use to create these tests. Of course, you can also use Pencil to create fully refined hand-drawn animations as well.

I include copies of Pencil for Linux, Windows, and Mac OS on this DVD. Be aware, though, that Pencil is a relatively young program — only at version 0.4.4b as of this writing. This means that you may run into a bug here or there. Fortunately, there is some very helpful information on Pencil at its Web site, `www.pencil-animation.org`.

✔ **Sintel:** *Creative Commons Attribution 3.0 License. For all operating systems. Sintel* is the third open movie project created by the Blender Institute. As with the previous open movies, the purpose was to assemble a small team of 3D artists and create a short movie with Blender. *Sintel* was the Institute's most ambitious project to date, and because of it, Blender gained quite a few features that you can now take full advantage of.

The video on the disc is a full HD encoding of the film, so you may want to copy it to your hard drive before playing. Also, I recommend that you use VLC (described next) to view it. You can read more about it and even download the project's .blend files for free at www.sintel.org.

✔ **VLC:** *GNU software. For Linux, Windows, and Mac OS.* VLC is short for Video LAN Client, and it's an excellent media player that plays nearly any sound or movie file that you throw at it. I include it on the DVD because occasionally Windows Media Player or QuickTime have trouble playing some movie formats. If you have problems playing any of the included videos on this DVD in one of those players, give VLC a try. For more information on VLC, check out www.videolan.org/vlc.

Troubleshooting

Blender works admirably on most computers with the minimum system requirements. Alas, your computer may differ, and Blender (or one of the other programs included on this DVD) may not work properly for some reason.

The two likeliest problems are that you don't have enough memory (RAM) for the programs you want to use, or you have other programs running that are affecting installation or running of a program. If you get an error message such as Not enough memory or Setup cannot continue, try one or more of the following suggestions and then try using the software again:

✔ **Turn off any antivirus software running on your computer.** Installation programs sometimes mimic virus activity and may make your computer incorrectly believe that a virus is infecting it.

✔ **Close all running programs.** The more programs you have running, the less memory is available to other programs. Installation programs typically update files and programs; so if you keep other programs running, installation may not work properly.

✔ **Have your local computer store add more RAM to your computer.** This is, admittedly, a drastic and somewhat expensive step. However, adding more memory can really help the speed of your computer and allow more programs to run at the same time.

You may also want to check with the official Web sites for any of these programs. Most of them have very active communities with user forums where you can get help for common (and even not-so-common) problems getting the software to run on your computer.

Customer Care

If you have trouble with the DVD, please call Wiley Product Technical Support at 800-762-2974. Outside the United States, call 317-572-3993. You can also contact Wiley Product Technical Support at `http://support.wiley.com`. Wiley Publishing will provide technical support only for installation and other general quality-control items. For technical support on the applications themselves, consult the program's vendor or author.

To place additional orders or to request information about other Wiley products, please call 877-762-2974.

Index

• N •

GNU General Public License

Version 3, 29 June 2007
Copyright © 2007 Free Software Foundation, Inc. <http://fsf.org/>

Everyone is permitted to copy and distribute verbatim copies of this license document, but changing it is not allowed.

Preamble

The GNU General Public License is a free, copyleft license for software and other kinds of works.

The licenses for most software and other practical works are designed to take away your freedom to share and change the works. By contrast, the GNU General Public License is intended to guarantee your freedom to share and change all versions of a program–to make sure it remains free software for all its users. We, the Free Software Foundation, use the GNU General Public License for most of our software; it applies also to any other work released this way by its authors. You can apply it to your programs, too.

When we speak of free software, we are referring to freedom, not price. Our General Public Licenses are designed to make sure that you have the freedom to distribute copies of free software (and charge for them if you wish), that you receive source code or can get it if you want it, that you can change the software or use pieces of it in new free programs, and that you know you can do these things.

To protect your rights, we need to prevent others from denying you these rights or asking you to surrender the rights. Therefore, you have certain responsibilities if you distribute copies of the software, or if you modify it: responsibilities to respect the freedom of others.

For example, if you distribute copies of such a program, whether gratis or for a fee, you must pass on to the recipients the same freedoms that you received. You must make sure that they, too, receive or can get the source code. And you must show them these terms so they know their rights.

Developers that use the GNU GPL protect your rights with two steps: (1) assert copyright on the software, and (2) offer you this License giving you legal permission to copy, distribute and/or modify it.

For the developers' and authors' protection, the GPL clearly explains that there is no warranty for this free software. For both users' and authors' sake, the GPL requires that modified versions be marked as changed, so that their problems will not be attributed erroneously to authors of previous versions.

Some devices are designed to deny users access to install or run modified versions of the software inside them, although the manufacturer can do so. This is fundamentally incompatible with the aim of protecting users' freedom to change the software. The systematic pattern of such abuse occurs in the area of products for individuals to use, which is precisely where it is most unacceptable. Therefore, we have designed this version of the GPL to prohibit the practice for those products. If such problems arise substantially in other domains, we stand ready to extend this provision to those domains in future versions of the GPL, as needed to protect the freedom of users.

Finally, every program is threatened constantly by software patents. States should not allow patents to restrict development and use of software on general-purpose computers, but in those that do, we wish to avoid the special danger that patents applied to a free program could make it effectively proprietary. To prevent this, the GPL assures that patents cannot be used to render the program non-free.

The precise terms and conditions for copying, distribution and modification follow.

Terms and Conditions

0. Definitions. "This License" refers to version 3 of the GNU General Public License. "Copyright" also means copyright-like laws that apply to other kinds of works, such as semiconductor masks. "The Program" refers to any copyrightable work licensed under this License. Each licensee is addressed as "you". "Licensees" and "recipients" may be individuals or organizations. To "modify" a work means to copy from or adapt all or part of the work in a fashion requiring copyright permission, other than the making of an exact copy. The resulting work is called a "modified version" of the earlier work or a work "based on" the earlier work. A "covered work" means either the unmodified Program or a work based on the Program.

To "propagate" a work means to do anything with it that, without permission, would make you directly or secondarily liable for infringement under applicable copyright law, except executing it on a computer or modifying a private copy. Propagation includes copying, distribution (with or without modification), making available to the public, and in some countries other activities as well.

To "convey" a work means any kind of propagation that enables other parties to make or receive copies. Mere interaction with a user through a computer network, with no transfer of a copy, is not conveying.

An interactive user interface displays "Appropriate Legal Notices" to the extent that it includes a convenient and prominently visible feature that (1) displays an appropriate copyright notice, and (2) tells the user that there is no warranty for the work (except to the extent that warranties are provided), that licensees may convey the work under this License, and how to view a copy of this License. If the interface presents a list of user commands or options, such as a menu, a prominent item in the list meets this criterion.

1. Source Code. The "source code" for a work means the preferred form of the work for making modifications to it. "Object code" means any non-source form of a work. A "Standard Interface" means an interface that either is an official standard defined by a recognized standards body, or, in the case of interfaces specified for a particular programming language, one that is widely used among developers working in that language.

The "System Libraries" of an executable work include anything, other than the work as a whole, that (a) is included in the normal form of packaging a Major Component, but which is not part of that Major Component, and (b) serves only to enable use of the work with that Major Component, or to implement a Standard Interface for which an implementation is available to the public in source code form. A "Major Component", in this context, means a major essential component (kernel, window system, and so on) of the specific operating system (if any) on which the executable work runs, or a compiler used to produce the work, or an object code interpreter used to run it.

The "Corresponding Source" for a work in object code form means all the source code needed to generate, install, and (for an executable work) run the object code and to modify the work, including scripts to control those activities. However, it does not include the work's System Libraries, or general-purpose tools or generally available free programs which are used unmodified in performing those activities but which are not part of the work. For example, Corresponding Source includes interface definition files associated with source files for the work, and the source code for shared libraries and dynamically linked subprograms that the work is specifically designed to require, such as by intimate data communication or control flow between those subprograms and other parts of the work.

The Corresponding Source need not include anything that users can regenerate automatically from other parts of the Corresponding Source.

The Corresponding Source for a work in source code form is that same work.

2. **Basic Permissions.** All rights granted under this License are granted for the term of copyright on the Program, and are irrevocable provided the stated conditions are met. This License explicitly affirms your unlimited permission to run the unmodified Program. The output from running a covered work is covered by this License only if the output, given its content, constitutes a covered work. This License acknowledges your rights of fair use or other equivalent, as provided by copyright law.

You may make, run and propagate covered works that you do not convey, without conditions so long as your license otherwise remains in force. You may convey covered works to others for the sole purpose of having them make modifications exclusively for you, or provide you with facilities for running those works, provided that you comply with the terms of this License in conveying all material for which you do not control copyright. Those thus making or running the covered works for you must do so exclusively on your behalf, under your direction and control, on terms that prohibit them from making any copies of your copyrighted material outside their relationship with you.

Conveying under any other circumstances is permitted solely under the conditions stated below. Sublicensing is not allowed; section 10 makes it unnecessary.

3. **Protecting Users' Legal Rights From Anti-Circumvention Law.** No covered work shall be deemed part of an effective technological measure under any applicable law fulfilling obligations under article 11 of the WIPO copyright treaty adopted on 20 December 1996, or similar laws prohibiting or restricting circumvention of such measures.

When you convey a covered work, you waive any legal power to forbid circumvention of technological measures to the extent such circumvention is effected by exercising rights under this License with respect to the covered work, and you disclaim any intention to limit operation or modification of the work as a means of enforcing, against the work's users, your or third parties' legal rights to forbid circumvention of technological measures.

4. **Conveying Verbatim Copies.** You may convey verbatim copies of the Program's source code as you receive it, in any medium, provided that you conspicuously and appropriately publish on each copy an appropriate copyright notice; keep intact all notices stating that this License and any non-permissive terms added in accord with section 7 apply to the code; keep intact all notices of the absence of any warranty; and give all recipients a copy of this License along with the Program.

You may charge any price or no price for each copy that you convey, and you may offer support or warranty protection for a fee.

5. **Conveying Modified Source Versions.** You may convey a work based on the Program, or the modifications to produce it from the Program, in the form of source code under the terms of section 4, provided that you also meet all of these conditions:

a) The work must carry prominent notices stating that you modified it, and giving a relevant date.

b) The work must carry prominent notices stating that it is released under this License and any conditions added under section 7. This requirement modifies the requirement in section 4 to "keep intact all notices".

c) You must license the entire work, as a whole, under this License to anyone who comes into possession of a copy. This License will therefore apply, along with any applicable section 7 additional terms, to the whole of the work, and all its parts, regardless of how they are packaged. This License gives no permission to license the work in any other way, but it does not invalidate such permission if you have separately received it.

d) If the work has interactive user interfaces, each must display Appropriate Legal Notices; however, if the Program has interactive interfaces that do not display Appropriate Legal Notices, your work need not make them do so.

A compilation of a covered work with other separate and independent works, which are not by their nature extensions of the covered work, and which are not combined with it such as to form a larger program, in or on a volume of a storage or distribution medium, is called an "aggregate" if the compilation and its resulting copyright are not used to limit the access or legal rights of the compilation's users beyond what the individual works permit. Inclusion of a covered work in an aggregate does not cause this License to apply to the other parts of the aggregate.

6. **Conveying Non-Source Forms.** You may convey a covered work in object code form under the terms of sections 4 and 5, provided that you also convey the machine-readable Corresponding Source under the terms of this License, in one of these ways:

a) Convey the object code in, or embodied in, a physical product (including a physical distribution medium), accompanied by the Corresponding Source fixed on a durable physical medium customarily used for software interchange.

b) Convey the object code in, or embodied in, a physical product (including a physical distribution medium), accompanied by a written offer, valid for at least three years and valid for as long as you offer spare parts or customer support for that product model, to give anyone who possesses the object code either (1) a copy of the Corresponding Source for all the software in the product that is covered by this License, on a durable physical medium customarily used for software interchange, for a price no more than your reasonable cost of physically performing this conveying of source, or (2) access to copy the Corresponding Source from a network server at no charge.

c) Convey individual copies of the object code with a copy of the written offer to provide the Corresponding Source. This alternative is allowed only occasionally and noncommercially, and only if you received the object code with such an offer, in accord with subsection 6b.

d) Convey the object code by offering access from a designated place (gratis or for a charge), and offer equivalent access to the Corresponding Source in the same way through the same place at no further charge. You need not require recipients to copy the Corresponding Source along with the object code. If the place to copy the object code is a network server, the Corresponding Source may be on a different server (operated by you or a third party) that supports equivalent copying facilities, provided you maintain clear directions next to the object code saying where to find the Corresponding Source. Regardless of what server hosts the Corresponding Source, you remain obligated to ensure that it is available for as long as needed to satisfy these requirements.

e) Convey the object code using peer-to-peer transmission, provided you inform other peers where the object code and Corresponding Source of the work are being offered to the general public at no charge under subsection 6d.

A separable portion of the object code, whose source code is excluded from the Corresponding Source as a System Library, need not be included in conveying the object code work.

A "User Product" is either (1) a "consumer product", which means any tangible personal property which is normally used for personal, family, or household purposes, or (2) anything designed or sold for incorporation into a dwelling. In determining whether a product is a consumer product, doubtful cases shall be resolved in favor of coverage. For a particular product received by a particular user, "normally used" refers to a typical or common use of that class of product, regardless of the status of the particular user or of the way in which the particular user actually uses, or expects or is expected to use, the product. A product is a consumer product regardless of whether the product has substantial commercial, industrial or non-consumer uses, unless such uses represent the only significant mode of use of the product.

"Installation Information" for a User Product means any methods, procedures, authorization keys, or other information required to install and execute modified versions of a covered work in that User Product from a modified version of its Corresponding Source. The information must suffice to ensure that the continued functioning of the modified object code is in no case prevented or interfered with solely because modification has been made.

If you convey an object code work under this section in, or with, or specifically for use in, a User Product, and the conveying occurs as part of a transaction in which the right of possession and use of the User Product is transferred to the recipient in perpetuity or for a fixed term (regardless of how the transaction is characterized), the Corresponding Source conveyed under this section must be accompanied by the Installation Information. But this requirement does not apply if neither you nor any third party retains the ability to install modified object code on the User Product (for example, the work has been installed in ROM).

The requirement to provide Installation Information does not include a requirement to continue to provide support service, warranty, or updates for a work that has been modified or installed by the recipient, or for the User Product in which it has been modified or installed. Access to a network may be denied when the modification itself materially and adversely affects the operation of the network or violates the rules and protocols for communication across the network.

Corresponding Source conveyed, and Installation Information provided, in accord with this section must be in a format that is publicly documented (and with an implementation available to the public in source code form), and must require no special password or key for unpacking, reading or copying.

7. **Additional Terms.** "Additional permissions" are terms that supplement the terms of this License by making exceptions from one or more of its conditions. Additional permissions that are applicable to the entire Program shall be treated as though they were included in this License, to the extent that they are valid under applicable law. If additional permissions apply only to part of the Program, that part may be used separately under those permissions, but the entire Program remains governed by this License without regard to the additional permissions.

When you convey a copy of a covered work, you may at your option remove any additional permissions from that copy, or from any part of it. (Additional permissions may be written to require their own removal in certain cases when you modify the work.) You may place additional permissions on material, added by you to a covered work, for which you have or can give appropriate copyright permission.

Notwithstanding any other provision of this License, for material you add to a covered work, you may (if authorized by the copyright holders of that material) supplement the terms of this License with terms:

a) Disclaiming warranty or limiting liability differently from the terms of sections 15 and 16 of this License; or

b) Requiring preservation of specified reasonable legal notices or author attributions in that material or in the Appropriate Legal Notices displayed by works containing it; or

c) Prohibiting misrepresentation of the origin of that material, or requiring that modified versions of such material be marked in reasonable ways as different from the original version; or

d) Limiting the use for publicity purposes of names of licensors or authors of the material; or

e) Declining to grant rights under trademark law for use of some trade names, trademarks, or service marks; or

f) Requiring indemnification of licensors and authors of that material by anyone who conveys the material (or modified versions of it) with contractual assumptions of liability to the recipient, for any liability that these contractual assumptions directly impose on those licensors and authors.

All other non-permissive additional terms are considered "further restrictions" within the meaning of section 10. If the Program as you received it, or any part of it, contains a notice stating that it is governed by this License along with a term that is a further restriction, you may remove that term. If a license document contains a further restriction but permits relicensing or conveying under this License, you may add to a covered work material governed by the terms of that license document, provided that the further restriction does not survive such relicensing or conveying.

If you add terms to a covered work in accord with this section, you must place, in the relevant source files, a statement of the additional terms that apply to those files, or a notice indicating where to find the applicab

Additional terms, permissive or non-permissive, may be stated in the form of a separately written license, or stated as exceptions; the above requirements apply either way.

8. **Termination.** You may not propagate or modify a covered work except as expressly provided under this License. Any attempt otherwise to propagate or modify it is void, and will automatically terminate your rights under this License (including any patent licenses granted under the third paragraph of section 11).

However, if you cease all violation of this License, then your license from a particular copyright holder is reinstated (a) provisionally, unless and until the copyright holder explicitly and finally terminates your license, and (b) permanently, if the copyright holder fails to notify you of the violation by some reasonable means prior to 60 days after the cessation.

Moreover, your license from a particular copyright holder is reinstated permanently if the copyright holder notifies you of the violation by some reasonable means, this is the first time you have received notice of violation of this License (for any work) from that copyright holder, and you cure the violation prior to 30 days after your receipt of the notice.

Termination of your rights under this section does not terminate the licenses of parties who have received copies or rights from you under this License. If your rights have been terminated and not permanently reinstated, you do not qualify to receive new licenses for the same material under section 10.

9. **Acceptance Not Required for Having Copies.** You are not required to accept this License in order to receive or run a copy of the Program. Ancillary propagation of a covered work occurring solely as a consequence of using peer-to-peer transmission to receive a copy likewise does not require acceptance. However, nothing other than this License grants you permission to propagate or modify any covered work. These actions infringe copyright if you do not accept this License. Therefore, by modifying or propagating a covered work, you indicate your acceptance of this License to do so.

10. **Automatic Licensing of Downstream Recipients.** Each time you convey a covered work, the recipient automatically receives a license from the original licensors, to run, modify and propagate that work, subject to this License. You are not responsible for enforcing compliance by third parties with this License.

An "entity transaction" is a transaction transferring control of an organization, or substantially all assets of one, or subdividing an organization, or merging organizations. If propagation of a covered work results from an entity transaction, each party to that transaction who receives a copy of the work also receives whatever licenses to the work the party's predecessor in interest had or could give under the previous paragraph, plus a right to possession of the Corresponding Source of the work from the predecessor in interest, if the predecessor has it or can get it with reasonable efforts.

You may not impose any further restrictions on the exercise of the rights granted or affirmed under this License. For example, you may not impose a license fee, royalty, or other charge for exercise of rights granted under this License, and you may not initiate litigation (including a cross-claim or counterclaim in a lawsuit) alleging that any patent claim is infringed by making, using, selling, offering for sale, or importing the Program or any portion of it.

11. **Patents.** A "contributor" is a copyright holder who authorizes use under this License of the Program or a work on which the Program is based. The work thus licensed is called the contributor's "contributor version".

A contributor's "essential patent claims" are all patent claims owned or controlled by the contributor, whether already acquired or hereafter acquired, that would be infringed by some manner, permitted by this License, of making, using, or selling its contributor version, but do not include claims that would be infringed only as a consequence of further modification of the contributor version. For purposes of this definition, "control" includes the right to grant patent sublicenses in a manner consistent with the requirements of this License.

Each contributor grants you a non-exclusive, worldwide, royalty-free patent license under the contributor's essential patent claims, to make, use, sell, offer for sale, import and otherwise run, modify and propagate the contents of its contributor version.

In the following three paragraphs, a "patent license" is any express agreement or commitment, however denominated, not to enforce a patent (such as an express permission to practice a patent or covenant not to sue for patent infringement). To "grant" such a patent license to a party means to make such an agreement or commitment not to enforce a patent against the party.

If you convey a covered work, knowingly relying on a patent license, and the Corresponding Source of the work is not available for anyone to copy, free of charge and under the terms of this License, through a publicly available network server or other readily accessible means, then you must either (1) cause the Corresponding Source to be so available, or (2) arrange to deprive yourself of the benefit of the patent license for this particular work, or (3) arrange, in a manner consistent with the requirements of this License, to extend the patent license to downstream recipients. "Knowingly relying" means you have actual knowledge that, but for the patent license, your conveying the covered work in a country, or your recipient's use of the covered work in a country, would infringe one or more identifiable patents in that country that you have reason to believe are valid.

If, pursuant to or in connection with a single transaction or arrangement, you convey, or propagate by procuring conveyance of, a covered work, and grant a patent license to some of the parties receiving the covered work authorizing them to use, propagate, modify or convey a specific copy of the covered work, then the patent license you grant is automatically extended to all recipients of the covered work and works based on it.

A patent license is "discriminatory" if it does not include within the scope of its coverage, prohibits the exercise of, or is conditioned on the non-exercise of one or more of the rights that are specifically granted under this License. You may not convey a covered work if you are a party to an arrangement with a third party that is in the business of distributing software, under which you make payment to the third party based on the extent of your activity of conveying the work, and under which the third party grants, to any of the parties who would receive the covered work from you, a discriminatory patent license (a) in connection with copies of the covered work conveyed by you (or copies made from those copies), or (b) primarily for and in connection with specific products or compilations that contain the covered work, unless you entered into that arrangement, or that patent license was granted, prior to 28 March 2007.

Nothing in this License shall be construed as excluding or limiting any implied license or other defenses to infringement that may otherwise be available to you under applicable patent law.

12. **No Surrender of Others' Freedom.** If conditions are imposed on you (whether by court order, agreement or otherwise) that contradict the conditions of this License, they do not excuse you from the conditions of this License. If you cannot convey a covered work so as to satisfy simultaneously your obligations under this License and any other pertinent obligations, then as a consequence you may not convey it at all. For example, if you agree to terms that obligate you to collect a royalty for further conveying from those to whom you convey the Program, the only way you could satisfy both those terms and this License would be to refrain entirely from conveying the Program.

13. **Use with the GNU Affero General Public License.** Notwithstanding any other provision of this License, you have permission to link or combine any covered work with a work licensed under version 3 of the GNU Affero General Public License into a single combined work, and to convey the resulting work. The terms of this License will continue to apply to the part which is the covered work, but the special requirements of the GNU Affero General Public License, section 13, concerning interaction through a network will apply to the combination as such.

14. **Revised Versions of this License.** The Free Software Foundation may publish revised and/or new versions of the GNU General Public License from time to time. Such new versions will be similar in spirit to the present version, but may differ in detail to address new problems or concerns.

Each version is given a distinguishing version number. If the Program specifies that a certain numbered version of the GNU General Public License "or any later version" applies to it, you have the option of following the terms and conditions either of that numbered version or of any later version published by the Free Software Foundation. If the Program does not specify a version number of the GNU General Public License, you may choose any version ever published by the Free Software Foundation.

If the Program specifies that a proxy can decide which future versions of the GNU General Public License can be used, that proxy's public statement of acceptance of a version permanently authorizes you to choose that version for the Program.

Later license versions may give you additional or different permissions. However, no additional obligations are imposed on any author or copyright holder as a result of your choosing to follow a later version.

15. **Disclaimer of Warranty.** THERE IS NO WARRANTY FOR THE PROGRAM, TO THE EXTENT PERMITTED BY APPLICABLE LAW. EXCEPT WHEN OTHERWISE STATED IN WRITING THE COPYRIGHT HOLDERS AND/OR OTHER PARTIES PROVIDE THE PROGRAM "AS IS" WITHOUT WARRANTY OF ANY KIND, EITHER EXPRESSED OR IMPLIED, INCLUDING, BUT NOT LIMITED TO, THE IMPLIED WARRANTIES OF MERCHANTABILITY AND FITNESS FOR A PARTICULAR PURPOSE. THE ENTIRE RISK AS TO THE QUALITY AND PERFORMANCE OF THE PROGRAM IS WITH YOU. SHOULD THE PROGRAM PROVE DEFECTIVE, YOU ASSUME THE COST OF ALL NECESSARY SERVICING, REPAIR OR CORRECTION.

16. **Limitation of Liability.** IN NO EVENT UNLESS REQUIRED BY APPLICABLE LAW OR AGREED TO IN WRITING WILL ANY COPYRIGHT HOLDER, OR ANY OTHER PARTY WHO MODIFIES AND/OR CONVEYS THE PROGRAM AS PERMITTED ABOVE, BE LIABLE TO YOU FOR DAMAGES, INCLUDING ANY GENERAL, SPECIAL, INCIDENTAL OR CONSEQUENTIAL DAMAGES ARISING OUT OF THE USE OR INABILITY TO USE THE PROGRAM (INCLUDING BUT NOT LIMITED TO LOSS OF DATA OR DATA BEING RENDERED INACCURATE OR LOSSES SUSTAINED BY YOU OR THIRD PARTIES OR A FAILURE OF THE PROGRAM TO OPERATE WITH ANY OTHER PROGRAMS), EVEN IF SUCH HOLDER OR OTHER PARTY HAS BEEN ADVISED OF THE POSSIBILITY OF SUCH DAMAGES.

17. **Interpretation of Sections 15 and 16.** If the disclaimer of warranty and limitation of liability provided above cannot be given local legal effect according to their terms, reviewing courts shall apply local law that most closely approximates an absolute waiver of all civil liability in connection with the Program, unless a warranty or assumption of liability accompanies a copy of the Program in return for a fee.

END OF TERMS AND CONDITIONS

John Wiley & Sons, Inc.
End-User License Agreement

5. Limited Warranty.

(a) WILEY warrants that the Software and Software Media are free from defects in materials and workmanship under normal use for a period of sixty (60) days from the date of purchase of this Book. If WILEY receives notification within the warranty period of defects in materials or workmanship, WILEY will replace the defective Software Media.

(b) WILEY AND THE AUTHOR(S) OF THE BOOK DISCLAIM ALL OTHER WARRANTIES, EXPRESS OR IMPLIED, INCLUDING WITHOUT LIMITATION IMPLIED WARRANTIES OF MERCHANTABILITY AND FITNESS FOR A PARTICULAR PURPOSE, WITH RESPECT TO THE SOFTWARE, THE PROGRAMS, THE SOURCE CODE CONTAINED THEREIN, AND/OR THE TECHNIQUES DESCRIBED IN THIS BOOK. WILEY DOES NOT WARRANT THAT THE FUNCTIONS CONTAINED IN THE SOFTWARE WILL MEET YOUR REQUIREMENTS OR THAT THE OPERATION OF THE SOFTWARE WILL BE ERROR FREE.

(c) This limited warranty gives you specific legal rights, and you may have other rights that vary from jurisdiction to jurisdiction.

6. Remedies.

(a) WILEY's entire liability and your exclusive remedy for defects in materials and workmanship shall be limited to replacement of the Software Media, which may be returned to WILEY with a copy of your receipt at the following address: Software Media Fulfillment Department, Attn.: *Blender For Dummies*, 2nd Edition, John Wiley & Sons, Inc., 10475 Crosspoint Blvd., Indianapolis, IN 46256, or call 1-800-762-2974. Please allow four to six weeks for delivery. This Limited Warranty is void if failure of the Software Media has resulted from accident, abuse, or misapplication. Any replacement Software Media will be warranted for the remainder of the original warranty period or thirty (30) days, whichever is longer.

(b) In no event shall WILEY or the author be liable for any damages whatsoever (including without limitation damages for loss of business profits, business interruption, loss of business information, or any other pecuniary loss) arising from the use of or inability to use the Book or the Software, even if WILEY has been advised of the possibility of such damages.

(c) Because some jurisdictions do not allow the exclusion or limitation of liability for consequential or incidental damages, the above limitation or exclusion may not apply to you.

7. U.S. Government Restricted Rights. Use, duplication, or disclosure of the Software for or on behalf of the United States of America, its agencies and/or instrumentalities "U.S. Government" is subject to restrictions as stated in paragraph (c)(1)(ii) of the Rights in Technical Data and Computer Software clause of DFARS 252.227-7013, or subparagraphs (c) (1) and (2) of the Commercial Computer Software - Restricted Rights clause at FAR 52.227-19, and in similar clauses in the NASA FAR supplement, as applicable.

8. General. This Agreement constitutes the entire understanding of the parties and revokes and supersedes all prior agreements, oral or written, between them and may not be modified or amended except in a writing signed by both parties hereto that specifically refers to this Agreement. This Agreement shall take precedence over any other documents that may be in conflict herewith. If any one or more provisions contained in this Agreement are held by any court or tribunal to be invalid, illegal, or otherwise unenforceable, each and every other provision shall remain in full force and effect.